FRAGMENTARY
REPUBLICAN LATIN

IV

LCL 541

FRAGMENTARY REPUBLICAN LATIN

ORATORY

PART 2

EDITED AND TRANSLATED BY

GESINE MANUWALD

HARVARD UNIVERSITY PRESS

CAMBRIDGE, MASSACHUSETTS

LONDON, ENGLAND

2019

First published 2019

LOEB CLASSICAL LIBRARY® is a registered trademark
of the President and Fellows of Harvard College

Library of Congress Control Number 2018962593
CIP data available from the Library of Congress

ISBN 978-0-674-99724-0

*Composed in ZephGreek and ZephText by
Technologies 'N Typography, Merrimac, Massachusetts.
Printed on acid-free paper and bound by
Maple Press, York, Pennsylvania*

CONTENTS

CONTENTS

CONTENTS

CONTENTS

CONTENTS

CONTENTS

ORATORY, PART 3 [LCL 542]

CONTENTS

CONTENTS

ORATORY
PART 2

70 L. MARCIUS PHILIPPUS

L. Marcius Philippus (cos. 91, censor 86 BC; RE Marcius 75) was an important politician in the first half of the first century BC. He became consul after two failed attempts; perhaps in connection with those, he was accused of bribery by Q. Servilius Caepio (85) in 92 BC (TLRR 95; Flor. 2.5.5). Philippus was an opponent of the laws of the Tribune of the People M. Livius Drusus (72) as well as of the senatorial policy at the time (Cic. De or. 1.24, 3.2; Val. Max. 6.2.2, 9.5.2; Flor. 2.5.8; Vir. ill. 66.9).

T 1 Cic. *Brut.* 173

[CICERO:] duobus igitur summis, Crasso et Antonio, L. Philippus proximus accedebat, sed longo intervallo tamen proximus. itaque eum, etsi nemo intercedebat qui se illi anteferret, neque secundum tamen neque tertium dixerim. nec enim in quadrigis eum secundum numeraverim aut tertium, qui vix e carceribus exierit, cum palmam iam primus acceperit, nec in oratoribus, qui tantum absit a primo, vix ut in eodem curriculo esse videatur. sed tamen erant ea in Philippo, quae qui sine comparatione illorum spectaret, satis magna diceret: summa libertas in oratione, multae facetiae, satis creber in reperiendis, solutus in explicandis sententiis; erat etiam in primis, ut temporibus

70 L. MARCIUS PHILIPPUS

*According to Cicero, as a speaker Philippus came after
the great orators L. Licinius Crassus (**66**) and M. Antonius
(**65**), though at a considerable distance (T 1, 3; Cic. Brut.
207, 301; Planc. 52). While Philippus surpassed others in
eloquence and nobility, some of these men were more successful in their political careers (T 2; Cic. Mur. 36). Philippus' learning in Greek culture and his charm, wittiness,
and resourcefulness in speaking are noted (T 1, 3, 5; Cic.
Off. 1.108).*

T 1 Cicero, *Brutus*

[CICERO:] To those two most outstanding men, then,
Crassus [L. Licinius Crassus (**66**)] and Antonius [M. Antonius (**65**)], L. Philippus came nearest, but nonetheless
nearest at a long distance. Therefore, though no one who
believed himself to surpass him stood in between, still I
would not call him second or third. For neither in a char-
iot race would I number as second or third someone who
has barely crossed the starting line when the first has already received the prize, nor among orators someone who
is so far from the first that he scarcely seems to be in the
same race. But still, there were those qualities in Philippus
which, if anyone looked at them without comparison with
those men, he would call rather considerable: there was
great outspokenness in his speech-making, many witti-
cisms; he was sufficiently resourceful in invention, uncon-
strained in outlining ideas; also, in relation to those times,

3

illis, Graecis doctrinis institutus; in altercando cum aliquo aculeo et maledicto facetus.

T 2 Cic. *Brut.* 166

[CICERO:] eodem tempore M. Herennius in mediocribus oratoribus Latine et diligenter loquentibus numeratus est; qui tamen summa nobilitate hominem, cognatione, sodalitate, conlegio, summa etiam eloquentia, L. Philippum in consulatus petitione superavit.

T 3 Cic. *Brut.* 186

[CICERO:] de populo si quem ita rogavisses: quis est in hac civitate eloquentissimus? in Antonio et Crasso aut dubitaret aut hunc alius, illum alius diceret. nemone Philippum tam suavem oratorem, tam gravem, tam facetum his anteferret, quem nosmet ipsi, qui haec arte aliqua volumus expendere, proximum illis fuisse diximus? nemo profecto

. . .

T 4 Cic. *Brut.* 326

[CICERO:] non probabantur haec senibus—saepe videbam cum inridentem tum etiam irascentem et stomachantem Philippum—sed mirabantur adulescentes, multitudo movebatur.

he was among the most versed in Greek learning; in the give and take of debate he was clever with a certain pungent abuse.

T 2 Cicero, *Brutus*

[CICERO:] In the same period [as Cn. Domitius Ahenobarbus (**69**)] M. Herennius [cos. 93 BC] was numbered among the orators of moderate ability, speaking a pure and exact Latin; yet, in the candidacy for the consulship, he defeated L. Philippus, a man of the highest nobility, family connections, membership in political associations and priestly colleges, and also of outstanding eloquence.

T 3 Cicero, *Brutus*

[CICERO:] If you had asked anyone of the common people thus: "Who is the most eloquent in this community?," either they might hesitate between Antonius [M. Antonius (**65**)] and Crassus [L. Licinius Crassus (**66**)], or one might say the latter, another the former. Would no one have expressed a preference for Philippus over them, such a charming, such a serious, such a witty orator, of whom we ourselves, who wish to weigh such qualities according to some theory, have said that he was nearest to them [T 1]? No one, certainly . . .

T 4 Cicero, *Brutus*

[CICERO:] These features [i.e., characteristics of the Asiatic style of speaking] were not looked upon with favor by older men—I have often seen Philippus listening with a derisive smile or even with anger and impatience—but the young men admired them, and the masses were carried away thereby.

T 5 Cic. *De or.* 2.316

[ANTONIUS:] in quo admirari soleo non equidem istos qui nullam huic rei operam dederunt, sed hominem in primis disertum atque eruditum, Philippum, qui ita solet surgere ad dicendum, ut quod primum verbum habiturus sit nesciat; et ait idem, cum brachium concalfecerit, tum se solere pugnare, neque attendit eos ipsos unde hoc simile ducat, primas illas hastas ita iactare leniter, ut et venustati vel maxime serviant et reliquis viribus suis consulant.

T 6 Cic. *De or.* 3.4
= **66** F 41.

T 7 Cic. *Off.* 2.59

L. quidem Philippus Q. f., magno vir ingenio in primisque clarus, gloriari solebat se sine ullo munere adeptum esse omnia quae haberentur amplissima.

On an Agrarian Bill (F 8)

F 8 Cic. *Off.* 2.73

in primis autem videndum erit ei qui rempublicam administrabit ut suum quisque teneat neque de bonis priva-

T 5 Cicero, *On the Orator*

[ANTONIUS:] In this respect I constantly wonder, not indeed at those people who have given no attention to this matter [i.e., an effective beginning of a speech], but at a man of outstanding eloquence and learning, Philippus, whose habit it is to get up to make a speech, in such a way that he does not know what he will utter as the first word; and he says that his way is to fight only once he has warmed up his arm, and he does not notice that even those men from whom he derives this comparison throw those first spears gently in such a way that they both pay attention to gracefulness as much as possible and look after the remainder of their strength.

T 6 Cicero, *On the Orator*

= **66** F 41.

T 7 Cicero, *On Duties*

To be sure, L. Philippus, Quintus' son, a man of great talent and particularly renowned, used to boast that without any handouts he had obtained all [the positions] that were regarded as the highest.

On an Agrarian Bill (F 8)

In about 104 BC, as Tribune of the People, Philippus proposed an agrarian bill, which was rejected (Rogatio Marcia agraria: LPPR, *pp. 26–27*).

F 8 Cicero, *On Duties*

And, first of all, the man who will administer political affairs will have to see to it that everyone shall keep what

7

torum publice deminutio fiat. perniciose enim Philippus in tribunatu, cum legem agrariam ferret, quam tamen antiquari facile passus est et in eo vehementer se moderatum praebuit, sed cum in agendo multa populariter, tum illud male, non esse in civitate duo milia hominum qui rem haberent. capitalis oratio est, ad aequationem bonorum pertinens! qua peste quae potest esse maior?

As Consul to the People (F 9–10)

F 9 Cic. *De or.* 1.24

cum igitur vehementius inveheretur in causam principum consul Philippus . . .

F 10 Cic. *De or.* 3.2

= **66** F 41.

they own and that there is no reduction of the property of private citizens by official actions. For Philippus acted in a ruinous fashion in his Tribunate, when he put forward an agrarian bill; yet when it was rejected, he took it with good grace and showed extraordinary moderation on this occasion. But in arguing for it, he said many things in a manner designed to appeal to the People and particularly badly this: that in the community there were not two thousand people who owned property. It is a pernicious speech, relating to an equal distribution of property! What plague can be greater than that one?

As Consul to the People (F 9–10)

As consul in 91 BC, Philippus criticized (CCMR, App. A: 219) *the Senate before the People (Val. Max. 6.2.2), to which L. Licinius Crassus responded (**66** F 41).*

F 9 Cicero, *On the Orator*

Then, at the time when the consul Philippus was assailing the cause of the leading men more strongly . . .[1]

[1] Because of the information included in another source (F 10), it is assumed that this statement refers to "assailing" at a meeting of the People.

F 10 Cicero, *On the Orator*

= **66** F 41.

Testimony under Lex Varia *(F 11)*

F 11 Cic. *Brut.* 304

= **61** F 2.

On Behalf of Cn. Pompeius Magnus (F 12–13)

When, as a young man, Cn. Pompeius Magnus (**111**) was
accused of having misappropriated booty obtained by his
father after the victory at Asculum (89 BC), Philippus, Q.
Hortensius Hortalus (**92** F 15), and Cn. Papirius Carbo

F 12 Cic. *Brut.* 230

= **92** T 1.

F 13 Plut. *Pomp.* 2.2

ἦν δέ τις καὶ ἀναστολὴ τῆς κόμης ἀτρέμα καὶ τῶν
περὶ τὰ ὄμματα ῥυθμῶν ὑγρότης τοῦ προσώπου
ποιοῦσα μᾶλλον λεγομένην ἢ φαινομένην ὁμοιότητα
πρὸς τὰς Ἀλεξάνδρου τοῦ βασιλέως εἰκόνας. ᾗ καὶ
τοὔνομα πολλῶν ἐν ἀρχῇ συνεπιφερόντων οὐκ ἔφευ-
γεν ὁ Πομπήιος, ὥστε καὶ χλευάζοντας αὐτὸν ἐνίους
ἤδη καλεῖν Ἀλέξανδρον. διὸ καὶ Λεύκιος Φίλιππος
ἀνὴρ ὑπατικός συνηγορῶν αὐτῷ μηδὲν ἔφη ποιεῖν
παράλογον, εἰ Φίλιππος ὢν φιλαλέξανδρός ἐστιν.

Testimony under Lex Varia *(F 11)*

In 90 BC Philippus was involved in court cases under the Lex Varia de maiestate *(see* **88***); he apparently provided testimony against L. Memmius (***61***) and Q. Pompeius Rufus (***83***)* (TLRR *101, 102).*

F 11 Cicero, *Brutus*

= **61** F 2.

On Behalf of Cn. Pompeius Magnus (F 12–13)

spoke on his behalf; Pompey was acquitted (TLRR *120; Sen.* Contr. *7.2.6; Plut.* Pomp. *4.1–6; Val. Max. 5.3.5, 6.2.8).*

F 12 Cicero, *Brutus*

= **92** T 1.

F 13 Plutarch, *Life of Pompey*

There was some slight lifting of his [Cn. Pompeius Magnus (**111**)] hair and suppleness of a well-proportioned shape around the eyes that produced a resemblance of his face, more talked about than actually apparent, to the portrait statues of king Alexander. Therefore, since many also applied the name to him in his earlier years, Pompey did not decline it, so that some now called him Alexander in derision. Hence, too, Lucius Philippus, a man of consular rank, when pleading on his behalf, said that he was doing nothing strange if, being Philip, he was a friend of Alexander.

11

On Behalf of Sex. Naevius (F 14)

F 14 Cic. *Quinct.* 72

". . . pro me pugnabit L. Philippus, eloquentia, gravitate, honore florentissimus civitatis, dicet Hortensius, excellens ingenio, nobilitate, existimatione, aderunt autem homines nobilissimi ac potentissimi, ut eorum frequentiam et consessum non modo P. Quinctius qui de capite decernit, sed quivis qui extra periculum sit perhorrescat."

Against M. Aemilius Lepidus in the Senate (F 14A)

F 14A Sall. *Hist.* 1.77 M. = 1.67 R.

Philippus criticizes M. Aemilius Lepidus' character and policies and describes it as appalling that he has been elected and is wielding great power. He claims that Lepidus is acting illegally to create a power base and that unrest is growing everywhere; the natural order of things is being inverted. Therefore, Philippus implores the senators

70 L. MARCIUS PHILIPPUS

On Behalf of Sex. Naevius (F 14)

In 81 BC Philippus appeared on behalf of Sex. Naevius, whose advocate was Q. Hortensius Hortalus (**92** F 16–18), while the opponent P. Quinctius was defended by Cicero (Cic. Quinct. 77, 80; TLRR 126).

F 14 Cicero, *Pro Quinctio*

[Sex. Naevius envisaged to be speaking:] ". . . for me L. Philippus will fight, a man of the greatest eminence in the community for his eloquence, dignity, and position; Hortensius [Q. Hortensius Hortalus (**92**), F 16–18] will speak, a man distinguished for his talent, nobility, and reputation; there will also be men of the highest rank and the greatest power, so that not only P. Quinctius, who is fighting for his life [as the accused], trembles at their numbers and presence, but even anyone who is beyond such danger."

Against M. Aemilius Lepidus in the Senate (F 14A)

In 77 BC Philippus was the leader of a faction in the Senate who wished to declare M. Aemilius Lepidus (**95**) a public enemy; a version of a speech given in this context is presented in Sallust.

F 14A Sallust, *Histories*

not to wait any longer and instead to take action to contain the spread of these developments. Philippus concludes with the motion that Ap. Claudius Pulcher (cos. 79, interrex 77 BC), the proconsul Q. Lutatius Catulus (cos. 78 BC), and others with military power provide protection for the city and see to it that the Republic suffers no harm.

Unplaced Fragments (F 15–17)

These utterances (cf. also Cic. Leg. Man. 62) come from the interrogation of a witness (F 16) and from verbal exchanges, not necessarily parts of set speeches (F 15, 17).

F 15

a Quint. *Inst.* 6.3.81

cui vicinum est non negare quod obicitur, cum et id palam falsum est et inde materia bene respondendi datur, ut Catulus dicenti Philippo: "quid latras?" "furem video" inquit.

b Cic. *De or.* 2.220

[CAESAR STRABO:] quid enim hic meus frater ab arte adiuvari potuit, cum a Philippo interrogatus quid latraret, furem se videre respondit?

Cf. Cic. *De or.* 2.255.

F 16 Cic. *De or.* 2.245

[CAESAR STRABO:] pusillus testis processit. "licet" inquit "rogare?" Philippus. tum quaesitor properans: "modo bre-

Unplaced Fragments (F 15–17)

Possible trials to which these remarks might refer have been suggested (TLRR 90, 359).

F 15

a Quintilian, *The Orator's Education*

Related to this [a pretended confession] is not to deny the charge, when it is patently false and thereby material for a good reply is supplied, for instance: when Philippus says "What are you barking at?," Catulus [Q. Lutatius Catulus (**63**)] answers "I see a thief."[1]

[1] *Latrare* ("to bark") can be applied to someone's style of speaking (e.g., Cic. *Brut.* 58), and, literally, is a pun on the meaning of Catulus' name ("a young dog"). In response, Catulus accepts the role of "watchdog" and comments on Philippus' behavior, which may refer to the extortion of money or the reduction of political rights.

b Cicero, *On the Orator*

[CAESAR STRABO:] For what help could my brother here [Q. Lutatius Catulus (**63**)] have gotten from art, when he was asked by Philippus what he [Catulus] was barking at, and answered that he saw a thief?[1]

[1] See note on F 15a, above.

F 16 Cicero, *On the Orator*

[CAESAR STRABO:] A very short witness came forward. "May I examine him?" said Philippus. There the president

15

viter." hic ille: "non accusabis. perpusillum rogabo." ridicule. sed sedebat iudex L. Aurifex brevior ipse quam testis
etiam: omnis est risus in iudicem conversus; visum est
totum scurrile ridiculum.

F 17 Cic. *De or.* 2.249

[CAESAR STRABO:] . . . at in male olentem: "video me a te
circumveniri"[1] subridicule Philippus.

1 circumveniri *vel* cumveniri *vel* conveniri *codd.*: cicrumveniri
non conveniri *Stephanus ex coniectura Strebaei*: non conveniri
sed circumveniri *Lambinus*: hirco veniri *Fleckeisen*: hircum veniri
Nencini

70A C. SEXTIUS CALVINUS

T 1 Cic. *Brut.* 130

[CICERO:] atque et acri[1] ingenio et sermone eleganti, valetudine incommoda C. Sextius Calvinus fuit; qui etsi, cum
remiserant dolores pedum, non deerat in causis, tamen id
non saepe faciebat. itaque consilio eius, cum volebant,
homines utebantur, patrocinio, cum licebat.

1 atque et acri *Friedrich*: atque etiam *codd.*: acuto etiam *Kayser*: atque etiam *Piderit*

16

of the court, hastening on, [said]: "Only briefly." Here he [said]: "You will not complain: I will make a very short examination." Funny. But L. Aurifex was sitting there as judge, even shorter than the witness: all the laughter turned toward the judge; the entire joke seemed buffoonish.

F 17 Cicero, *On the Orator*

[CAESAR STRABO:] . . . but to a malodorous individual Philippus [said] with a spark of humor: "I perceive that I am encircled by you."[1]

---

[1] Presumably a pun on *circum* ("round about") and *hircus* ("he-goat," applied to a person's smell; e.g., Hor. *Sat.* 1.2.27), that is, both cheated and surrounded by a bad smell.

70A C. SEXTIUS CALVINUS

C. Sextius Calvinus (RE Sextius 21) was probably a contemporary of M. Antonius (65) and L. Licinius Crassus (66). In Cicero's view (T 1), Calvinus could have been a good pleader if he had been of better health (cf. 58b F 3).

T 1 Cicero, *Brutus*

[CICERO:] Another man of keen mind and careful speech, but of unfavorable health, was C. Sextius Calvinus: even though he would not be neglectful with respect to trials if the pain of his feet had relaxed, yet he did not do it often. Therefore, people availed themselves of his counsel when they would, of his help in court when they could.

On Appius (F 2)

F 2 Cic. *De or.* 2.246

[CAESAR STRABO:] ut iste qui se volt dicacem—et mehercule est, Appius, sed nonnumquam in hoc vitium scurrile delabitur—: "cenabo" inquit "apud te" huic lusco, familiari meo, C. Sextio; "uni enim locum esse video." est hoc scurrile et quod sine causa lacessivit et tamen id dixit, quod in omnes luscos conveniret. ea, quia meditata putantur esse, minus ridentur. illud egregium Sexti et ex tempore: "manus lava" inquit "et cena."

71 HELVIUS MANCIA

Helvius Mancia (RE Helvius 15), from Formiae (modern Formia in Lazio) and a son of a freedman, was active in the first half of the first century BC.

On C. Antonius (F 1A)

F 1A Cic. *De or.* 2.274

[CAESAR STRABO:] genus hoc levius, et, ut dixi, mimicum; sed habet nonnumquam aliquid etiam apud nos loci, ut vel

On Appius (F 2)

F 2 Cicero, *On the Orator*

[CAESAR STRABO:] For instance, that Appius, who wants to be witty—and, by Hercules, actually is, but occasionally slips into this fault of buffoonery—said to my one-eyed friend here, C. Sextius: "I will have dinner at your house, for I see that there is room for one." This is buffoonery; for he attacked unprovoked, and even so he only said what would apply to all one-eyed individuals. Such remarks, as they seem to be thought out in advance, win less laughter. The retort of Sextius was brilliant and spontaneous: "Wash your hands," he said, "and then dine."

71 HELVIUS MANCIA

*Cicero mentions that Helvius Mancia was mocked in an exchange with C. Iulius Caesar Strabo (**73** F 15).*

On C. Antonius (F 1A)

*Helvius Mancia made a witty comment about M. Antonius (**65**) while censor (97 BC), when Antonius was prosecuted by M. Duronius (**68**) for* ambitus *(TLRR 83).*

F 1A Cicero, *On the Orator*

[CAESAR STRABO:] This kind [of joke: comic, somewhat absurd] is rather trivial, and, as I said [earlier in the paragraph], fit for farces; but occasionally there is some room for it even among us [orators], with the result that even a

non stultus quasi stulte cum sale dicat aliquid; ut tibi,
Antoni, Mancia,[1] cum audisset te censorem a M. Duronio
de ambitu postulatum, "aliquando" inquit "tibi tuum ne-
gotium agere licebit."

[1] Mancia *vel* minima *codd.*

In Response to Cn. Pompeius Magnus (F 1)

*In old age, Helvius Mancia accused L. Scribonius Libo
(cos. 34 BC; RE Scribonius 20) before the censors (probably at the census of 55–54 BC). Libo was supported by*

F 1 Val. Max. 6.2.8

Helvius Mancia Formianus, libertini filius ultimae senec-
tutis, L. Libonem apud censores accusabat. in quo certamine cum Pompeius Magnus humilitatem ei aetatemque
exprobrans ab inferis illum ad accusandum remissum dixisset, "non mentiris" inquit, "Pompei: venio enim ab inferis, in L. Libonem accusator venio. sed dum illic moror,
vidi cruentum Cn. Domitium Ahenobarbum deflentem,
quod summo genere natus, integerrimae vitae, amantissimus patriae, in ipso iuventae flore tuo iussu esset occisus. vidi pari claritate conspicuum M. Brutum ferro lace-

man who is no fool says something in the manner of a fool, but with humor, as Mancia did to you, Antonius [M. Antonius (**65**)], when he had heard that you, as censor, were being prosecuted by M. Duronius [**68**] for corrupt practices: "At last," he said, "it will be possible for you to attend to your own business."

In Response to Cn. Pompeius Magnus (F 1)

*Cn. Pompeius Magnus (**111** F 26), whose son was married to Libo's daughter (on this altercation see Steel 2013).*

F 1 Valerius Maximus, *Memorable Doings and Sayings*

Helvius Mancia of Formiae, son of a freedman, in extreme old age, was accusing L. Libo before the censors. When in that altercation Pompey [Cn. Pompeius Magnus (**111**), F 26], reproaching him with his lowly status and his age, had said that the other had been sent back from the underworld to make the charge, he said: "You are not lying, Pompey: truly I come from the underworld, I come as L. Libo's accuser. But while I was there, I saw Cn. Domitius Ahenobarbus[1] all bloody, lamenting that he, a man of the noblest birth, of an entirely unblemished life, a great lover of his country, had been put to death on your order in the very flower of youth. I saw M. Brutus,[2] notable for the

---

[1] Cn. Domitius Ahenobarbus (*RE* Domitius 22), promagistrate in 82–81 BC, defeated and put to death by Pompey in Africa (*MRR* II 77). [2] M. Iunius Brutus, besieged by Pompey at Mutina and put to death, after having surrendered, in 78 BC (*MRR* II 90).

ratum, querentem id sibi prius perfidia deinde etiam crudelitate tua accidisse. vidi Cn. Carbonem acerrimum pueritiae tuae bonorumque patris tui defensorem, in tertio consulatu catenis, quas tu ei inici iusseras, vinctum, obtestantem se[1] adversus omne fas ac nefas, cum in summo esset imperio, a te equite Romano trucidatum. vidi eodem habitu et quiritatu praetorium virum Perpernam[2] saevitiam tuam exsecrantem, omnesque eos una voce indignantes, quod indemnati sub te adulescentulo carnifice occidissent." obducta iam vetustis cicatricibus bellorum civilium vastissima vulnera municipali homini, servitutem paternam redolenti, effrenatae temeritatis, intolerabilis spiritus, impune revocare licuit. itaque eodem tempore et fortissimum erat Cn. Pompeio maledicere et tutissimum.

---

[1] se *Kempf*: te *codd.*   [2] Perpernam *cod. epit., unus cod.* *corr.*: Perpennam *codd.*

72 M. LIVIUS DRUSUS

M. Livius Drusus (tr. pl. 91 BC; RE Livius 18), a son of M. Livius Drusus (42), was known as an energetic Tribune of the People and a powerful orator (T 1–6; Cic. Brut. 182;

same distinction, lacerated with steel, complaining that this happened to him first by your treachery, then also by your cruelty. I saw Cn. Carbo,[3] the most zealous defender of your boyhood and of your father's property [cf. **70** F 12–13], bound in his third consulship by the chains that you ordered to be placed upon him, protesting that against all things lawful and unlawful he, while holding highest authority, was slaughtered by you, a Roman knight. I saw Perperna,[4] an ex-praetor, in the same condition and with the same protest, cursing your savagery, and all of them with one voice indignant that without judicial sentence they perished on your orders, a mere youth as an executioner." The huge wounds of the civil wars, already overlaid with shriveled scars, could be recalled with impunity by a man from a country town, smelling of his father's slavery, unbridled in his impetuosity, unbearable in his arrogance. Therefore, at the same time it was both very brave and very safe to insult Pompey.

[3] Cn. Papirius Carbo (cos. 85, 84, 82 BC), captured and put to death by Pompey in Sicily in 82/81 BC (*MRR* II 66).   [4] ?M. Perperna Vento (praet. 82 BC), leader of the conspiracy to kill Sertorius, captured and put to death by Pompey in 72 BC (*MRR* II 120).

72 M. LIVIUS DRUSUS

Sen. Dial. *6.16.4); some of his measures were controversial, and he was eventually killed. Drusus was friends with the poet Archias (Cic.* Arch. *6) and an acquaintance of the orator L. Licinius Crassus (**66**) (Cic.* De or. *1.97).*

T 1 Cic. *Brut.* 222

[CICERO:] . . . M. Drusum tuum magnum avunculum, gravem oratorem ita dumtaxat cum de re publica diceret . . .

T 2 Vell. Pat. 2.13.1

deinde interiectis paucis annis tribunatum iniit M. Livius Drusus, vir nobilissimus eloquentissimus sanctissimus, meliore in omnia ingenio animoque quam fortuna usus.

T 3 Sen. *Dial.* 10.6.1–2

Livius Drusus, vir acer et vehemens, cum leges novas et mala Gracchana movisset stipatus ingenti totius Italiae coetu . . . execratus inquietam a primordiis vitam dicitur dixisse uni sibi ne puero quidem umquam ferias contigisse. ausus est enim et pupillus adhuc et praetextatus iudicibus reos commendare et gratiam suam foro interponere, tam efficaciter quidem ut quaedam iudicia constet ab illo rapta. [2] . . . sero itaque querebatur nullas sibi ferias contigisse, a puero seditiosus et foro gravis. disputatur an ipse sibi manus attulerit; subito enim vulnere per inguen accepto conlapsus est, aliquo dubitante an mors eius voluntaria esset, nullo an tempestiva.

T 1 Cicero, *Brutus*

[CICERO:] . . . M. Drusus, your great-uncle [of M. Iunius Brutus (**158**)], an orator of weight, at least when he spoke about political issues . . .

T 2 Velleius Paterculus, *Compendium of Roman History*

Then, after an interval of a few years, M. Livius Drusus entered the Tribunate, a very noble, very eloquent, and very upright man; in all his acts he had more talent and good intentions than success.

T 3 Seneca, *Dialogues. De Brevitate Vitae*

When Livius Drusus, a bold and energetic man, had proposed new laws and Gracchan evils [i.e., measures reminiscent of Ti. Sempronius Gracchus (**34**) and C. Sempronius Gracchus (**48**)], surrounded by a huge crowd drawn from all Italy . . . he is said to have cursed the life of unrest he had had from the beginning and to have said that he was the only person who had never had a holiday, not even as a boy. For, while he was still a ward and wearing the dress of a boy, he had had the courage to commend the accused to the favor of judges and to make his influence felt in the Forum, so powerfully indeed, that it is well known that certain trials were seized by him. [2] . . . And so he complained too late that he had never had a holiday, when from boyhood onward he had been a troublemaker and a nuisance in the Forum. It is debated whether he laid hands on himself; for he fell from a sudden wound received in his groin, some doubting whether his death was voluntary, no one whether it was timely.

T 4 [Aurel. Vict.] *Vir. ill.* 66.1

Marcus Livius Drusus, genere et eloquentia magnus, sed ambitiosus et superbus, aedilis munus magnificentissimum dedit.

T 5 Diod. Sic. 37.10.1

ὅτι Μάρκος Λίβιος Δροῦσος ἀνὴρ νέος μὲν ἦν τὴν ἡλικίαν, κεκοσμημένος δὲ πᾶσι τοῖς πρωτείοις. . . . αὐτὸς δὲ ὑπῆρχε λόγῳ μὲν δεινότατος τῶν ἡλικιωτῶν, πλούτῳ δὲ πάντας τοὺς πολίτας ὑπερβάλλων, μεγάλην δὲ ἀξιοπιστίαν ἔχων καὶ κατὰ τὰς ὑποσχέσεις ὧν βεβαιότατος, ἔτι δὲ πλήρης εὐγενοῦς φρονήματος.

T 6 Plut. *Cat. min.* 1.2

καὶ πάντες οὗτοι παρὰ Λιβίῳ Δρούσῳ τροφὴν καὶ δίαιταν εἶχον, θείῳ μὲν ὄντι τῆς μητρός, ἄγοντι δὲ τὴν πολιτείαν τότε· καὶ γὰρ εἰπεῖν δεινότατος ἦν, καὶ τἆλλα σώφρων ἀνὴρ ἐν τοῖς μάλιστα, καὶ φρονήματος οὐδενὶ Ῥωμαίων ὑφιέμενος.

About L. Marcius Philippus in the Senate (F 7)

When Drusus was Tribune of the People (91 BC), he attacked the consul, L. Marcius Philippus (70 F 9–10) in the Senate because he had criticized the Senate at a meeting

T 4 [Aurelius Victor], *On Famous Men*

Marcus Livius Drusus, outstanding in ancestry and eloquence, but ambitious and haughty, when aedile,[1] gave
most magnificent games.

[1] There may be an error in the source; it is uncertain whether
Drusus ever held the aedileship (Sumner 1973, 110–11).

T 5 Diodorus Siculus, *Library of History*

Marcus Livius Drusus was a young man in terms of age,
yet endowed with all great advantages. . . . in oratory, he
himself was the most competent among his contemporaries; in wealth he surpassed all citizens; he commanded
great trustworthiness and was most faithful to his promises; moreover, he was imbued with a noble-minded spirit.

T 6 Plutarch, *Life of Cato the Younger*

And all these [M. Porcius Cato (**126**) and his siblings]
enjoyed board and lodging in the home of Livius Drusus,
their maternal uncle, who at that time was running public
affairs; for he was most powerful in speaking, in other
respects a prudent man to the greatest degree, and yield-
ing to none of the Romans in spirit.

About L. Marcius Philippus in the Senate (F 7)

*of the People (CCMR, App. A: 218; cf. Val. Max. 9.5.2),
which was also commented on by L. Licinius Crassus (**66**
F 41).*

F 7 Cic. *De or.* 3.2

= **66** F 41.

72A CN. OCTAVIUS

Cn. Octavius (cos. 87 BC; RE Octavius 20), when consul, clashed with his colleague L. Cornelius Cinna, as the latter wished to recall C. Marius and grant citizenship to tribes all over Italy. This led to a civil conflict (called bellum Octavianum *by Cicero); Cinna and Marius besieged Rome, and eventually Octavius was killed.*

As Consul to the People (F 1)

F 1 Cic. *Brut.* 176

[CICERO:] Cn. autem Octavi eloquentia, quae fuerat ante consulatum ignorata, in consulatu multis contionibus est vehementer probata. sed ab eis, qui tantum in dicentium numero, non in oratorum fuerunt, iam ad oratores revertamur.

72B CN. POMPONIUS

Cn. Pomponius (tr. pl. 90 BC; RE Pomponius 3) died during the civil war in the 80s BC.

Pomponius is mentioned several times in Cicero's Brutus: *there he is described as an able, well-known orator in*

F 7 Cicero, *On the Orator*
= **66** F 41.

72A CN. OCTAVIUS

Speeches to the People during Octavius' consulship are mentioned in Cicero (CCMR, App. A: 224): these showcased his hitherto unnoticed eloquence; still, he is counted among those well able to speak, not the true orators (F 1).

As Consul to the People (F 1)

F 1 Cicero, *Brutus*

[CICERO:] And the eloquence of Cn. Octavius, which before his consulship had not been known, found high favor through many speeches to the People during his consulship. But let us return now from those who were accounted only among the competent speakers, not among the true orators, to the true orators.

72B CN. POMPONIUS

the early first century BC, who had a great effect on audiences (T 1–2; Cic. Brut. 182, 308, 311). In De oratore *it is noted that his speeches suffered from a lack of organization and were therefore difficult to understand (T 3).*

T 1 Cic. *Brut.* 207

[CICERO:] his duobus eiusdem aetatis adnumerabatur nemo tertius, sed mihi placebat Pomponius maxime, vel dicam, minime displicebat.

T 2 Cic. *Brut.* 221

[CICERO:] . . . fortis vero actor et vehemens et verbis nec inops nec abiectus et quem plane oratorem dicere auderes, Cn. Pomponius lateribus pugnans, incitans animos, acer acerbus criminosus.

T 3 Cic. *De or.* 3.50
= **75** T 3.

Speeches to the People (F 4)

F 4 Cic. *Brut.* 305
= **87** T 2.

T 1 Cicero, *Brutus*

[CICERO:] To these two [C. Aurelius Cotta (**80**) and P. Sulpicius Rufus (**76**)] no one of the same generation was added as third in rank; but Pomponius pleased me most or, I should rather say, displeased me least.

T 2 Cicero, *Brutus*

[CICERO:] . . . but a vigorous and energetic performer and neither lacking abundance nor mean in his diction was Cn. Pomponius, a man whom you would absolutely venture to call an orator, fighting with lungpower, rousing the auditors, sharp, harsh, accusatory.

T 3 Cicero, *On the Orator*

= **75** T 3.

Speeches to the People (F 4)

According to Cicero, Pomponius delivered frequent speeches to the People (CCMR, App. A: 220).

F 4 Cicero, *Brutus*

= **87** T 2.

73 C. IULIUS CAESAR STRABO

C. Iulius Caesar Strabo / Vopiscus / Sesquiculus (aed. cur.
90 BC; RE Iulius 135) was quaestor, curule aedile, mili-
tary tribune, decemvir, *and* pontifex, *but was unsuccessful*
when he stood for the consulship in 88 BC (Cic. Phil.
11.11); in 87 BC he was killed by the Marians. Caesar
*Strabo was also a tragic poet (*TrRF *1:130–33) and is a*
speaker in Cicero's De oratore, *where he discusses jokes*
and witticism (Cic. Att. *13.19.4;* De or. *2.12, 2.216–90).*

T 1 Cic. *Brut.* 177

"festivitate igitur et facetiis, inquam [CICERO], C. Iulius
L. f. et superioribus et aequalibus suis omnibus praestitit
oratorque fuit minime ille quidem vehemens, sed nemo
umquam urbanitate, nemo lepore, nemo suavitate condi-
tior. sunt eius aliquot orationes, ex quibus sicut ex eiusdem
tragoediis lenitas eius ⟨non⟩[1] sine nervis perspici potest. . . ."

[1] *add. Friedrich (cf. Cic. De or. 3.199)*

T 2 Cic. *Off.* 1.108

erat in L. Crasso, in L. Philippo multus lepos, maior etiam
magisque de industria in C. Caesare L. f. . . .

73 C. IULIUS CAESAR STRABO

In Cicero the wittiness and charm of Caesar Strabo's
speeches are highlighted (T 1–4, 6); it is also noted that
he was able to mix tones without the result turning into
something inappropriate (T 5). Some of Caesar Strabo's
speeches and tragedies were extant in Cicero's time (T 1).
Caesar Strabo was said to be an advocate in demand in his
time and regarded as one of those in second place after M.
Antonius (65) and L. Licinius Crassus (66) (Cic. Brut.
207; Vell. Pat. 2.9.2).

T 1 Cicero, *Brutus*

"With regard to liveliness and wittiness, then," I [CICERO]
said, "C. Iulius, Lucius' son, surpassed all his predecessors
and contemporaries. And as an orator he was not at all
vehement, but nobody ever was more seasoned in humor,
nor in grace, nor in charm. Some of his orations are extant,
from which, as from his tragedies, his smooth style, ‹not›
without vigor, may be discerned. . . ."

T 2 Cicero, *On Duties*

There was a lot of wit in L. Crassus [L. Licinius Crassus
(**66**)] and in L. Philippus [L. Marcius Philippus (**70**)], even
more in C. Caesar, Lucius' son, and employed more delib-
erately . . .

33

T 3 Cic. *Off.* 1.133

sale vero et facetiis Caesar, Catuli patris frater, vicit omnes, ut in illo ipso forensi genere dicendi contentiones aliorum sermone vinceret.

T 4 Cic. *De or.* 2.98

[ANTONIUS:] . . . quod et in vobis animum adverti recte potest, Caesar et Cotta, quorum alter inusitatum nostris quidem oratoribus leporem quendam et salem, alter acutissimum et subtilissimum dicendi genus est consecutus . . .

T 5 Cic. *De or.* 3.30

[CRASSUS:] quid, noster hic Caesar nonne novam quandam rationem attulit orationis et dicendi genus induxit prope singulare? quis umquam res, praeter hunc, tragicas paene comice, tristis remisse, severas hilare, forenses scenica prope venustate tractavit atque ita, ut neque iocus magnitudine rerum excluderetur nec gravitas facetiis minueretur?

T 6 Cic. *Tusc.* 5.55

[M.:] . . . M. Antoni, omnium eloquentissimi quos ego audierim, C. Caesaris, in quo mihi videtur specimen fuisse humanitatis salis suavitatis leporis.

T 3 Cicero, *On Duties*

But in humor and wittiness Caesar, the elder Catulus' [Q. Lutatius Catulus (**63**)] [half-]brother, surpassed everyone, so that even in that forensic type of speaking he would defeat the vigorous orations of others with his conversational style.

T 4 Cicero, *On the Orator*

[ANTONIUS:] . . . and that [developing characteristics as an orator without imitating anyone] may truly be observed also in the two of you, Caesar and Cotta [C. Aurelius Cotta (**80**)], one of whom has acquired an unusual kind of humor and wit, at least among our orators, and the other a very shrewd and very subtle type of oratory . . .

T 5 Cicero, *On the Orator*

[CRASSUS:] Again, has not our friend Caesar here brought forward some novel method of oratory and introduced an almost unique type of speaking? Who except him has handled tragic themes in a manner almost proper to comedy, gloomy topics lightheartedly, severe ones cheerfully, and forensic ones almost with the charm of the stage, and in such a way that neither was a jest excluded by the importance of the subject matter nor the seriousness reduced by wittiness?

T 6 Cicero, *Tusculan Disputations*

[M.:] . . . of M. Antonius [**65**], the most eloquent of all I have myself heard, of C. Caesar, who seemed to me to be a model of courtesy, wit, grace, and charm.

On Behalf of the Sardinians (F 7–10)

F 7 Cic. *Off.* 2.50

sed hoc quidem non est saepe faciendum, nec umquam nisi aut reipublicae causa . . . aut ulciscendi gratia . . . aut patrocinii, ut nos pro Siculis, pro Sardis {pro M. Albucio}[1] Iulius.

[1] *del. Lambinus*: pro m. albutio *vel sim. codd.*

F 8 Cic. *Div. Caec.* 63

itaque neque L. Philoni in C. Servilium nominis deferendi potestas est data, neque M. Aurelio Scauro in L. Flaccum, neque Cn. Pompeio in T. Albucium; quorum nemo propter indignitatem repudiatus est, sed ne libido violandae necessitudinis auctoritate iudicum comprobaretur. atque ille Cn. Pompeius ita cum C. Iulio contendit, ut tu mecum; quaestor enim Albuci fuerat, ut tu Verris; Iulius hoc secum

On Behalf of the Sardinians (F 7–10)

Having been asked by the Sardinians, Caesar Strabo pros-
*ecuted T. Albucius (**64**), shortly after the latter's return*
from his propraetorship in Sardinia, for his behavior in
that province (TLRR 67; cf. Cic. Pis. 92; Scaur. 40).

F 7 Cicero, *On Duties*

But this [an accusation] should not be done often, never,
in fact, except for the sake of the Republic . . . or for taking
revenge . . . or for offering support as a patron, as we [did]
on behalf of the Sicilians [against C. Verres] or Iulius on
behalf of the Sardinians {on behalf of M. Albucius}.

F 8 Cicero, *Against Caecilius*

For this reason L. Philo[1] was not given permission to prosecute C. Servilius [praet. in Sicily in 102 BC], nor M.
Aurelius Scaurus [M. Aurelius Scaurus (**59**)] to prosecute
L. Flaccus [L. Valerius Flaccus, cos. 100 BC], nor Cn.
Pompeius [Cn. Pompeius Strabo, cos. 89 BC] to prosecute
T. Albucius [**64**]. None of them were rejected because of
unworthiness, but rather so that the desire to violate the
bonds between people [former quaestors turning against
their superiors] should not be endorsed by the authority
of the judges. And that Cn. Pompeius [Cn. Pompeius
Strabo] competed with C. Iulius in the same way as you
do with me; for he [Pompeius] had been quaestor to Al-

[1] Perhaps L. Veturius Philo (quaest. 102 BC, according to this
passage), but the *nomen* is not certain (*RE* Veturius 21; *MRR* I
569 n. 5).

auctoritatis ad accusandum adferebat quod, ut hoc tempore nos ab Siculis, sic tum ille ab Sardis rogatus ad causam accesserat.

F 9 Suet. *Iul.* 55.2
= **121** T 10.

F 10 Apul. *Apol.* 66.4
= **65** F 15.

As Aedile to the People (F 11)

F 11 Cic. *Brut.* 305
[CICERO:] . . . C. etiam Iulius aedilis curulis cottidie fere accuratas contiones habebat.

Against C. Scribonius Curio (F 12)

F 12 Cic. *Brut.* 216
= **86** T 2.

bucius, as you have been to Verres; Iulius brought this weighty claim to the right of prosecution because he had then undertaken the case at the request of the Sardinians, as we are now doing at the request of the Sicilians.

F 9 Suetonius, *Life of Caesar*

= **121** T 10.

F 10 Apuleius, *Apologia*

= **65** F 15.[1]

[1] If Sauppe's conjecture *C. Iulius T. Albucium* for *C. Mucius A. Albucium* is accepted, the present case is referred to in this passage.

As Aedile to the People (F 11)

As aedile in 90 BC, Caesar Strabo is said to have delivered many speeches to the People (CCMR, App. A: 220).

F 11 Cicero, *Brutus*

[CICERO:] . . . C. Iulius too, when curule aedile, delivered almost daily elaborate speeches before the People.

Against C. Scribonius Curio (F 12)

*The mocking question asked of C. Scribonius Curio (**86**) may not have been part of a set speech.*

F 12 Cicero, *Brutus*

= **86** T 2.

Before the Censors (F 13)

F 13 Varro, *Rust.* 1.7.10

Caesar Vopiscus aedilicius, causam cum ageret apud censores, campos Roseae Italiae dixit esse sumen, in quo relicta pertica postridie non appareret propter herbam.

Cf. Plin. *HN* 17.32.

In Response to P. Sulpicius Rufus (F 14)

When Caesar Strabo was a candidate for the consulship (without having been praetor) in 88 BC, he was taken to court by the Tribunes of the People P. Sulpicius Rufus (76

F 14 Prisc., *GL* II, p. 170.21–23

Caesar Strabo in oratione, qua Sulpicio respondit: "deinde propinquos nostros Messalas domo deflagrata penore volebamus privare."

Cf. Prisc., *GL* II, p. 261.4–6: Caesar Strabo contra Sulpicium tribunum plebis: ". . ."

Before the Censors (F 13)

After his aedileship, Caesar Strabo acted in a case before the censors.

F 13 Varro, *On Agriculture*

Caesar Vopiscus, an ex-aedile, when he was pleading a case before the censors, said that the plains of Rosea [extremely fertile plains near Reate] were the nursing-ground of Italy, where a rod left there would not be visible the next day because of the grass.

In Response to P. Sulpicius Rufus (F 14)

*F 17–18) and P. Antistius (**78**) (Asc. in Cic. Scaur. II.2 [p. 25.6–8 C.]) and replied to the accusations.*

F 14 Priscian

[on *penus / penum*, "provisions"]: Caesar Strabo in the speech in which he responded to Sulpicius [P. Sulpicius Rufus (**76**)]: "then we wanted to deprive our neighbors, the Messallae, after the house had burned down, of provisions."[1]

[1] The clause might comment on an accusation.

Cf. Priscian: Caesar Strabo against Sulpicius, a Tribune of the People [88 BC]: ". . ."

Against Helvius Mancia (F 15)

F 15 Cic. *De or.* 2.266

[CAESAR STRABO:] valde autem ridentur etiam imagines, quae fere in deformitatem aut in aliquod vitium corporis ducuntur cum similitudine turpioris; ut meum illud in Helvium Manciam: "iam ostendam cuius modi sis;" cum ille: "ostende quaeso," demonstravi digito pictum Gallum in Mariano scuto Cimbrico sub Novis distortum, eiecta lingua, buccis fluentibus; risus est commotus: nihil tam Manciae simile visum est . . .

Cf. Quint. *Inst.* 6.3.38.

On Behalf of Sextilius (F 16)

F 16 Val. Max. 5.3.3

quo enim nimbo qua procella verborum impium Sextili caput obrui meretur, quod C. Caesarem, a quo cum studiose tum etiam feliciter gravissimi criminis reus defensus

Against Helvius Mancia (F 15)

The altercation with Helvius Mancia (71), not necessarily part of a set speech, provides an example of Caesar Strabo's wittiness.

F 15 Cicero, *On the Orator*

[CAESAR STRABO:] And images also provoke much laughter: they are generally directed toward disfigurement or some physical defect and involve comparison with something even more unseemly, such as my remark to Helvius Mancia: "I will now show what manner of man you are"; when he said: "Show me, please," I pointed out with my finger a Gaul depicted on a Cimbrian shield of Marius [C. Marius, seven-time consul and victorious general against the Cimbri, a Germanic tribe], hanging below the New Shops, with the body deformed, the tongue protruding, the cheeks baggy; laughter was raised: for nothing so similar to Mancia was ever seen . . .

On Behalf of Sextilius (F 16)

At an unknown date (before the rule of Cinna in 87–84 BC), Caesar Strabo defended a Sextilius (TLRR 112), who later betrayed him (Cic. De or. 3.10).

F 16 Valerius Maximus, *Memorable Doings and Sayings*

With what a downpour, what a storm of words does the impious head of Sextilius deserve to be overwhelmed? When C. Caesar, by whom he had been zealously and also successfully defended on a very serious charge, was a fugi-

fuerat, Cinnanae proscriptionis tempore profugum, prae-
sidium suum in fundo Tarquiniensi cladis condicione im-
plorare beneficii iure repetere coactum, a sacris perfidae
mensae et altaribus nefandorum penatium avolsum tru-
culento victori iugulandum tradere non exhorruit? finge
accusatorem eius fortuna publica in supplicis nomen con-
versum tam luctuosam illam opem genibus adnixum
orasse; crudeliter tamen repulsus videretur, quia etiam
quos iniuriae invisos faciunt, gratiosos miseriae reddunt.
verum Sextilius non accusatorem sed patronum saevissi-
mae inimici violentiae suis manibus obiecit, si metu mortis, vita indignus, si praemii spe, dignissimus morte.

To Pomponius (F 17)

F 17 Quint. *Inst.* 6.3.75

elevandi ratio est duplex, ut aut nimiam[1] quis iactantiam
minuat (quem ad modum C. Caesar Pomponio ostendenti
vulnus ore exceptum in seditione Sulpiciana, quod is se
passum pro Caesare pugnantem gloriabatur, "numquam
fugiens respexeris?" inquit) aut . . .

---

[1] nimiam *Deffner (ap. Halm)*: ueniam *vel* uerecundiam *codd.*

tive at the time of the Cinnan proscription, he was forced
by his calamitous plight to beg for protection at his [Sex-
tilius'] property near Tarquinii [in Etruria] and to claim it
by right of his benefaction: Sextilius did not shudder to
tear him from the rites of a treacherous table and the altars
of abominable household gods and hand him over for
slaughter to the savage victor. Imagine that his accuser,
turned by public fortune into the category of suppliant,
had begged on his knees for that mournful succor; still, he
would have seemed cruel to reject him, because even
those whom injuries make odious win favor by miseries.
But Sextilius with his own hands offered not his accuser
but his advocate to the most ruthless violence of an enemy;
if from fear of death, he was unworthy to live, if in hope
of reward, he was very worthy to die.

*Further witty remarks are attested directed against Pom-
ponius (F 17) and an unidentified witness (F 18).*

To Pomponius (F 17)

F 17 Quintilian, *The Orator's Education*

The method of weakening is twofold: either someone
chops up too much boasting (as C. Caesar said to Pomponius, displaying a wound on his face received in Sulpicius' [P. Sulpicius Rufus (**76**)] insurrection [88 BC],
because he boasted of having suffered it while fighting
for Caesar: "Would you have never looked back when flee-
ing?") or . . .

To a Witness (F 18)

F 18 Quint. *Inst.* 6.3.91

est et illa ex ironia fictio, qua usus est C. Caesar. nam cum testis diceret a reo femina sua ferro petita, et esset facilis reprehensio, cur illam potissimum partem corporis vulnerare voluisset, "quid enim faceret," inquit, "cum tu galeam et loricam haberes?"

74 L. AELIUS STILO PRAECONINUS

L. Aelius Stilo Praeconinus (RE Aelius 144) was not an orator himself; instead, he wrote speeches for others (T 1–2; Cic. Brut. *169). He was a Roman knight, learned in Greek and Roman literature, and a student of grammar (T 2; Suet.* Gram. et rhet. *2.1–2; Gell. NA 1.18.2, 16.8.2); he was a teacher of Cicero and Varro (Cic.* Brut. *207; Gell. NA 16.8.2). Aelius Stilo sympathized with the Stoics (T 2) and produced works on grammar, etymology, and literary criticism (GRF, pp. 51–76).*

T 1 Suet. *Gram. et rhet.* 3.2

= **58** T 2.

T 2 Cic. *Brut.* 205–6

[CICERO:] fuit is omnino vir egregius et eques Romanus cum primis honestus idemque eruditissimus et Graecis

To a Witness (F 18)

F 18 Quintilian, *The Orator's Education*

That which C. Caesar used is also something made up based on irony. For when a witness said that the accused had aimed at his thighs with a sword, and it would have been a straightforward point of criticism [to ask] why he should have wanted to strike that part of the body in particular, he [Caesar] said: "Well, what else could he do since you were wearing a helmet and a breastplate?"

74 L. AELIUS STILO PRAECONINUS

Aelius Stilo wrote speeches for, among others, Q. Metellus (cf. 58 T 3) (F 3) (TLRR 82 [with different identification of Metellus]), Q. Servilius Caepio (85) (F 3, 4), C. Aurelius Cotta (80) (F 5–6; cf. App. B Civ. 1.37.167) (TLRR 105), and Q. Pompeius Rufus (83) (F 7) (TLRR 101). At least some of these speeches were intended for men charged under the Lex Varia de maiestate (see 88), which seems to have required the accused to defend themselves.

T 1 Suetonius, *Lives of Illustrious Men. Grammarians and Rhetoricians*

= **58** T 2.

T 2 Cicero, *Brutus*

[CICERO:] He [Aelius] was in all respects an outstanding man, a Roman knight respectable to the highest degree, and equally thoroughly learned in both Greek and Latin

47

litteris et Latinis, antiquitatisque nostrae et in inventis rebus et in actis scriptorumque veterum litterate peritus. . . . [206] sed idem Aelius Stoicus ⟨esse⟩ voluit,[1] orator autem nec studuit umquam nec fuit. scribebat tamen orationes, quas alii dicerent . . .

[1] Stoicus ⟨esse⟩ voluit *edd.*: Stoicus voluit *codd.*: Stoicus studuit *Martha*: Stoicum se voluit *Stangl*

For Q. Metellus (F 3)

F 3 Cic. *Brut.* 206–7

[CICERO:] scribebat tamen orationes, quas alii dicerent; ut Q. Metello ⟨. . .⟩ f.,[1] ut Q. Caepioni,[2] ut Q. Pompeio Rufo; quamquam is etiam ipse scripsit eas, quibus pro se est usus, sed non sine Aelio. [207] his enim scriptis[3] etiam ipse interfui, cum essem apud Aelium adulescens eumque audire perstudiose solerem.

[1] ⟨L.⟩ f. *Martha*: Balearici filio *Lambinus* [2] Caepioni *edd.*: Caepione *codd.* [3] scriptis *om. unus cod.[1]*: scribendis *Lambinus*: scribentibus *Kraffert*

For Q. Servilius Caepio (F 4)

F 4 Cic. *Brut.* 169 (cf. F 3)

[CICERO:] . . . omnium autem eloquentissimus extra hanc urbem T. Betutius Barrus Asculanus, cuius sunt aliquot orationes Asculi habitae; una[1] Romae contra Caepionem

[1] una *Madvig*: illa *codd.*: et illa *Bake*

letters, and, as a well-read man, well versed in our past history, with respect to both discoveries and actions, and in ancient writers. . . . [206] And the same Aelius wished ‹to be› a Stoic, and he never aimed to be an orator nor was one. Yet he wrote orations for others to deliver . . . [continued by F 3]

For Q. Metellus (F 3)

F 3 Cicero, *Brutus*

[Cicero:] [continuing from T 2] Yet he [Aelius] wrote orations for others to deliver, as, for example, for Q. Metellus, son of ‹. . .› [cf. Q. Caecilius Metellus Numidicus (**58**), T 3], for Q. Caepio [Q. Servilius Caepio (**85**)], for Q. Pompeius Rufus [**83**], though the last also wrote himself those [orations] that he used in his own defense, but not without Aelius. [207] For I was even present myself as these were written, since, as a young man, I was in Aelius' company and accustomed to listen to him with the greatest enthusiasm. [continued by F 6]

For Q. Servilius Caepio (F 4)

F 4 Cicero, *Brutus* (cf. F 3)

[Cicero:] . . . but the most eloquent of all outside of this city [of Rome] was T. Betutius Barrus of Asculum [**84**], of whom some orations are extant delivered at Asculum [modern Ascoli]; a single speech [delivered] at Rome [**84** F 1], against Caepio [Q. Servilius Caepio (**85**), F 8], well

nobilis sane, quo‹i›[2] orationi Caepionis ore respondit
Aelius, qui scriptitavit orationes multis, orator ipse numquam fuit.

[2] cui *edd.*: quo *codd.*

For C. Aurelius Cotta (F 5–6)

F 5 Cic. *Brut.* 205

[CICERO:] Cottae pro se lege Varia quae inscribitur, eam
L. Aelius scripsit Cottae rogatu.

F 6 Cic. *Brut.* 207

[CICERO:] Cottam autem miror summum ipsum oratorem
minimeque ineptum Aelianas levis oratiunculas voluisse
existimari suas.

For Q. Pompeius Rufus (F 7)

F 7 Cic. *Brut.* 206

= F 3.

75 L. FUFIUS

*L. Fufius (RE Fufius 5) was an orator in the first half of
the first century BC (T 1). His qualities as a speaker are
not regarded highly in Cicero's* De oratore *(T 2–3), while*

known to be sure, to which Aelius replied through Caepio's mouth, Aelius, who was in the habit of writing speeches for many, but never was an orator himself.

For C. Aurelius Cotta (F 5–6)

F 5 Cicero, *Brutus*

[CICERO:] The oration entitled "Cotta in his own defense under the *Lex Varia*" was composed at Cotta's [C. Aurelius Cotta (**80**), F 10] request by L. Aelius.

F 6 Cicero, *Brutus*

[CICERO:] [continuing from F 3] But I wonder that Cotta [C. Aurelius Cotta (**80**), T 7], himself a most distinguished orator and far from devoid of taste, should have wanted the trivial speeches of Aelius be thought his own.

For Q. Pompeius Rufus (F 7)

F 7 Cicero, *Brutus*

= F 3.

75 L. FUFIUS

elsewhere at least his diligence and industry are praised (F 4–5).

T 1 Cic. *Brut.* 182
= **76** T 1.

T 2 Cic. *De or.* 2.91
= **55** T 2.

T 3 Cic. *De or.* 3.50

[CRASSUS:] isti enim, qui ad nos causas deferunt, ita nos plerumque ipsi docent, ut non desideres plenius dici. easdem res autem simulac Fufius aut vester aequalis Pomponius agere coepit, non aeque quid dicant, nisi admodum attendi, intellego; ita confusa est oratio, ita perturbata, nihil ut sit primum, nihil ut secundum tantaque insolentia ac turba verborum, ut oratio, quae lumen adhibere rebus debet, ea obscuritatem et tenebras adferat atque ut quodam modo ipsi sibi in dicendo obstrepere videantur.

Against M'. Aquillius (F 4–6)

*Fufius prosecuted M'. Aquillius (cos. 101 BC) for extortion, after the latter had concluded the servile war in Sicily following his consulship; M. Antonius (***65*** *F 19–21) defended the accused and managed to get him acquitted (TLRR 84).*

T 1 Cicero, *Brutus*

= **76** T 1.

T 2 Cicero, *On the Orator*

= **55** T 2.

T 3 Cicero, *On the Orator*

[CRASSUS:] In fact, those who bring their lawsuits to us themselves usually inform us in such a way that you would not want more to be said. But as soon as Fufius or your contemporary Pomponius [Cn. Pomponius (**72B**)] has begun to plead the same cases, I do not understand equally well what they are saying, unless I pay close attention; their speech is so muddled up, so confused that there is no first point, no second point, and there is such a flood of unusual words that the speech, which should throw light on the facts, brings darkness and shadows, and that they seem somehow to be shouting themselves down when speaking.

Against M'. Aquillius (F 4–6)

Fufius was also engaged in a civil suit with M. Buculeius (Cic. De or. 1.179; TLRR 361).

F 4 Cic. *Brut.* 222

[CICERO:] multum ab his aberat L. Fufius, tamen ex accusatione M'. Aquilli diligentiae fructum ceperat.

F 5 Cic. *Off.* 2.50

in accusando etiam M'. Aquillio[1] L. Fufi cognita industria est.

[1] Manio Aquillio *Langius, Lambinus post Manutium*: aquilio *vel* manilio *codd.*

F 6 Apul. *Apol.* 66.4
= **65** F 15.

75A M. OCTAVIUS

M. Octavius (RE Octavius 32) was presumably a Tribune of the People in the early first century BC. He is known only from references (also Cic. Off. 2.72) to his successful initiative to abrogate C. Sempronius Gracchus' (48) grain

Against Lex Sempronia frumentaria *(F 1)*

F 1 Cic. *Brut.* 222

[CICERO:] . . . M. Octavium Cn. f., qui tantum auctoritate dicendoque valuit ut legem Semproniam frumentariam populi frequentis suffragiis abrogaverit . . . abducamus ex

54

F 4 Cicero, *Brutus*

[CICERO:] Far inferior to these [the orators just mentioned: C. Papirius Carbo Arvina (**87**), Q. Varius Hybrida (**88**), Cn. Pomponius (**72B**)] was L. Fufius; yet from the accusation of M'. Aquillius he had earned the reward of diligence.

F 5 Cicero, *On Duties*

In the accusation of M'. Aquillius too the diligence of L. Fufius was recognized.

F 6 Apuleius, *Apologia*

= **65** F 15.

75A M. OCTAVIUS

law (Lex Sempronia frumentaria: LPPR, *pp. 307–8*); *Cicero's report suggests that this result was partly due to Octavius' powerful oratory.*

Against Lex Sempronia frumentaria *(F 1)*

F 1 Cicero, *Brutus*

[CICERO:] . . . M. Octavius, Gnaeus' son, who was so influential through his authority and speaking that he abrogated the Sempronian grain law by the votes of the People present in large numbers . . . let us withdraw them from

acie, id est a iudiciis, et in praesidiis rei publicae, cui facile
satis facere possint, collocemus.

75B T. IUNIUS

*T. Iunius (RE Iunius 32) was a Tribune of the People in
the early first century BC; he did not obtain higher offices
owing to ill health (F 1).*

Against P. Sextius (F 1)

F 1 Cic. *Brut.* 180

[CICERO:] fuit etiam facilis et expeditus ad dicendum et
vitae splendore multo et ingenio sane probabili T. Iunius
L. f. tribunicius, quo accusante P. Sextius praetor designatus damnatus est ambitus; is processisset honoribus
longius, nisi semper infirma atque etiam aegra valetudine
fuisset.

76 P. SULPICIUS RUFUS

*P. Sulpicius Rufus (tr. pl. 88 BC; RE Sulpicius 92) was a
legate in the Social War in 89 BC (Cic. Brut. 304). As
Tribune of the People in 88 BC, he supported C. Marius
and proposed a number of laws, for instance on citizen
rights and financial issues; in the same year, he was killed
on the orders of L. Cornelius Sulla.*

the battle line, that is from the courts, and station them [the orators just listed] on the ramparts of the Republic, whose demands they are easily able to meet.

75B T. IUNIUS

Iunius' only attested public appearance is his prosecution of P. Sextius on a charge of bribery (TLRR 107). In Cicero, Iunius is described as a fluent and talented speaker (F 1).

Against P. Sextius (F 1)

F 1 Cicero, *Brutus*

[CICERO:] An easy and fluent speaker, of much distinction in life and certainly of commendable talent, was also T. Iunius, Lucius' son, a former Tribune; under his prosecution P. Sextius, a praetor designate, was convicted of bribery. He [Iunius] would have gone further in public office had he not always suffered from unstable and even bad health.

76 P. SULPICIUS RUFUS

In Cicero, Sulpicius is described as a great orator in his time; his natural talent is highlighted (T 1–4, 6, 7, 9; Cic. Brut. 201, 207, 214, 297; cf. Vell. Pat. 2.9.2). Sulpicius' style is described as full and elevated, with charm and brevity, his delivery as vigorous and dignified (T 2, 5, 7, 8). Sulpicius is a speaker in Cicero's De oratore. *None of*

T 1 Cic. *Brut.* 182–83

[CICERO:] isdem fere temporibus aetate inferiores paulo quam Iulius, sed aequales propemodum fuerunt C. Cotta P. Sulpicius Q. Varius Cn. Pomponius C. Curio L. Fufius M. Drusus P. Antistius; nec ulla aetate uberior oratorum fetus fuit. [183] ex his Cotta et Sulpicius cum meo iudicio tum omnium facile primas tulerunt.

T 2 Cic. *Brut.* 203–4

[CICERO:] "fuit enim Sulpicius vel maxime omnium, quos quidem ego audiverim, grandis et, ut ita dicam, tragicus orator. vox cum magna tum suavis et splendida; gestus et motus corporis ita venustus ut tamen ad forum, non ad scaenam institutus videretur; incitata et volubilis nec ea redundans tamen nec circumfluens oratio. Crassum hic volebat imitari; Cotta malebat Antonium; sed ab hoc vis aberat Antoni, Crassi ab illo lepos." [204] . . . "atque in his oratoribus illud animadvertendum est, posse esse summos, qui inter se sint dissimiles. nihil enim tam dissimile quam Cotta Sulpicio, et uterque aequalibus suis plurimum praestitit."

his speeches were extant in Cicero's time; P. Cannutius (114 F 4) was said to have written some in Sulpicius' name after the latter's death (T 10; Cic. Orat. 132: 80 T 6).

T 1 Cicero, *Brutus*

[CICERO:] To about the same time, a little younger than Iulius [C. Iulius Caesar Strabo (**73**)], but almost contemporary, belong C. Cotta [C. Aurelius Cotta (**80**)], P. Sulpicius, Q. Varius [Q. Varius Hybrida (**88**)], Cn. Pomponius [Cn. Pomponius (**72B**)], C. Curio [C. Scribonius Curio (**86**)], L. Fufius [L. Fufius (**75**)], M. Drusus [M. Livius Drusus (**72**)], P. Antistius [P. Antistius (**78**)]; in no period was the brood of orators more copious. [183] Of these Cotta and Sulpicius easily achieved the first place, both in my judgment and also in that of everyone.

T 2 Cicero, *Brutus*

[CICERO:] "Sulpicius, in fact, was of all whom I at least have heard the most elevated in style, and, so to speak, the most theatrical orator. His voice was strong and at the same time of pleasing and brilliant timbre; his gesture and bodily movement was graceful, in such a way, though, that it seemed made for the Forum, not for the stage; his language was swift and of easy flow and still not redundant or overflowing. He wished to imitate Crassus [L. Licinius Crassus (**66**)]; Cotta [C. Aurelius Cotta (**80**), T 2] preferred Antonius [M. Antonius (**65**)]. But the latter lacked the force of Antonius, the former the charm of Crassus." [204] . . . "Yes, and in these orators this is to be noticed, that those may be supreme who are unlike each other. For nothing was so unlike as Cotta to Sulpicius, and each of them surpassed their contemporaries by far."

T 3 Cic. *De or.* 1.99

[CRASSUS:] . . . praesertim cum te unum ex omnibus ad dicendum maxime natum, aptumque cognossem . . .

T 4 Cic. *De or.* 1.131–32

tum ille [CRASSUS] "ego vero" inquit "quod in vobis egregiam quandam ac praeclaram indolem ad dicendum esse cognovi, idcirco haec exposui omnia, nec magis ad eos deterrendos qui non possent, quam ad vos qui possetis exacuendos accommodavi orationem meam; et quamquam in utroque vestrum summum esse ingenium studiumque perspexi, tamen haec quae sunt in specie posita, de quibus plura fortasse dixi quam solent Graeci dicere, in te, Sulpici, divina sunt. [132] ego enim neminem nec motu corporis neque ipso habitu atque forma aptiorem nec voce pleniorem aut suaviorem mihi videor audisse . . ."

T 5 Cic. *De or.* 2.96

[ANTONIUS:] hanc igitur similitudinem qui imitatione adsequi volet, cum exercitationibus crebris atque magnis tum scribendo maxime persequatur. quod si haec noster Sulpicius faceret, multo eius oratio esset pressior; in qua nunc interdum, ut in herbis rustici solent dicere, in summa ubertate inest luxuries quaedam, quae stilo depascenda est.

T 3 Cicero, *On the Orator*

[CRASSUS:] . . . especially since I had recognized that you [Sulpicius] alone out of all men were eminently born for speaking and adapted to it . . .

T 4 Cicero, *On the Orator*

Then he [CRASSUS] said: "For my part, because I recognized in the two of you [Sulpicius and C. Aurelius Cotta (**80**)] a certain remarkable and splendid natural disposition for speaking, for that reason I have outlined all this; not to discourage those who are not able rather than to stimulate you who are able, I have shaped my discourse; and although I have noted that in both of you there is the greatest talent and industry, still, as regards these advantages that are based on appearance, about which I have perhaps said more than the Greeks are accustomed to do, in yourself, Sulpicius, they are divine. [132] For never, I think, have I listened to anyone better qualified by his bodily movement or by his very bearing and appearance, or to one with a voice more resonant and pleasing . . ."

T 5 Cicero, *On the Orator*

[ANTONIUS:] Let him, then, who wishes to attain such a similarity by imitation [of great models], pursue it by frequent and extended practice and particularly by writing. If our Sulpicius here were to do so, his diction would be far more condensed; at present, as countrymen are wont to say of grass, amid the greatest fertility there occasionally is some immoderate growth, which should be grazed off by the pen.

T 6 Cic. *De or.* 3.11

[CICERO:] . . . Sulpicius autem, qui in eadem invidiae flamma fuisset, quibuscum privatus coniunctissime vixerat, hos in tribunatu spoliare instituit omni dignitate; cui quidem ad summam gloriam eloquentiae florescenti ferro erepta vita est et poena temeritatis non sine magno rei publicae malo constituta.

T 7 Cic. *De or.* 3.31

[CRASSUS:] ecce praesentes duo prope aequales Sulpicius et Cotta. quid tam inter se dissimile? quid tam in suo genere praestans? . . . Sulpicius autem fortissimo quodam animi impetu, plenissima et maxima voce, summa contentione corporis et dignitate motus, verborum quoque ea gravitate et copia est, ut unus ad dicendum instructissimus a natura esse videatur.

T 8 Cic. *Har. resp.* 41

nam quid ego de Sulpicio[1] loquar? cuius tanta in dicendo gravitas, tanta iucunditas, tanta brevitas fuit, ut posset vel ut prudentes errarent vel ut boni minus bene sentirent perficere dicendo.

[1] Sulpicio *vel* P. Sulpicio *codd.*

T 6 Cicero, *On the Orator*

[CICERO:] . . . and Sulpicius, who had been affected by the
same outburst of hatred [as C. Aurelius Cotta (**80**)], in his
Tribunate set about robbing of every honorable position
the very persons with whom he had associated very closely
as a private individual; from him indeed, when just ap-
proaching the prime of the highest distinction in eloquence, his life was snatched away by the sword, and the
penalty for his rashness was instituted, not without great
damage to the Republic.

T 7 Cicero, *On the Orator*

[CRASSUS:] In present company, consider these two, almost contemporaries, Sulpicius and Cotta [C. Aurelius
Cotta (**80**), T 5]. What is so unlike each other? What so
eminent, each in their own way? . . . Sulpicius, on the other
hand, is characterized by an extremely bold mental vigor,
a very resonant and very loud voice, extreme exertion of
body and dignity of gesture, also such a weight and pro-
fuseness of language that he alone seems to be best
equipped by nature for speaking.

T 8 Cicero, *De Haruspicum Responsis*

For what shall I say about Sulpicius? He had such weight,
such charm, such brevity in speaking that he could bring
it about by speaking that the wise erred or that the loyal
felt less loyal.

T 9 Vell. Pat. 2.18.5–6

. . . P. Sulpicius tribunus pl., disertus, acer, opibus, gratia, amicitiis, vigore ingenii atque animi celeberrimus, cum antea rectissima voluntate apud populum maximam quaesisset dignitatem, quasi pigeret eum virtutum suarum et bene consulta ei male cederent, [6] subito pravus se[1] praeceps C. Mario . . . addixit[2] . . .

[1] se *Watt*: et *cod., ed. princ.*: praeceps ⟨se⟩ *Puteanus*
[2] addixit *cod.[2], ed. princ.*: dedit *cod.[1]*: ⟨se⟩ addixit *Heinsius*

T 10 Cic. *Brut.* 205

[CICERO:] Sulpici orationes quae feruntur, eas post mortem eius scripsisse P. Cannutius putatur aequalis meus, homo extra nostrum ordinem meo iudicio disertissimus. ipsius Sulpici nulla oratio est, saepeque ex eo audivi, cum se scribere neque consuesse neque posse diceret.

On a Petty Case (F 11)

F 11 Cic. *De or.* 2.88–89

[ANTONIUS:] atque ut a familiari nostro exordiar, hunc ego, Catule, Sulpicium primum in causa parvola adulescentulum audivi voce et forma et motu corporis et reliquis rebus aptis ad hoc munus, de quo quaerimus, oratione

T 9 Velleius Paterculus, *Compendium of Roman History*

. . . P. Sulpicius, a Tribune of the People, eloquent, energetic, very renowned for his wealth, his influence, his friendships, the vigor of his native ability and his mind, although he had previously sought the greatest influence with the People by the most honorable attitude, now, as if he regretted his virtues and the good actions turned out badly for him, [6] suddenly misguided, he impetuously attached himself to C. Marius . . .

T 10 Cicero, *Brutus*

[CICERO:] The orations of Sulpicius that are in circulation are believed to have been written after his death by P. Cannutius [**114** F 4], my contemporary, the most eloquent man outside our rank [i.e., the senatorial] in my judgment. No oration by Sulpicius himself is extant, and I often heard him say that he had never had the habit of writing and could not do it.

On a Petty Case (F 11)

Sulpicius first appeared as an advocate in a petty case when he was still a fairly young man (TLRR 85, 88), about a year before a more significant intervention (F 12–15).

F 11 Cicero, *On the Orator*

[ANTONIUS:] And so as to begin with our friend, Catulus [Q. Lutatius Catulus (**63**)], I first heard this Sulpicius here, when he was a very young man, in a petty case: voice, appearance, movement of the body, and the other matters were well suited to this role that we are investigating, but

autem celeri et concitata, quod erat ingenii, sed verbis effervescentibus et paulo nimium redundantibus, quod erat aetatis. non sum aspernatus; volo enim se efferat in adulescente fecunditas. . . . [89] vidi statim indolem neque dimisi tempus et eum sum cohortatus ut forum sibi ludum putaret esse ad discendum, magistrum autem quem vellet eligeret; me quidem si audiret, L. Crassum.

Against C. Norbanus (F 12–15)

About a year after the case described in F 11 (also after M. Antonius' (65) censorship in 97 BC [cf. 65 F 22]), Sulpicius prosecuted C. Norbanus (cos. 83 BC), when M. Anto-

F 12 Cic. *De or.* 2.89

[ANTONIUS:] vix annus intercesserat ab hoc sermone cohortationis meae, cum iste accusavit C. Norbanum, defendente me. non est credibile quid interesse mihi sit visum inter eum, qui tum erat et qui anno ante fuerat. omnino in illud genus eum Crassi magnificum atque praeclarum natura ipsa ducebat, sed ea non satis proficere potuisset, nisi eodem studio atque imitatione intendisset atque ita dicere consuesset, ut tota mente Crassum atque omni animo intueretur.

F 13 Cic. *De or.* 2.197–98

= **65** F 22.

his delivery was rapid and impetuous, which was a matter of his nature, while his diction was agitated and a little too exuberant, which was a matter of his age. I did not object to it; for I am well content that fecundity should come to the fore in a young man. . . . [89] I instantly perceived his natural qualities and did not miss the opportunity; I urged him to regard the Forum as his school of instruction and to choose what master he pleased, though if he listened to me, L. Crassus [L. Licinius Crassus (**66**)].

Against C. Norbanus (F 12–15)

*nius (**65** F 22–30), whose quaestor in Sicily C. Norbanus had been, defended him (TLRR 86; cf. Cic. De or. 2.107, 2.109, 2.124, 2.201–3, 2.305).*

F 12 Cicero, *On the Orator*

[ANTONIUS:] Scarcely a year had elapsed after this conversation of advice with me [cf. F 11], when he [Sulpicius] prosecuted C. Norbanus, while I was the defense. It is incredible what a difference there seemed to me to be between him as he was then and how he had been a year earlier. Assuredly nature herself was leading him to that grand and glorious style of Crassus [L. Licinius Crassus (**66**)], but she could never have made him sufficiently proficient, had he not pressed forward to the same goal with eagerness and imitation and had got used to speaking in such a way that he contemplated Crassus with all his mind and all his soul.

F 13 Cicero, *On the Orator*

= **65** F 22.

F 14 Cic. *Off.* 2.49

etiam P. Sulpici eloquentiam accusatio inlustravit, cum
seditiosum et inutilem civem, C. Norbanum, in iudicium
vocavit.

F 15 Apul. *Apol.* 66.4
= **65** F 15.

On a Law Recalling Those Expelled (F 16)

*As Tribune of the People in 88 BC, Sulpicius proposed a
bill on the recall of those expelled without trial, while he
had opposed a similar bill earlier (Liv.* Epit. 77; Vell. Pat.

F 16 *Rhet. Her.* 2.45

item vitiosum est de nomine et vocabulo controversiam
struere, quam rem consuetudo optime potest iudicare;
velut Sulpicius, qui intercesserat, ne exulis, quibus causam
dicere non licuisset, reducerentur, idem posterius inmu-
tata voluntate, cum eandem legem ferret, alio se ferre
dicebat propter nominum commutationem: nam non
exules, sed vi eiectos se reducere aiebat. proinde quasi id
fuisset in controversia, quo illi nomine appellarentur, aut
proinde[1] quasi non omnes, quibus aqua et igni interdictum est, exules appellentur. verum illi fortasse ignoscimus
si cum causa fecit . . .

[1] appellarentur aut proinde *Kayser*: appellarentur a. p. r. aut
proinde *vel* a populo romano appellarentur aut proinde *vel* appellarentur aut p̌r. dnde s. s. ei *vel* appellarentur deinde *vel* appellarentur a p̌r deinde *vel* appellarentur a. pp̌. ř. *vel* appellarentur
codd.

F 14 Cicero, *On Duties*

A prosecution too brought glory to the eloquence of P. Sulpicius, when he took a seditious and harmful citizen, C. Norbanus, to court.

F 15 Apuleius, *Apologia*

= **65** F 15.

On a Law Recalling Those Expelled (F 16)

2.18.5–6; Rogatio ut exules quibus causam dicere non licuisset revocarentur: LPPR, *p. 343*; Lex Sulpicia de revocandis vi eiectis: LPPR, *p. 345*).

F 16 *Rhetorica ad Herennium*

Equally it is a fault to build on a name or appellation a dispute about a matter that usage can best decide. For example, Sulpicius had opposed his veto to the recall of the exiles who had not been permitted to plead their case; later, the same man, having changed his mind, when he proposed the same law, said he was proposing it with a different intention, because of the change of terms. For he said, he was recalling not "exiles," but "those ejected by violence," just so as though the dispute had concerned the point by which name to call those people, or just so as though not all to whom water and fire have been formally forbidden are called exiles. True, we perhaps excuse him if he did this with a reason . . .

Against C. Iulius Caesar Strabo (F 17–18)

F 17 Cic. *Brut.* 226

= **78** T 2.

F 18 Cic. *Har. resp.* 43

. . . Sulpicium ab optima causa profectum Gaioque Iulio[1] consulatum contra leges petenti resistentem longius quam voluit popularis aura provexit.

1 Iulio *Manutius*: totio *vel* tutio *vel* tucio *codd.*

As Tribune to the People (F 19–20)

F 19 Cic. *Brut.* 306

[CICERO:] tum P. Sulpici in tribunatu cottidie contionantis totum genus dicendi penitus cognovimus . . .

Against C. Iulius Caesar Strabo (F 17–18)

*During his Tribunate (88 BC), Sulpicius charged C. Iulius Caesar Strabo (**73** F 14), standing for the consulship without having been praetor, as did his colleague P. Antistius (**78** F 4A).*

F 17 Cicero, *Brutus*

= **78** T 2.

F 18 Cicero, *De Haruspicum Responsis*

. . . Sulpicius started from a very good cause and resisted Gaius Iulius, aiming for the consulship against the laws; then the breeze of popular support carried him further than he wished.

As Tribune to the People (F 19–20)

Sulpicius is said to have made frequent speeches at public meetings when Tribune of the People (88 BC) (CCMR, App. A: 222).

F 19 Cicero, *Brutus*

[CICERO:] Then, in the Tribunate of P. Sulpicius, who daily spoke before the People, we got to know this entire kind of speaking thoroughly . . .

F 20 Iul. Exup. 3.20

statim ut Romam venit, resistentem sibi Sulpicium et seditiosis contionibus rem publicam disturbantem cum multis,
quos sibi socios adsciverat, trucidavit . . .

77 L. ANTISTIUS

Nothing is known about L. Antistius (RE Antistius 12)
other than what can be inferred from Cicero's comments.
It has been suggested that L. Antistius is identical with P.

Against T. Matrinius of Spoletium (F 1)

L. Antistius prosecuted T. Matrinius of Spoletium (modern
Spoleto in Umbria) for holding Roman citizenship re-
ceived from C. Marius and exercising its rights (TLRR 89).
Antistius is said to have argued that the grant was invalid,
as the precondition, a law of L. Appuleius Saturninus
*(**64A**) on giving Roman citizenship to people in colonies,*

F 1 Cic. *Balb.* 48

itaque cum paucis annis post hanc civitatis donationem
acerrima de civitate quaestio Licinia et Mucia lege venisset, num quis eorum, qui de foederatis civitatibus esset
civitate donatus, in iudicium est vocatus? nam Spoletinus
T. Matrinius, unus ex iis quos C. Marius civitate donasset,

F 20 Iulius Exuperantius

Immediately after he [L. Cornelius Sulla] had come to Rome, he slew Sulpicius, who was opposing him and throwing the Republic into disorder with seditious speeches before the People, along with many whom he had attached to himself as followers . . .

77 L. ANTISTIUS

Antistius (78), since the latter is recognized as an orator in Cicero's Brutus *and personal names often get confused in the manuscripts.*

Against T. Matrinius of Spoletium (F 1)

had been annulled in the meantime. One of Appuleius' laws on colonization and land distribution (e.g., Lex Appuleia de coloniis in Siciliam Achaiam Macedoniam deducendis*: LPPR, p. 332) must have included regulations for awarding citizenship.*

F 1 Cicero, *Pro Balbo*

And so, when a few years after this gift of citizenship [by C. Marius to people in Italy] a most severe investigation concerning citizenship had come to take place under the *Lex Licinia et Mucia* [*Lex Licinia Mucia de civibus redigundis*, 95 BC: *LPPR*, p. 335], was anyone of those who, from allied states, had been presented with citizenship, ever brought to trial? For T. Matrinius of Spoletium was the only one of those whom C. Marius had presented with

dixit causam ex colonia Latina in primis firma et inlustri.
quem cum disertus homo L. Antistius accusaret, non dixit
fundum Spoletinum populum non esse factum—videbat
enim populos de suo iure, non de nostro fondos fieri solere—sed cum lege Apuleia coloniae non essent deductae,
qua lege Saturninus C. Mario tulerat ut in singulas colo-
nias ternos civis Romanos facere posset, negabat hoc
beneficium re ipsa sublata valere debere.

78 P. ANTISTIUS

*P. Antistius (tr. pl. 88 BC; RE Antistius 18) was killed in
82 BC on the orders of consul C. Marius the son (Vell. Pat.
2.26.2; App. B Civ. 1.88.403–4; Cic. Brut. 311: 102 T 3).*

*In Cicero, P. Antistius is mentioned as a good (though
late to be recognized) orator in the first half of the first*

T 1 Cic. *Brut.* 182

= **76** T 1.

T 2 Cic. *Brut.* 226–27

[CICERO:] coniunctus igitur Sulpici aetati P. Antistius fuit,
rabula sane probabilis, qui multos cum tacuisset annos
neque contemni solum sed inrideri etiam solitus esset, in
tribunatu primum contra C. Iuli illam consulatus peti-

citizenship to plead his case, and he came from a Latin colony particularly powerful and distinguished. When an eloquent man, L. Antistius, prosecuted him, he did not say that the people of Spoletium had not ratified it—for he knew that peoples were accustomed to ratify laws concerning their own rights, not ours—but, since colonies had not been founded under the *Lex Appuleia*, a law that Saturninus [L. Appuleius Saturninus (**64A**)] had proposed for C. Marius, so that in each colony he could make three men Roman citizens, he maintained that this grant could not be valid when the measure itself had been annulled.

78 P. ANTISTIUS

century BC and an active lawyer; his accurate argumentation, strong memory, and elegance in a middle style are highlighted, while his delivery is described as less polished (T 1–3).

T 1 Cicero, *Brutus*

= **76** T 1.

T 2 Cicero, *Brutus*

[CICERO:] Associated then with the time of Sulpicius [P. Sulpicius Rufus (**76**)] was P. Antistius, a ranting speaker but certainly quite decent, who, after he had been silent for many years and was customarily treated not only with contempt but even with ridicule, first won favor in his Tribunate [88 BC] by carrying to success a just indictment against that irregular candidacy of C. Iulius [C. Iulius Cae-

tionem extraordinariam veram causam agens est probatus;
et eo magis quod eandem causam cum ageret eius conlega
ille ipse Sulpicius, hic plura et acutiora dicebat. itaque
post tribunatum primo multae ad eum causae, deinde omnes maximae quaecumque erant deferebantur. [227] rem
videbat acute, componebat diligenter, memoria valebat;
verbis non ille quidem ornatis utebatur sed tamen non
abiectis; expedita autem erat et perfacile currens oratio;
et erat eius quidam[1] tamquam habitus non inurbanus;
actio paulum cum vitio vocis tum etiam ineptiis claudica-
bat. hic temporibus floruit eis[2] quibus inter profectionem
reditumque L. Sullae sine iure fuit et sine ulla dignitate
res publica; hoc etiam magis probabatur, quod erat ab
oratoribus quaedam in foro solitudo. Sulpicius occiderat,
Cotta aberat et Curio, vivebat e reliquis patronis eius aetatis nemo praeter Carbonem et Pomponium, quorum
utrumque facile superabat.

[1] quidam *Manutius*: quidem *codd.*   [2] eis *edd.*: his *codd.*

T 3 Cic. *Brut.* 308

[CICERO:] triennium fere fuit urbs sine armis, sed oratorum aut interitu aut discessu aut fuga—nam aberant etiam
adulescentes M. Crassus et Lentuli duo—primas in causis

sar Strabo (**73**), F 14] for the consulship. And this all the
more because, while his colleague, the famous Sulpicius
himself [**76** F 17–18] pleaded the same case, he [Antistius]
said more and more penetrating things. Therefore, after
his Tribunate, first many cases were brought to him, at that
time all the most important of whatever sort. [227] He
found the point at issue acutely, arranged his argument
carefully, and had a strong memory. He used words not at
all embellished, yet still not commonplace; and his speech
was unencumbered and easily flowing; and its entire appearance, as it were, was not without a certain urbanity;
his delivery was hampered a little by a flaw in his voice and
especially from some tasteless mannerisms. He flourished
in the period [87–82 BC] when, between the departure
and the return of L. Sulla [L. Cornelius Sulla], the Republic was without law and without any dignity. For this reason, he won even more favor because there was a certain
emptiness of orators in the Forum: Sulpicius had fallen,
Cotta [C. Aurelius Cotta (**80**)] and Curio [C. Scribonius
Curio (**86**)] were away, and of the remaining advocates of
that generation no one was still alive apart from Carbo [C.
Papirius Carbo Arvina (**87**)] and Pomponius [Cn. Pomponius (**72B**)], both of whom he surpassed easily.

T 3 Cicero, *Brutus*

[CICERO:] For a period of about three years [86–84 BC]
the city was free from arms; but because of the death or
absence or exile of orators—for even young men like
Crassus [M. Licinius Crassus Dives (**102**)] and the two
Lentuli [Cn. Cornelius Lentulus Clodianus (**99**) and P.
Cornelius Lentulus Sura (**100**)] were away—Hortensius

77

agebat Hortensius, magis magisque cottidie probabatur
Antistius, Piso saepe dicebat, minus saepe Pomponius,
raro Carbo, semel aut iterum Philippus.

Against C. Iulius Caesar Strabo (F 4A)

F 4A Cic. *Brut.* 226

= T 2.

79 C. ERUCIUS

Nothing further is known about C. Erucius (RE Erucius)
other than what can be inferred from the passages below.
If a comment mentioned in one of Cicero's fragmentary
speeches, where an Erucius is called an "Antoniaster," that

T 1 Cic. *Pro Vareno*, F 17 Puccioni = 10 Crawford (Prisc.,
GL II, p. 112.19–23; cf. Quint. *Inst.* 8.3.22)

excipitur "Antonius," quod "Antoniaster" facit diminuti-
vum. Cicero pro Vareno: "Lucius ille Septimius diceret,
etenim est ad L. Crassi eloquentiam gravis et vehemens
et volubilis: Erucius hic noster Antoniaster est."

[Q. Hortensius Hortalus (**92**)] held the first place in pleadings, Antistius enjoyed a reputation increasing on a daily basis, Piso [M. Pupius Piso Frugi Calpurnianus (**104**)] spoke often, less often Pomponius [Cn. Pomponius (**72B**)], Carbo [C. Papirius Carbo Arvina (**87**)] rarely, Philippus once or twice [L. Marcius Philippus (**70**)].

Against C. Iulius Caesar Strabo (F 4A)

*Like P. Sulpicius Rufus (**76** F 17–18), P. Antistius, when Tribune of the People in 88 BC, spoke against C. Iulius Caesar Strabo's (**73** F 14) candidacy for the consulship.*

F 4A Cicero, *Brutus*

= T 2.

79 C. ERUCIUS

*is, apparently a poor imitator of the great orator M. Antonius (**65**), refers to this Erucius (T 1), it suggests that his oratorical style was not rated highly by everyone.*

T 1 Cicero, *Pro Vareno* (quoted in Priscian)

"Antonius" is an exception [from the rule of how diminutives of the second declension are formed] since it forms the diminutive "Antoniaster." Cicero, *Pro Vareno* [Crawford 1994, 7–18]: "That famous Lucius Septimius [*RE* Septimius 8] would say, for he is serious and energetic and fluent according to the model of L. Crassus' [L. Licinius Crassus (**66**)] eloquence: 'Our Erucius here is a little Antonius.'"

T 2 Cic. *Rosc. Am.* 46

si tibi fortuna non dedit ut patre certo nascerere ex quo
intellegere posses qui animus patrius in liberos esset, at
natura certe dedit ut humanitatis non parum haberes; eo
accessit studium doctrinae ut ne a litteris quidem alienus
esses.

Against Sex. Roscius from Ameria (F 3–4)

F 3 Schol. Gron. ad Cic. *Rosc. Am.*, *arg.* (p. 301.22–24
Stangl)

interim Sextus Roscius adulescens parricidii accusatus est
ab Erucio quodam ex novis accusatoribus et absolutus.

F 4 Cic. *Rosc. Am.* 35, 37, 38, 39, 40, 42–45, 50, 52, 58–
60, 61, 74, 80, 82

criminis confictionem accusator Erucius suscepit . . . [37]
occidisse patrem Sex. Roscius arguitur. . . . [38] in hoc
tanto, tam atroci, tam singulari maleficio, quod ita raro
exstitit ut, si quando auditum sit, portenti ac prodigi simile
numeretur, quibus tandem tu,[1] C. Eruci, argumentis accu-

[1] tu *Klotz*: te *codd.*

T 2 Cicero, *Pro Sexto Roscio Amerino*

If fortune did not grant that you [Erucius] were born of a father concerning whom there is no doubt, from whom you could have learned the essence of paternal feeling toward one's children, yet at least nature granted that you have no small share of humanity; to this is added an eagerness to study, so that you are not even a stranger to literature.

Against Sex. Roscius from Ameria (F 3–4)

In 81 BC C. Erucius prosecuted Sex. Roscius from Ameria (in Umbria) on a charge of parricide; Cicero acted for the defense (Cic. Rosc. Am.) and includes references to what the prosecutor allegedly said in his speech (TLRR 129).

F 3 Scholia Gronoviana to Cicero, *Pro Sexto Roscio Amerino*

In the meantime the young Sextus Roscius was accused of parricide by a certain Erucius from among the new prosecutors and was found not guilty.

F 4 Cicero, *Pro Sexto Roscio Amerino*

The accuser Erucius has undertaken the fabrication of the charge . . . [37] Sex. Roscius is accused of having killed his father. . . . [38] With respect to such a grave, such an atrocious, such a unique misdeed, which has happened so rarely that, if it is heard of once in a while, it is regarded as similar to a portent and a monstrosity, what arguments do you, C. Erucius, actually think the accuser ought to

satorem censes uti oportere? nonne et audaciam eius qui
in crimen vocetur singularem ostendere et mores feros
immanemque naturam et vitam vitiis flagitiisque omnibus
deditam, {et}[2] denique omnia ad perniciem profligata atque perdita? quorum tu nihil in Sex. Roscium ne obiciendi
quidem causa contulisti. [39] patrem occidit Sex. Roscius.
qui homo? adulescentulus corruptus et ab hominibus ne-
quam inductus? annos natus maior quadraginta. vetus videlicet sicarius, homo audax et saepe in caede versatus. at
hoc ab accusatore ne dici quidem audistis. luxuries igitur
hominem nimirum et aeris alieni magnitudo et indomitae
animi cupiditates ad hoc scelus impulerunt. de luxuria
purgavit Erucius, cum dixit hunc ne in convivio quidem
ullo fere interfuisse. nihil autem umquam debuit. cupiditates porro quae possunt esse in eo qui, ut ipse accusator
obiecit, ruri semper habitarit et in agro colendo vixerit?
. . . [40] quae res igitur tantum istum furorem Sex. Roscio
obiecit? "patri" inquit "non placebat." quam ob causam?
. . . [42] "nescio" inquit "quae causa odi fuerit; fuisse
odium intellego quia antea, cum duos filios haberet, illum
alterum qui mortuus est secum omni tempore volebat
esse, hunc in praedia rustica relegarat." . . . ille quo modo
crimen commenticium confirmaret non inveniebat, ego
res tam levis qua ratione infirmem ac diluam reperire non
possum. [43] quid ais, Eruci? tot praedia, tam pulchra,
tam fructuosa Sex. Roscius filio suo relegationis ac suppli-

[2] *del. Madvig*

employ? Ought he not to show the remarkable audacity of
the man who is accused of the crime, his savage manners
and brutal nature, a life given over to every kind of vice
and infamy, {and} in short, everything utterly ruined to destruction and desperate? You have brought none of these
points against Sex. Roscius, not even for the sake of reproaching him. [39] Sex. Roscius killed his father. What
kind of person is he? A very young man, depraved and led
astray by worthless people? He is more than forty years
old. He is doubtless a veteran assassin, an audacious person and often involved in murder. But you have not heard
this even hinted at by the accuser. No doubt, then, indulgent living, the size of his debt, and his unbridled desires
drove the man to commit this crime. As for the charge of
indulgent living, Erucius cleared him from that when he
said that he hardly ever even attended any dinner party.
And as for debts, he never had any. Further, as for greed,
how could it exist in someone who, as the prosecutor himself has put forward as criticism, has always lived in the
country and spent his time in the cultivation of his land?
. . . [40] What then suggested such an enormous act of
madness as that to Sex. Roscius? "By his father," he says,
"he was not liked." For what reason? . . . [42] "I do not
know," he says, "what the reason for the hatred was; I
recognize that there was hatred, since previously, when he
had two sons alive, he wanted the one who is now dead to
be with him at all times, but banished this one to the farms
in the country." . . . That man could not find anything by
which to support his fabricated charge; I can discover no
means by which to invalidate and refute such trifling matters. [43] What are you saying, Erucius? Did Sextus Roscius hand over so many farms, so beautiful and so abound-

cii gratia colenda ac tuenda tradiderat? . . . [44] . . . quid?
si constat hunc non modo colendis praediis praefuisse sed
certis fundis patre vivo frui solitum esse, tamenne haec a
te vita eius[3] rusticana relegatio atque amandatio appella-
bitur? vides, Eruci, quantum distet argumentatio tua ab
re ipsa atque a veritate. quod consuetudine patres faciunt,
id quasi novum reprehendis; quod benevolentia fit, id odio
factum criminaris; quod honoris causa pater filio suo con-
cessit, id eum supplici causa fecisse dicis. [45] neque haec
tu non intellegis, sed usque eo quid arguas non habes, ut
non modo tibi contra nos dicendum putes verum etiam
contra rerum naturam contraque consuetudinem hominum contraque opiniones omnium. . . . [50] ne tu, Eruci,
accusator esses ridiculus, si illis temporibus natus esses
cum ab aratro arcessebantur qui consules fierent. etenim
qui praeesse agro colendo flagitium putes, profecto illum
Atilium quem sua manu spargentem semen qui missi
erant convenerunt hominem turpissimum atque inhones-
tissimum iudicares. . . . [52] odium igitur acerrimum patris
in filium ex hoc, opinor, ostenditur, Eruci, quod hunc ruri
esse patiebatur. numquid est aliud? "immo vero" inquit
"est; nam istum exheredare in animo habebat." audio;
nunc dicis aliquid quod ad rem pertineat; nam illa, opinor,

---

[3] a te vita eius *Vahlen*: a te vita et *vel* attente vita et *codd.*:
attenta vita et *Naugerius*

ing in produce, to his son to cultivate and look after for the
sake of getting him out of the way and punishing him? . . .
[44] . . . What? If it is established that he not only oversaw
the cultivation of the farms, but, during his father's lifetime, was accustomed to have the usufruct of certain estates, will you still continue to call this life of his a banish-
ment to the country and relegation? You see, Erucius, how
far your reasoning differs from the very facts and from the
truth. What fathers are in the habit of doing, you find fault
with as if it were something novel; what happens through
kindness, you denounce as done because of hatred; what
a father has granted his son as a mark of esteem, you assert
he has done for the sake of punishment. [45] And it is not
that you do not understand this, but you are so far from
having anything to argue that you think yourself obliged
to speak not only against us, but even against the nature
of the facts, against the custom of mankind, and against
universally held opinions. . . . [50] In truth, Erucius, you
would have been an absurd accuser if you had been born
in those times when men were summoned from the plow
to be made consuls. For, you who you consider it an out-
rage to superintend the cultivation of the land, you would
assuredly have judged the famous Atilius, whom the dep-
utation found scattering seed with his own hand [C. Atilius
Regulus Serranus, cos. 257 BC; cf. Plin. *HN* 18.20], a most
base and most dishonorable man. . . . [52] So then, this
violent hatred of the father against the son is shown, I
suppose, Erucius, by the fact that he allowed him to remain in the country! Is there anything else? "Certainly
there is," he says: "for he intended to disinherit him." I
hear that; now you are saying something to do with the
case, for, I think, even you admit the following arguments

85

tu quoque concedis levia esse atque inepta: "convivia cum patre non inibat." . . . "domum suam istum non fere quisquam vocabat." . . . [58] quid mihi ad defendendum dedisti, bone accusator? quid hisce autem ad suspicandum? "ne exheredaretur veritus est." audio, sed qua de causa vereri debuerit nemo dicit. "habebat pater in animo." planum fac. nihil est; non quicum deliberarit quem certiorem fecerit, unde istud vobis suspicari in mentem venerit. cum hoc modo accusas, Eruci, nonne hoc palam dicis: "ego quid acceperim scio, quid dicam nescio; unum illud spectavi quod Chrysogonus aiebat neminem isti patronum futurum; de bonorum emptione deque ea societate neminem esse qui verbum facere auderet hoc tempore"? haec te opinio falsa in istam fraudem impulit; non me hercules verbum fecisses, si tibi quemquam responsurum putasses. [59] operae pretium erat, si animadvertistis, iudices, neglegentiam eius in accusando considerare. credo, cum vidisset qui homines in hisce subselliis sederent, quaesisse num ille aut ille defensurus esset; de me ne suspicatum quidem esse, quod antea causam publicam nullam dixerim. postea quam invenit neminem eorum qui possunt et solent ita neglegens esse coepit ut, cum in mentem veniret ei, resideret, deinde spatiaretur, non numquam etiam puerum vocaret, credo, cui cenam imperaret, prorsus ut vestro consessu et hoc conventu pro summa solitudine abuteretur. peroravit aliquando, adsedit; surrexi ego.

---

1 Chrysogonus was a freedman of L. Cornelius Sulla. Cicero claims that he had Sex. Roscius' father put on the proscription list after the latter's death, so that he could easily acquire the dead man's property.

to be trifling and absurd: "He never went to any dinner parties with his father." . . . "Hardly anyone asked him to their house." . . . [58] What then have you given me to refute, you worthy accuser? What grounds for suspicion have you given these gentlemen? "He was afraid of being disinherited." I hear that, but no one says why he should have been afraid. "His father had this in mind." Make this obvious. There is no proof; [you do] not [say] with whom he took counsel, whom he informed, whence such a suspicion has come into your minds. When you bring an accusation in this manner, Erucius, do you not openly declare: "I know what I have received; what I am to say, I do not know; I have only taken into account the single point that Chrysogonus[1] said that no one would act as the defense for that man, that there would be no one in these times who would dare to utter a word about the purchase of the goods and about that partnership"? This false expectation led you to that deception; by Hercules, you would not have said a word if you had thought that anyone would reply to you. [59] It was worthwhile, if you noticed it, judges, to consider this man's carelessness in making the accusation. I believe that, when he saw who the men were sitting on these benches, he asked whether this man or that man was likely to undertake the defense; that he never even thought of me, because I had never pleaded a criminal case before. After he had found no one of those who are able and so accustomed, he began to be so careless that, when it occurred to him, he sat down, then walked about, sometimes even called for his slave (I suppose, to order him to prepare dinner); in fact, he treated your council and this assembly with no respect, as if he had been absolutely alone. At last he concluded and sat down;

[60] respirare visus est quod non alius potius diceret. coepi dicere. usque eo animadverti, iudices, eum iocari atque alias res agere ante quam Chrysogonum nominavi; quem simul atque attigi, statim homo se erexit, mirari visus est. intellexi quid eum pepugisset. iterum ac tertio nominavi. . . . [61] . . . de parricidio causa dicitur; ratio ab accusatore reddita non est quam ob causam patrem filius occiderit. . . . [74] quo modo occidit? ipse percussit an aliis occidendum dedit? si ipsum arguis, Romae non fuit; si per alios fecisse dicis, quaero quos?⁴ servosne an liberos? ‹si liberos›,⁵ quos homines? indidemne Ameria an hosce ex urbe sicarios? si Ameria, qui sunt ei? cur non nominantur? si Roma{e},⁶ unde eos noverat Roscius qui Romam multis annis non venit neque umquam plus triduo fuit? ubi eos convenit? qui conlocutus⁷ est? quo modo persuasit? "pretium dedit"; cui dedit? per quem dedit? unde aut quantum dedit? nonne his vestigiis ad caput malefici perveniri solet? et simul tibi in mentem veniat facito quem ad modum vitam huiusce depinxeris; hunc hominem ferum atque agrestem fuisse, numquam cum homine quoquam conlocutum esse, numquam in oppido constitisse. [75] . . . [80] quid ergo est quo tamen accusator inopia argumentorum confugerit? "eius modi tempus erat" inquit "ut homines volgo impune occiderentur; qua re hoc tu propter multi-

---

⁴ quos *unus cod., Richter*: om. cett.   ⁵ *add. Madvig*: om. codd.   ⁶ Roma{e} *ed. R. Stephani*: Romae *codd.*   ⁷ qui conlocutus *G. Krüger*: quicum locutus *codd.*

I got up. [60] He seemed to breathe again because no other person was going to speak instead. I began to speak. I observed, judges, that he was joking and did other things until I mentioned Chrysogonus by name; as soon as I referred to him, this man immediately jumped up; he seemed to be astonished. I understood what had stung him. I mentioned him [Chrysogonus] a second and a third time. . . . [61] . . . The trial is about parricide; the prosecutor has given no account of the reason why the son should have killed his father. . . . [74] How did he kill him? Did he strike the blow himself or entrust the task of killing to others? If you maintain that he did it himself, he was not in Rome; if you say that he did it through others, I ask who were they? Slaves or free men? <If free men,> who are they? From the same place, Ameria, or assassins here from the city [of Rome]? If from Ameria, who are they? Why are their names not given? If from Rome, how did Roscius, who for many years did not come to Rome and never stayed there for more than three days, make their acquaintance? Where did he meet them? How did he talk to them? How did he persuade them? "He gave them a bribe": to whom did he give it? Through whom did he give it? Where did the money come from, or how much was it? Is it not by following up all such traces that the starting point of the crime is usually reached? And at the same time make sure that you remember how you described the life of this man: that he had been a boor and a savage person, that he had never talked to any human being, that he had never stayed in a town. [75] . . . [80] What then? Where, nonetheless, has the prosecutor taken refuge amid the dearth of arguments? "The times were such," he says, "that men were killed as an ordinary occurrence with im-

tudinem sicariorum nullo negotio facere potuisti." . . . [82]
. . . Eruci criminatio tota, ut arbitror, dissoluta est; nisi
forte exspectatis ut illa diluam quae de peculatu ac de eius
modi rebus commenticiis inaudita nobis ante hoc tempus
ac nova obiecit; quae mihi iste visus est ex alia oratione
declamare quam in alium reum commentaretur; ita neque
ad crimen parricidi neque ad eum qui causam dicit per-
tineba⟨n⟩t;[8] de quibus quoniam verbo arguit, verbo satis
est negare.

[8] pertineba⟨n⟩t *Naugerius*: pertinebat *codd.*

80 C. AURELIUS COTTA

*C. Aurelius Cotta (cos. 75 BC; RE Aurelius 96) was pros-
ecuted in 90 BC under the* Lex Varia de maiestate *(see 88)
and had to go into exile, although he had defended himself
with a speech written by L. Aelius Stilo Praeconinus (74
F 5–6; cf. T 7; Cic. De or. 3.11; Brut. 205, 303, 305; App.
B Civ. 1.37.167). Cotta returned to Rome after L. Cornelius Sulla's victory in 82 BC (Cic. Brut. 311: 102 T 3).
When consul in 75 BC, Cotta restored to the Tribunes of
the People the right (taken away by Sulla) to obtain ad-
ditional offices (Asc. in Cic. Corn. [pp. 66.21–67.5, 78.23–
25 C.]: Sall. Hist. 2.49 M. = 2.44 R.). Afterward, he was
proconsul in Cisalpine Gaul in 74 BC; he was awarded a
triumph, but died before it could take place (Cic. Pis. 62;
Asc. in Cic. Pis. 62 [p. 14.22–24 C.]; Cic. Brut. 318).*

punity; therefore, because of the large number of assassins, you could have done this without any effort." . . . [82] . . . Erucius' entire accusation, I believe, has been overthrown, unless perhaps you are waiting for me to refute the charge of embezzlement[2] and other fabricated accusations of this kind, charges that we never heard of before today and that are novel. He seemed to me to be declaiming them taken from another speech that he was preparing against another accused person, so little did they apply to the charge of parricide or to the man who is on trial. Since he asserts them merely with a word, it is sufficient to deny them with a word.

[2] That is, embezzlement of public money or property, if Sex. Roscius kept some of his father's confiscated assets.

80 C. AURELIUS COTTA

*In Cicero, Cotta is described as a great speaker in the first half of the first century BC (T 1, 4, 7; Cic. Brut. 297, 333; cf. Asc. in Cic. Pis. 62 [p. 14.20–21 C.]; Vell. Pat. 2.36.2); he is said to have had a sharp grasp of the subject matter, a refined style, a detailed and precise exposition, and a measured delivery adapted to his physical ability, effective in its own way. His oratory is defined as different from that of his contemporary P. Sulpicius Rufus (**76**), these two men being the main orators in the generation after M. Antonius (**65**) and L. Licinius Crassus (**66**) (T 2–3, 5; Cic. Brut. 189, 202–4, 317, 333; De or. 2.98). Cotta is a speaker in Cicero's* De oratore *and* De natura deorum *(Cic. De or. 1.25; Nat. D. 1.15; Div. 1.8); he is introduced as an adherent of the philosophical school of the Academy*

91

T 1 Cic. *Brut.* 182–83
= **76** T 1.

T 2 Cic. *Brut.* 202–3

[CICERO:] inveniebat igitur acute Cotta, dicebat pure ac solute; et ut ad infirmitatem laterum perscienter contentionem omnem remiserat, sic ad virium imbecillitatem dicendi accommodabat genus. nihil erat in eius oratione nisi sincerum, nihil nisi siccum atque sanum; illudque maximum, quod cum contentione orationis flectere animos iudicum vix posset nec omnino eo genere diceret, tractando tamen impellebat ut idem facerent a se commoti quod a Sulpicio concitati. [203] . . . Crassum hic volebat imitari; Cotta malebat Antonium; sed ab hoc vis aberat Antoni, Crassi ab illo lepos.

T 3 Cic. *Brut.* 204
= **76** T 2.

T 4 Cic. *Brut.* 317
= **92** T 3.

(Cic. Nat. D. *2.147). Nothing by him was left in writing in Cicero's time (T 6).*

T 1 Cicero, *Brutus*

= **76** T 1.

T 2 Cicero, *Brutus*

[CICERO:] As for Cotta, then, he was acute in invention, pure and facile in diction; and as he had very wisely learned to relax all exertion in relation to a weakness of the lungs, so he accommodated his style of speaking to his physical weakness. In his oratory there was nothing that was not genuine, nothing not sober and healthy; and that most of all that, since he was scarcely able to move the minds of the judges by the vehemence of the oration and indeed never used that style, he still swayed them by artful management, so that they did the same aroused by him as incited on by Sulpicius [P. Sulpicius Rufus (**76**), T 2]. [203] . . . He [Sulpicius] wished to imitate Crassus [L. Licinius Crassus (**66**)]; Cotta preferred Antonius [M. Antonius (**65**)]. But the latter lacked the force of Antonius, the former the charm of Crassus.

T 3 Cicero, *Brutus*

= **76** T 2.

T 4 Cicero, *Brutus*

= **92** T 3.

T 5 Cic. *De or.* 3.31

[CRASSUS:] ecce praesentes duo prope aequales Sulpicius et Cotta. quid tam inter se dissimile? quid tam in suo genere praestans? limatus alter et subtilis, rem explicans propriis aptisque verbis. haeret in causa semper et quid iudici probandum sit cum acutissime vidit, omissis ceteris argumentis, in eo mentem orationemque defigit.

T 6 Cic. *Orat.* 132

uterer exemplis domesticis, nisi ea legisses, uterer alienis vel Latinis, si ulla reperirem, vel Graecis, si deceret. sed Crassi perpauca sunt nec ea iudiciorum, nihil Antonii, nihil Cottae, nihil Sulpicii . . .

T 7 Cic. *Brut.* 207

[CICERO:] Cottam autem miror summum ipsum oratorem minimeque ineptum Aelianas levis oratiunculas voluisse existimare suas. his duobus eiusdem aetatis adnumerabatur nemo tertius, sed mihi placebat Pomponius maxime, vel dicam, minime displicebat. locus erat omnino in maximis causis praeter eos de quibus supra dixi nemini, prop-

T 5 Cicero, *On the Orator*

[CRASSUS:] In present company, consider these two, almost contemporaries, Sulpicius [P. Sulpicius Rufus (**76**), T 7] and Cotta. What is so unlike each other? What is so eminent, each in their own way? The one [Cotta] polished and precise, unfolding the matter in appropriate and suitable words. He always sticks to the case, and, having discerned with supreme acumen the point that has to be proved to the judge, he leaves out all other arguments and fixes his thoughts and utterances on that.

T 6 Cicero, *Orator*

I would use examples [for passionate speeches designed to arouse emotions] from my own [speeches] if you had not read those; I would use those of others, in Latin if I could find any, or in Greek if it were fitting to do so. But there is very little of Crassus [L. Licinius Crassus (**66**)], and this is not from the courts; nothing of Antonius [M. Antonius (**65**)], nothing of Cotta, nothing of Sulpicius [P. Sulpicius Rufus (**76**)] . . .

T 7 Cicero, *Brutus*

[CICERO:] But I wonder that Cotta, himself a most distinguished orator and far from devoid of taste, should have wanted the trivial speeches of Aelius [L. Aelius Stilo Praeconinus (**74**), F 6] be thought his own. To these two [P. Sulpicius Rufus (**76**) and Cotta] no one of the same generation was added as third in rank; but Pomponius [Cn. Pomponius (**72B**)] pleased me most or, I should rather say, displeased me least. In the most important cases there was in fact no place for anyone except those of whom I have

95

terea quod Antonius, qui maxime expetebatur, facilis in causis recipiendis erat; fastidiosior Crassus, sed tamen recipiebat. horum qui neutrum habebat, confugiebat ad Philippum fere aut ad Caesarem; † Cotta † Sulpicius expetebantur.[1] ita ab his sex patronis causae inlustres agebantur . . .

[1] ⟨rarius⟩ Cotta ⟨et⟩ Sulpicius expetebantur *Eberhard*: ⟨post⟩ Cotta Sulpicius⟨que⟩ expetebantur *Martha*: ⟨tum⟩ C. ⟨et⟩ S. expetebantur *Piderit*: Cotta ⟨raro, rarius⟩ S. expetebatur *Stangl*: *alii alia*

On Behalf of P. Rutilius Rufus (F 8–9)

F 8 Cic. *Brut.* 115

= **44** F 3.

F 9 Cic. *De or.* 1.229

[ANTONIUS:] nam cum esset ille vir exemplum, ut scitis, innocentiae cumque illo nemo neque integrior esset in civitate neque sanctior, non modo supplex iudicibus esse noluit, sed ne ornatius quidem aut liberius causam dici suam quam simplex ratio veritatis ferebat. paulum huic Cottae tribuit partium, disertissimo adulescenti, sororis suae filio; dixit item causam illam quadam ex parte Q. Mucius, more suo, nullo apparatu, pure et dilucide.

spoken above; for Antonius [M. Antonius (**65**)], who was
most in demand, was always ready to undertake cases;
Crassus [L. Licinius Crassus (**66**)] was harder to please,
but still undertook them. Those who could get neither of
them had recourse usually to Philippus [L. Marcius Philippus (**70**)] or to Caesar [C. Iulius Caesar Strabo (**73**)];
‹more rarely› [?], Cotta and Sulpicius were sought. Thus,
all prominent cases were handled by these six advocates
. . .

On Behalf of P. Rutilius Rufus (F 8–9)

*Cotta supported P. Rutilius Rufus (**44** F 3–6), who also*
spoke on his own behalf and was aided by Q. Mucius Scae-
*vola (**67** F 7–8), in a case of extortion (*TLRR 94).

F 8 Cicero, *Brutus*

= **44** F 3.

F 9 Cicero, *On the Orator*

[Antonius:] For though, as you know, that man [Rutilius]
was a pattern of righteousness and though there was no
one either more honorable or more blameless than he in
the community, he not only did not wish to behave like a
suppliant before the judges, but not even to be defended
more eloquently or elaborately than the simple consideration of truth permitted. To Cotta here, a very eloquent
young man and his sister's son, he allotted only a small
share of the role. Q. Mucius [Q. Mucius Scaevola (**67**),
F 7–8] too spoke in that case to a certain extent, in his own
way, with no pomp, with unadorned and clear diction.

On His Own Behalf (F 10)

F 10 Cic. *Brut.* 205

= **74** F 5.

Against a Woman from Arretium (F 11)

Probably in 79 BC, Cotta spoke before the decemviri
*against a woman from Arretium (modern Arezzo) in a case
concerning her freedom and citizenship. Cicero defended
her (Cic.* Pro muliere Arretina: *Crawford 1984, 33–34)
and won the case at the second hearing (TLRR 132). According to the legal procedure of* legis actio sacramento
*(see Kaser and Hackl 1996, 81–113) applied here, the for-
mula* aio hanc mulierem esse liberam ex iure Quiritium

F 11 Cic. *Caec.* 97

atque ego hanc adulescentulus causam cum agerem contra hominem disertissimum nostrae civitatis, ⟨C.⟩[1] Cottam, probavi. cum Arretinae mulieris libertatem defende-
rem et Cotta xviris religionem[2] iniecisset non posse
nostrum sacramentum iustum iudicari, quod Arretinis
adempta civitas esset, et ego vehementius contendissem
civitatem adimi non posse, xviri prima actione non iudi-

---

[1] *add. Baiter*   [2] religionem *ed.* V: religionis *codd.*

On His Own Behalf (F 10)

In 90 BC Cotta delivered a speech in his own defense when accused under the Lex Varia de maiestate *(see* **88***); allegedly, the speech was written by L. Aelius Stilo Praeconinus (***74** *F 5–6) (TLRR 105).*

F 10 Cicero, *Brutus*

= **74** F 5.

Against a Woman from Arretium (F 11)

("I declare that this woman is free on the basis of citizen rights") has to be pronounced. Cotta argued that this claim was invalid since citizenship had been taken away from the people of Arretium, while Cicero maintained that neither liberty nor citizenship could be removed without consent (cf. Cic. Caec. 96; on the arguments see Frier 1985, 99–101).

F 11 Cicero, *Pro Caecina*

And I established this point as a rather young man, when I was pleading a case against a very eloquent man of our community, ‹C.› Cotta. I was defending the freedom of a woman from Arretium, and Cotta had raised the scruples of the *decemviri*, saying that our solemn promise could not be judged to be valid because citizenship had been taken away from the people of Arretium, while I had argued rather forcefully that citizenship could not be taken away: the *decemviri* did not come to a decision at the first hearing. Later, after an examination and discussion of the case,

caverunt; postea re quaesita et deliberata sacramentum nostrum iustum iudicaverunt. atque hoc et contra dicente Cotta et Sulla vivo iudicatum est.

On Behalf of M. Canuleius (F 12)

F 12 Cic. *Brut.* 317
= **92** T 3.

On Behalf of Cn. Cornelius Dolabella (F 13–14)

*In 77 BC Cn. Cornelius Dolabella (**94**) was accused of extortion with regard to his proconsulship in Macedonia by C. Iulius Caesar (**121** F 15–23); defended by Cotta and*

F 13 Cic. *Brut.* 317
= **92** T 3.

F 14 Val. Max. 8.9.3
= **121** F 19.

they judged our solemn promise to be valid. And this judgment was reached although both Cotta opposed it and Sulla [L. Cornelius Sulla] was still alive [who had disenfranchised Arretium].

On Behalf of M. Canuleius (F 12)

As on other occasions, in the case of M. Canuleius, Cotta shared the defense with Q. Hortensius Hortalus (92 F 20) (TLRR 146).

F 12 Cicero, *Brutus*

= **92** T 3.

On Behalf of Cn. Cornelius Dolabella (F 13–14)

Q. Hortensius Hortalus (92 F 20A), Dolabella was acquitted (TLRR 140).

F 13 Cicero, *Brutus*

= **92** T 3.

F 14 Valerius Maximus, *Memorable Doings and Sayings*

= **121** F 19.

As Consul to the People (F 14A)

F 14A Sall. *Hist.* 2.47 M. = 2.43 R.

Cotta reflects on his deeds and misfortunes in the past as
well as the present situation. He points out that he has
sacrificed himself for the Republic, has been restored, is
now full of gratitude and will offer his support for the sake
of the Republic again. At the same time, he advises the

On Behalf of Titinia (F 15)

Early in Cicero's career, Cotta seems to have defended a
lady called Titinia in a private suit, along with Cicero (Cic.
Pro Titinia Cottae: *Crawford 1984, 35–36), against the*

F 15 Cic. *Brut.* 217

[CICERO:] memoria autem ita fuit nulla, ut aliquotiens,
tria cum proposuisset, aut quartum adderet aut tertium
quaereret; qui in iudicio privato vel maximo, cum ego pro
Titinia Cottae peroravissem, ille contra me pro Ser. Nae-
vio diceret, subito totam causam oblitus est idque venefi-
ciis et cantionibus Titiniae factum esse dicebat.

---

1 The construction of the Latin is uncertain (*Cottae* gen. or
dat.) and possibly unusual (see Douglas 1966, *ad loc.*): it is most
likely to mean that both L. Aurelius Cotta and Cicero spoke on
behalf of Titinia and that Cicero gave the final speech.

As Consul to the People (F 14A)

Sallust puts in Cotta's mouth a speech allegedly given by him as consul (75 BC) at a meeting of the People (CCMR, App. A: 235).

F 14A Sallust, *Histories*

People to behave responsibly, endure adversity, and take counsel for the Republic as they see wars being waged all around them and the sacrifice of a consul may not be a lasting solution.

On Behalf of Titinia (F 15)

*prosecution of Ser. Naevius, who was supported by C. Scribonius Curio (**86** F 10–11) (TLRR 133).*

F 15 Cicero, *Brutus*

[CICERO:] And as for memory, it was so completely lacking that sometimes, when he [C. Scribonius Curio (**86**), T 2] had announced three points, he would either add a fourth or want a third: in a private suit of the greatest importance, when I had wound up the case on behalf of Titinia in support of Cotta,[1] and he [Curio] was speaking against me on behalf of Ser. Naevius, he suddenly forgot the whole case and said that this was caused by Titinia's potions and incantations.

On the Annulment of His Laws in the Senate (F 16)

F 16

a Cic. *Corn.* I, F 20 Puccioni = Crawford

possum dicere hominem summa prudentia spectatum, C. Cottam, de suis legibus abrogandis ipsum ad senatum rettulisse.

b Asc. in Cic. *Corn.* (pp. 58–59 KS = 66.19–67.5 C.)

hic est Cotta de quo iam saepe diximus, magnus orator habitus et compar in ea gloria P. Sulpicio et C. Caesari . . .[1] videntur autem in rebus parvis fuisse leges illae, quas cum tulisset, rettulit de eis abrogandis ad senatum. nam neque apud Sallustium neque apud Livium neque apud Fenestellam ullius alterius latae ab eo legis est mentio praeter eam quam in consulatu tulit invita nobilitate magno populi studio, ut eis qui tr. pl. fuissent alios quoque magistratus capere liceret; quod lex a dictatore L. Sulla paucis ante annis lata prohibebat: neque eam Cottae legem abrogatam esse significat.

[1] *lac. vel lac. om. codd.*: ⟨aequalibus⟩ *suppl. KS*

*On the Annulment of His Laws in the
Senate (F 16)*

F 16

a Cicero, *Pro Cornelio*

I can say that a man distinguished for his outstanding wisdom, C. Cotta, himself brought the matter of the annulment of his laws before the Senate.

b Asconius on Cicero, *Pro Cornelio*

This is the Cotta about whom we have already spoken frequently; he was regarded as a great orator and comparable in reputation for that with P. Sulpicius [P. Sulpicius Rufus (**76**)] and C. Caesar [C. Iulius Caesar Strabo (**73**)] ⟨. . .⟩ And those laws that he, although he had proposed them, put forward for annulment in the Senate seem to have concerned minor matters. For neither in Sallust nor in Livy nor in Fenestella is there mention of any second law proposed by him except for that one that he proposed during his consulship, against the wishes of the nobility and with much support of the People, that it should be allowed for those who had been Tribunes of the People to take up other magistracies too; this was forbidden by a law carried by the dictator L. Sulla a few years previously: he [Cicero] does not indicate that this law of Cotta's was annulled.

On Behalf of Cn. Veturius (F 17)

F 17 Charis., *GL* I, p. 220.1–3 = p. 284.10–12 B.

sponte nomen quidem est aptoton, ideoque[1] C. Cotta
⌊pro⌋[2] Cn. Veturio[3] libro I: "tu solus hic cum optimis,[4] tu
de tua sponte hic cum religione."

 [1] ideoque *Keil*: et eo q *cod.*: et eo utitur *Putschen*   [2] *add.*
Putschen (sec. excerpta ex deperdito cod.)   [3] Veturio *H.*
Meyer: ueterio *cod.*   [4] Tu solus hic cum tua religione *Cau-*
chii ex deperdito cod. excerpta

80A P. CORNELIUS CETHEGUS

*P. Cornelius Cethegus (RE Cornelius 97) was proscribed
by Sulla in 88 BC and fled to Africa with C. Marius; after
Sulla's return he joined his cause (App. B Civ. 1.80.369).
Cethegus was notorious for his bad morals and debauched*

T 1 Cic. *Brut.* 178

[CICERO:] eius aequalis P. Cethegus, cui de re publica
satis suppeditabat oratio—totam enim tenebat eam peni-
tusque cognoverat; itaque in senatu consularium auctoritatem adsequebatur—; sed in causis publicis nihil, ‹in›[1]
privatis satis veterator videbatur.

 [1] *add. edd.*

On Behalf of Cn. Veturius (F 17)

*If C. Aurelius Cotta (**80**) is the C. Cotta mentioned, he defended Cn. Veturius (F 17) in more than one speech.*

F 17 Charisius

sponte ["of one's own accord"] certainly is an indeclinable noun, and therefore C. Cotta [says in the speech] ‹On behalf of› Cn. Veturius, in book one: "you [sg.] alone [are] here with the best men, you [are] here out of your own accord in connection with a religious obligation."

80A P. CORNELIUS CETHEGUS

lifestyle, but still was an influential figure in Roman politics of the period (Cic. Parad. 40; Plut. Luc. 5.4).

In Cicero it is noted that Cethegus was influential as a speaker in the Senate and a decent pleader in private cases, but not able to deal with criminal cases (T 1).

T 1 Cicero, *Brutus*

[CICERO:] His [C. Iulius Caesar Strabo's (**73**); continued from **73** T 1] contemporary was P. Cethegus, who possessed an oratory adequate for the treatment of political matters—of these, to be sure, he had complete mastery and had achieved profound understanding; therefore, in the Senate he obtained the influence of men of consular rank—; but in criminal cases he was nothing at all; ‹in› private suits he appeared as an adequate experienced pleader.

107

80B T. IUVENTIUS

T 1 Cic. *Brut.* 178–79

[CICERO:] in eodem genere causarum multum erat T. Iuventius nimis ille quidem lentus in dicendo et paene frigidus, sed et callidus et in capiendo adversario versutus et praeterea nec indoctus et magna cum iuris civilis intellegentia. [179] cuius auditor P. Orbius meus fere aequalis in dicendo non nimis exercitatus, in iure autem civili non inferior quam magister fuit.

81 Q. SERTORIUS

*Q. Sertorius (*RE *Sertorius 3), having served under C. Marius, was a military tribune in Hispania in the 90s BC. He then became a quaestor in Gallia Cisalpina and a general in the Social War. In the civil war he supported Cinna and C. Marius; afterward, he fought against Roman generals in Hispania for a long time until he lost the support of his followers and fell victim to a conspiracy.*

T 1 Cic. *Brut.* 180

[CICERO:] sed omnium oratorum sive rabularum, qui et plane indocti et inurbani aut rustici etiam fuerunt, quos quidem ego cognoverim, solutissimum in dicendo et acu-

80B T. IUVENTIUS

T. Iuventius (RE Iuventius 10) was active as a pleader in the Sullan period and noted for his knowledge of civil law.

T 1 Cicero, *Brutus*

[CICERO:] With the same type of cases [private lawsuits] T. Iuventius was much occupied; he was much too slow and almost cold in his way of speaking, but shrewd and clever in trapping the opponent, and besides not untrained, and with great knowledge of the civil law. [179] His student P. Orbius, a man of about my age, was not greatly experienced in speaking, but as regards civil law not inferior to his master.

81 Q. SERTORIUS

In Cicero it is acknowledged that Q. Sertorius was a ready and shrewd speaker, but his oratory is not rated highly (T 1); in Plutarch he is described as an able speaker with some influence (T 2). A fragment from Sallust's Histories *may come from a speech put into Sertorius' mouth (Sall. Hist. 1.93 M. = 1.81 R.); Plutarch's biography includes a few short utterances ascribed to Sertorius (Plut. Sert. 5.4, 16.9–10).*

T 1 Cicero, *Brutus*

[CICERO:] But of all those orators or ranting speakers, who were quite without training and without manners, or even uncouth, whom I at least have known, I regard as the

tissimum iudico nostri ordinis Q. Sertorium, equestris C. Gargonium.

T 2 Plut. *Sert.* 2.2

ἤσκητο μὲν οὖν καὶ περὶ δίκας ἱκανῶς καί τινα καὶ δύναμιν ἐν τῇ πόλει μειράκιον ὢν ἀπὸ τοῦ λέγειν ἔσχεν· αἱ δὲ περὶ τὰ στρατιωτικὰ λαμπρότητες αὐτοῦ καὶ κατορθώσεις ἐνταῦθα τὴν φιλοτιμίαν μετέστησαν.

81A C. GARGONIUS

T 1 Cic. *Brut.* 180

= **81** T 1.

82 C. MARCIUS CENSORINUS

*C. Marcius Censorinus (RE Marcius 43) was a supporter of C. Marius in the civil war and a mint master in 88 BC. He attacked and killed the consul Cn. Octavius in 87 BC (App. B Civ. 1.71.327–28); in 82 BC Censorinus himself was killed (App. B Civ. 1.88.401; Cic. Brut. 311: **102** T 3).*

readiest and shrewdest in speaking, of our order [i.e., senatorial], Q. Sertorius, of the equestrian order, C. Gargonius [**81A**].

T 2 Plutarch, *Life of Sertorius*

He [Sertorius] was sufficiently versed in judicial procedure and also acquired some influence in the city [of Rome] from his eloquence while a young man; but his brilliant successes in war turned his ambition in that direction.

81A C. GARGONIUS

C. Gargonius (RE Gargonius 4) is an otherwise unknown equestrian. Among the men of that class, he is presented in Cicero as the readiest and shrewdest of the uneducated ranting speakers (T 1).

T 1 Cicero, *Brutus*

= **81** T 1.

82 C. MARCIUS CENSORINUS

According to Cicero, Censorinus was familiar with Greek literature and able to provide a clear argument and to offer a pleasant delivery, but not industrious and not drawn to activity in the Forum (T 1).

T 1 Cic. *Brut.* 237

[CICERO:] C. Censorinus Graecis litteris satis doctus, quod proposuerat explicans expedite, non invenustus actor, sed iners et inimicus fori.

Against L. Cornelius Sulla (F 2–3)

F 2 Firm. Mat. *Math.* 1.7.28

hunc ⟨quem⟩[1] sciebamus in praeturae {PR.} petitione[2] deiectum, cui gravissimus Censorinus veris ac firmis accusationibus spoliatae provinciae crimen obiecit . . .

   [1] *add. Kroll*   [2] in praeturae {PR.} petitione *Kroll*: impraetura. ṖṘ. petitione *vel* in pretura prepetitione *codd.*

F 3 Plut. *Sull.* 5.12

ἀναχωρήσαντι δὲ αὐτῷ δίκην ἔλαχε δώρων Κηνσωρῖνος, ὡς πολλὰ χρήματα συνειλοχότι παρὰ τὸν νόμον ἐκ φίλης καὶ συμμάχου βασιλείας. οὐ μὴν ἀπήντησεν ἐπὶ τὴν κρίσιν, ἀλλ᾽ ἀπέστη τῆς κατηγορίας.

T 1 Cicero, *Brutus*

[CICERO:] C. Censorinus was reasonably well educated in Greek literature, able to present lucidly what he had set out to, a not ungraceful performer, but lazy and hostile to the Forum.

Against L. Cornelius Sulla (F 2–3)

In the 90s BC Censorinus charged L. Cornelius Sulla, after the latter had returned from his provincial governorship in Cilicia, with extortion, but then dropped the charges (TLRR 92).

F 2 Firmicus Maternus, *Mathesis*

He [Sulla], ‹whom› we knew had been turned down in his candidacy for the praetorship [of 98 BC], against whom the very respected Censorinus had brought forward the reproach of having robbed the province in true and strong accusations . . .

F 3 Plutarch, *Life of Sulla*

When he [Sulla] came back, Censorinus brought a suit against him for bribery, alleging that he had collected large sums of money illegally from a friendly and allied kingdom. Yet he did not appear at the trial, but abandoned the prosecution.

83 Q. POMPEIUS RUFUS

*Q. Pompeius Rufus (cos. 88 BC; RE Pompeius 39), probably a son of Q. Pompeius (**30**), supported his consular colleague L. Cornelius Sulla and was killed during internal conflicts in 88 BC (App. B Civ. 1.63.283–84; Liv. Epit. 77).*

T 1 Cic. *Brut.* 206

= **74** F 3.

On His Own Behalf (F 2)

F 2 Cic. *Brut.* 304

= **61** F 2.

Unplaced Fragment (F 3)

F 3 Prisc., *GL* II, p. 385.10–11

Quintus Pompeius: "me miserum, quem illae feminae despicari ausae sunt." "despicor" commune accipiebant.

83 Q. POMPEIUS RUFUS

L. Aelius Stilo Praeconinus (74 F 7) is said to have writ-ten speeches for Q. Pompeius Rufus and helped him in composing his own.

T 1 Cicero, *Brutus*

= **74** F 3.

On His Own Behalf (F 2)

In 90 BC Q. Pompeius Rufus spoke in his own defense when accused under the Lex Varia de maiestate *(see 88) (TLRR 101).*

F 2 Cicero, *Brutus*

= **61** F 2.

Unplaced Fragment (F 3)

F 3 Priscian

Quintus Pompeius: "Poor me, whom those women have dared to despise!"[1] *despicor* ["I despise"; normally depo-nent] they accepted as a verb in both forms [i.e., active and passive voice].

[1] It is uncertain to which Q. Pompeius this statement belongs and what the context might be.

115

84 T. BETUTIUS BARRUS ASCULANUS

Nothing is known about T. Betutius Barrus of Asculum (modern Ascoli) other than what Cicero says about him (RE Betutius 1): in addition to speeches delivered in his

Against Q. Servilius Caepio (F 1)

F 1 Cic. *Brut.* 169

= **74** F 4.

85 Q. SERVILIUS CAEPIO

T 1 Cic. *Brut.* 222–23

[CICERO:] . . . abducamus ex acie, id est a iudiciis, et in praesidiis rei publicae, cui facile satis facere possint, collocemus. [223] eodem Q. Caepionem referrem, nisi nimis equestri ordini deditus a senatu dissedisset.

84 T. BETUTIUS BARRUS ASCULANUS

hometown (on orators from outside Rome see David 1985),
Betutius prosecuted Q. Servilius Caepio (85 F 8) in Rome
(TLRR 88, 106).

Against Q. Servilius Caepio (F 1)

F 1 Cicero, *Brutus*

= **74** F 4.

85 Q. SERVILIUS CAEPIO

Q. Servilius Caepio (quaest. 100 BC; RE Servilius 50), a
son of Q. Servilius Caepio (62), is listed as an orator more
suited to political than to forensic speeches in Cicero (T 1);
he died fighting in the Social War.

T 1 Cicero, *Brutus*

[CICERO:] . . . let us withdraw them from the battle line,
that is from the courts, and station them [the orators just
listed] on the ramparts of the Republic, whose demands
they are easily able to meet. [223] To this same place I
would assign Q. Caepio, had he not through excessive devotion to the equestrian order set himself apart from the
Senate.

Against Appuleius Saturninus' Grain Law (F 2)

When quaestor in 100 BC, Caepio spoke against a grain
law (Lex Appuleia frumentaria: LPPR, p. 332) proposed
by the Tribune of the People L. Appuleius Saturninus

F 2 *Rhet. Her.* 1.21

cum Lucius Saturninus legem frumentariam de semissi-
bus et trientibus laturus esset, Q. Caepio,[1] qui per id temporis quaestor urbanus erat, docuit senatum aerarium pati
non posse largitionem tantam.

[1] Q. cepio *vel* Q. cipio *vel* caepio *codd.*

*On His Own Behalf Against M. Aemilius
Scaurus (F 3)*

F 3 Asc. in Cic. *Scaur.* I.2 (p. 19 KS = 21.18–24 C.)
= **43** F 8.

Against M. Aemilius Scaurus (F 4–7)

In 90 BC Caepio got the Tribune of the People Q. Varius
Hybrida (**88**) to summon M. Aemilius Scaurus (**43**) to
court under the Lex Varia de maiestate (Val. Max. 3.7.8;

Against Appuleius Saturninus' Grain Law (F 2)

(**64A**) *(Sall.* Hist. *1.62 M. = 1.54 R.) and prevented the People from voting on the bill.*

F 2 *Rhetorica ad Herennium*

When Lucius Saturninus [L. Appuleius Saturninus (**64A**), F 3] was about to put forward the grain law concerning the five-sixths *as* [i.e., 5/6ths of an *as* (Roman coin) as price per *modius* (Roman grain measure)], Q. Caepio, who was city quaestor during that time, explained to the Senate that the treasury could not endure so great a largesse [i.e., reducing the price].

On His Own Behalf Against M. Aemilius
Scaurus (F 3)

*In late 92 or early 91 BC, Caepio took M. Aemilius Scaurus (**43** F 8) to court for extortion (TLRR 96). M. Aemilius Scaurus (**43** F 8–10) then took Caepio to court on the same charge (TLRR 97).*

F 3 Asconius on Cicero, *Pro Scauro*

= **43** F 8.

Against M. Aemilius Scaurus (F 4–7)

Quint. Inst. *5.12.10; Vir. ill. 72.11) (TLRR 100); Caepio delivered a speech against the accused, who defended himself (**43** F 11).*

119

F 4 Cic. *Scaur.* F I(e)

ab eodem etiam lege Varia custos ille rei publicae prodi-
tionis est in crimen vocatus; vexatus a Q. Vario tribuno
plebis est.

F 5 Asc. in Cic. *Scaur.* I.3 (p. 19 KS = 22.5–11 C.)

= **43** F 11.

F 6 Charis., *GL* I, p. 196.7–9 = p. 255.7–9 B.

cotidio ut falso pro cotidie Q. Caepio in M. Aemilium
Scaurum lege Varia: "cum ab isto viderem cotidio consiliis
hosteis adiuvari."

Cf. Charis., *GL* I, p. 193.19–20 = p. 251.12–15 B.

F 7 Charis., *GL* I, p. 224.21–22 = p. 289.15–17 B.

vehementer Caepio in M. Aemilium Scaurum lege Varia:
"Q. Albius vir bonus est et vehementer idoneus."

*In Response to T. Betutius Barrus of
Asculum (F 8)*

F 8 Cic. *Brut.* 169

= **74** F 4.

F 4 Cicero, *Pro Scauro*

By the same person [Caepio] also, under the *Lex Varia*, that guardian of the Republic [Scaurus] was taken to court for treason; he was attacked by the Tribune of the People Q. Varius [Q. Varius Hybrida (**88**)].

F 5 Asconius on Cicero, *Pro Scauro*

= **43** F 11.

F 6 Charisius

cotidio ["daily"], wrongly instead of *cotidie* [usual form], Q. Caepio [in the speech] against M. Aemilius Scaurus under the *Lex Varia*: "when I saw the enemy helped daily by that man with pieces of advice."

F 7 Charisius

vehementer ["strongly"], Caepio [in the speech] against M. Aemilius Scaurus under the *Lex Varia*: "Q. Albius [not in *RE*] is a good man and strongly of the right qualities."

In Response to T. Betutius Barrus of
Asculum (F 8)

Caepio was prosecuted by T. Betutius Barrus of Asculum (**84** F 1) *and replied with a speech allegedly written by L. Aelius Stilo Praeconinus* (**74** F 4) *(TLRR 88, 106).*

F 8 Cicero, *Brutus*

= **74** F 4.

121

Unplaced Fragment (F 9)

F 9 Charis., *GL* I, p. 145.29–30 = p. 184.28–29 B.

tores Servilius, ut etiam Fl. Pomponianus notat, "aurem[1] tores," pro torques.

> [1] aurem *Barwick*: aureum *cod.*: aureus tores *Keil*

86 C. SCRIBONIUS CURIO PATER

*C. Scribonius Curio pater (cos. 76 BC; RE Scribonius 10) was the son and the father of a C. Scribonius Curio (**47** + **170**; cf. F 8; **47** T 4). He fought with Sulla in the Mithridatic Wars. After his consulship he administered the province of Macedonia and brought the wars there to an end, for which he was awarded a triumph (Sall. Hist. 2.80 M. = 2.66 R.; Liv. Epit. 92, 95). In 63 BC he was among the senators who demanded punishment for the Catilinarians (Cic. Att. 12.21.1). Afterward, Curio defended P. Clodius Pulcher (**137**); in turn, this provoked Cicero's speech* In Clodium et Curionem *in the Senate in 61 BC (Crawford 1994, 233–69; for Cicero's report on the trial, see Cic. Att. 1.16.1–6). Later, Curio was reconciled with Cicero.*

T 1 Cic. *Brut.* 182

= **76** T 1.

Unplaced Fragment (F 9)

F 9 Charisius

tores ["you twist / torture"; unusual form], Servilius, as Fl.
Pomponianus [grammarian] also notes, "you torture the
ear,"[1] instead of *torques* [usual form].

---

[1] Since the identity of Servilius is uncertain, the fragment is
also given as a possible fragment for the historian M. Servilius
Nonianus (*FRHist* 79 [F 3]).

86 C. SCRIBONIUS CURIO PATER

*Curio wrote a dialogue including an invective against
Caesar (Cic. Brut. 218; cf. FRHist A 35), and seems to
have discussed geographical matters, since Pliny the Elder
lists him among the sources for his Book 3 (Plin. HN 1).*

*In Cicero, Curio is mentioned as a respectable orator in
the first half of the first century BC (T 1). It is noted that
he had little education in literature, history, and law, but
spoke a polished and educated Latin, such as he might
have learned at home; his memory and delivery are described as ridiculous and his arrangement as disorderly,
but his speeches were regarded as worth reading because
of their language and style (T 2; Cic. De or. 2.98).*

T 1 Cicero, *Brutus*

= **76** T 1.

T 2 Cic. *Brut.* 210–34

[CICERO:] erant tamen quibus videretur illius aetatis tertius Curio, quia splendidioribus fortasse verbis utebatur
et quia Latine non pessime loquebatur, usu, credo, aliquo
domestico. nam litterarum admodum nihil sciebat . . .
[211] . . . [213] . . . similiter igitur suspicor, ut conferamus
parva magnis, Curionis, etsi pupillus relictus est, patrio
fuisse instituto puro sermone adsuefactam domum; et eo
magis hoc iudico quod neminem ex his quidem, qui aliquo
in numero fuerunt, cognovi in omni genere honestarum
artium tam indoctum, tam rudem. [214] nullum ille poe-
tam noverat, nullum legerat oratorem, nullam memoriam
antiquitatis conlegerat; non publicum ius, non privatum et
civile cognoverat. . . . [216] itaque in Curione hoc veris-
sime iudicari potest, nulla re una magis oratorem com-
mendari quam verborum splendore et copia. nam cum
tardus in cogitando tum in struendo dissipatus fuit. reliqua
duo sunt, agere et meminisse: in utroque cachinnos inri-
dentium commovebat. motus erat is, quem et C. Iulius in
perpetuum notavit, cum ex eo in utramque partem toto
corpore vacillante quaesivit quis loque⟨re⟩tur[1] e luntre,[2]
et . . . [217] . . . memoria autem ita fuit nulla, ut aliquotiens, tria cum proposuisset, aut quartum adderet aut tertium quaereret . . . [218] magna haec immemoris ingeni

---

[1] loque⟨re⟩tur *edd.*: loquetur *codd.*   [2] eluntre *vel* e lintre
vel cluntre *vel* eli intre *codd.*: in luntre *Quint. Inst. 11.3.129*

T 2 Cicero, *Brutus*

[CICERO:] There were, however, some to whom Curio seemed to be the third in that time, perhaps because he employed more brilliant words and because he was not the worst speaker of Latin, as a result of, I believe, some training at home. For he did not know anything whatsoever about literature . . . [211] . . . [213] . . . In the same way [as in other families of orators], then, I suppose, to compare small with great, the house of Curio, though he was left an orphan, became accustomed to a pure idiom by his father's practice; and I believe this even more because, out of all those [orators] of any rank at any rate, I have not known anyone so completely uneducated and so unskilled in every kind of liberal arts. [214] That man knew no poet, had read no orator, had acquired no knowledge of the past, had no acquaintance with public law, none with private and civil law. . . . [216] Therefore, in the case of Curio it may be concluded with singular truth that an orator wins commendation by nothing more than by the excellence and wealth of his diction. For he was both slow in invention and also in arrangement disorderly. There remain two points, delivery and memory: for both of them he evoked the laughter and ridicule of the audience. His movement was of a kind that both C. Iulius [C. Iulius Caesar Strabo (**73**), F 12] branded it forever, when, as he [Curio] was reeling and swaying his whole body from side to side, he asked him "who is talking from a skiff?" and . . . [F 7] . . . [217] . . . And as for memory, it was so completely lacking that sometimes, when he had announced three points, he would either add a fourth or want a third . . . [F 10] . . . [218] That sort of thing is significant evidence of a feeble

125

signa; sed nihil turpius quam quod etiam in scriptis obli-
viscebatur quid paulo ante posuisset . . . [219] . . . iam, qui
hac parte animi, quae custos est ceterarum ingeni partium, tam debilis esset ut ne in scripto quidem meminisset
quid paulo ante posuisset, huic minime mirum est ex tempore dicenti solitam effluere mentem. [220] itaque cum ei
nec officium deesset et flagraret studio dicendi, perpaucae
ad eum causae deferebantur. orator autem {vivis eius ae-
qualibus}[3] proximus optimis numerabatur propter verborum bonitatem, ut ante dixi, et expeditam ac profluentem
quodam modo celeritatem. itaque eius orationes aspicien-
das tamen censeo. sunt illae quidem languidiores, verum
tamen possunt augere et quasi alere id bonum quod in illo
mediocriter fuisse concedimus: quod habet tantam vim ut
solum sine aliis in Curione speciem oratoris alicuius effecerit. . . . [234] . . . ita, tamquam Curio copia non nulla
verborum, nullo alio bono, tenuit oratorum locum: sic . . .

[3] *del. Kayser*: vivis eius aequalibus *codd.*: vivis eius <aetatis>
aequalibus *Friedrich*: a temporis eius aequalibus *Madvig*: a suis
aequalibus *Piderit*: vivis etiam aequalibus *Stangl*

T 3 Quint. *Inst.* 6.3.76

hoc genus dicti consequens vocant quidam, estque[1] illi
simile quod Cicero Curionem, semper ab excusatione
aetatis incipientem, facilius cotidie prohoemium habere
dixit, quia ista natura sequi et cohaerere videantur.

[1] estque *Radermacher*: atque *cod.*: atque est *Meister*

memory; but nothing is worse than that he would forget even in his writings what he had set down a little earlier . . . [219] . . . Now, if someone is so feeble in that part of the mind that is the custodian of the remaining parts of his intelligence, that even in a written work he could not recall what he had set down a little earlier, it is not at all surprising that his memory often deserted him in extempore speech. [220] Therefore, though he did not lack readiness to help and was zealous in cultivating oratory, very few cases were brought to him. Still, as an orator he was reckoned as next in rank to the best {among his living peers}, because of the excellence of his diction, as I have said before, and his somehow unencumbered ease and fluency. Therefore, I still consider his orations worth looking at. Those are, to be sure, somewhat spiritless, but they may still augment and in a sense feed that excellence that we acknowledge he possessed in moderate degree: it has such a force that by itself and without other merits it gave to Curio the semblance of an orator of some sort. . . . [234] . . . Thus, as Curio by some wealth of diction, without any other good quality, held the rank of orator: so . . .

T 3 Quintilian, *The Orator's Education*

Some call this type of witticism "a consequence," and similar to that is what Cicero said about Curio, who always began by apologizing for his age, that he had an easier prooemium day by day, because those things seem to follow and be connected naturally.

*Against Q. Caecilius Metellus Nepos Baliarici
filius (F 4–5)*

F 4 Asc. in Cic. *Corn.* (p. 56 KS = 63.11–21 C.)

res autem tota se sic habet: in qua quidem illud primum explicandum est, de quo Metello hoc dicit. fuerunt enim tunc plures Quinti Metelli, ex quibus duo consulares, Pius et Creticus, de quibus apparet eum non dicere, duo autem adulescentes Nepos et Celer, ex quibus nunc Nepotem significat. eius enim patrem Q. Metellum Nepotem, Baliarici filium, Macedonici nepotem qui consul fuit cum T. Didio, Curio is de quo loquitur accusavit: isque Metellus moriens petiit ab hoc filio suo Metello ut Curionem accusatorem suum accusaret, et id facturum esse iure iurando adegit.

F 5 Apul. *Apol.* 66.4

= **65** F 15.

On Behalf of the Brothers Cossi (F 6)

F 6 Cic. *De or.* 2.98

= **65** F 32.

Against Q. Caecilius Metellus Nepos Baliarici
filius (F 4–5)

Curio prosecuted Q. Caecilius Metellus Nepos Baliarici
filius (cos. 98 BC) in what was apparently a famous case
(TLRR 82).

F 4 Asconius on Cicero, *Pro Cornelio*

And the whole matter stands as follows: therein that point
has to be explained first, about which Metellus he [Cicero]
says this. For at that time there were several Quinti Metelli, of whom two were ex-consuls, Pius and Creticus,
about whom it is clear that he is not talking, and two young
men, Nepos and Celer, of whom he now means Nepos.
For his father Q. Metellus Nepos, son of Baliaricus, grand-
son of Macedonicus, who was consul with T. Didius [98
BC], was accused by the Curio about whom he talks; and
that Metellus, on his deathbed, entreated his son, this
Metellus, that he should accuse Curio, his own accuser,
and he bound him by oath that he would do so.

F 5 Apuleius, *Apologia*

= **65** F 15.

On Behalf of the Brothers Cossi (F 6)

Curio supported the brothers Cossi in the centumviral
*court, when they were prosecuted by M. Antonius (**65***
F 32) (TLRR 360).

F 6 Cicero, *On the Orator*

= **65** F 32.

As Consul to the People (F 7)

F 7 Cic. *Brut.* 216–17 (cf. T 2)

[Cicero:] motus erat is, quem et C. Iulius in perpetuum notavit, cum ex eo in utramque partem toto corpore vacillante quaesivit quis loque‹re›tur[1] e luntre,[2] et Cn. Sicinius homo impurus, sed admodum ridiculus—neque aliud in eo oratoris simile quicquam. [217] is cum tribunus plebis Curionem et Octavium consules produxisset Curioque multa dixisset sedente Cn. Octavio conlega, qui devinctus erat fasciis et multis medicamentis propter dolorem artuum delibutus, "numquam," inquit, "Octavi, conlegae tuo gratiam referes: qui nisi se suo more iactavisset, hodie te istic muscae comedissent."

[1] loque‹re›tur *edd.*: loquetur *codd.*   [2] eluntre *vel* e lintre *vel* cluntre *vel* eli intre *codd.*: in luntre *Quint.*

Cf. Quint. *Inst.* 11.3.129.

On Behalf of P. Clodius Pulcher (F 8)

*In 61 BC Curio defended P. Clodius Pulcher (**137**), charged with sexual impurity after having been discovered among women celebrating the festival of Bona Dea (TLRR 236). Despite many testimonies against him, including one*

As Consul to the People (F 7)

*As consul in 76 BC, Curio spoke before a meeting of the People (CCMR, App. A: 234) when mocked by the Tribune of the People Cn. Sicinius (**98**).*

F 7 Cicero, *Brutus* (cf. T 2)

[CICERO:] His movement was of a kind that both C. Iulius [C. Iulius Caesar Strabo (**73**), F 12] branded it forever, when, as he [Curio] was reeling and swaying his whole body from side to side, he asked him "who is talking from a skiff?" and Cn. Sicinius [**98** T 1], a coarse man, but rather funny—and nothing else resembling an orator in him—made a jest to the same effect. [217] When, as Tribune of the People, he [Sicinius] had presented the consuls Curio and Octavius [76 BC] to a meeting of the People, and Curio had spoken at great length, while his colleague Cn. Octavius sat by, who was swathed in bandages and anointed with many medicinal salves because of the pain in his joints, he said: "You, Octavius, will never repay the debt to your colleague: if he had not moved about in his way, the flies would have eaten you here and now."

On Behalf of P. Clodius Pulcher (F 8)

*by Cicero, Clodius was acquitted due to alleged corruption among the judges; Curio then published a piece against Cicero, and Clodius spoke against Cicero (**137** F 1–2, 3).*

F 8 Schol. Bob. ad Cic. *Clod. et Cur.* (p. 85.16–19 Stangl)

post quod reus de incesto factus est P. Clodius accusante
L. Lentulo, defendente C. Curione patre. nam tres illis
temporibus Curiones inlustri nomine extiterunt atque ita
in libris adhuc feruntur: Curio avus . . . et hic Curio pater
qui P. Clodio adfuit, et tertius ille Curio tribunicius.

On Cn. Pompeius Magnus (F 9)

F 9 Suet. *Iul.* 50.1

nam certe Pompeio et a Curionibus patre et filio et a multis exprobratum est, quod cuius causa post tres liberos
exegisset uxorem et quem gemens Aegisthum appellare
consuesset, eius postea filiam potentiae cupiditate in ma-
trimonium recepisset.

F 8 Scholia Bobiensia to Cicero, *Against Clodius and Curio*

Afterward P. Clodius was charged with sexual impurity, with L. Lentulus acting as the prosecution [L. Cornelius Lentulus Crus (**157**), F 3–4] and C. Curio the father as the defense. For in those times there were three men called Curio with an illustrious name, and they are still referred to in the books thus: Curio the grandfather [**47**] . . . and this Curio the father, who assisted P. Clodius, and the third, that Curio of tribunician rank [**170**].

On Cn. Pompeius Magnus (F 9)

*In 59 BC or shortly afterward, Curio, like others (Plut. Caes. 14.8), expressed disapproval of the fact that Cn. Pompeius Magnus (**111**) had married the daughter of C. Iulius Caesar (**121**).*

F 9 Suetonius, *Life of Caesar*

For there is no doubt that Pompey was taken to task by Curio the father and Curio the son [**170** F 11] as well as by many others, because, through a desire for power, he had later married the daughter [Iulia] of a man [C. Iulius Caesar (**121**)] on whose account he had divorced a wife [Mucia Tertia], after having had three children with her, and whom, with a groan, he had been accustomed to call Aegisthus.[1]

[1] That is, implying that Caesar started a relationship with Mucia Tertia, Pompey's wife, while the latter was absent in the war against Mithridates, as did the mythical Aegisthus with Agamemnon's wife, Clytemnestra, during the Trojan War.

On Behalf of Ser. Naevius Against Titinia
(F 10–11)

At an unknown date, Curio spoke in a private suit on be-
half of Ser. Naevius against a lady called Titinia, who was
apparently defended by C. Aurelius Cotta (80 F 15) and

F 10 Cic. *Brut.* 217

= **80** F 15.

F 11 Cic. *Orat.* 129

. . . nobis privata in causa magna et gravi cum coepisset
Curio pater respondere, subito assedit, cum sibi venenis
ereptam memoriam diceret.

On C. Iulius Caesar (F 12–16)

F 12 Suet. *Iul.* 9.1–3

nec eo setius maiora mox in urbe molitus est: siquidem
ante paucos dies quam aedilitatem iniret, venit in suspicionem conspirasse cum Marco Crasso consulari, item

On Behalf of Ser. Naevius Against Titinia
(F 10–11)

Cicero (Cic. Pro Titinia Cottae*: Crawford 1984, 35–36)*
(TLRR 133).

F 10 Cicero, *Brutus*

= **80** F 15.

F 11 Cicero, *Orator*

. . . when in a major and serious private case[1] Curio the
father had begun his reply to us, he suddenly sat down,
while he said that his memory had been taken away by
magical potions.

[1] The case is not identified, but the details given suggest that
the comment refers to the case of Titinia.

On C. Iulius Caesar (F 12–16)

*Curio made critical remarks about C. Iulius Caesar (**121**).*
Whether all of them come from speeches is unclear; for
some, even the attribution to this Curio and the context are
uncertain.

F 12 Suetonius, *Life of Caesar*

But nonetheless he [C. Iulius Caesar (**121**)] soon undertook something greater in the city [of Rome]: for indeed
a few days before he entered upon the aedileship [65 BC],
he came under the suspicion of having conspired with

Publio Sulla et L. Autronio post designationem consulatus
ambitus condemnatis, ut principio anni senatum adorirentur, et trucidatis quos placitum esset, dictaturam Crassus
invaderet, ipse ab eo magister equitum diceretur constitutaque ad arbitrium re publica Sullae et Autronio consulatus restitueretur. [2] meminerunt huius coniurationis
Tanusius Geminus in historia, Marcus Bibulus in edictis,
C. Curio pater in orationibus. de hac significare videtur et
Cicero in quadam ad Axium epistula referens Caesarem
in consulatu confirmasse regnum, de quo aedilis cogitarat.
Tanusius adicit Crassum paenitentia vel metu diem caedi
destinatum non obisse et idcirco ne Caesarem quidem
signum, quod ab eo dari convenerat, dedisse; convenisse
autem Curio ait, ut togam de umero deiceret. [3] idem
Curio sed et M. Actorius Naso auctores sunt conspirasse
eum etiam cum Gnaeo Pisone adulescente, cui ob suspicionem urbanae coniurationis provincia Hispania ultro
extra ordinem data sit; pactumque ut simul foris ille, ipse
Romae ad res novas consurgerent, per † Ambranos[1] et
Transpadanos; destitutum utriusque consilium morte Pisonis.

[1] Lambranos *Sabellicus*: Ambrones *Beroaldus* (-as *al.*): Ambarros *Urlichs*: Aruernos *Mommsen*: Campanos *Madvig*

---

[1] It is uncertain to which nation the corrupt word *Ambrani*
refers; the *Transpadani* lived beyond the river Po in northern
Italy.

Marcus Crassus [M. Licinius Crassus Dives (**102**)], an ex-consul, likewise with Publius Sulla [P. Cornelius Sulla] and L. Autronius [i.e., P. Autronius Paetus], who, after their election to the consulship [for 65 BC], had been found guilty of bribery; their plan was to attack the Senate at the beginning of the year and, having killed those whom they had resolved to kill, Crassus was to usurp the dictatorship, he himself was to be named by him as master of the horse, and, when they had organized the Republic according to their pleasure, the consulship was to be restored to Sulla and Autronius. [2] This plot is mentioned by Tanusius Geminus in his history [*FRHist* 44 F 2], by Marcus Bibulus in edicts [M. Calpurnius Bibulus (**122**), F 2–6], and by C. Curio the father in speeches. Cicero too seems to hint at it in some letter to Axius [not preserved], where he says that Caesar in his consulship established the kingly rule that he had had in mind as aedile. Tanusius adds that Crassus, out of conscience or fear, did not appear on the day appointed for the massacre and therefore Caesar then did not give the signal that, as had been agreed, was to be given by him; and Curio says that it was agreed that he should let his toga fall from his shoulder. [3] The same Curio, but also M. Actorius Naso [*FRHist* 43 F 1] are witnesses that he [Caesar] also made a plot with the young Gnaeus Piso [Cn. Calpurnius Piso, quaestor pro praetore in Hispania citerior in 65/64 BC], to whom, because he was suspected of political intrigues in the city [of Rome], the province of Hispania had been assigned unasked and out of the regular order; and that it was agreed to rise in revolt at the same time, the latter abroad and he himself at Rome, aided by the Ambrani [?] and the Transpadani;[1] that the designs of both of them were rendered void by Piso's death.

137

F 13 Suet. *Iul.* 49.1

pudicitiae eius famam nihil quidem praeter Nicomedis
contubernium laesit, gravi tamen et perenni obprobrio et
ad omnium convicia exposito. . . . praetereo actiones Dolabellae et Curionis patris, in quibus eum Dolabella "pae-
licem reginae, spondam interiorem regiae lecticae," at
Curio "stabulum Nicomedis et Bithynicum fornicem" di-
cunt.

F 14 Suet. *Iul.* 52.3

at[1] ne cui dubium omnino sit et impudicitiae et adulterio-
rum flagrasse infamia, Curio pater quadam eum oratione
"omnium mulierum virum et omnium virorum mulierem"
appellat.

[1] ac *edd. fere cum Erasmo*

F 15 Prisc., *GL* II, p. 385.11–13

Curio pater: "nusquam demolitur, nusquam exoneratur
pecunia," "demolitur" passive dixit.

F 13 Suetonius, *Life of Caesar*

Nothing damaged his reputation for chastity except his intimate companionship with Nicomedes [king of Bithynia], though that was a deep and lasting reproach and exposed to insults from everyone.... I pass over the speeches of Dolabella [Cn. Cornelius Dolabella (**94**), F 1] and of Curio the father, in which Dolabella calls him [Caesar] "the queen's rival, the inner side of the royal couch,"[1] but Curio "the stable of Nicomedes and the brothel of Bithynia."

[1] *lectica* is literally a "litter," but here seems to refer to a bed (diminutive of *lectus*). The "inner side" is the bed's "open" side, the place for the second person (cf. Ov. *Am.* 3.14.32: *cur pressus prior est interiorque torus?*).

F 14 Suetonius, *Life of Caesar*

But so that there is no doubt at all for anyone that he was ablaze with a bad reputation for both sexual impurity [with men] and adultery, Curio the father, in some oration, calls him [Caesar] "every woman's man and every man's woman."

F 15 Priscian

Curio the father: "under no circumstances is he removed, under no circumstances is he relieved of [paying / accepting] the money," *demolitur* ["is removed"] he used in passive sense [normally deponent with active meaning].

F 16 Prisc., *GL* II, pp. 384.13–85.1

Curio:[1] "eum tam invidiosa fortuna conplecti," passive.

[1] Curio *Hertz*: Curio. cupio *Lipsius*: Cicero. Cupio *vel* cupio *codd.*

87 C. PAPIRIUS CARBO ARVINA

*C. Papirius Carbo Arvina (tr. pl. 90, praet. before 82 BC; RE Papirius 40), a son of C. Papirius Carbo (**35**), was killed by L. Iunius Brutus Damasippus in the Curia Hostilia in 82 BC (Cic. Fam. 9.21.3; Brut. 311: **102** T 3; De or. 3.10; Vell. Pat. 2.26.2; Val. Max. 9.2.3; Oros. 5.20.4; App. B Civ. 1.88.403).*

T 1 Cic. *Brut.* 221

[CICERO:] in eodem igitur numero eiusdem aetatis C. Carbo fuit illius eloquentissimi viri filius. non satis acutus orator, sed tamen orator numeratus est. erat in verbis gravitas et facile dicebat et auctoritatem naturalem quandam habebat oratio.

T 2 Cic. *Brut.* 305

[CICERO:] . . . diserti autem Q. Varius C. Carbo Cn. Pomponius, et hi quidem habitabant in rostris . . .

F 16 Priscian

Curio: "he being implicated in such invidious fortune," in passive sense [normally deponent with active meaning].

87 C. PAPIRIUS CARBO ARVINA

In Cicero, Carbo is mentioned among the respectable, yet not outstanding orators of his period and as someone who delivered many speeches to the People (T 1–2; Cic. Brut. 227, 308). A passage from one of these contiones, *given when Carbo was Tribune of the People, survives (F 4; CCMR, App. A: 220).*

T 1 Cicero, *Brutus*

[CICERO:] To the same group of that same period [of P. Sulpicius Rufus (**76**) and C. Aurelius Cotta (**80**)], then, belonged C. Carbo, a son of the great orator of that name [C. Papirius Carbo (**35**)]. He was not an orator of much acumen, but still he was accounted an orator. There was dignity in his diction, and he spoke readily, and his speech possessed a certain natural authority.

T 2 Cicero, *Brutus*

[CICERO:] . . . but eloquent men were Q. Varius [Q. Varius Hybrida (**88**), T 3], C. Carbo, Cn. Pomponius [Cn. Pomponius (**72B**), F 4], and these indeed lived on the Rostra . . .

T 3 Sacerd., *GL* VI, p. 461.23–30

astismos fit tribus modis: . . . per similitudinem, quo modo
dictum est de Carbone, qui mortuo Crasso, homine felice,
inimico suo, ante obscurus florere coepit, "postquam
Crassus carbo factus est," id est periit, "Carbo crassus factus est," id est res ante mortua revixit, id est ad florem
pervenit . . .

As Tribune to the People (F 4)

F 4 Cic. *Orat.* 213–14

= **42** F 3.

88 Q. VARIUS HYBRIDA

*Q. Varius Hybrida, also called Sucronensis (tr. pl. 90 BC;
RE Varius 7), introduced a law ordering investigation of
those men through whose support allies had taken up arms
against the Roman People (Val. Max. 8.6.4; Asc. in Cic.
Scaur. I.3 [p. 22.5–8 C.]; Lex Varia de maiestate: LPPR,
pp. 339–40). On this basis many eminent men (having to
defend themselves) were taken to court (Cic. Brut. 304).*

T 1 Cic. *Brut.* 182

= **76** T 1.

T 3 Sacerdos

A witticism occurs in three ways: . . . through similarity, as is said about Carbo, who, when Crassus [L. Licinius Crassus (**66**)], a fortunate man, his enemy [because of the prosecution of his father: **66** F 13–14], was dead, began to flourish, having been undistinguished previously, "after Crassus was turned into charcoal [*carbo*]," that is, perished, "Carbo was made thick [*crassus*]," that is, a matter previously dead, came to life again, that is, reached a flourishing state . . .

As Tribune to the People (F 4)

F 4 Cicero, *Orator*

= **42** F 3.

88 Q. VARIUS HYBRIDA

In 89 BC Q. Varius Hybrida was himself prosecuted under the same law, found guilty, and went into exile (Cic. Brut. 305; Val. Max. 8.6.4) (TLRR 109).

In Cicero, Varius Hybrida is regarded as an able and active orator, while the employment of his faculties is regretted (T 1–4).

T 1 Cicero, *Brutus*

= **76** T 1.

T 2 Cic. *Brut.* 221

[CICERO:] acutior Q. Varius rebus inveniendis nec minus verbis expeditus . . .

T 3 Cic. *Brut.* 305

= **87** T 2.

T 4 Cic. *De or.* 1.117

[CRASSUS:] quis vestrum aequalem Q. Varium, vastum hominem atque foedum, non intellegit illa ipsa facultate, quamcumque habet, magnam esse in civitate gratiam consecutum?

89 L. CORNELIUS SISENNA

L. Cornelius Sisenna (praet. 78 BC; RE Cornelius 374) was praetor urbanus *and* peregrinus *in 78 BC and afterward apparently propraetor in Sicilia (on his life, see FRHist 1:306–7). In the war against the pirates, he was a legate of Pompey's (App. Mithr. 95); when he came to Crete, he fell ill and died in 67 BC (Cass. Dio 36.18.1–19.1). Sisenna was a friend of T. Pomponius Atticus (**103**) (F 5).*

T 1 Cic. *Brut.* 228

[CICERO:] inferioris autem aetatis erat proximus L. Sisenna, doctus vir et studiis optimis deditus, bene Latine loquens, gnarus rei publicae, non sine facetiis, sed neque

T 2 Cicero, *Brutus*

[CICERO:] Shrewder in invention [than C. Papirius Carbo Arvina (**87**)] was Q. Varius and no less ready in diction . . .

T 3 Cicero, *Brutus*

= **87** T 2.

T 4 Cicero, *On the Orator*

[CRASSUS:] Who does not know that Q. Varius, your contemporary [of P. Sulpicius Rufus (**76**) and C. Aurelius Cotta (**80**)], an unrefined and repulsive man, has attained great popularity in the community through that very ability [oratory] to the extent he possesses it?

89 L. CORNELIUS SISENNA

Sisenna wrote a work on the history of Rome in at least twenty-three books (FRHist 26) and Milesian novels on the model of Aristides' Greek tales (HRR I, p. 297). In Cicero Sisenna is described as a learned man with good Latinity and knowledge of politics, but not a great orator, lacking in industry and legal experience (T 1–2).

T 1 Cicero, *Brutus*

[CICERO:] But of the younger generation the nearest [to P. Antistius (**78**) in oratorical ability] was L. Sisenna, a man of scholarly training and devoted to the best studies, speaking well a pure Latin, well acquainted with political

laboris multi nec satis versatus in causis; interiectusque
inter duas aetates Hortensi et Sulpici nec maiorem[1] consequi poterat et minori necesse erat cedere. huius omnis
facultas ex historia ipsius perspici potest, quae cum facile
omnis vincat superiores, tum indicat tamen quantum absit
a summo quamque genus hoc scriptionis nondum sit satis
Latinis litteris inlustratum.

[1] maiorem *edd.*: maioris *codd.*

T 2 Cic. *Leg.* 1.7

[ATTICUS:] Sisenna, eius amicus, omnes adhuc nostros
scriptores . . . facile superavit; is tamen neque orator in
numero vestro umquam est habitus, et in historia puerile
quiddam consectatur, ut unum Clitarchum neque praeterea quemquam de Graecis legisse videatur, eum tamen
velle dumtaxat imitari; quem si assequi posset, aliquantum
ab optimo tamen abesset.

On Behalf of C. Verres (F 3–4)

F 3 Cic. *Verr.* 2.2.110

. . . nihil enim minus libenter de Sthenio commemoro,
nihil aliud in eo quod reprehendi possit invenio nisi quod

matters, not without wit; but he had neither great industry nor adequate experience in the courts; falling between the two generations of Hortensius [Q. Hortensius Hortalus (**92**)] and Sulpicius [P. Sulpicius Rufus (**76**)], he was not able to catch up with the elder and was obliged to yield before the younger. All his ability can be seen from his history, which, while easily surpassing all predecessors, yet reveals how far from perfection this type of writing is and how inadequately as yet it has been given glory in Latin letters.

T 2 Cicero, *On the Laws*

[ATTICUS:] [continued from **110** T 2] Sisenna, his [C. Licinius Macer's (**110**)] friend, has easily surpassed all our historians up to the present time. . . . Still, he has never been considered an orator of your rank [i.e., of you, Cicero, and your colleagues], and, in his historical writing, he seeks something childish, so that he seems to have read Clitarchus [*FGrHist / BNJ* 137] only, and nobody from the Greeks besides, and still to wish to imitate just him; and even if he were able to equal him, he would still be a considerable distance away from the best.

On Behalf of C. Verres (F 3–4)

*In 70 BC Sisenna, along with Q. Hortensius Hortalus (**92** F 23–28) and others, defended C. Verres, when Cicero prosecuted him (Cic. Verr.) (TLRR 177).*

F 3 Cicero, *Verrine Orations*

. . . for there is nothing that I am more unwilling to record about Sthenius [of Thermae], nor can I observe anything

homo frugalissimus atque integerrimus te, hominem plenum stupri, flagiti, sceleris, domum suam invitavit, nisi quod, qui C. Mari, Cn. Pompei, C. Marcelli, L. Sisennae, tui defensoris, ceterorum virorum fortissimorum hospes fuisset atque esset, ad eum numerum clarissimorum hominum tuum quoque nomen adscripsit.

F 4 Cic. *Verr.* 2.4.43

tu porro posses facere ut Cn. Calidio non redderes? praesertim cum is L. Sisenna, defensore tuo, tam familiariter uteretur, et cum ceteris familiaribus Sisennae reddidisses.

On Behalf of C. Hirtilius (F 5)

F 5 Cic. *Brut.* 259–60

[ATTICUS:] ". . . Sisenna autem quasi emendator sermonis usitati cum esse vellet, ne a C. Rusio quidem accusatore deterreri potuit quo minus inusitatis verbis uteretur." [260] "quidnam istuc est?" inquit BRUTUS; "aut quis est iste C. Rusius?" et ille [ATTICUS]: "fuit accusator," inquit, "vetus, quo accusante C. Hirtilium[1] Sisenna defendens

---

[1] Chirtilium *codd.*: C. Herennium *Martha*

else in him that could be criticized, other than that this most upright and most honest man invited you [Verres], a man full of sexual promiscuity, outrageous conduct, and crime, to his house; than that, having been and still being the host of C. Marius [the seven-time consul], Pompey [Cn. Pompeius Magnus (**111**)], C. Marcellus [governor of Sicily in 79 BC], L. Sisenna, your advocate, and other very courageous gentlemen, he has added to that roll of very illustrious people your [Verres'] name as well.

F 4 Cicero, *Verrine Orations*

And further, could you [Verres] act in such a way that you did not give them [special silver drinking vessels] back to Cn. Calidius [a Roman knight]? Especially since that man was so intimate with L. Sisenna, your advocate, and you had given back [their possessions] to Sisenna's other intimate friends.

On Behalf of C. Hirtilius (F 5)

*Sisenna appeared as the defense for C. Hirtilius against C. Rusius (*TLRR 191*).*

F 5 Cicero, *Brutus*

[ATTICUS:] ". . . But when Sisenna wanted to be a reformer, as it were, of commonly used language, he could not be deterred even by C. Rusius, a prosecutor, from using less common words." [260] "What is this," said BRUTUS; "and who was that C. Rusius?" And he [ATTICUS] said: "He was a veteran prosecutor; when he prosecuted C. Hirtilius, Sisenna, who defended him, said that certain

149

dixit quaedam eius sputatilica esse crimina. tum C. Rusius: 'circumvenior,' inquit, 'iudices, nisi subvenitis. Sisenna quid dicat[2] nescio; metuo insidias. sputatilica, quid est hoc? sputa quid sit scio, tilica nescio.' maximi risus; sed ille tamen familiaris meus recte loqui putabat esse inusitate loqui. . . ."

[2] dicat *edd.*: dicas *codd.*

90 L. LICINIUS LUCULLUS

*L. Licinius Lucullus (cos. 74 BC; RE Licinius 104), a brother of M. Licinius Lucullus (**91**), was a supporter of L. Cornelius Sulla and served in the Social War; in his youth he composed a work on the war in Greek as a* jeu d'esprit *(FRHist 23). After his consulship in 74 BC, he received the provinces of Asia and Cilicia, which he reorganized and where he fought against the kings Mithridates VI and Tigranes; thereupon, he eventually celebrated a triumph in 63 BC, having faced opposition to his policies (cf. **125** F 3–6). L. Lucullus supported the death penalty for the arrested Catilinarian conspirators in 63 (Cic. Att. 12.21.1) and testified against his former brother-in-law P. Clodius Pulcher (**137**) at the Bona Dea trial of 61 BC (on Lucullus' life, see van Ooteghem 1959; Schütz 1994).*

T 1 Cic. *Brut.* 222

[CICERO:] . . . L. autem Lucullum etiam acutum, patremque tuum, Brute, iuris quoque et publici et privati sane peritum, M. Lucullum . . . abducamus ex acie, id est a

accusations of his were *sputatilica* ['execrable'; rendering κατάπτυστά, 'to be spat upon, abominable']. Thereupon C. Rusius said: 'I am encircled, judges, unless you come to my rescue. What Sisenna is saying I do not understand; I fear a trap. *Sputatilica*, what is that? What *sputa* [past participle of *spuo* or imperative of *sputo*, 'to spit'] is, I know, but *tilica* I do not understand.' There was great laughter; but still that good friend of mine believed that speaking correctly was speaking in an uncommon way. . . ."

90 L. LICINIUS LUCULLUS

L. Lucullus was regarded as extremely rich (Diod. Sic. 4.21.4) and as a very learned and cultured man. L. Cornelius Sulla dedicated his commentarii *to him as an able writer (T 2; FRHist 23 T 3). L. Lucullus was on familiar terms with the poet Archias (Cic. Arch. 5–6) and the philosopher Antiochus of Ascalon, and himself interested in philosophy: accordingly, the second book of one version of Cicero's* Academica *is named after him. L. Lucullus was recognized as an able orator, though described as more suited to political oratory in Cicero (T 1–3).*

Both brothers were attacked by C. Memmius (125 F 2–6), when the latter was Tribune of the People in 66 BC, but the charges were dropped (TLRR 206).

T 1 Cicero, *Brutus*

[CICERO:] . . . L. Lucullus too, also a shrewd man, and your father [M. Iunius Brutus, tr. pl. 83 BC], Brutus, well versed indeed in both public and private law, M. Lucullus, . . . let us withdraw them from the battle line, that is from

151

iudiciis, et in praesidiis rei publicae, cui facile satis facere possint, collocemus.

T 2 Plut. *Luc.* 1.4–5

ὁ δὲ Λεύκολλος ἤσκητο καὶ λέγειν ἱκανῶς ἑκατέραν γλῶτταν, ὥστε καὶ Σύλλας τὰς αὑτοῦ πράξεις ἀναγράφων ἐκείνῳ προσεφώνησεν ὡς συνταξομένῳ καὶ διαθήσοντι τὴν ἱστορίαν ἄμεινον. [5] ἦν γὰρ οὐκ ἐπὶ τὴν χρείαν μόνην ἐμμελὴς αὐτοῦ καὶ πρόχειρος ὁ λόγος, καθάπερ ὁ τῶν ἄλλων, τὴν μὲν ἀγορὰν "θύννος βολαῖος πέλαγος ὡς διεστρόβει" [Ad. F 391 *TrGF*], γενόμενος δὲ τῆς ἀγορᾶς ἐκτὸς "αὖος, ἀμουσίᾳ τεθνηκώς," ἀλλὰ καὶ τὴν ἐμμελῆ ταύτην καὶ λεγομένην ἐλευθέριον ἐπὶ τῷ καλῷ προσεποιεῖτο παιδείαν ἔτι καὶ μειράκιον ὤν . . .

T 3 Plut. *Luc.* 33.3

ταῦτα γὰρ ὑπάρξαι Λευκόλλῳ κακὰ λέγουσιν ἐν πᾶσι τοῖς ἄλλοις ἀγαθοῖς· καὶ γὰρ μέγας καὶ καλὸς καὶ δεινὸς εἰπεῖν καὶ φρόνιμος ὁμαλῶς ἐν ἀγορᾷ καὶ στρατοπέδῳ δοκεῖ γενέσθαι.

Against Servilius the Augur (F 4–6)

*To great acclaim (though without immediate success), the brothers Luculli (cf. **91** F 2A), as young men, prosecuted Servilius the augur (TLRR 71), who had prosecuted their father upon his return from Sicily in 102 BC (TLRR 69;*

the courts, and station them [the orators just listed] on the ramparts of the Republic, whose demands they are easily able to meet.

T 2 Plutarch, *Life of Lucullus*

Lucullus was trained also to speak fluently both languages, so that Sulla [L. Cornelius Sulla], writing his own memoirs, dedicated them to him, as a man who would set in order and duly arrange the narrative in a better way. [5] For his style was suitable not for practical needs alone and ready, like that of the others, "it stirred up" the Forum "like smitten tunny-fish the sea" [Ad. F 391 *TrGF*], yet outside of the Forum it became "withered, dead without refinement"; but he [Lucullus], even while still a young man, also attached himself to that harmonious and so-called liberal culture directed toward the beautiful . . .

T 3 Plutarch, *Life of Lucullus*

These bad qualities [e.g., discourteous and arrogant behavior] Lucullus is said to have had among all the other good qualities: for he seems to have been tall and handsome and powerful in speaking, and equally prudent in the Forum and the camp.

Against Servilius the Augur (F 4–6)

on the trials and the identity of Servilius, see also van Ooteghem 1959, 14–16; Gruen 1968a, 176–78; Schütz 1994, 38–49).

F 4 Plut. *Luc.* 1.2

αὐτὸς δ' ὁ Λεύκολλος ἔτι μειράκιον ὤν, πρὶν ἀρχήν
τινα μετελθεῖν καὶ πολιτείας ἅψασθαι, πρῶτον ἔργον
ἐποιήσατο τὸν τοῦ πατρὸς κατήγορον κρῖναι Σερ-
ουίλιον αὔγουρα{ν},[1] λαβὼν ἀδικοῦντα δημοσίᾳ. καὶ
τὸ πρᾶγμα λαμπρὸν ἐφάνη Ῥωμαίοις, καὶ τὴν δίκην
ἐκείνην ὥσπερ ἀριστείαν διὰ στόματος ἔσχον. ἐδόκει
δὲ καὶ ἄλλως αὐτοῖς ἄνευ προφάσεως οὐκ ἀγεννὲς
εἶναι τὸ τῆς κατηγορίας ἔργον, ἀλλὰ καὶ πάνυ τοὺς
νέους ἐβούλοντο τοῖς ἀδικοῦσιν ἐπιφυομένους ὁρᾶν
ὥσπερ θηρίοις εὐγενεῖς σκύλακας. οὐ μὴν ἀλλὰ με-
γάλης περὶ τὴν δίκην ἐκείνην φιλονικίας γενομένης,
ὥστε καὶ τρωθῆναί τινας καὶ πεσεῖν, ἀπέφυγεν ὁ Σερ-
ουίλιος.

[1] αὔγουρα{ν} *Coraes:* αὔγουραν *codd.*

F 5 Cic. *Acad.* 2.1

magnum ingenium L. Luculli magnumque optimarum
artium studium, tum omnis liberalis et digna homine nobili ab eo percepta doctrina quibus temporibus florere in
foro maxime potuit, caruit omnino rebus urbanis.[1] ut enim
{urbanis}[2] admodum adulescens cum fratre pari pietate et
industria praedito paternas inimicitias magna cum gloria
est persecutus, in Asiam quaestor profectus ibi permultos
annos admirabili quadam laude provinciae praefuit . . .

[1] urbanis *ed. Veneta 1493 vel 1496:* humanis *codd.*
[2] urbanis *vel* urbanus *vel om. codd.*

F 4 Plutarch, *Life of Lucullus*

Lucullus himself, while still a young man, before he had stood for any office and turned to political activity, made it his first business to bring to trial his father's prosecutor, Servilius the augur, whom he found doing wrong on public service. And the matter seemed to be brilliant to the Romans, and they had that case in their mouths, like a great deed of prowess. Indeed, generally, the business of prosecution, without special provocation, did not seem ignoble to them; instead, they very much wished to see their young men fastening themselves on malefactors like highbred whelps on wild beasts. Around that case, however, great animosity arose, so that some were wounded and slain; Servilius was acquitted.

F 5 Cicero, *Prior Academics*

The great talent of L. Lucullus and his great devotion to the best arts, also all the liberal learning suited to a man of high rank that he had acquired, were entirely separated from public life in the city [of Rome] in the period in which he could have flourished greatly in the Forum. For when he {in the city}, while only a youth, together with his brother [M. Licinius Lucullus (**91**)] possessed of equal filial affection and devotion, had carried on with great distinction the personal feuds of his father, he set off as quaestor to Asia [87–80 BC], and there for a great many years he presided over the province with quite remarkable credit . . .

155

F 6 Cic. *Prov. cons.* 22

multa praetereo, quod intueor coram haec lumina atque
ornamenta rei publicae, P. Servilium et M. Lucullum.
utinam etiam L. Lucullus illic adsideret![1] quae fuerunt
inimicitiae in civitate graviores quam Lucullorum atque
Servili? quas in viris fortissimis non solum exstinxit rei
publicae ‹utilitas›[2] dignitasque ipsorum, sed etiam ad
amicitiam consuetudinemque traduxit.

[1] illic adsideret *Madvig*: ille desiderat *codd. pler.*: ille deside-
ret *unus cod. corr.*: ille viveret *unus cod., Angelius*: ille desineret
tres codd.   [2] rei publicae ‹utilitas› *Baiter*: res publica *unus
cod.*: rei publicae *codd. cet.*

Against L. Cotta [?] (F 7)

F 7 Ps.-Asc. in Cic. *Verr.* 1.55 (p. 222.14–18 Stangl)

"faciam hoc ‹non›[1] novum, sed ab his, qui nunc principes
nostrae civitatis sunt, ante factum." verum dicit; etenim L.
Lucullus et item M. Lucullus ambo consulares, Marcus
vero et triumphalis fuit. hi cum accusarent L. Cottam, non

[1] *coniectura ex codd. Poggianis recc. sumpta*

---

[1] The name is often regarded as a mistake for C. Servilius, but
Gruen (1971, 54–55) argues that it is unlikely to be a scribal error
and that other details in this note are correct. Gruen therefore
assumes another prosecution by the brothers Luculli, perhaps of
the L. Cotta who was a Tribune of the People in 103 and a praetor in the 90s BC (see also Schütz 1994, 49–50). Such a trial would

F 6 Cicero, *De Provinciis Consularibus*

I pass over many examples, since I see here present those lights and ornaments of the Republic, P. Servilius[1] and M. Lucullus [M. Licinius Lucullus (**91**)]. Would that L. Lucullus also were sitting there! What enmities in this community were ever more bitter than those between the Luculli and Servilius? And yet, in such most worthy men, their regard for public ‹benefit› and their own honor not only extinguished those [enmities], but even transformed them into friendship and intimacy.

[1] Seen as a mistake for C. Servilius (the augur) or as a reference to another Servilius, most likely P. Servilius Vatia Isauricus (cos. 79 BC). A mistake does not have to be assumed: the trials involving the Luculli and Servilius are alluded to by the mention of "enmities" later in this passage.

Against L. Cotta [?] (F 7)

F 7 Pseudo-Asconius on Cicero, *Verrine Orations*

"I shall do this ‹not› as something novel, but it has previously been done by those who are now leading men in our community." He [Cicero] says what is true; for L. Lucullus and equally M. Lucullus [M. Licinius Lucullus (**91**)] were both ex-consuls, and Marcus was also a former triumphator. When these men accused L. Cotta,[1] they did not use

have to be dated to a later stage in the careers of the Luculli since according to F 5 Lucullus was not active in the Forum or even in Rome for some time as a younger man, apart from the personally motivated prosecution of Servilius. That Lucullus is seen as a forensic speaker and as someone appearing in the Forum (T 1, 2, 3) might suggest that he was involved in more than the single trial securely attested.

usi sunt oratione perpetua, sed interrogatione testium causam peregerunt.

Testimony Against C. Cornelius (F 7A)

F 7A Val. Max. 8.5.4

= **92** F 32.

91 M. LICINIUS LUCULLUS

*M. Licinius Lucullus (cos. 73 BC; RE Licinius 109), a brother of L. Licinius Lucullus (**90**), was called M. Terentius M. f. Varro Lucullus after his adoption. In the civil war he supported L. Cornelius Sulla against the Marians. After his consulship he was governor of Macedonia, defeated the Thracians, and celebrated a triumph in 71 BC.*

Like his brother, M. Lucullus was on familiar terms with the poet Archias (Cic. Arch. 5–6; cf. TLRR 235). He was recognized as an orator, even though he was more suited

T 1 Cic. *Brut.* 222

= **90** T 1.

a continuous speech, but carried the case through by questioning witnesses.[2]

[2] This procedure is a precedent for Cicero's approach in the trial of Verres in 70 BC.

Testimony Against C. Cornelius (F 7A)

L. Lucullus may have provided testimony against C. Cornelius (TLRR 209), *as his brother M. Licinius Lucullus* (**91** F 2B) *did.*

F 7A Valerius Maximus, *Memorable Doings and Sayings* = **92** F 32.[1]

[1] See note on **92** F 32.

91 M. LICINIUS LUCULLUS

to political speeches than to forensic ones, according to Cicero (T 1).

*On several occasions M. Lucullus made oratorical appearances (F 2A–B) with his brother (**90**) (TLRR 71, 209). Moreover, in 99 BC he intervened in favor of the return from exile of their uncle Q. Caecilius Metellus Numidicus (cos. 109 BC) (Cic. Red. sen. 37; Red. pop. 6). As pontifex, M. Lucullus supported Cicero's plans for rebuilding his house in 57 BC (Cic. Har. resp. 12; Att. 4.2.4).*

T 1 Cicero, *Brutus* = **90** T 1.

Against Servilius the Augur and L. Cotta [?] (F 2A)

F 2A Plut. *Luc.* 1.2; Cic. *Acad.* 2.1; *Prov. cons.* 22; Ps.-Asc. in Cic. *Verr.* 1.55 (p. 222.15–18 Stangl)

= **90** F 4–7.

Testimony Against C. Cornelius (F 2B)

F 2B Asc. in Cic. *Corn.*, *arg.* (pp. 53 KS = 60.19–61.5 C.); Val. Max. 8.5.4

= **92** F 31–32.

92 Q. HORTENSIUS HORTALUS

Q. Hortensius Hortalus (114–50 BC; cos. 69 BC; RE Hortensius 13) was regarded as the greatest orator before Cicero and as his only rival (T 1, 9–10). According to ancient authorities, mainly Cicero, Hortensius was a promising orator from an early age (T 1–2). He trained assiduously, but he relaxed this regime after his consulship; the lack of exercise and the fact that the Asiatic style of speaking was seen as more appropriate for young men meant that the elder Hortensius was less highly regarded (T 2, 4–5). Hortensius' style is described as full and elaborate, in line with the Asiatic genre, and characterized by an immaculate structure, comprehensiveness, and energetic delivery (T 2–3); elsewhere, he is seen as the representative of a single type of style, the middle style (Cic. Orat. 106). He had an excellent memory (T 2; Cic. De or. 3.230; Sen. Contr. 1, praef. 19).

Hortensius' delivered speeches were felt to be more effective than the written versions (T 7, 10); published

Against Servilius the Augur and L. Cotta [?] (F 2A)

F 2A Plutarch; Cicero; Pseudo-Asconius
= **90** F 4–7.

Testimony Against C. Cornelius (F 2B)

F 2B Asconius; Valerius Maximus
= **92** F 31–32.

92 Q. HORTENSIUS HORTALUS

*speeches were known in the time of Cicero (e.g., F 51) and
of Valerius Maximus (F 52). When Hortensius was han-
dling a case together with Cicero, the latter typically gave
the final speech (Cic.* Brut. *190;* Orat. *130).*

*In addition to speeches, Hortensius apparently pro-
duced playful verses (Plin. Ep. 5.3.5; Ov. Tr. 2.441; Catull.
95.3; Gell. NA 19.9.7), a work on oratorical commonplaces
(Quint. Inst. 2.1.11, 2.4.27), and a historical piece on the
Social War (Vell. Pat. 2.16.2–3; FRHist 31 T 2). Hortensius
may not have been very interested in philosophy (Cic.
Acad. 2.61; Fin. 1.2). Cicero's (lost) philosophical dialogue*
Hortensius *is named after him: it advocates the study of
philosophy, while "Hortensius" supports oratory (on Hortensius in* Brutus, *see Garcea and Lomanto 2014).*

*There are only a few references to oratorical interven-
tions by Hortensius in the Senate, indicating the circumstances, not providing details of the speeches (Cic. Att.
4.3.3; Fam. 1.1.3, 1.2.1–2; Cass. Dio 39.37.3). In 61 BC*

*Hortensius commented on a bill proposed by the consul M. Pupius Piso Frugi Calpurnianus (**104**) concerning P. Clodius Pulcher (**137**) (cf. **126** F 17). In 54 BC Hortensius, along with Cicero (Cic. Planc.), defended Cn. Plancius against L. Cassius Longinus (**168** F 1) and M. Iuventius*

T 1 Cic. *Brut.* 228–30

[CICERO:] nam Q. Hortensi admodum adulescentis ingenium ut Phidiae signum simul aspectum et probatum est. [229] is L. Crasso Q. Scaevola consulibus primum in foro dixit et apud hos ipsos quidem consules, et cum eorum qui adfuerunt, tum ipsorum consulum qui omnis intellegentia anteibant, iudicio discessit probatus. undeviginti annos natus erat eo tempore, est autem L. Paullo C. Marcello consulibus mortuus: ex quo videmus eum in patronorum numero annos quattuor et quadraginta fuisse. hoc de oratore paulo post plura dicemus; hoc autem loco voluimus aetatem ‹eius›[1] in disparem oratorum aetatem includere. quamquam id quidem omnibus usu venire necesse fuit, quibus paulo longior vita contigit, ut et cum multo maioribus natu quam essent ipsi et cum aliquanto minoribus compararentur. . . . [230] sic Hortensius non cum suis aequalibus solum sed et mea cum aetate et cum tua, Brute, et cum aliquanto superiore coniungitur, si quidem et Crasso vivo dicere solebat et magis iam etiam vigebat Antonio et {cum}[2] Philippo iam sene pro Cn. Pompei

[1] *add. Stephanus*: aetatem *del. Schütz, om. unus cod.*

[2] Antonio et {cum} *Martha*: Antonio et cum *codd.*: cum Antonio et *Madvig*

*Laterensis (**167** F 1–2; Alexander 2002, 128–47); the defendant was acquitted (TLRR 293). Previously, Hortensius had spoken in the Senate about the selection of judges,
an issue presented as relevant to the case by Cicero (Cic.
Planc. 37; see Linderski 1961).*

T 1 Cicero, *Brutus*

[CICERO:] For the talent of the young Q. Hortensius, like
a statue of Phidias, won approval immediately upon being
seen. [229] In the consulship of L. Crassus and Q. Scaevola [95 BC] he spoke in the Forum for the first time
[F 12], and indeed in the presence of these same consuls,
and he came away from the trial having won the approval
not only of all who were present, but of the consuls themselves, who surpassed everyone in discernment. At that
time he was nineteen years old; and he died in the consulship of L. Paullus and C. Marcellus [50 BC]: from that we
see that he was among the advocates for forty-four years.
Of his character as an orator I shall say more a little later;
at this point I wished to insert <his> dates between the
ranks of orators of different generations. Yet this happens
naturally to all who enjoy a slightly longer life that they are
compared both with men much older than they are themselves and with those somewhat younger. . . . [230] Thus
Hortensius is associated not only with his contemporaries,
but also with my time and with yours, Brutus, as well as
with a somewhat earlier time, if, indeed, he used to speak
even while Crassus [L. Licinius Crassus (**66**)] was alive,
and flourished already even more in the time of Antonius
[M. Antonius (**65**)] and when Philippus [L. Marcius
Philippus (**70**), F 12–13], already an old man, spoke on

163

bonis dicente, in illa causa, adulescens cum esset, princeps
fuit et in eorum quos in Sulpici aetate posui, numerum
facile pervenerat et suos inter aequalis M. Pisonem M.
Crassum Cn. Lentulum P. Lentulum Suram longe praestitit et me adulescentem nactus octo annis minorem
quam erat ipse multos annos in studio eiusdem laudis
⟨se⟩[3] exercuit et tecum simul, sicut ego pro multis, sic ille
pro Appio Claudio dixit paulo ante mortem.

[3] *add. Douglas in comm.*

T 2 Cic. *Brut.* 301–3

[CICERO:] Hortensius igitur cum admodum adulescens
orsus esset in foro dicere, celeriter ad maiores causas adhi-
beri coeptus est: ⟨et⟩[1] quamquam inciderat in Cottae et
Sulpici aetatem, qui annis decem maiores ⟨erant⟩,[2] excel-
lente tum Crasso et Antonio, dein Philippo, post Iulio,
cum his ipsis dicendi gloria comparabatur. primum memoria tanta quantam in nullo[3] cognovisse me arbitror, ut
quae secum commentatus esset, ea sine scripto verbis

[1] *add. Ellendt*   [2] *add. Rau*   [3] in nullo *edd.*: in nullo
viro *vel* in viro *vel* invito *codd.*

behalf of the property of Pompey [Cn. Pompeius Magnus (**111**)]; in that case, he was, although he was a young man, the principal speaker [F 15], and in the ranks of those whom I have placed in the period of Sulpicius [P. Sulpicius Rufus (**76**)] he had easily found a place, and among his own contemporaries, M. Piso [M. Pupius Piso Frugi Calpurnianus (**104**)], Crassus [M. Licinius Crassus Dives (**102**)], Cn. Lentulus [Cn. Cornelius Lentulus Clodianus (**99**)], P. Lentulus Sura [P. Cornelius Lentulus Sura (**100**)], he was by far superior, and, encountering me, as young man, eight years younger than he was himself, he exerted ⟨himself⟩ in eagerness for the same prize for many years, and, shortly before his death, he spoke alongside you [M. Iunius Brutus (**158**), F 22], as did I on behalf of many, so did he [F 53–54] on behalf of Appius Claudius [Ap. Claudius Pulcher (**130**)].

T 2 Cicero, *Brutus*

[CICERO:] Hortensius, then, when as just a young man he had started to speak in the Forum, soon began to be called upon in cases of greater importance. ⟨And⟩ though his beginnings had fallen in the period of Cotta [C. Aurelius Cotta (**80**)] and Sulpicius [P. Sulpicius Rufus (**76**)], who ⟨were⟩ ten years older, when Crassus [L. Licinius Crassus (**66**)] and Antonius [M. Antonius (**65**)], then Philippus [L. Marcius Philippus (**70**)], and afterward Iulius [C. Iulius Caesar Strabo (**73**)], were preeminent, in renown as a speaker he was constantly compared with these very men. First of all, he possessed so great a memory as I believe I have never known in anyone; thus, what he had prepared in private, he could reproduce without notes in the same

eisdem redderet quibus cogitavisset. hoc adiumento ille
tanto sic utebatur ut sua et commentata et scripta et nullo
referente omnia omnium[4] adversariorum dicta meminisset. [302] ardebat autem cupiditate sic ut in nullo umquam
flagrantius studium viderim. nullum enim patiebatur esse
diem quin aut in foro diceret aut meditaretur extra forum.
saepissime autem eodem die utrumque faciebat. attulerat-
que minime vulgare genus dicendi; duas quidem res quas
nemo alius: partitiones quibus de rebus dicturus esset et
conlectiones,[5] memor et[6] quae essent dicta contra quaeque ipse dixisset. [303] erat in verborum splendore elegans, compositione aptus, facultate copiosus; eaque erat
cum summo ingenio tum exercitationibus maximis consecutus. rem complectebatur memoriter, dividebat acute,
nec praetermittebat fere quicquam quod esset in causa aut
ad confirmandum aut ad refellendum. vox canora et suavis, motus et gestus etiam plus artis habebat quam erat
oratori satis.

[4] omnia omnium *Stangl*: omnia omnia *vel* omnia *codd.*
[5] conlectiones *edd.*: coniectiones *codd.*   [6] memor et *vel*
memor *codd.*: memor eorum *Orelli*: {memor} eorum *Jahn*

T 3 Cic. *Brut.* 317

[CICERO:] duo tum excellebant oratores qui me imitandi
cupiditate incitarent, Cotta et Hortensius; quorum alter
remissus et lenis et propriis verbis comprendens solute et
facile sententiam, alter ornatus, acer et non talis qualem

words in which he had thought it out. This great means of support he used in such a way that he recalled his own words, both thought out and written down, and also, without any prompting, all utterances of all opponents. [302] He was fired too with such ambition that I have never seen more eager study in anyone. For he did not suffer a day to go by without either speaking in the Forum or practicing outside the Forum. Very often indeed he would do both on the same day. And he had brought with him a kind of speaking in no way commonplace, two things in fact that nobody else [did in the same way]: divisions of the matters about which he was going to speak and summaries, recalling both what had been said in opposition and what he himself had said [cf. Cic. *Quinct.* 35; *Div. Caec.* 45]. [303] In the brilliance of his words he was fastidious, felicitous in composition, resourceful in his command; and he had achieved that by his very great talent and particularly by his most extensive exercising. He always knew his case by heart, divided it sharply into its parts, and hardly ever overlooked anything concerning the case either for confirmation or for refutation. His voice was melodious and agreeable; his delivery and gesture even a little too studied than was sufficient for an orator.

T 3 Cicero, *Brutus*

[CICERO:] At that time two orators were preeminent who spurred me on through a desire to emulate them, Cotta [C. Aurelius Cotta (**80**)] and Hortensius. One of them [Cotta] was relaxed and quiet, constructing his sentences smoothly and easily, with words in their literal meaning; the other [Hortensius] was ornate, passionate, and not like

167

tu eum, Brute, iam deflorescentem cognovisti, sed verborum et actionis genere commotior. itaque cum Hortensio
mihi magis arbitrabar rem esse, quod et dicendi ardore
eram propior et aetate coniunctior. etenim videram in
isdem causis, ut pro M. Canuleio, pro Cn. Dolabella consulari, cum Cotta princeps adhibitus esset, priores tamen
agere partis Hortensium. acrem enim oratorem, ⟨et⟩[1] in-
censum et agentem et canorum concursus hominum fo-
rique strepitus desiderat.

[1] *add. Bake*

T 4 Cic. *Brut.* 319–20

[CICERO:] sed quoniam omnis hic sermo noster non solum
enumerationem oratorum[1] verum etiam praecepta quaedam desiderat, quid tamquam notandum et animadvertendum sit in Hortensio breviter licet dicere. [320] nam is
post consulatum—credo quod videret ex consularibus
neminem esse secum comparandum, neglegeret autem
eos qui consules non fuissent—summum illud suum studium remisit quo a puero fuerat incensus, atque in omnium rerum abundantia voluit beatius, ut ipse putabat,
remissius certe vivere. primus et secundus annus et tertius
tantum quasi de picturae veteris colore detraxerat, quantum non quivis unus ex populo, sed existimator doctus et
intellegens posset cognoscere. longius autem procedens
ut in ceteris eloquentiae partibus, tum maxime in celeri-
tate et continuatione verborum adhaerescens, sui dissimi-
lior videbatur fieri cottidie.

[1] oratorum *Lambinus*: oratoriam *codd.*

the man as you knew him, Brutus, in his decline, but live-
lier in the style of diction and delivery. Therefore, I felt
that Hortensius rather was the man I had to do with, since
in the ardor of speaking I was more like him and nearer in
age. For indeed I had noted that in shared cases, such as
for M. Canuleius [**80** F 12] or for Cn. Dolabella, the ex-
consul [**80** F 13–14], though Cotta was called upon as
the chief advocate, yet Hortensius [F 20, 20A] played the
leading role. For a great throng of people and the din of
the Forum call for an orator of energy, of fire, of action,
and of full voice.

T 4 Cicero, *Brutus*

[CICERO:] But since this entire conversation of ours aims
not merely to enumerate orators, but to teach some lessons, let me point out briefly what little there is in Hortensius that may be open to criticism or censure. [320]
For, after his consulship—because, I believe, he saw that
no one from the ex-consuls was comparable with him, and
he ignored those who had not been consuls—he relaxed
that great eagerness of his by which he had been enflamed
from his boyhood; and he wished, in an abundance of
all things, to live with greater enjoyment, as he himself
thought, or at least in a more relaxed way. One year, a
second, and a third had taken away something, as from the
color of an old picture, not so much as any single person
from the People, but as a trained and knowledgeable critic
would be able to perceive. But continuing further in this
way, coming to a standstill in all aspects of eloquence and
especially in the swift and smooth flow of language, he
seemed to become more unlike himself daily.

169

T 5 Cic. *Brut.* 325–27

[CICERO:] sed si quaerimus cur adulescens magis floruerit dicendo quam senior Hortensius, causas reperiemus verissimas duas. primam,[1] quod genus erat orationis Asiaticum adulescentiae magis concessum quam senectuti. genera autem Asiaticae dictionis duo sunt . . . [326] haec autem, ut dixi, genera dicendi aptiora sunt adulescentibus, in senibus gravitatem non habent. itaque Hortensius utroque genere florens clamores faciebat adulescens. habebat enim et Meneclium illud studium crebrarum venustarumque sententiarum, in quibus, ut in illo Graeco, sic in hoc erant quaedam magis venustae dulcesque sententiae quam aut necessariae aut interdum utiles; et erat oratio cum incitata et vibrans tum etiam accurata et polita. . . . [327] erat excellens iudicio vulgi et facile primas tenebat adulescens. etsi enim genus illud dicendi auctoritatis habebat parum, tamen aptum esse aetati videbatur. et certe, quod et ingeni quaedam forma ⟨e⟩lucebat[2] {et}[3] exercitatione[4] perfecta eratque verborum[5] astricta comprehensio,[6] summam hominum admirationem excitabat. sed cum iam honores et illa senior auctoritas gravius quiddam requireret, remanebat idem nec decebat idem; quodque exercitationem studiumque dimiserat, quod in eo

---

[1] primam *Ernesti*: primum *codd.*   [2] ⟨e⟩lucebat *Lambinus*: lucebat *codd.*   [3] *del. Schütz*   [4] exercitatione *codd.*: exercitatio *Martha*: et exercitatio plane perfecta *Reis*: ⟨et studio⟩ et exercitatione *Barwick*: ⟨lucubratione⟩ et exercitatione *Alfonsi*: et exercitatione perfecta ⟨erat sententiarum concinnitas⟩ *Fuchs*: ⟨usu⟩ et exercitatione perfecta *Malcovati*   [5] eratque verborum *edd.*: verborum. eratque *codd.*: erat{que} *Douglas*: ⟨erat⟩ verborum eratque *Friedrich*: erat ⟨sententiarum concinnitas⟩

T 5 Cicero, *Brutus*

[CICERO:] But if we ask why, as a young man, Hortensius enjoyed a more brilliant reputation for speaking than at a more advanced age, we shall find two very good reasons: first, because the Asiatic style of speaking was more permissible for youth than for old age. Of the Asiatic style there are two types . . . [326] And these styles of speaking, as I have said, are better suited to young men; with old men they lack weightiness. Therefore Hortensius, skilled in both styles, won great applause as a young man. For, on the one hand, he had that desire for frequent and gracefully pointed phrases in the manner of Menecles [Greek rhetorician, 2nd / 1st cent. BC]; among them, as with that Greek man, so with him, some phrases were more graceful and pleasant-sounding than either necessary or sometimes useful; on the other hand, his language was swift and vibrant, and also meticulous and polished. . . . [327] He was preeminent in the judgment of the public and easily held the first place as a young man. For even though that type of speaking had little authority, still, it seemed suited to his age. And at any rate, because also some beauty of talent shone forth, perfected by practice, and the arrangement of words was compact, he provoked the greatest admiration from people. But when honorable positions and that authority of age already called for something weightier, he remained the same, and the same was no longer fitting. And because he had relaxed that practice

---

verborumque *Bake*: verborum erat ‹at›que astricta *Sydow*: verborumque erat ‹arte› astricta *Hendrickson*   6 comprehensio *codd.*: comprehensio‹ne› *Martha*

fuerat acerrimum, concinnitas illa crebritasque sententiarum pristina manebat, sed ea vestitu illo orationis quo
consuerat ornata non erat. hoc tibi ille, Brute, minus fortasse placuit quam placuisset, si illum flagrantem studio et
florentem facultate audire potuisses.

T 6 Cic. *Brut.* 324

[CICERO:] dicendi autem genus quod fuerit in utroque,
orationes utriusque etiam posteris nostris indicabunt.

T 7 Cic. *Orat.* 132

. . . dicebat melius quam scripsit Hortensius.

T 8 Cic. *Brut.* 190

tum BRUTUS: "quid tu," inquit, "quaeris alios? de te ipso
nonne quid optarent rei, quid ipse Hortensius iudicaret
videbamus? qui cum partiretur tecum causas—saepe
enim interfui—perorandi locum, ubi plurimum pollet oratio, semper tibi relinquebat."

T 9 Gell. *NA* 1.5.2

ad eundem modum Q. Hortensius omnibus ferme oratoribus aetatis suae, nisi M. Tullio, clarior, quod multa
munditia et circumspecte compositeque indutus et amic-

and eagerness, which had been most intense in him, that earlier habit of frequent elegant expressions of thought remained, but it was not adorned with that dress of language that it used to have. For this reason, perhaps, Brutus, he pleased you less than he would have pleased you if you had been able to hear him burning with eagerness and flourishing in his ability. [continued by F 51]

T 6 Cicero, *Brutus*

[CICERO:] And as for the style of oratory that marked each of the two of us [Hortensius and Cicero], the speeches of either will indicate that also to people who come after us.

T 7 Cicero, *Orator*

. . . Hortensius generally spoke better than he wrote [up his speeches].

T 8 Cicero, *Brutus*

Then BRUTUS said: "Why do you look for others? As regards yourself, have we not seen repeatedly what clients chose, what Hortensius himself judged? When he shared cases with you—for I was often present—the place of the concluding speech, where oratory makes the greatest impact, he always left to you."

T 9 Gellius, *Attic Nights*

In the same way [as Demosthenes] Q. Hortensius, more renowned than almost all orators of his time except for M. Tullius [Cicero], because he dressed and arranged his clothing with great refinement and with care and exact-

tus esset manusque eius inter agendum forent argutae
admodum et gestuosae, maledictis compellationibusque
probris iactatus est, multaque in eum, quasi in histrionem,
in ipsis causis atque iudiciis dicta sunt.

T 10 Quint. *Inst.* 11.3.7–8

. . . et M. Cicero unam in dicendo actionem dominari
putat. [8] hac . . . tradit . . . Antonium et Crassum multum
valuisse, plurimum vero Q. Hortensium. cuius rei fides
est, quod eius scripta tantum infra famam sunt, qua diu
princeps orator, aliquando aemulus Ciceronis existimatus
est, novissime, quoad vixit, secundus, ut appareat pla-
cuisse aliquid eo dicente quod legentes non invenimus.

T 11 Apul. *Apol.* 95

quamcumque orationem struxerit Avitus, ita illa erit undi-
que sui perfecte absoluta, ut in illa neque Cato gravitatem
requirat neque Laelius lenitatem nec Gracchus impetum
nec Caesar calorem nec <H>ortensius distributionem nec
Calvus argutias nec parsimoniam Salustius nec opulen-
tiam Cicero: prorsus, inquam, ne omnis persequar, si Avi-
tum audias, neque additum quicquam velis neque detrac-
tum neque autem aliquid commutatum.

ness, and during the action his hands were rather expressive and gesturing, was assailed with gibes and shameful charges; and many taunts were hurled at him, as if at an actor, during the trials and court cases themselves.

T 10 Quintilian, *The Orator's Education*

. . . and M. [Tullius] Cicero believes [like Demosthenes] that delivery alone rules in oratory [cf. Cic. *De or.* 3.213]. [8] He transmits that therein . . . Antonius [M. Antonius (**65**)] and Crassus [L. Licinius Crassus (**66**)] were very powerful, but Q. Hortensius most. Testimony to this matter is that his [Hortensius'] written works are far below the reputation on account of which he was long regarded as the leading orator, for a time as Cicero's rival, and finally, for the rest of his life, as the second, so that it is obvious that there was something pleasing in his speaking that we do not find when we read him.

T 11 Apuleius, *Apologia*

Whatever oration Avitus [L. Hedius Rufus Lollianus Avitus, cos. 144 AD] has put together, it will be so perfectly executed in all its aspects that in it neither would Cato [M. Porcius Cato (**8**)] miss dignity nor Laelius [C. Laelius Sapiens (**20**)] smoothness nor Gracchus [C. Sempronius Gracchus (**48**)] vigor nor Caesar [C. Iulius Caesar (**121**)] passion nor ‹H›ortensius arrangement nor Calvus [C. Licinius Macer Calvus (**165**)] wittiness nor Sallust [C. Sallustius Crispus (**152**)] economy nor Cicero sumptuousness. In fact, I say, so as not to run through all of them, if you should hear Avitus, you would not wish anything added or removed or indeed anything changed.

On Behalf of Africa (F 12–13)

Hortensius first appeared as an orator in 95 BC, as a young man (cf. Quint. Inst. 12.7.3), when he spoke both in the Forum (F 12) and in the Senate (F 13) in support of

F 12 Cic. *Brut.* 229

= T 1.

F 13 Cic. *De or.* 3.228–29

= F 14.

On Behalf of the King of Bithynia (F 14)

F 14 Cic. *De or.* 3.228–29

[CATULUS:] ". . . ac vellem, ut meus gener, sodalis tuus, Hortensius, adfuisset; quem quidem ego confido omnibus istis laudibus, quas tu oratione complexus es, excellentem fore." [229] et CRASSUS: "fore dicis?" inquit; "ego vero esse iam iudico et tum iudicavi, cum me consule in senatu causam defendit Africae nuperque etiam magis, cum pro Bithyniae rege dixit. . . ."

On Behalf of Africa (F 12–13)

*the cause of Africa (details unclear), unless the speech in
the Forum refers to a different case (TLRR 90).*

F 12 Cicero, *Brutus*

= T 1.

F 13 Cicero, *On the Orator*

= F 14

On Behalf of the King of Bithynia (F 14)

Shortly before the dramatic date of Cicero's De oratore *(91
BC), Hortensius spoke on behalf of a king of Bithynia, who
might be Nicomedes IV Philopator, involved in a quarrel
about claims to the country's throne.*

F 14 Cicero, *On the Orator*

[CATULUS:] "... and I only wish my son-in-law Hortensius
[married to Catulus' daughter Lutatia], a companion of
yours [L. Licinius Crassus (**66**)], had been here: he, I am
convinced, will certainly be outstanding in all those accomplishments that you have covered in your speech."
[229] And CRASSUS said: "Will be, you say? In my judgment in fact he is there already, and I formed this judgment when he defended the cause of Africa in the Senate
[F 13] during my consulship [95 BC], and even more
so recently, when he spoke on behalf of the king of
Bithynia. . . ."

On Behalf of Cn. Pompeius Magnus (F 15)

F 15 Cic. *Brut.* 230
= T 1.

On Behalf of Sex. Naevius (F 16–18)

*In 81 BC, again with L. Marcius Philippus (**70** F 14), Hortensius supported Sex. Naevius against P. Quinctius, who was defended by Cicero (Cic. Quinct.) (TLRR 126;*

F 16 Cic. *Quinct.* 1

quae res in civitate duae plurimum possunt, eae contra nos ambae faciunt in hoc tempore, summa gratia et eloquentia; quarum alteram, C. Aquilli, vereor, alteram metuo. eloquentia Q. Hortensi ne me in dicendo impediat, non nihil commoveor, gratia Sex. Naevi ne P. Quinctio noceat, id vero non mediocriter pertimesco.

F 17 Cic. *Quinct.* 8

nam quid hoc iniquius aut indignius, C. Aquilli, dici aut commemorari potest, quam me qui caput alterius, famam

On Behalf of Cn. Pompeius Magnus (F 15)

*Like L. Marcius Philippus (**70** F 12–13), Hortensius supported the young Cn. Pompeius Magnus (**111**), accused
of having appropriated booty inherited from his father
(TLRR 120).*

F 15 Cicero, *Brutus*

= T 1.

On Behalf of Sex. Naevius (F 16–18)

*Gell. NA 15.28.3; Cic. Quinct. 1–2, 7–8, 34–35, 44–45, 63,
68, 80).*

F 16 Cicero, *Pro Quinctio*

Those two things that have most power in the community,
enormous influence and eloquence, are both working
against us on this occasion; one of these, C. Aquillius [C.
Aquillius Gallus, praet. 66 BC, the judge], fills me with
apprehension, the other with fear. That the eloquence of
Q. Hortensius may impede me in my pleading does not
leave me calm; that the influence of Sex. Naevius may do
harm to P. Quinctius, of that indeed I am not insignifi-
cantly afraid.

F 17 Cicero, *Pro Quinctio*

For can anything more iniquitous or more scandalous be
spoken of or recalled, C. Aquillius [C. Aquillius Gallus,
praet. 66 BC, the judge], than the fact that I, who am

179

fortunasque defendam priore loco causam dicere? cum
praesertim Q. Hortensius qui ⟨in⟩[1] hoc iudicio partis accusatoris obtinet contra me sit dicturus, cui summam co-
piam facultatemque dicendi natura largita est.

[1] *add. Baiter*

F 18 Cic. *Quinct.* 72

= **70** F 14.

On Behalf of Cn. Cornelius Dolabella Against
M. Aemilius Scaurus [?] (F 19)

According to Pseudo-Asconius, Hortensius supported Cn.
Cornelius Dolabella (praet. 81 BC) when the latter re-
turned from a provincial governorship in Cilicia, taken up
after his praetorship, and was prosecuted by M. Aemilius
*Scaurus (**139** F 1–3) for extortion (TLRR 135). Pseudo-*
Asconius, however, confuses two Dolabellae distinguished

F 19 Ps.-Asc. in Cic. *Div. Caec.* 24 (p. 194.6–8 Stangl)

significat sane etiam Scaurum, qui alterum Dolabellam
consularem triumphalemque accusavit: et potuit eidem
Hortensius resistere.

defending the life, the good name, and the property of another, should have to plead my cause first—above all, when Q. Hortensius, who <in> this trial fulfills the part of the prosecutor, upon whom nature has lavishly bestowed the greatest command of the resources of oratory and the greatest ability to speak, is going to speak against me?

F 18 Cicero, *Pro Quinctio*

= **70** F 14.

On Behalf of Cn. Cornelius Dolabella Against M. Aemilius Scaurus [?] (F 19)

*by Asconius (cf. **121** F 20; also Ps.-Asc. in Cic. Verr. 2.1.41 [p. 234.26–32 St.]): the Cn. Cornelius Dolabella (**94**) who was an ex-consul and former triumphator was defended by Hortensius (F 20A) in another trial (TLRR 140). Hortensius, therefore, might not have appeared against Scaurus.*

F 19 Pseudo-Asconius on Cicero, *Against Caecilius*

He [Cicero] certainly means also Scaurus [M. Aemilius Scaurus (**139**), F 1–3], who accused the younger Dolabella, an ex-consul and former triumphator; and Hortensius was able to offer opposition to the same person [Scaurus].

On Behalf of M. Canuleius (F 20)

F 20 Cic. *Brut.* 317

= T 3.

On Behalf of Cn. Cornelius Dolabella (F 20A)

*This Cn. Cornelius Dolabella (**94**; cf. F 19), charged upon his return from his provincial governorship by the young C. Iulius Caesar (**121** F 15–23), was successfully defended*

F 20A Cic. *Brut.* 317

= T 3.

On Behalf of Terentius Varro (F 21–22)

*Hortensius defended his relative Terentius Varro, who had been a legate in Asia: upon his return, Varro was charged with extortion by Ap. Claudius Pulcher (**130** F 4), first before the praetor L. Furius (or Turius: see MRR II 97) in 75 BC and then before the praetor P. Cornelius Lentulus*

On Behalf of M. Canuleius (F 20)

*Hortensius and C. Aurelius Cotta (**80** F 12) spoke on behalf of M. Canuleius (TLRR 146).*

F 20 Cicero, *Brutus*

= T 3.

On Behalf of Cn. Cornelius Dolabella (F 20A)

*by Hortensius, in association with C. Aurelius Cotta (**80** F 13–14) (TLRR 140).*

F 20A Cicero, *Brutus*

= T 3.

On Behalf of Terentius Varro (F 21–22)

*Sura (**100**) in 74 BC. The accused was acquitted as a result of the intervention of Hortensius, who employed bribery and colored voting tablets (TLRR 144, 158; Schol. Gron. ad Cic. Verr. 1.17 [p. 349.15–16 St.]; Ps.-Acro in Hor. Sat. 2.1.49).*

F 21 Ps.-Asc. in Cic. *Div. Caec.* 24 (p. 193.19–26 Stangl)

⟨Marcus Terentius⟩[1] Varro, consobrinus frater Hortensi, reus[2] ex Asia apud L.[3] Furium praetorem primo de pecuniis repetundis, deinde apud P. Lentulum Suram, est accusatus; absolutusque est a Q. Hortensio, qui corruptis iudicibus hunc metum adiunxit ad gratiam, ut discoloribus[4] ceris insignitas iudices tabulas accipiant et timeret unusquisque eorum ne fidem pactionis[5] non servare videretur, si non in tabula, quam unicuique datam meminisset Hortensius, ex nota cerae scilicet discoloris, absolutum Varronem reperiret.

[1] ⟨Marcus Terentius⟩ *Stangl*: *lac. in codd.*: Terentius *Robortellus*: Marcus *Baiter* [2] Hortensii, reus *Robortellus*: huic censi reus *vel* censireus *codd.* [3] lucium *vel* .l. *codd.* [4] ut his color—*nonnulli codd.* [5] fidem pact—*ed. Lodoici Tiletani*: si de (*cum lac.*) act—*codd.*

F 22 Ps.-Asc. in Cic. *Div. Caec.* 24 (pp. 193.29–94.1 Stangl)

"a pueris nobilibus": Appio Claudio adulescente nobili: qui cum accusaret M. Terentium Varronem repetundarum ex Asia, victus ab Hortensio est; in quo iudicio discoloribus ceris signa sententiarum notabantur.

F 21 Pseudo-Asconius on Cicero, *Against Caecilius*

‹Marcus[1] Terentius› Varro, a cousin of Hortensius, upon his return from Asia, was first accused with respect to the extortion of money before the praetor L. Furius, then before P. Lentulus Sura [P. Cornelius Lentulus Sura (**100**)]; and he was acquitted because of Q. Hortensius, who added for the corrupt judges this fear to the bribery: the judges received tablets marked with wax of different colors,[2] and each of them feared that he would be seen not to keep the faith of the pact, if Hortensius did not find, on the tablet that he remembered as given to each (on the basis of the sign of the differently colored wax, obviously), Varro clearly acquitted.

[1] Elsewhere, Pseudo-Asconius calls the defendant Marcus (F 22); therefore, this name has been restored here. Actually, it is probably A. Terentius Varro, a legate under L. Licinius Murena in Asia in 82 BC (*MRR* II 72; *RE* Terentius 82), unless one assumes an otherwise unknown governor of Asia (*MRR* II 91). [2] By distributing tablets with wax of different color for the two options of "condemned" and "released," Hortensius was able to see whether the judges voted in the way that was agreed when they took the bribe (cf. Cic. *Div. Caec.* 24; *Verr.* 1.17, 1.40; *Clu.* 130).

F 22 Pseudo-Asconius on Cicero, *Against Caecilius*

"from noble boys": Appius Claudius [mentioned as an example], a noble young man [Ap. Claudius Pulcher (**130**), F 4]: when he accused M. Terentius Varro of extortion upon [the latter's] return from Asia, he was defeated by Hortensius; in that trial the signs of the votes were marked by wax of different colors.

185

On Behalf of C. Verres (F 23–28)

*In 70 BC, along with L. Cornelius Sisenna (**89** F 3–4) and Q. Caecilius Metellus Pius Scipio Nasica (**154**), Hortensius was among the defense advocates of his friend C. Verres against Cicero (TLRR 177; Cic. Div. Caec. 23; Plin. HN 34.48; Quint. Inst. 6.3.98; Plut. Cic. 7.8; Apophth. Cic. 11). An altercation between the two pleaders at the trial is*

F 23 Cic. *Brut.* 319

[CICERO:] cum igitur essem in plurimis causis et in principibus patronis quinquennium fere versatus, tum in patrocinio Siciliensi maximum[1] in certamen veni designatus aedilis cum designato consule Hortensio.

 [1] maximum *Rau*: maxime *codd.*

F 24 Ps.-Asc. in Cic. *Div. Caec.*, *arg.* (p. 185.11–16 Stangl)

accessit eis non ignobilis futura ideo de Verre victoria, quia a Metellis, Scipionibus et multis aliis nobilibus viris et praecipue ab Hortensio ipso defenderetur, facile et principe in senatu propter nobilitatem et in foro ob eloquentiam rege causarum et eodem consule designato cum Q. Metello fratre Metellorum, alterius praetoris Siculi, alterius praetoris urbani.

On Behalf of C. Verres (F 23–28)

reported (F 27); a speech is mentioned by Quintilian (F 28), while other sources say that Hortensius did not say anything in reply to Cicero (F 25–26). What Quintilian refers to might be a separate, written version, perhaps not even by Hortensius himself.

F 23 Cicero, *Brutus*

[CICERO:] Thus, after I had been involved in very many cases and been among the leading pleaders for about five years, then, in support of the Sicilians, as aedile designate [70 BC], I entered a duel of the highest magnitude with the consul designate, Hortensius.

F 24 Pseudo-Asconius on Cicero, *Against Caecilius*

To these [reasons for asking Cicero to act as the prosecutor] was added that a victory [by Cicero] concerning Verres would not be undistinguished for the reason that he was defended by the Metelli, the Scipiones and many other noblemen and especially by Hortensius himself, easily both the foremost man in the Senate because of his nobility and the king of trials in the Forum because of his eloquence, and also a consul designate with Q. Metellus [Q. Caecilius Metellus Creticus, cos. 69 BC], the brother of the Metelli, of whom one was praetor in Sicily and the other praetor in the city.

F 25 Cic. *Orat.* 129

nobis pro familiari reo summus orator non respondit Hortensius . . .

F 26 Ps.-Asc. in Cic. *Verr.* 1, *arg.* (p. 205.7–15 Stangl)

iam repente adveniens cum videret id agi, ut a ⟨M'.⟩[1] Glabrione praetore et ab his iudicibus qui tunc erant ad alium annum aliumque praetorem res tota transiret eripereturque sibi reus patrocinio Hortensii ac Metelli, qui tunc consules futuri erant (per hos omnem Verres eludendi iudicii fiduciam sumpserat), hoc commentus est rationis, ut orationem longam praetermitteret neque in criminibus declamatione cumulandis tempus absumeret, sed tantummodo citaret testes ad unumquodque crimen expositum et eos Hortensio interrogandos daret: qua arte ita est fatigatus Hortensius, ut nihil contra quod diceret inveniret, ipse etiam Verres desperato patrocinio suo sponte discederet in exilium.

[1] *add. Schuetz*

F 27 Plin. *HN* 34.48

signis quae vocant Corinthia plerique in tantum capiuntur ut secum circumferant, sicut Hortensius orator sphingem Verri reo ablatam, propter quam Cicero illo iudicio in altercatione neganti ei aenigmata se intellegere respondit debere, quoniam sphingem domi haberet.

Cf. Plut. *Cic.* 7.8.

F 25 Cicero, *Orator*

Hortensius, a consummate orator, made no reply to us [Cicero] on behalf of the defendant, his friend . . .

F 26 Pseudo-Asconius on Cicero, *Against Verres*

Now arriving quickly, since he [Cicero] saw that this was being aimed for, namely that from the praetor ⟨M'.⟩ Glabrio [M'. Acilius Glabrio, praet. urb. 70, cos. 67 BC] and from those judges who were in post at the time the whole matter was to be deferred to another year and another praetor and the defendant to be snatched away from him through the support of Hortensius and Metellus, who were then future consuls [for 69 BC] (on account of them Verres had assumed complete confidence of evading the trial), he devised this plan, namely that he forwent a long speech and did not take up time on piling up reproaches in a set speech, but merely called witnesses for each crime listed and presented them to Hortensius for questioning: by this artifice Hortensius was so worn out that he could not find anything to say in opposition; even Verres himself, despairing of his support, went off into exile of his own accord.

F 27 Pliny the Elder, *Natural History*

By the figurines that they call Corinthian most people are so enamored that they carry them about with them, like the orator Hortensius the sphinx taken away from Verres when on trial; because of that, in an altercation at that trial, when he [Hortensius] denied that he understood riddles, Cicero replied to him that he ought to, since he had a sphinx at home.

189

F 28 Quint. *Inst.* 10.1.22–23

illud vero utilissimum, nosse eas causas quarum orationes
in manus sumpserimus, et, quotiens continget, utrimque
habitas legere actiones: ut Demosthenis et Aeschinis inter
se contrarias, et Servi Sulpici atque Messalae, quorum
alter pro Aufidia, contra dixit alter, et Pollionis et Cassi reo
Asprenate, aliasque plurimas. [23] quin etiam si minus
pares videbuntur aliquae, tamen ad cognoscendam litium
quaestionem recte requirentur, ut contra Ciceronis orationes Tuberonis in Ligarium et Hortensi pro Verre.

Against Lex Gabinia *(F 29)*

*Although both the former consul Q. Lutatius Catulus (**96**
F 5–6) and Hortensius (in the Senate and before the People) spoke against the bill proposed by A. Gabinius (tr. pl.
67 BC) granting Cn. Pompeius Magnus (**111**) sole procon-*

F 29 Cic. *Leg. Man.* 52

nam tu idem, Q. Hortensi, multa pro tua summa copia ac
singulari facultate dicendi et in senatu contra virum for-
tem, A. Gabinium, graviter ornateque dixisti, cum is de
uno imperatore contra praedones constituendo legem

F 28 Quintilian, *The Orator's Education*

In fact, that is most useful, to have learned about those cases from which we have taken up speeches and, whenever possible, to read the pleadings delivered on both sides, like the opposing [speeches] of Demosthenes and Aeschines, and of Servius Sulpicius [Ser. Sulpicius Rufus (**118**), F 7–10] and Messalla [M. Valerius Messalla Corvinus (**176**), F 12–13], of whom one spoke for Aufidia and the other against, and of Pollio [C. Asinius Pollio (**174**), F 35–38] and Cassius [Cassius Severus] in the case of Asprenas, and many others. [23] Indeed, even if some [speeches] seem not quite equal, still, they will be rightly sought out with a view to understanding the issue of the cases: such as, against the speeches of Cicero [Cic. *Lig.*; *Verr.*], that of Tubero [Q. Aelius Tubero (**175**), F 3–7] prosecuting Ligarius and that of Hortensius in defense of Verres.

Against Lex Gabinia *(F 29)*

sular command in the war against the pirates, it was carried (Cic. Leg. Man. *56; Corn.* I, *F 31 Puccioni = 31 Crawford; App.* Mithr. *94; Lex Gabinia de bello piratico: LPPR, pp. 371–72).*

F 29 Cicero, *Pro Lege Manilia*

For you yourself, Q. Hortensius, with your outstanding oratorical command and unique ability in speaking, said a lot against that courageous man, A. Gabinius [tr. pl. 67 BC], weightily and brilliantly in the Senate, when he had proposed a law on the appointment of a single commander against the pirates, and you also delivered very many

promulgasset, et ex hoc ipso loco permulta item contra
eam legem verba fecisti.

Against Lex Manilia *(F 30)*

*Q. Lutatius Catulus (**96** F 7–8) and Hortensius were again
unsuccessful in speaking (CCMR, App. A: 252) against a
bill, proposed by C. Manilius (tr. pl. 66 BC) and supported
by Cicero, granting supreme command to Cn. Pompeius*

F 30 Cic. *Leg. Man.* 51–52

at enim vir clarissimus, amantissimus rei publicae, vestris
beneficiis amplissimis adfectus, Q. Catulus, itemque summis ornamentis honoris, fortunae, virtutis, ingeni praeditus, Q. Hortensius, ab hac ratione dissentiunt. quorum ego
auctoritatem apud vos multis locis plurimum valuisse et
valere oportere confiteor; sed in hac causa, tametsi cognostis[1] auctoritates contrarias virorum fortissimorum et
clarissimorum, tamen omissis auctoritatibus ipsa re ac ratione exquirere possumus veritatem, atque hoc facilius
quod ea omnia quae a me adhuc dicta sunt idem isti vera
esse concedunt, et necessarium bellum esse et magnum
et in uno Cn. Pompeio summa esse omnia. [52] quid igitur
ait Hortensius? si uni omnia tribuenda sint, dignissimum
esse Pompeium, sed ad unum tamen omnia deferri non
oportere. obsolevit iam ista oratio re multo magis quam
verbis refutata.

[1] cognostis *Halm*: cognoscitis *codd. Clarki*: cognoscetis *unus
cod. det.*

Cf. Cic. *Leg. Man.* 56, 66.

words from this very place [i.e., from the Rostra before the People] against that law.

Against Lex Manilia *(F 30)*

*Magnus (**111**) in what came to be known as the Third Mithridatic War (Cic.* Leg. Man.*; Lex Manilia de imperio Cn. Pompei:* LPPR, *pp. 375–76).*

F 30 Cicero, *Pro Lege Manilia*

But indeed, a very distinguished man, a great lover of the Republic, honored with the greatest benefits from you [the People], Q. Catulus [Q. Lutatius Catulus (**96**), F 7–8], and also a man endowed with the highest gifts of position, fortune, character, and talent, Q. Hortensius, disagree with this measure. I admit that the authoritative opinion of these men has had on many occasions and ought to have the greatest weight with you; but in this case, although you have noticed that the authoritative opinions of the bravest and most illustrious men are opposed, still, we can set authoritative opinions to one side and find out the truth by considering the actual facts, and this the more easily because even these very men admit that everything that I have said hitherto is true, namely that the war is necessary and great and that in Pompey [Cn. Pompeius Magnus (**111**)] alone are all the highest qualifications. [52] What then does Hortensius say? That if the entire power is to be given to a single man, the worthiest man is Pompey; but that nevertheless the entire power ought not to be given to one man. That line of argument is now out of date, refuted by the situation far more than by words.

Testimony Against C. Cornelius (F 31–32)

*After his Tribunate, in 66 BC, C. Cornelius (tr. pl. 67 BC) was prosecuted by the brothers P. and C. Cominius (**143 + 144** F 2–6); the trial was disrupted, and the charges were dropped (TLRR 203). In the following year, the brothers took up the charge of treason; on that occasion*

F 31 Asc. in Cic. *Corn.*, *arg.* (pp. 53 KS = 60.19–61.5 C.)

dixerunt in eum infesti testimonia principes civitatis qui plurimum in senatu poterant Q. Hortensius, Q. Catulus, Q. Metellus Pius, M.[1] Lucullus, Mam.[2] Lepidus. dixerunt autem hoc: vidisse se cum Cornelius in tribunatu codicem pro rostris ipse recitaret, quod ante Cornelium nemo fecisse existimaretur. volebant videri se iudicare eam rem magnopere ad crimen imminutae maiestatis tribuniciae pertinere; etenim prope tollebatur intercessio, si id tribunis permitteretur.

[1] M. *vel* L. *codd.*   [2] Mam. *Sumner 1964*: M. *vel* L. *codd.*:
M'. *Manutius*

Testimony Against C. Cornelius (F 31–32)

(TLRR 209) *several noblemen, including Hortensius, pro-*
vided testimonies (Asc. in Cic. Corn. *[p. 79.20–24 C.]).*
Cicero defended the accused, who was acquitted (Cic. Pro
C. Cornelio I *and* II: *Crawford 1994, 65–144).*

F 31 Asconius on Cicero, *Pro Cornelio*

Witness statements against him [C. Cornelius] were made
in hostile fashion by leaders of the community, who were
very powerful in the Senate: Q. Hortensius, Q. Catulus [Q.
Lutatius Catulus (**96**), F 8A], Q. Metellus Pius [Q. Caecilius Metellus Pius, cos. 80 BC], M. Lucullus [M. Licinius
Lucullus (**91**), F 2B], Mam. Lepidus [Mam. Aemilius
Lepidus Livianus, cos. 77 BC].[1] And they said this: that
they had watched when in his Tribunate Cornelius read
out a document in person from the front of the Rostra,
which before Cornelius nobody was believed to have
done. They wished to be seen as being of the opinion that
this matter very much concerned the crime of diminishing
tribunician power; for intercession was all but annulled if
this was granted to Tribunes.[2]

[1] The reading of the name and the identity of Lepidus are
uncertain. The text follows Sumner's (1964) emendation and interpretation.   [2] The text and thus the offense are controversial (cf. also Quint. *Inst.* 4.4.8, 10.5.13): the most likely scenario
is (Marshall 1985, 228): "to read the text of a bill in the face of a
colleague's veto is to destroy intercession; to destroy intercession
is to diminish tribunician power; to diminish tribunician power is
to diminish the majesty of the Roman people."

F 32 Val. Max. 8.5.4

age, Q. Metellus Pius L. et M. Luculli[1] Q. Hortensius M'.[2]
Lepidus C. Corneli maiestatis rei quam non onerarunt
tantummodo testes salutem, sed etiam, negantes illo inco-
lumi stare rem publicam posse, depoposcerunt! quae de-
cora civitatis, pudet referre, umbone iudiciali repulsa
sunt.

[1] L. et *vel* L. *codd.*: L. Lucullus (*om.* M.) *Halm*: *fort.* M. Lucullus (*om.* L.) *Briscoe*   [2] M'. *Sigonius (ad Asc.)*: M. *codd.*

On Behalf of L. Vargunteius (F 33)

F 33 Cic. *Sull.* 6

quis nostrum adfuit Vargunteio? nemo, ne hic quidem Q.
Hortensius, praesertim qui illum solus antea de ambitu

F 32 Valerius Maximus, *Memorable Doings and Sayings*

Again, how did Q. Metellus Pius [Q. Caecilius Metellus Pius, cos. 80 BC], L. and M. Lucullus [L. Licinius Lucullus (**90**), F 7A; M. Licinius Lucullus (**91**), F 2B], Q. Hortensius, and M'. Lepidus [?] as witnesses[1] not only encumber the well-being of C. Cornelius, charged with treason, but even call him down for punishment, asserting that the Republic could not survive if he remained unharmed! What ornaments of the community (I am ashamed to relate it) were repelled by a judicial shield.[2]

[1] In comparison with Asconius (F 31), Valerius Maximus lists L. Lucullus, but not Q. Catulus. Since L. Licinius Lucullus (**90**) came back to Rome from his promagistracy only in 66 BC, it is regarded as improbable that he appeared as a witness for events that took place in Rome in 67 BC.—If Sumner's arguments (1964) are accepted, Lepidus here too (cf. F 31) should be Mam. Aemilius Lepidus Livianus (cos. 77 BC) rather than M'. Aemilius Lepidus (cos. 66 BC).   [2] That is, Cornelius was acquitted despite statements of eminent men against him.

On Behalf of L. Vargunteius (F 33)

Hortensius defended L. Vargunteius on a charge of bribery. The defendant is known to have been a supporter of the Catilinarian Conspiracy (Sall. Cat. 17.3, 28.1), but the trial seems to have happened prior to that (TLRR 202).

F 33 Cicero, *Pro Sulla*

Which of us supported Vargunteius? Nobody, not even Q. Hortensius here, especially as he was the only one to have defended him previously on a charge of bribery. For he

defendisset. non enim iam se ullo officio cum illo coniunctum arbitrabatur, cum ille tanto scelere commisso omnium
officiorum societatem diremisset.

On Behalf of C. Rabirius (F 34–35)

The Roman knight C. Rabirius had been prosecuted by C.
*Licinius Macer (**110** F 4), because he had killed L. Ap-*
*puleius Saturninus (**64A**), and had been acquitted. When*
Rabirius was again prosecuted for the same reason by T.

F 34 Cic. *Rab. perd.* 18

arguis occisum esse a C. Rabirio L. Saturninum. at[1] id C.
Rabirius multorum testimoniis, Q. Hortensio copiosissime
defendente, antea falsum esse docuit . . .

[1] at *Turnebus*: et *codd.*

F 35 Charis., *GL* I, p. 125.1–2 = p. 159.6–8 B.

cicatricum, non cicatricium. Hortensius pro G. Rabirio
"cicatricum mearum," quod emendate dictum sit.

On Behalf of L. Licinius Murena (F 36–37)

*In 63 BC Ser. Sulpicius Rufus (**118** F 6), one of the unsuc-*
cessful candidates in the elections to the consulship for 62
*BC, along with M. Porcius Cato (**126** F 11–12), prosecuted*
one of the elected candidates, L. Licinius Murena (cos. 62

did not think that he was bound by any obligation to that man any longer when by committing so great a crime he had broken the bond of all obligations.

On Behalf of C. Rabirius (F 34–35)

*Labienus (**133** F 1–2) in 63 BC, he was defended by Hortensius and Cicero (Cic. Rab. perd.); this trial was eventually abandoned (TLRR 221; Cass. Dio 37.26–28).*

F 34 Cicero, *Pro Rabirio Perduellionis Reo*

You maintain that L. Saturninus [L. Appuleius Saturninus (**64A**)] was killed by C. Rabirius. But C. Rabirius has previously shown, on the evidence of many witnesses and with the most ample defense by Q. Hortensius, that this is false . . .

F 35 Charisius

cicatricum ["of scars"; standard form of genitive plural], not *cicatricium*. Hortensius [in the speech] on behalf of C. Rabirius: "of my scars [*cicatricum*]," which is said faultlessly.

On Behalf of L. Licinius Murena (F 36–37)

BC), for ambitus *(Alexander 2002, 121–27); defended by M. Licinius Crassus Dives (**102** F 8–9), Hortensius, and Cicero (Cic. Mur.), Murena was acquitted (TLRR 224).*

F 36 Plut. *Cic.* 35.4

Λικινίῳ δὲ Μουρήνᾳ φεύγοντι δίκην ὑπὸ Κάτωνος βο-
ηθῶν, καὶ φιλοτιμούμενος Ὁρτήσιον ὑπερβαλεῖν εὐη-
μερήσαντα, μέρος οὐδὲν ἀνεπαύσατο τῆς νυκτός,
ὥσθ' ὑπὸ τοῦ σφόδρα φροντίσαι καὶ διαγρυπνῆσαι
κακωθεὶς ἐνδεέστερος αὑτοῦ φανῆναι.

F 37 Cic. *Mur.* 48

atque ex omnibus illa plaga est iniecta petitioni tuae non
tacente me maxima, de qua ab homine ingeniosissimo et
copiosissimo, ⟨Q.⟩[1] Hortensio, multa gravissime dicta
sunt. quo etiam mihi durior locus est dicendi datus ut,
cum ante me et ille dixisset et vir summa dignitate et diligentia et facultate dicendi, M. Crassus, ego in extremo
non partem aliquam agerem causae sed de tota re dicerem
quod mihi videretur. itaque in isdem rebus fere versor et
quoad possum, iudices, occurro vestrae satietati.[2]

[1] *add. Klotz*   [2] satietati *unus cod.,* Hotoman: sapietati
alter cod.: sapientiae *codd. cet.*

On Behalf of P. Cornelius Sulla (F 38–39)

*In 62 BC L. Manlius Torquatus (**146** F 2–2A) prosecuted
P. Cornelius Sulla (RE Cornelius 386) under the Lex Plautia de vi, after Sulla had been prevented from holding the
consulship in 65 BC by an accusation of ambitus and had*

F 36 Plutarch, *Life of Cicero*

When he [Cicero] was supporting Licinius Murena in a case brought against him by Cato [M. Porcius Cato (**126**), F 11–12] and was ambitious to surpass Hortensius, who had made a successful plea, he did not rest for any part of the night before, so that he was harmed by his exceeding concern and lack of sleep and was thought inferior to himself.

F 37 Cicero, *Pro Murena*

And that blow [i.e., preparing the prosecution and not focusing entirely on the election] was, as I pointed out, the greatest of all to be struck at your campaign [of Ser. Sulpicius Rufus (**118**)], about which a lot has been said by an extremely talented and very eloquent man, ‹Q.› Hortensius, with great authority. Therefore, an even harder position of speaking has been assigned to me, in the sense that, since both he and a man of immense prestige, diligence, and ability to speak, Crassus [M. Licinius Crassus Dives (**102**), F 8–9], have spoken before me, I, in the final position, am not dealing with any one part of the case but am saying about the whole matter what I feel is required. For that reason I am mostly dealing with the same matters and, as far as I can, judges, checking your boredom.

On Behalf of P. Cornelius Sulla (F 38–39)

been involved in the Catilinarian Conspiracy in 63 BC. Defended by Hortensius and Cicero (Cic. Sull.*), Sulla was acquitted (*TLRR 234; Schol. Bob. ad Cic.* Sull. *[pp. 77–84 St.]).*

F 38 Cic. *Sull.* 11, 12, 14

duae coniurationes abs te, Torquate, constituuntur, una
quae Lepido et Volcatio consulibus patre tuo consule designato facta esse dicitur, altera quae me consule; harum
in utraque Sullam dicis fuisse. . . . [12] quis ergo intererat
vestris consiliis? omnes hi quos vides huic adesse et in
primis Q. Hortensius; qui cum propter honorem ac dignitatem atque animum eximium in rem publicam, tum propter summam familiaritatem summumque amorem in patrem tuum cum communibus tum praecipuis patris tui
periculis commovebatur. ergo istius coniurationis crimen
defensum ab eo est qui interfuit, qui cognovit, qui parti-
ceps et consili vestri fuit et timoris; cuius in hoc crimine
propulsando cum esset copiosissima atque ornatissima
oratio, tamen non minus inerat auctoritatis in ea quam
facultatis. . . . [14] et quoniam de criminibus superioris
coniurationis Hortensium diligenter audistis, de hac coni-
iuratione quae me consule facta est hoc primum attendite.

F 39 Gell. *NA* 1.5.3

sed cum L. Torquatus, subagresti homo ingenio et infes-
tivo, gravius acerbiusque apud consilium iudicum, cum de
causa Sullae quaereretur, non iam histrionem eum esse
diceret, sed gesticulariam Dionysiamque eum notissimae

F 38 Cicero, *Pro Sulla*

You posit two conspiracies, Torquatus [L. Manlius Torquatus (**146**)]: one that is said to have been formed in the consulship of Lepidus and Volcatius [66 BC], when your father [L. Manlius Torquatus (**109**)] was consul designate, the other during my consulship [63 BC]. You say that Sulla was involved in both of them. . . . [12] Who, then, was party to your [the Torquatii] deliberations? All these men whom you see here present in support of him [Sulla] and especially Q. Hortensius; because of his high office, his prestige, and his exceptional devotion to the Republic, as well as particularly because of his very close friendship and very great affection for your father, he was moved by the dangers affecting all and especially by those confronting your father individually. So the charge of that earlier conspiracy has been refuted by a man [Hortensius] who was party to it, who got to know it, who shared both your deliberations and your fear. While his speech in repelling this charge was very detailed and very elaborate, yet there was no less authoritativeness in it than technical skill. . . . [14] And since you heard Hortensius with attention on the charges relating to the earlier conspiracy, now, concerning the later conspiracy that was formed during my consulship, first listen to this.

F 39 Gellius, *Attic Nights*

But when L. Torquatus [L. Manlius Torquatus (**146**), F 2], a man of somewhat boorish and uncouth nature, said rather strongly and bitterly before the assembled judges, when the case of Sulla was being investigated, not just that that man [Hortensius] was an actor, but called him a pos-

saltatriculae nomine appellaret, tum voce molli atque demissa Hortensius "Dionysia," inquit, "Dionysia malo equidem esse quam quod tu, Torquate, ἄμουσος, ἀναφρό- διτος, ἀπροσδιόνυσος."

On Behalf of Valerius (F 40)

F 40 Cic. *Att.* 2.3.1

primum, ut opinor, εὐαγγελία. Valerius absolutus est Hortensio defendente. id iudicium Auli filio[1] condonatum putabatur; et Epicratem suspicor, ut scribis, lascivum fuisse. etenim mihi caligae eius et[2] fasciae cretatae non placebant.

---

[1] Auli filio *Tunstall*: Afilio *vel* at(t)ilio *vel* athilio *vel* hati- *vel* haci- *vel* Kati- *vel* K. Ati- *codd.*   [2] et *Orelli*: ut *codd.*

On Behalf of L. Valerius Flaccus (F 41–42)

turer and a Dionysia (by the name of a most notorious dancing girl), then Hortensius replied in a soft and gentle tone: "I would rather be a Dionysia, yes, a Dionysia, than what you are, Torquatus, a stranger to the Muses, to Aphrodite, and to Dionysus."

On Behalf of Valerius (F 40)

A Valerius, perhaps M. Valerius Messalla Rufus (cos. 53 BC), was successfully defended by Hortensius in 60 BC (TLRR 239).

F 40 Cicero, *Letters to Atticus*

First, as I imagine, good news. Valerius has been acquitted, with Hortensius defending. The verdict was thought to have been a gift for Aulus' son [i.e., L. Afranius, cos. 60 BC]. And I suspect that Epicrates [Athenian politician; viz., Cn. Pompeius Magnus (**111**)] was, as you write, frolicking. At any rate his leather shoes and white bands do not please me.[1]

[1] Mockery of Pompey's clothing for its nonmilitary affectation (on these pieces of clothing associated with Pompey, cf. Val. Max. 6.2.7; Amm. Marc. 17.11.4).

On Behalf of L. Valerius Flaccus (F 41–42)

In 59 BC L. Valerius Flaccus (praet. 63 BC), accused of extortion in relation to his provincial governorship in Asia (Alexander 2002, 78–97), was successfully defended by Hortensius and Cicero (Cic. Flacc.) (TLRR 247).

F 41 Cic. *Att.* 2.25.1–2

at hercule alter tuus familiaris Hortalus quam plena manu, quam ingenue, quam ornate nostras laudes in astra sustulit cum de Flacci praetura et de illo tempore Allobrogum diceret! sic habeto, nec amantius nec honorificentius nec copiosius potuisse dici. [2] ei te hoc scribere a me tibi esse missum sane volo.

F 42 Cic. *Flacc.* 41

sed quoniam de hoc teste totoque Mithridatico crimine disseruit subtiliter et copiose Q. Hortensius, nos, ut instituimus, ad reliqua pergamus.

On Behalf of P. Sestius (F 43–45)

*In 56 BC Cicero (Cic. Sest.), M. Licinius Crassus Dives (**102** F 11), C. Licinius Macer Calvus (**165** F 29), and Hortensius successfully defended P. Sestius (**135**), when he was accused after his Tribunate (57 BC) under the* Lex

F 43 Cic. *Sest.* 3

et quamquam a Q. Hortensio, clarissimo viro atque eloquentissimo, causa est P. Sesti perorata, nihilque ab eo praetermissum est quod aut pro re publica conquerendum fuit aut pro reo disputandum, tamen adgrediar ad dicen-

F 41 Cicero, *Letters to Atticus*

But, by Hercules, your other friend, Hortalus, how un-
grudgingly, how candidly, how eloquently he lauded our
merits to the stars when he spoke of Flaccus' praetorship
[63 BC] and that situation of the Allobroges [during the
Catilinarian Conspiracy]! You can take my word, it could
not have been presented in friendlier or more flattering or
more ample terms. [2] I certainly want you to write to him
that this has been sent to you by me.

F 42 Cicero, *Pro Flacco*

But since Q. Hortensius has spoken in detail and at length
about this witness and the entire charge concerning Mithridates [king of Pontus], let us move on, as we set out, to
what remains.

On Behalf of P. Sestius (F 43–45)

Plautia de vi *by P. Albinovanus on the instigation of P.
Clodius Pulcher (137)* (TLRR 271; Cic. Vat. 3, 41; Q Fr.
2.3.5, 2.4.1; Schol. Bob. ad Cic. Sest. [pp. 125–44 St.];
Plut. Cic. 26.8).

F 43 Cicero, *Pro Sestio*

And although the case of P. Sestius has been fully dealt
with by Q. Hortensius, a very distinguished and very eloquent man, and nothing has been omitted by him that
either had to be complained about in the interest of the
Republic or to be argued in defense of the accused, nevertheless, I shall get ready to speak, so that my protection

dum, ne mea propugnatio ei potissimum defuisse videatur per quem est perfectum ne ceteris civibus deesset.

F 44 Cic. *Sest.* 14

de quo quidem tribunatu ita dictum est a Q. Hortensio ut eius oratio non defensionem modo videretur criminum continere, sed etiam memoria dignam iuventuti[1] rei publicae capessendae auctoritatem disciplinamque praescribere.

1 dignam iuventuti *Madvig*: dignam iuti *vel* digna uti *codd.*

F 45 Schol. Bob. ad Cic. *Sest.*, *arg.* (p. 125.15–26 Stangl)

postquam tamen Cicero ab exilio rediit, accusare de vi P. Clodius Sextium coepit inmisso velut principe delationis P. Albinovano et testimonium dicente P. Vatinio . . . hanc igitur eandem causam plurimi defenderunt, in quis fuit Q. Hortensius, M. Crassus, C.[1] Licinius Calvus, partibus inter se distributis quas in agendo tuerentur.

1 C. *Meyer*: L. *cod.*

Against a lex sumptuaria *(F 46)*

does not seem to have failed that man in particular, thanks to whom it was accomplished that it would not fail other citizens [since P. Sestius contributed to Cicero's recall from exile].

F 44 Cicero, *Pro Sestio*

About this Tribunate [of P. Sestius], indeed, Q. Hortensius has spoken in such a manner that his speech appeared not only to contain a defense against the charges, but also to prescribe for the young an authoritative pattern of engaging in political life well worth remembering.

F 45 Scholia Bobiensia to Cicero, *Pro Sestio*

Yet, after Cicero had returned from exile, P. Clodius [P. Clodius Pulcher (**137**)] began to accuse Sestius of violence, with P. Albinovanus let loose almost as leader of the denunciation and P. Vatinius providing a witness statement . . . This same case therefore was defended by very many men, among whom were Q. Hortensius, Crassus [M. Licinius Crassus Dives (**102**), F 11], and C. Licinius Calvus [C. Licinius Macer Calvus (**165**), F 29], after they had divided among themselves the parts that they would see to in the case.

Against a lex sumptuaria *(F 46)*

In 55 BC Hortensius' intervention contributed to a planned sumptuary law not coming into effect.

F 46 Cass. Dio 39.37.2–4

ἐπεχείρησαν μὲν γὰρ καὶ τὰ ἀναλώματα ⟨τὰ κατὰ⟩
τὴν[1] δίαιταν ἐπὶ μακρότατον προηγμένα[2] συστεῖλαι,
καίπερ ἐς πᾶν αὐτοὶ καὶ τρυφῆς καὶ ἁβρότητος προ-
κεχωρηκότες, ἐκωλύθησαν δὲ ὑπὸ αὐτοῦ τούτου δια-
νομοθετῆσαι. [3] ὁ γὰρ Ὁρτήσιος φιλαναλωτὴς[3] ἐν
τοῖς μάλιστα ὢν ἔπεισεν αὐτούς, τό τε μέγεθος τῆς
πόλεως ἐπεξιών, καὶ ⟨αὐτοὺς⟩[4] ἐπί τε τῇ οἴκοι πολυ-
τελείᾳ καὶ ἐπὶ τῇ ἐς τοὺς ἄλλους μεγαλοφροσύνῃ
ἐπαινῶν, καταβαλεῖν[5] τὴν γνώμην, ἅτε καὶ συναγωνιστῇ[6] τῶν λόγων τῷ βίῳ σφῶν χρώμενος. [4] τήν τε
γὰρ ἐναντίωσιν αἰδεσθέντες, καὶ προσέτι καὶ κατο-
κνήσαντες φθόνῳ τινὶ τοὺς ἄλλους, ὧν αὐτοὶ ἐποίουν,[7]
δοκεῖν ἀπείργειν, ἑκόντες ἀφῆκαν τὴν ἐσήγησιν.

[1] ἀναλώματα ⟨τὰ κατὰ⟩ τὴν Reiske praeeunte Leunclavio
(ἀναλώατα τὴν cod.): ἀναλώτατα τὴν cod.   [2] προηγμένα Leunclavius: προσηγμένα cod.   [3] φιλαναλωτὴς
Pflugk: φιλανάλωτος cod.   [4] add. Leunclavius   [5] καταβαλεῖν Xylander: καταλαβεῖν cod.   [6] συναγωνιστῇ R.
Stephanus: συναγωνιστὴν cod.   [7] ἐποίουν Bekker: ἐποι-
οῦντο cod.

On Behalf of Procilius (F 47)

*In 54 BC Procilius was prosecuted by P. Clodius Pulcher
(**137** F 8), apparently for murder of a pater familias (which
may be linked to the disturbances in 56 BC), and defended*

F 46 Cassius Dio, *Roman History*

For they [the consuls of 55 BC] undertook to curtail even personal expenditure, which had increased to an enormous extent, although they themselves went to every length of luxury and indulgence; but they were prevented by this very circumstance from enacting the law: [3] Hortensius, among those most fond of expensive living, by reviewing the great size of the city and praising ⟨them⟩ because of the costliness of their homes and their generosity toward others, persuaded them to give up their intention, as he made use of their own mode of life as support for his arguments. [4] They were brought to shame by his opposition and also shrank from appearing to debar others through jealousy from what they themselves enjoyed; so, they voluntarily withdrew their motion.

On Behalf of Procilius (F 47)

by Hortensius; Procilius was found guilty by a narrow majority (TLRR 284; cf. Cic. Att. 4.16.5).

F 47 Cic. *Att.* 4.15.4

a. d. III<I>[1] Non. Quint. Sufenas et Cato absoluti, Procilius condemnatus. ex quo intellectum est τρισαρεοπα-γίτας[2] ambitum, comitia, interregnum, maiestatem, totam denique rem publicam flocci non facere, patrem familias domi suae occidi[3] nolle, neque tamen id ipsum abunde; nam absolverunt XXII, condemnarunt XXVIII. Publius sane diserto epilogo criminans[4] mentis iudicum moverat. Hortalus[5] in ea causa fuit cuius modi solet. nos verbum nullum; verita{s}[6] est enim pusilla, quae nunc laborat, ne animum Publi offenderet.

[1] III<I> *Manutius*: III *codd.*   [2] τρισ- *Bosius*: tres *nonnulli codd.*: om. *unus cod.*   [3] occidi *Schütz*: occidere *codd.*

[4] criminans *vel* criminari *vel* cruminar *codd.*: <la>crim{in}ans *Shackleton Bailey*   [5] Hortalus *Manutius*: hotal(l)us *vel sim. codd.*: hortensius *unus cod.*

[6] verita{s} *Manutius*: veritas *codd.*

On Behalf of M. Aemilius Scaurus (F 48)

*Hortensius, like Cicero (Cic. Scaur.), was among the six advocates who defended M. Aemilius Scaurus (**139**), when P. Valerius Triarius (**148** F 1–2) prosecuted him for extor-*

F 48 Asc. in Cic. *Scaur.*, arg. (p. 18 KS = 20.13–18 C.)

defenderunt Scaurum sex patroni, cum ad id tempus raro quisquam pluribus quam quattuor uteretur: at post bella civilia ante legem Iuliam ad duodenos patronos est perven-

F 47 Cicero, *Letters to Atticus*

On the fourth day before the Nones of Quintilis [July 4] Sufenas [Nonius Sufenas] and Cato [C. Porcius Cato (**136**)] were acquitted [tr. pl. 56 BC], Procilius found guilty. From this it can be seen that the judges, Areopagites thrice over,[1] do not care in the least about bribery, elections, interregnum, high treason, or indeed the entire political system, but do not want a *pater familias* to be slaughtered in his own house, yet not, however, overwhelmingly, even in this case; for twenty-two acquitted him, and twenty-eight found him guilty. Publius [P. Clodius Pulcher (**137**), F 8] had moved the minds of the judges, presenting the accusation in a quite eloquent peroration. Hortalus in that case was as he usually is. As for us, no word; for the little girl [Cicero's daughter Tullia], who is not very well at present, was afraid it might annoy the feelings of Publius.

[1] That is, stern judges, alluding to the Areopagus in Athens and the judicial function of the council meeting there.

On Behalf of M. Aemilius Scaurus (F 48)

tion (*Asc. in Cic.* Scaur., arg. [pp. 18–20 C.]); *Scaurus* (**139** F 5) *also spoke on his own behalf and was acquitted* (TLRR 295; cf. **148**).

F 48 Asconius on Cicero, *Pro Scauro*

Six advocates defended Scaurus [M. Aemilius Scaurus (**139**)] although until that time rarely anyone engaged more than four: but after the civil wars, before the *Lex Iulia* [probably *Leges Iuliae iudiciorum publicorum et privatorum*: *LPPR*, pp. 448–50; dated to 17 BC], one got

213

tum. fuerunt autem hi sex: P. Clodius Pulcher, M. Marcellus, M. Calidius, M. Cicero, M. Messala Niger, Q. Hortensius.

In Support of T. Annius Milo (F 49–50)

*In 52 BC Hortensius, along with others, spoke in support of T. Annius Milo (**138**) in connection with one of the trials in that year (F 49; TLRR 306). He also argued in the*

F 49 Asc. in Cic. *Mil.*, *arg.* (p. 30 KS = 34.15–21 C.)

adfuerunt Miloni Q. Hortensius, M. Cicero, M. Marcellus, M. Calidius, M. Cato, Faustus Sulla. verba pauca Q. Hortensius dixit, liberos esse eos qui pro servis postularentur; nam post recentem caedem manu miserat eos Milo sub hoc titulo quod caput suum ulti essent. haec agebantur mense intercalari.

F 50 Asc. in Cic. *Mil.* 14 (pp. 39 KS = 44.8–45.4 C.)
= **150** F 6.

On Behalf of M. Valerius Messalla Rufus (F 51–52)

In 51 BC M. Valerius Messalla Rufus (cos. 53 BC), Hortensius' nephew, was accused of having employed bribery while standing for the consulship in 54 BC (Cic. Q Fr.

as far as twelve advocates at a time. And they were the following six: P. Clodius Pulcher [P. Clodius Pulcher (**137**), F 9], M. Marcellus [M. Claudius Marcellus (**155**), F 5], M. Calidius [M. Calidius (**140**), F 9], M. Cicero, M. Messalla Niger [M. Valerius Messalla Niger (**124**), F 4], Q. Hortensius.

In Support of T. Annius Milo (F 49–50)

Senate for an investigation of the matter by a special court (F 50; Schol. Bob. ad Cic. Mil. *[p. 117.17–18 St.]).*

F 49 Asconius on Cicero, *Pro Milone*

Milo [T. Annius Milo (**138**)] was supported by Q. Hortensius, M. Cicero, M. Marcellus [M. Claudius Marcellus (**155**), F 6], M. Calidius [M. Calidius (**140**), F 10], M. Cato [M. Porcius Cato (**126**), F 26] and Faustus Sulla [Faustus Cornelius Sulla (**156**), F 2]. Q. Hortensius said a few words: that those who were demanded in the capacity of slaves were free; for after the recent bloodbath Milo had set them free under the pretext that they had avenged his life. This was being done in the intercalary month [between February and March 52 BC].

F 50 Asconius on Cicero, *Pro Milone*

= **150** F 6.

On Behalf of M. Valerius Messalla Rufus (F 51–52)

*2.14.4, 3.9.3; Att. 4.15.7, 5.12.2); Hortensius managed to get him acquitted, to the dismay of the People (*TLRR 329; Cael. ap. Cic. *Fam. 8.2.1, 8.4.1).*

F 51 Cic. *Brut.* 328

tum BRUTUS: "ego vero," inquit, "et ista quae dicis video
qualia sint et Hortensium magnum oratorem semper pu-
tavi maximeque probavi pro Messalla dicentem, cum tu
afuisti." "sic ferunt," inquam [CICERO], "idque declarat
totidem quot dixit, ut aiunt, scripta verbis oratio. . . ."

F 52 Val. Max. 5.9.2

Q. autem Hortensi, qui suis temporibus ornamentum
Romanae eloquentiae fuit, admirabilis in filio patientia
exstitit: cum enim eo usque impietatem eius suspectam
et nequitiam invisam haberet ut Messalam sororis suae
filium heredem habiturus, ambitus reum defendens iudicibus diceret, si illum damnassent, nihil sibi praeter os-
culum nepotum, in quibus adquiesceret, superfuturum,
hac scilicet sententia, quam etiam editae orationi inseruit,
filium potius in tormentis animi quam in voluptatibus
reponens, tamen, ne naturae ordinem confunderet, non
nepotes, sed filium heredem reliquit, moderate usus ad-
fectibus suis, quia et vivus moribus eius verum testimonium et mortuus sanguini honorem debitum reddidit.

F 51 Cicero, *Brutus*

[continued from T 5] Then BRUTUS said: "On the one hand I recognize indeed the nature of what you [Cicero] say; on the other hand I have always thought Hortensius a great orator, and I admired him particularly speaking on behalf of Messalla while you were away [as governor in Cilicia]." "So they say," I [CICERO] said, "and the written speech, reproduced, as they maintain, exactly with the words as spoken, confirms this. . . ."

F 52 Valerius Maximus, *Memorable Doings and Sayings*

And Q. Hortensius, who in his day was an ornament of Roman eloquence, was admirable in his patience toward his son: for to such an extent did he regard the latter's undutiful behavior as suspicious and his worthlessness as offensive that he intended to make his sister's son, Messalla, his heir; in defending him, accused of bribery in the election campaign, he told the judges that, if they condemned that man, nothing would be left for him [Hortensius] except the kisses of his grandchildren, in which he found comfort. With that sentiment, which he also included in the published speech, he placed his son among his mind's afflictions rather than its delights. Nonetheless, so as not to confuse nature's order, he left not his grandsons, but his son as his heir, controlling his feelings with discretion, in that he both in his lifetime bore true testimony to his [the son's] character and in death rendered due respect to the claims of blood.

On Behalf of Ap. Claudius Pulcher (F 53–54)

*Ap. Claudius Pulcher (**130**) was prosecuted for* maiestas *and* ambitus *by P. Cornelius Dolabella (**173**) when he returned from his provincial governorship in Cilicia. Defended by Hortensius, shortly before the latter's death in*

F 53 Cic. *Brut.* 230

= T 1.

F 54 Cic. *Brut.* 324

[CICERO:] . . . idem quarto ⟨et⟩[1] sexagensimo anno, perpaucis ante mortem diebus, una tecum socerum tuum defendit Appium.

　[1] *add. edd.*

Unplaced Fragments (F 55–56)

F 55 Prisc., *GL* II, p. 381.10–11

Q. Hortensius: "abusis iam omnibus locis," "abusis" κατα-
χρησθέντων.

F 56 Quint. *Inst.* 1.5.12

nam duos in uno nomine faciebat barbarismos Tinga Placentinus, si reprehendenti Hortensio credimus, "precu-

On Behalf of Ap. Claudius Pulcher (F 53–54)

*50 BC, and by his son-in-law M. Iunius Brutus (**158** F 22), presumably on the latter charge, Appius was acquitted (TLRR 344, 345; Sumner 1973, 122–23; Cic. Fam. 3.11.1–3, 3.12.1, 8.6.1).*

F 53 Cicero, *Brutus*

= T 1.

F 54 Cicero, *Brutus*

[CICERO:] . . . in his sixty-fourth year, a few days before his death, he [Hortensius] defended, together with you [Brutus], your father-in-law Appius.

Unplaced Fragments (F 55–56)

F 55 Priscian

Q. Hortensius: "with all topoi already used up," "used up," used up [in Greek: Latin deponent used in passive sense].

F 56 Quintilian, *The Orator's Education*

For Tinga of Placentia[1] (if we are to believe Hortensius finding fault with it) committed two barbarisms in a single word, saying *precula* for *pergula* ["a more or less open

---

[1] Probably T. Tinca Placentinus, mentioned by Cicero among orators from outside Rome (Cic. *Brut.* 172); he seems to have flourished during the late second / early first century BC.

lam" pro "pergula" dicens, et inmutatione, cum c pro g uteretur, et transmutatione, cum r praeponeret antecedenti.

93 HORTENSIA

*Hortensia (RE Hortensius 16) was the daughter of Q. Hortensius Hortalus (**92**) and his wife Lutatia.*

In 42 BC Hortensia successfully delivered a speech (admired by later ancient authors) before the triumviri, *who*

Before the triumviri *(F 1–2A)*

F 1 Val. Max. 8.3.3

Hortensia vero Q. Hortensi filia, cum ordo matronarum gravi tributo a triumviris esset oneratus nec quisquam virorum patrocinium eis accommodare auderet, causam feminarum apud triumviros et constanter et feliciter egit: repraesentata enim patris facundia impetravit ut maior pars imperatae pecuniae his remitteretur. revixit tum muliebri stirpe Q. Hortensius verbisque filiae aspiravit, cuius si virilis sexus posteri vim sequi voluissent, Hortensianae eloquentiae tanta hereditas una feminae actione abscissa non esset.

attachment to the front of a building"], both by change, since he used *c* for *g*, and by transposition, since he put *r* before the preceding letter.

93 HORTENSIA

were planning to force wealthy women to make a financial contribution to the running of the state (F 1–2). A version of the oration is put into Hortensia's mouth in Appian (F 2A).

Before the triumviri *(F 1–2A)*

F 1 Valerius Maximus, *Memorable Doings and Sayings*

Hortensia, the daughter of Q. Hortensius [Q. Hortensius Hortalus (**92**)], indeed pleaded the case of the women before the *triumviri* both resolutely and successfully, when the class of married women had been burdened by the *triumviri* with a heavy tax and none of the men ventured to lend them their advocacy. For reviving her father's eloquence, she achieved that the greater part of the money requested was remitted for them. Q. Hortensius then lived again in his female progeny and inspired his daughter's words; if his male descendants had chosen to follow his force, the great heritage of Hortensian eloquence would not have been cut short with a single speech by a woman.

F 2 Quint. *Inst.* 1.1.6

. . . et Hortensiae Q. filiae[1] oratio apud triumviros habita legitur non tantum in sexus honorem.

[1] Hortensiae Q. filiae *Meyer*: hortensiae que filiae *vel* hortensie filie *codd.*

F 2A App. *B Civ.* 4.32.135–33.146

After the triumviri *have proposed that the wealthiest 1,400 women should contribute to the war effort and resistance would be fined, the women protest and appoint Hortensia as their spokesperson to voice their feelings in the Forum: on behalf of the group Hortensia points out (according to Appian) that the women have already lost a number of their male relatives; if their property is taken away too, this will reduce them to a situation unbecoming to their position, especially since the women cannot be accused of*

94 CN. CORNELIUS DOLABELLA

Cn. Cornelius Dolabella (cos. 81 BC; RE Cornelius 134), a supporter of L. Cornelius Sulla in the civil war, served as consul in 81 BC; afterward, he governed the province of Macedonia (80–77 BC) and celebrated a triumph upon his return (Cic. Pis. 44).

Against C. Iulius Caesar (F 1)

*The context of Dolabella's critical remark about C. Iulius Caesar (***121***) is uncertain. It is sometimes assumed that*

F 2 Quintilian, *The Orator's Education*

... and the speech of Hortensia, Quintus' [Q. Hortensius Hortalus (**92**)] daughter, delivered in front of the *triumviri*, is read not only in honor of her sex.

F 2A Appian, *Civil Wars*

having done any wrongs and did not participate in politics. Hortensia recalls that their mothers have once contributed voluntarily in a war with an external enemy. At the same time, she affirms that the women will never support civil war; moreover, she notes that they have not been forced to pay in previous civil wars, only now by these men, claiming that they are reestablishing the Republic. The triumviri *are angry about this political intervention by women.*

94 CN. CORNELIUS DOLABELLA

*Upon coming back from the province, Dolabella was charged with extortion by C. Iulius Caesar (**121** F 15–23), but was acquitted, defended by C. Aurelius Cotta (**80** F 13–14) and Q. Hortensius Hortalus (**92** F 20A) (TLRR 140).*

Against C. Iulius Caesar (F 1)

Dolabella spoke in his own defense when taken to court by Caesar and that the comment was made on that occasion.

F 1 Suet. *Iul.* 49.1

= **86** F 13.

95 M. AEMILIUS LEPIDUS

M. Aemilius Lepidus (cos. 78 BC; RE Aemilius 72) seems
to have enlarged his fortune in the Sullan proscriptions;
when propraetor in Sicily (80 BC), he administered the
province in such a way that he was able to erect sumptuous
buildings and the basilica bearing his name in Rome (Cic.
Verr. 2.3.212; Plin. HN 35.13, 36.49, 36.109). He was
therefore accused of extortion by Q. Caecilius Metellus
*Celer (**119** F 2) and Q. Caecilius Metellus Nepos (**120***
F 2A); yet they are said to have dropped the case after a
pretrial hearing (TLRR 131).

As Consul to the People (F 1–2A)

F 1 Gran. Licin. 36.33–35 (pp. 27.4–28.2 Criniti)

verum ⟨ubi⟩ con⟨v⟩enera⟨nt⟩ tribuni plebis, co⟨nsu⟩les
uti tribuniciam ⟨po⟩testatem restitue⟨rent⟩, negavit prior
Lepid⟨us⟩, et in contione m⟨ag⟩na pars adsensa ⟨e⟩st
⟨dicen⟩ti non esse utile re⟨sti⟩tui tribuniciam p⟨otes⟩ta-
tem. et extat ora⟨tio. et le⟩gem frumentari⟨am⟩ nullo
resistente t⟨uta⟩tus est, ut annon⟨ae⟩ quinque modi⟨i⟩
popu⟨lo da⟩rentur, et alia mul⟨ta pol⟩licebatur: exules
r⟨edu⟩cere, res gestas a Sul⟨la rescindere⟩, in quorum
agro⟨s mil⟩ites deduxerat, re⟨sti⟩tuere.

---

[1] The transmitted text is rather corrupt but has been plausibly
restored (specific textual notes have been omitted).

F 1 Suetonius, *Life of Caesar*
= **86** F 13.

95 M. AEMILIUS LEPIDUS

*During his consulship (78 BC), Lepidus disagreed with his colleague Q. Lutatius Catulus (**96**) (Cic. Cat. 3.24). He delivered speeches to the People, in which, among other things, he argued for a repeal of some of Sulla's laws, but rejected a restitution of tribunician powers (F 1–2; CCMR, App. A: 233). The only "example" of a consular contio is a speech put in M. Aemilius Lepidus' mouth by Sallust (F 2A). Toward the end of his consulship, Lepidus joined those dissatisfied with Sulla's land distributions in Etruria; in 77 BC he marched on Rome and was defeated by Q. Lutatius Catulus.*

As Consul to the People (F 1–2A)

F 1 Granius Licinianus

But as soon as the Tribunes of the People had agreed that the consuls should reinstate tribunician powers, first Lepidus rejected it, and at a public meeting a large proportion agreed with him when he said that it was not useful to reinstate tribunician powers. And his speech is extant. And he defended the grain law with nobody in opposition, so that grain for subsistence to the amount of five pecks would be given to the People, and he promised many other things: to recall exiles, to abolish arrangements introduced by Sulla, to reinstate those in whose lands he [L. Cornelius Sulla] had settled soldiers.[1]

F 2 Flor. 2.11(3.23).5

ergo cum turbidis contionibus velut classico civitatem ter-
ruisset, profectus in Etruriam arma inde et exercitum urbi
admovebat.

F 2A Sall. *Hist.* 1.55 M. = 1.49 R.

*Lepidus warns the People about Sulla: he describes Sulla
and his minions negatively, criticizes the fact that everything is in the power of one man, and alleges that success
is exploited as a screen for vices. Therefore, Lepidus calls
the People to resistance; he reminds them that a state of
tranquility combined with freedom no longer exists and
that at the present time one has to be either enslaved or in
command. The Roman People, however, have been stripped*

96 Q. LUTATIUS CATULUS MINOR

*Q. Lutatius Catulus minor (cos. 78, censor 65 BC; RE
Lutatius 8), a son of Q. Lutatius Catulus (**63**), is praised
by Cicero for his character and political views (Cic. Verr.
1.44, 2.3.210; Leg. Man. 51; Cat. 3.24; Balb. 35). He
moved that Cicero should be called* pater patriae *after the
suppression of the Catilinarian Conspiracy (T 3; Cic. Sest.
121; cf. Red. sen. 9; Dom. 113).*

*In the civil wars of the 90s and 80s BC, Catulus fought
on the side of C. Marius. In 78 BC he was consul with M.
Aemilius Lepidus (**95**), with whom he disagreed during
their term of office (Cic. Cat. 3.24). Catulus was respon-
sible for buildings at Rome, especially the rebuilding of the
temple of Iuppiter Capitolinus (Varro ap. Gell. NA 2.10.2;*

F 2 Florus

Thus, after he [Lepidus] had frightened the populace with turbulent speeches to the People as with a war trumpet, he set off for Etruria and from there led arms and an army toward the city [of Rome].

F 2A Sallust, *Histories*

of their former power, glory, and rights. Lepidus justifies his previous behavior and announces his intention to put an end to civil war and crimes; he affirms that freedom is better than wealth and stresses that the Roman People should end their lack of resolve and stop waiting for a leader. Lepidus closes by encouraging the People to follow him, the consul, as the leader and advocate for the recovery of freedom.

96 Q. LUTATIUS CATULUS MINOR

Cic. Verr. 2.4.69; Val. Max. 6.9.5), whence he is sometimes called "Capitolinus."

In Cicero, Catulus is described as a decent orator, but not of the first rank and more suited to political orations, even though he had a refined and cultivated manner of speech (T 1–2). He is a speaker in the first version of Cicero's Academica, *with one of the books named after him (Cic. Att. 13.32.3, 13.19.5; Acad. 2.9, 2.80). Like his father, he was a friend of the poet Archias (Cic. Arch. 6).*

*In 73 BC Catulus, along with M. Pupius Piso Frugi Calpurnianus (**104**), seems to have supported L. Sergius Catilina (**112**), when Catiline was accused of sexual intercourse with a Vestal Virgin (TLRR 167; Oros. 6.3.1). In*

T 1 Cic. *Brut.* 133

[CICERO:] nam de sono vocis et suavitate appellandarum litterarum, quoniam filium cognovisti, noli exspectare quid dicam. quamquam filius quidem non fuit in oratorum numero, sed non deerat ei tamen in sententia dicenda cum prudentia tum elegans quoddam et eruditum orationis genus.

T 2 Cic. *Brut.* 222

[CICERO:] . . . Q. etiam Catulum filium abducamus ex acie, id est a iudiciis, et in praesidiis rei publicae, cui facile satis facere possint, collocemus.

T 3 Cic. *Pis.* 6

me Q. Catulus, princeps huius ordinis et auctor publici consili, frequentissimo senatu parentem patriae nominavit.

On Tribunician Powers in the Senate (F 4)

In 70 BC the consuls consulted the Senate about the restitution of tribunician powers taken away by L. Cornelius Sulla, in preparation for a law (Lex Pompeia Licinia de

the 60s BC Catulus supported a clerk taken to court for
fraud by M. Porcius Cato when quaestor (126 F 9A).

T 1 Cicero, *Brutus*

[CICERO:] For about the sound of his [Catulus' father's: Q.
Lutatius Catulus (**63**), T 1] voice and the charm of his
pronouncing the letters, do not expect me to say anything
since you knew his son. Admittedly, the son was not in the
ranks of orators, but, still, in voicing his opinion in the
Senate, he lacked neither practical wisdom nor a certain
refined and cultivated manner of speech.

T 2 Cicero, *Brutus*

[CICERO:] . . . also Q. Catulus the son, let us withdraw
them from the battle line, that is from the courts, and station them [the orators just listed] on the ramparts of the
Republic, whose demands they are easily able to meet.

T 3 Cicero, *Against Piso*

Q. Catulus, leader of this order and a guiding voice in political deliberations, before a very well attended meeting
of the Senate, named me "father of the fatherland."

On Tribunician Powers in the Senate (F 4)

tribunicia potestate: LPPR, *p. 369); Catulus commented*
on the proposal.

F 4 Cic. *Verr.* 1.44

neque enim ullam aliam ob causam populus Romanus tribuniciam potestatem tanto studio requisivit; quam cum
poscebat, verbo illam poscere videbatur, re vera iudicia
poscebat. neque hoc Q. Catulum, hominem sapientissimum atque amplissimum, fugit, qui Cn. Pompeio, viro
fortissimo et clarissimo, de tribunicia potestate referente
cum esset sententiam rogatus, hoc initio est summa cum
auctoritate usus, patres conscriptos iudicia male et flagi-
tiose tueri; quodsi in rebus iudicandis populi Romani exis-
timationi satis facere voluissent, non tanto opere homines
fuisse tribuniciam potestatem desideraturos.

*Like Q. Hortensius Hortalus (**92** F 29, 30, 31–32), Catulus
spoke (F 5–6, 7–8, 8A) against the bills proposed by the
Tribunes of the People A. Gabinius (tr. pl. 67 BC) and C.*

Against Lex Gabinia *(F 5–6)*

F 5 Cic. *Leg. Man.* 59

reliquum est ut de Q. Catuli auctoritate et sententia dicendum esse videatur. qui cum ex vobis quaereret, si in
uno Cn. Pompeio omnia poneretis, si quid eo factum esset, in quo spem essetis habituri, cepit magnum suae virtutis fructum ac dignitatis, cum omnes una prope voce in
eo ipso vos spem habituros esse dixistis. etenim talis est

F 4 Cicero, *Verrine Orations*

For no other reason [other than that there is no confidence in the law courts] have the Roman People requested tribunician power with such eagerness. When they demanded this, they appeared to demand that nominally; in fact, they demanded law courts. And this fact did not escape Q. Catulus, that very wise and very eminent individual: when Pompey [Cn. Pompeius Magnus (**111**), F 12], that very valiant and very distinguished man, was putting forward a proposal on tribunician power, he [Catulus], when he was asked for his opinion, had recourse to this opening with the greatest authority: that the members of the Senate were guarding the courts ineffectively and immorally; and if they had chosen, when judging cases, to satisfy the honor of the Roman People, people would not have desired tribunician powers to such an extent.

Manilius (tr. pl. 66 BC) before the People (CCMR, App. A: 246, 252) and provided testimony against C. Cornelius (TLRR 209).

Against Lex Gabinia *(F 5–6)*

F 5 Cicero, *Pro Lege Manilia*

It remains that it seems appropriate to speak about Q. Catulus' authority and opinion. When he asked you on whom you would set your hopes if you staked everything upon Pompey [Cn. Pompeius Magnus (**111**)] alone, if anything should happen to him, he received a great tribute to his own high character and position when almost with one voice you all asserted that you would set your hopes upon

vir ut nulla res tanta sit ac tam difficilis quam ille non et
consilio regere et integritate tueri et virtute conficere possit.

Cf. Vell. Pat. 2.32.1; Val. Max. 8.15.9; Plut. *Pomp.* 25.4; Cass. Dio
36.36a.

F 6 Arus., *GL* VII, p. 470.25–26

evenit in illo, Sal. hist. V [F 5.24 M. = 5.20 R.]: "nam si in
Pompeio quid humani evenisset."

Against Lex Manilia *(F 7–8)*

F 7 Cic. *Leg. Man.* 51–52
= **92** F 30.

F 8 Plut. *Pomp.* 30.4–5

ἐνστάντος δὲ τοῦ καιροῦ, τὸν δῆμον φοβηθέντες ἐξ-
έλιπον καὶ κατεσιώπησαν οἱ λοιποί, Κάτλος δὲ τοῦ
νόμου πολλὰ κατηγορήσας καὶ τοῦ δημάρχου, μη-
δένα δὲ πείθων, ἐκέλευε τὴν βουλὴν ἀπὸ τοῦ βήματος
κεκραγὼς πολλάκις ὄρος ζητεῖν ὥσπερ οἱ πρόγονοι
καὶ κρημνόν, ὅπου καταφυγοῦσα διασώσει τὴν ἐλευ-
θερίαν. [5] ἐκυρώθη δ᾽ οὖν ὁ νόμος ὡς λέγουσι πάσαις
ταῖς φυλαῖς, καὶ κύριος ἀποδέδεικτο μὴ παρὼν ὁ

that very man [Catulus]. For he is indeed a man of such a character that there is no undertaking so huge and so difficult that he could not direct it by his counsel, defend it by his uprightness, and complete it by his ability.

F 6 Arusianus Messius

"it happens" in that phrase, Sallust, *Histories* 5 [F 5.24 M. = 5.20 R.]: "for if anything human had happened in Pompey's case."[1]

[1] This excerpt may come from the speech of Catulus as reported in Sallust's *Histories*.

Against Lex Manilia (F 7–8)

F 7 Cicero, *Pro Lege Manilia*

= **92** F 30.

F 8 Plutarch, *Life of Pompey*

But when the time [for discussing and voting on the bill] came, the others, fearing the People, left off and kept silent; but Catulus denounced the law and the Tribune at great length; when he did not persuade anyone, he urged the Senate, calling out in loud tones from the Rostra again and again, to seek out a mountain, like their forefathers, or a lofty rock, where they might fly for refuge and preserve their freedom. [5] Still, then, the law was passed by all the tribes, as they say, and Pompey [Cn. Pompeius Magnus (**111**)], in his absence, was proclaimed master of

Πομπήϊος ἁπάντων σχεδὸν ὢν ὁ Σύλλας ὅπλοις καὶ πολέμῳ τῆς πόλεως κρατήσας.

Testimony Against C. Cornelius (F 8A)

F 8A Asc. in Cic. *Corn.*, *arg.* (pp. 53 KS = 60.19–61.5 C.) = **92** F 31.

On the Catilinarian Conspirators (F 9)

F 9 Plut. *Cic.* 21.4

εἰρημένης δὲ τῆς γνώμης πρῶτος ἀντέκρουσεν αὐτῇ Κάτλος Λουτάτιος . . .

97 L. PLOTIUS GALLUS

L. Plotius Gallus (RE *Plotius* 16) *was the first to teach Latin oratory at Rome, in the time of Cicero's youth (Suet.* Gram. et rhet. *26.1; Schol. Bob. ad Cic.* Arch. *[p. 178.11 St.]; Sen.* Contr. *2, praef. 5; Quint.* Inst. *2.4.42; Hieron.* Ab Abr. *1929 = 88 BC [p. 150f Helm]). C. Marius is said to have felt that Plotius was well qualified to record his*

almost all the powers that Sulla [L. Cornelius Sulla] had exercised after subduing the city [of Rome] in armed warfare.

Testimony Against C. Cornelius (F 8A)

F 8A Asconius on Cicero, *Pro Cornelio*
= **92** F 31.

On the Catilinarian Conspirators (F 9)

*At the meeting of the Senate in December 63 BC concerning the fate of the Catilinarian conspirators, Catulus spoke against the view of C. Iulius Caesar (**121** F 32–36A) (Plut. Caes. 8.1; Cic. Att. 12.21.1).*

F 9 Plutarch, *Life of Cicero*
After the view [of C. Iulius Caesar (**121**), F 32–36A] had been presented, Lutatius Catulus was the first to oppose it . . .

97 L. PLOTIUS GALLUS

achievements (Cic. Arch. 20). In fact, Plotius wrote about oratorical gestures (Quint. Inst. 11.3.143) and composed speeches for the accused.

*In 56 BC Plotius produced a speech for L. Sempronius Atratinus (**171** F 1–7), who prosecuted M. Caelius Rufus (**162** F 23–28) (TLRR 275).*

For L. Sempronius Atratinus (F 1)

F 1 Suet. *Gram. et rhet.* 26.2

hunc eundem—nam diutissime vixit—M. Caelius in oratione quam pro se de vi habuit significa{ba}t[1] dictasse
Atratino accusatori suo actionem subtractoque nomine
hordearium eum rhetorem appellat, deridens ut inflatum
ac levem et sordidum.

> [1] significa{ba}t *Muretus*: significabat *codd.*

98 CN. SICINIUS

*Cn. Sicinius (tr. pl. 76 BC; RE Sicinius 9; praenomen L.
at Sall. Hist. 3.48.8 M. = 3.15.8 R.) was rather funny according to Cicero, but otherwise lacking in oratorical*

T 1 Cic. *Brut.* 216–17

= **86** F 7.

99 CN. CORNELIUS LENTULUS
CLODIANUS

*Cn. Cornelius Lentulus Clodianus (cos. 72, censor 70 BC;
RE Cornelius 216) was a contemporary of Q. Hortensius
Hortalus (**92**) (T 1). As consuls, he and his colleague L.
Gellius Poplicola (**101**) put forward several bills (e.g., Sall.
Hist. 4.1 M. = 4.1 R.); these initiatives included a motion
for not trying people in the provinces in their absence,*

For L. Sempronius Atratinus (F 1)

F 1 Suetonius, *Lives of Illustrious Men. Grammarians and Rhetoricians*

M. Caelius [M. Caelius Rufus (**162**), F 23–28], in a speech that he delivered in his own defense on a charge of violence, implies that this same man [Plotius]—for he lived very long—supplied his accuser, Atratinus [L. Sempronius Atratinus (**171**), F 1–7], with the plea; and without mentioning him by name, he [Caelius] calls him a barley-bread rhetorician, mocking him as puffy, light, and coarse.

98 CN. SICINIUS

qualities (T 1). A witty remark about the consuls of 76 BC is reported (T 1; Quint. Inst. 11.3.129).

T 1 Cicero, *Brutus*

= **86** F 7.

99 CN. CORNELIUS LENTULUS CLODIANUS

presented in the Senate (F 4). When the two men were censors, they expelled a number of individuals from the Senate (e.g., Liv. Epit. 98; Cic. Clu. 120).

*In 67 BC Lentulus was a legate of Cn. Pompeius Magnus (**111**) in the war against the pirates; in the following year he supported the* Lex Manilia de imperio Cn. Pompei

(LPPR, pp. 375–76) (Cic. Leg. Man. *68). In the same period Lentulus seems to have been involved in the trial of a Popillius (*TLRR *185; Cic.* Clu. *132).*

T 1 Cic. *Brut.* 230

= **92** T 1.

T 2 Cic. *Brut.* 308

= **78** T 3.

T 3 Cic. *Brut.* 234

[CICERO:] Cn. autem Lentulus multo maiorem opinionem dicendi actione faciebat quam quanta in eo facultas erat; qui cum esset nec peracutus, quamquam et ex facie et ex vultu videbatur, nec abundans verbis, etsi fallebat in eo ipso: sic intervallis, exclamationibus, voce suavi et canora, † admirando inridebat †, calebat[1] in agendo, ut ea quae deerant non desiderarentur. ita, tamquam Curio copia non nulla verborum, nullo alio bono, tenuit oratorum locum: sic Lentulus ceterarum virtutum dicendi mediocritatem actione occultavit, in qua excellens fuit.

[1] admirando inridebat calebat *codd.*: admirando ore dicebat *Friedrich*: admirantes inretiebat *Schütz*: admirandus incedebat {calebat} *Martha*: admirando irridendo latebat *Lambinus*: ad mirandum illiciebat <ita> calebat *Madvig*: *alii alia*

Lentulus is noted for his excellent delivery and an ability thereby to hide his lesser faculties in other areas of oratory (T 3; Quint. Inst. 11.3.8).

T 1 Cicero, *Brutus*

= **92** T 1.

T 2 Cicero, *Brutus*

= **78** T 3.

T 3 Cicero, *Brutus*

[CICERO:] But Cn. Lentulus won a much higher reputation for eloquence through his delivery than by the amount of ability he had. He was neither very acute, though he seemed to be on the basis of his expression and of his countenance, nor resourceful in language, even though he deceived in that very matter: thus, by pauses, exclamations, a voice agreeable and sonorous, he caused admiration [?] and was fiery in delivery, so that what he lacked was not missed. Thus, as Curio [C. Scribonius Curio (**86**)], by some wealth of diction, without any other good quality, held the rank of orator, so Lentulus, by his delivery, in which he was excellent, cloaked his mediocrity in the other virtues of speaking.

As Consul in the Senate (F 4)

F 4 Cic. *Verr.* 2.2.95

itaque in senatu continuo Cn. Lentulus et L. Gellius consules faciunt mentionem placere statui, si patribus conscriptis videretur, ne absentes homines in provinciis rei
fierent rerum capitalium; causam Stheni totam et istius
crudelitatem et iniquitatem senatum docent.

100 P. CORNELIUS LENTULUS SURA

P. Cornelius Lentulus Sura (praet. 74, 63, cos. 71 BC; RE
Cornelius 240), like others, was expelled from the Senate
in 70 BC, because of his lifestyle (Plut. Cic. 17.1; Cass. Dio
37.30.4); later, he was reinstated (cf. **99, 101***). He was*
praetor again in 63 BC (Plut. Cic. 17.1; Cass. Dio 37.30.4).
In that year he was involved in the Catilinarian Conspir-
acy and was expecting a leading role because of a prophecy
in the Sibylline Books, announcing that three Cornelii
would rule in Rome (Sall. Cat. 47.2); at the end of the year

T 1 Cic. *Brut.* 230

= **92** T 1.

T 2 Cic. *Brut.* 308

= **78** T 3.

As Consul in the Senate (F 4)

F 4 Cicero, *Verrine Orations*

Therefore, immediately, Cn. Lentulus and L. Gellius [L. Gellius Poplicola (**101**), F 4], the consuls [72 BC], moved the following resolution in the Senate to be approved, if it seemed good to the senators, that people should not be prosecuted in the provinces for capital charges in their absence; they gave the Senate a full account of the case of Sthenius [of Thermae, wronged by C. Verres] and the iniquitous cruelty of that man [Verres].

100 P. CORNELIUS LENTULUS SURA

he was killed along with the other captured conspirators (Sall. Cat. 55.5–6).

In Cicero it is noted that Lentulus had a pleasant voice and an elegant style of delivery but did not possess any other oratorical accomplishments (T 3; cf. Cic. Cat. 3.11). Some of Lentulus' speeches were apparently included in an anthology compiled by C. Licinius Mucianus (Tac. Dial. 37.3). Letters by Lentulus are mentioned (Cic. Cat. 3.12; Sall. Cat. 44.4–6).

T 1 Cicero, *Brutus*

= **92** T 1.

T 2 Cicero, *Brutus*

= **78** T 3.

T 3 Cic. *Brut.* 235

[CICERO:] nec multo secus P. Lentulus, cuius et excogitandi et loquendi tarditatem tegebat formae dignitas, corporis motus plenus et artis et venustatis, vocis et suavitas et magnitudo. sic in hoc nihil praeter actionem fuit, cetera etiam minora quam in superiore.

101 L. GELLIUS POPLICOLA

L. Gellius Poplicola (cos. 72, censor 70 BC; RE Gellius 17) was consul with Cn. Cornelius Lentulus Clodianus (99); in that year the consuls put forward a number of bills. When the two men were censors, they expelled several individuals from the Senate (e.g., Liv. Epit. 98; Cic. Clu. 120). In 67 BC Poplicola was a legate of Cn. Pompeius Magnus (111) in the war against the pirates (App. Mithr. 95; Flor. 1.41.9). In 63 BC he supported a harsh verdict on the Catilinarian conspirators (Cic. Att. 12.2.1) and was one of those who suggested honoring Cicero (Cic. Pis. 6; Gell. NA 5.6.15). Poplicola lived to a rather advanced age

T 1 Cic. *Brut.* 174

[CICERO:] horum aetati prope coniunctus L. Gellius non tam vendibilis orator, quamvis[1] nescires quid ei deesset; nec enim erat indoctus nec tardus ad excogitandum nec Romanarum rerum immemor et verbis solutus satis; sed in magnos oratores inciderat eius aetas; multam tamen

---

[1] quamvis *Jeep*: quam ut *codd.*

T 3 Cicero, *Brutus*

[CICERO:] And not very different [from Cn. Cornelius Lentulus Clodianus (**99**)] was the case of P. Lentulus, whose slowness of thought and speech was covered up by dignity of bearing, bodily movement full of art and grace, and the sweetness and strength of his voice. Thus, in him there was nothing but delivery; everything else was even inferior to the preceding [Cn. Lentulus].

101 L. GELLIUS POPLICOLA

(T 1; F 7); he still participated in meetings of the Senate in 59 BC (F 7) and 55 BC (F 5) and spoke at a contio in 58/57 BC (F 8).

In Cicero, Poplicola is described as a decent orator, with some education and elegance in speaking, and as a great supporter of his friends, but not able to compete with the outstanding orators of his age (T 1; Cic. Brut. 176). A speech to the philosophers in Athens as well as several forensic and political speeches in Rome are attested (F 2–8; on F 3 see TLRR 156; on F 8 see CCMR, App. A: 307).

T 1 Cicero, *Brutus*

[CICERO:] Nearly contemporary with the period of these men [M. Antonius (**65**); L. Licinius Crassus (**66**); L. Marcius Philippus (**70**)] was L. Gellius, an orator who did not greatly commend himself, though you would not know what he lacked; for he was not uneducated, nor slow in invention, nor unfamiliar with Roman matters, and sufficiently fluent in his diction; but his time had fallen upon an age of great orators; still, he provided much useful

operam amicis et utilem praebuit, atque ita diu vixit ut multarum aetatum oratoribus implicaretur.

To the Philosophers in Athens (F 2)

F 2 Cic. *Leg.* 1.53

ATTICUS: qu<i>a m<e>[1] Athenis audire ex Phaedro meo memini Gellium familiarem tuum, cum pro consule ex praetura in Graeciam venisset, essetque[2] Athenis, philosophos qui tum erant in locum unum convocasse, eisque[3] magnopere auctorem fuisse ut aliquando controversiarum aliquem facerent modum; quodsi essent eo animo ut nollent aetatem in litibus conterere, posse rem convenire; et simul operam suam illis esse pollicitum, si posset inter eos aliquid convenire.

[1] qu<i>a m<e> *Poggius*: quam *codd.*   [2] venisset essetque *Vahlen*: venissetque *vel* venisset et *vel* venisset *vel* venisseque *vel* venisse et *codd.*   [3] eisque *Halm*: ipse i(i)sque (hisque) *vel* ipsisque *codd.*

On Behalf of M. Octavius Ligus (F 3)

F 3 Cic. *Verr.* 2.1.125

C. Sulpicius Olympus fuit; is mortuus est C. Sacerdote praetore, nescio an antequam Verres praeturam petere coeperit; fecit heredem M. Octavium Ligurem. Ligus hereditatem adiit; possedit Sacerdote praetore sine ulla controversia. posteaquam Verres magistratum iniit, ex edicto istius, quod edictum Sacerdos non habuerat, Sul-

support to friends, and he lived so long that he came into
contact with orators of many periods.

To the Philosophers in Athens (F 2)

F 2 Cicero, *On the Laws*

ATTICUS: For I remember that in Athens I heard from my
friend Phaedrus [Epicurean philosopher] that your friend
Gellius, when, after his praetorship [94 BC], he had gone
to Greece as proconsul and was in Athens, called together
in one place the philosophers who were there at the time
and urgently advised them to come at last to some settlement of their controversies. If they were of the opinion
that they did not wish to waste their lives in argument, the
matter could be settled; and at the same time he promised
his support to them if some settlement could be agreed
among them.

On Behalf of M. Octavius Ligus (F 3)

F 3 Cicero, *Verrine Orations*

There was a man called C. Sulpicius Olympus; he died
during the praetorship of C. Sacerdos [75 BC], possibly
before Verres began canvassing for the praetorship. He
made M. Octavius Ligus his heir. Ligus accepted the inheritance; while Sacerdos was praetor, he held on to it
without any controversy. After Verres had entered office,
on the basis of an edict of his that Sacerdos had not maintained, the daughter of Sulpicius' patron began to claim

pici patroni filia sextam partem hereditatis ab Ligure
petere coepit. Ligus non aderat. L. frater eius causam
agebat; aderant amici, propinqui. dicebat iste, nisi cum
muliere decideretur, in possessionem se ire iussurum. L.
Gellius causam Liguris defendebat; docebat edictum eius
non oportere in eas hereditates valere quae ante eum
praetorem venissent; si hoc tum fuisset edictum, fortasse
Ligurem hereditatem aditurum non fuisse. aequa postu-
latio, summa hominum auctoritas pretio superabatur.

As Consul in the Senate (F 4)

F 4 Cic. *Verr.* 2.2.95

= **99** F 4.

On Cicero in the Senate (F 5–6)

F 5 Cic. *Pis.* 6

mihi hic vir clarissimus qui propter te sedet, L. Gellius,
his audientibus civicam coronam deberi a re publica dixit.

F 6 Gell. *NA* 5.6.15

hac corona civica L. Gellius, vir censorius, in senatu Ciceronem consulem donari a republica censuit, quod eius
opera esset atrocissima illa Catilinae coniuratio detecta
vindicataque.

246

from Ligus one-sixth of the inheritance. Ligus was not present. His brother Lucius argued his case; friends and relatives were there. That man [Verres] announced that, unless the matter was settled with the lady, he would make an order for her to take possession. L. Gellius defended the case of Ligus; he pointed out that his [Verres'] edict ought not to apply to those inheritances that had happened before his praetorship; if this edict had existed then, perhaps Ligus would not have accepted the inheritance. The equity of the plea and the prestige of the men were defeated by money.

As Consul in the Senate (F 4)

F 4 Cicero, *Verrine Orations*
= **99** F 4.

On Cicero in the Senate (F 5–6)

F 5 Cicero, *Against Piso*

This very illustrious man, who sits next to you [Q. Lutatius Catulus (**96**)], L. Gellius, said in the hearing of these men that a civic crown was due to me from the Republic.

F 6 Gellius, *Attic Nights*

It was this civic crown that L. Gellius, an ex-censor, proposed in the Senate that the consul Cicero [63 BC] should be awarded by the Republic, because through his efforts that most dreadful conspiracy of Catiline had been detected and punished.

247

On Lex Iulia agraria *(F 7)*

F 7 Plut. *Cic.* 26.4

ἐπεὶ δὲ Καίσαρι ψηφισαμένῳ τὴν ἐν Καμπανίᾳ χώραν
κατανεμηθῆναι τοῖς στρατιώταις πολλοὶ μὲν ἐδυσχέ-
ραινον ἐν τῇ βουλῇ, Λεύκιος δὲ Γέλλιος ὁμοῦ τι
πρεσβύτατος ὢν εἶπεν ὡς οὐ γενήσεται τοῦτο ζῶντος
αὐτοῦ, "περιμείνωμεν" ὁ Κικέρων ἔφη· "μακρὰν γὰρ
οὐκ αἰτεῖται Γέλλιος ὑπέρθεσιν."

On Cicero Before the People (F 8)

F 8 Cic. *Red. pop.* 17

sed audistis eo tempore clarissimi viri non solum auctoritatem, sed etiam testimonium, L. Gelli: qui quia suam
classem adtemptatam magno cum suo periculo paene sen-
sit, dixit in contione vestrum, si ego consul cum fui non
fuissem, rem publicam funditus interituram fuisse.

102 M. LICINIUS CRASSUS DIVES

*M. Licinius Crassus Dives (cos. 70, 55, censor 65 BC; RE
Licinius 68) was an active political figure from his youth
onward. After he had suffered losses in the proscriptions
by C. Marius and L. Cornelius Cinna as a supporter of L.
Cornelius Sulla, he made a fortune as a result of the Sullan
proscriptions and became proverbially rich. In 60 BC
Crassus formed an alliance with Cn. Pompeius Magnus*

On Lex Iulia agraria *(F 7)*

F 7 Plutarch, *Life of Cicero*

And when Caesar got a decree passed [59 BC] that the land in Campania should be divided among his soldiers [*Lex Iulia agraria campana* (?): *LPPR*, pp. 387–88], and many in the Senate were dissatisfied, and Lucius Gellius, who was about the oldest of them, declared that it should never happen while he was alive, Cicero said: "Let us wait, since Gellius does not ask for a long postponement."

On Cicero Before the People (F 8)

F 8 Cicero, *Post Reditum ad Quirites*

Moreover, you heard at that time [of discussions about Cicero's recall from exile in 57 BC] not only the authoritative opinion, but also the testimony of a very illustrious man, L. Gellius: since he almost felt that his fleet had been tampered with to his own great danger, he said at one of your public meetings that, if I had not been consul when I was [63 BC], the Republic would have perished entirely.

102 M. LICINIUS CRASSUS DIVES

*(**111**) and C. Iulius Caesar (**121**); he died in the battle of Carrhae in 53 BC (on his life see, e.g., Marshall 1976).*

*In Cicero it is noted that Crassus, a contemporary of Q. Hortensius Hortalus (**92**), was a popular lawyer, having achieved this position by hard work and his personal standing, as he had only moderate training and natural ability (T 1, 4, 6, 7). His speeches were characterized by a*

pure Latinity, a careful structure, and liveliness of thought, but his delivery was rather monotonous (T 4).

T 1 Cic. *Brut.* 230

= **92** T 1.

T 2 Cic. *Brut.* 308

= **78** T 3.

T 3 Cic. *Brut.* 311

[CICERO:] tumultus interim ⟨in⟩[1] recuperanda re publica et crudelis interitus oratorum trium Scaevolae Carbonis Antisti, reditus Cottae Curionis Crassi Lentulorum Pompei, leges et iudicia constituta, recuperata res publica; ex numero autem oratorum Pomponius Censorinus Murena sublati.

[1] *add. Orelli*

T 4 Cic. *Brut.* 233

[CICERO:] verum interponam, ut placet, alios et a M. Crasso, qui fuit aequalis Hortensi, exordiar. is igitur mediocriter a doctrina instructus, angustius etiam a natura,

*Crassus was prosecuted for sexual relations with a Vestal Virgin, but was acquitted (*TLRR *169; Plut.* Crass. *1.4;* De cap. ex inimicis util. *89D).*

T 1 Cicero, *Brutus*

= **92** T 1.

T 2 Cicero, *Brutus*

= **78** T 3.

T 3 Cicero, *Brutus*

[CICERO:] Meanwhile, ⟨in⟩ the process of restoring the Republic, there was violence; the cruel death of three orators, Scaevola [Q. Mucius Scaevola (**67**)], Carbo [C. Papirius Carbo Arvina (**87**)], and Antistius [P. Antistius (**78**)]; the return of Cotta [C. Aurelius Cotta (**80**)], Curio [C. Scribonius Curio (**86**)], Crassus, the Lentuli [Cn. Cornelius Lentulus Clodianus (**99**) and P. Cornelius Lentulus Sura (**100**)], and Pompey [Cn. Pompeius Magnus (**111**)]; the setting up of laws and courts; and the restoration of the Republic; from the ranks of orators, however, Pomponius [Cn. Pomponius (**72B**)], Censorinus [C. Marcius Censorinus (**82**)], and Murena [P. Licinius Murena] had been removed.

T 4 Cicero, *Brutus*

[CICERO:] I will, however, insert, if it is all right, some others, and I will begin with Crassus, who was a contemporary of Hortensius [Q. Hortensius Hortalus (**92**)]. That man, then, with moderate training from formal teaching

labore et industria et quod adhibebat ad obtinendas causas curam etiam et gratiam, in principibus patronis aliquot annos fuit. in huius oratione sermo Latinus erat, verba non abiecta, res compositae diligenter, nullus flos tamen neque lumen ullum, animi magna, vocis parva contentio, omnia fere ut similiter atque uno modo dicerentur.

T 5 Tac. *Dial.* 37.2–3

= **47** T 5.

T 6 Plut. *Crass.* 3.3–6

παιδείας δὲ τῆς περὶ λόγον μάλιστα μὲν τὸ ῥητορικὸν καὶ χρειῶδες εἰς ⟨τοὺς⟩¹ πολλοὺς ἤσκησε, καὶ γενό-μενος δεινὸς ἐπεῖν ἐν τοῖς μάλιστα Ῥωμαίων, ἐπιμε-λείᾳ καὶ πόνῳ τοὺς εὐφυεστάτους ὑπερέβαλεν. [4] οὐδεμίαν γὰρ οὕτω δίκην φασὶ μικρὰν οὐδ᾽ εὐκατα-φρόνητον γενέσθαι πρὸς ἣν ἀπαράσκευος ἦλθεν, ἀλλὰ καὶ Πομπηίου πολλάκις ὀκνοῦντος καὶ Καίσα-ρος ἐξαναστῆναι καὶ Κικέρωνος, ἐκεῖνος ἀνεπλήρου τὴν συνηγορίαν. καὶ διὰ τοῦτο μᾶλλον ἤρεσκεν ὡς ἐπιμελὴς καὶ βοηθητικός. [5] . . . [6] λέγεται δὲ καὶ πολυμαθὴς καθ᾽ ἱστορίαν γενέσθαι καί τι καὶ φιλο-σοφῆσαι, τοῖς Ἀριστοτέλους λόγοις προσθέμενος, ὧν διδάσκαλον εἶχεν Ἀλέξανδρον, ἄνθρωπον εὐκολίας καὶ πραότητος ἀπόδειξιν διδόντα τὴν πρὸς Κράσσον συνήθειαν.

¹ *add.* Schaefer

and with even less natural endowment, through hard work and industry, and since he applied also care and his personal influence to be successful in his cases, was for some years among the best advocates. In his oratory there was a pure Latinity, a vocabulary not vulgar, a careful arrangement of matter, yet no flower nor any luster of ornament, much liveliness of thought, little exertion of voice, so that nearly everything was said similarly and in a uniform manner.

T 5 Tacitus, *Dialogue on Oratory*

= **47** T 5.

T 6 Plutarch, *Life of Crassus*

As for his literary culture, he [Crassus] practiced particularly the art of speaking, useful toward ⟨the⟩ many, and after becoming one of the most powerful Roman speakers, he surpassed through care and industry those who were most gifted by nature. [4] For there was no case, they say, however trifling and even contemptible, to which he came unprepared, but often, when Pompey [Cn. Pompeius Magnus (**111**)] and Caesar [C. Iulius Caesar (**121**)] and Cicero were unwilling to plead, he would perform all the duties of an advocate. And for this reason he became more popular, being regarded as careful and ready to help. [5] . . . [6] It is said also that he was well versed in history and also somewhat in philosophy, following the doctrines of Aristotle, in which he had Alexander [Peripatetic philosopher] as a teacher, a man showing proof of contentedness and meekness by his intimacy with Crassus.

T 7 Plut. *Crass.* 7.4

ὁ δὲ Κράσσος ἐνδελεχέστερον τὸ χρήσιμον ἔχων, καὶ σπάνιος οὐκ ὢν οὐδὲ δυσπρόσοδος, ἀλλ᾽ ἐν μέσαις ἀεὶ ταῖς σπουδαῖς ἀναστρεφόμενος, τῷ κοινῷ καὶ φιλανθρώπῳ περιεγίνετο τῆς ἐκείνου σεμνότητος. σώματος δ᾽ ἀξίωμα καὶ λόγου πειθὼ καὶ προσώπου χάριν ἀγωγὸν ἀμφοτέροις ὁμοίως προσεῖναι λέγουσιν.

On Behalf of L. Licinius Murena (F 8–9)

In 63 BC Crassus defended L. Licinius Murena, who was charged with ambitus *in his campaign for the consulship (of 62 BC) by the unsuccessful Ser. Sulpicius Rufus (***118**

F 8 Cic. *Mur.* 10

etenim si me tua familiaritas ab hac causa removisset, et si hoc idem Q. Hortensio, M. Crasso, clarissimis viris, si item ceteris a quibus intellego tuam gratiam magni aestimari accidisset, in ea civitate consul designatus defensorem non haberet in qua nemini umquam infimo maiores nostri patronum deesse voluerunt.

F 9 Cic. *Mur.* 48
= **92** F 37.

T 7 Plutarch, *Life of Crassus*

But Crassus was more continuously ready with his services, and not aloof nor difficult to access, instead always moving in the thick of things, and so through his universal kindness prevailed over the other's [Cn. Pompeius Magnus (**111**)] solemn bearing. But they say that dignity of person, persuasiveness of speech, and pleasantness of features were equally present in both [Crassus and Pompey].

On Behalf of L. Licinius Murena (F 8–9)

*F 6), supported by M. Porcius Cato (***126*** F 11–12); Q. Hortensius Hortalus (***92*** F 36–37) and Cicero (Cic. Mur.) also acted for the defense (TLRR 224).*

F 8 Cicero, *Pro Murena*

For if friendship with you [the prosecutor] had kept me out of this case, and if the same had happened to Q. Hortensius [Q. Hortensius Hortalus (**92**), F 36–37] and Crassus, very distinguished men, if likewise to others by whom, I know, your agreeableness is highly regarded, a consul designate [L. Licinius Murena, cos. 62 BC] would not have someone to defend him in that community in which our ancestors did not wish anyone, even the humblest man, ever to be without an advocate.

F 9 Cicero, *Pro Murena*

= **92** F 37.

On Cicero in the Senate (F 10)

F 10 Cic. *Att.* 1.14.3

Crassus, postea quam vidit illum excepisse laudem ex eo, quod {hi}[1] suspicarentur homines ei consulatum meum placere, surrexit ornatissimeque de meo consulatu locutus est, ut[2] ita diceret, se quod esset senator, quod civis, quod liber, quod viveret, mihi acceptum referre; quotiens coniugem, quotiens domum, quotiens patriam videret, totiens se beneficium meum videre. quid multa? totum hunc locum, quem ego varie meis orationibus, quarum tu Aristarchus es, soleo pingere, de flamma, de ferro (nosti illas ληκήθους), valde graviter pertexuit.

[1] *del. Lambinus*   [2] cum *Wesenberg*

On Behalf of P. Sestius (F 11)

F 11 Schol. Bob. ad Cic. *Sest.*, *arg.* (p. 125.15–26 Stangl) = **92** F 45.

On Cicero in the Senate (F 10)

In 61 BC Crassus spoke in praise of Cicero's consulship in the Senate.

F 10 Cicero, *Letters to Atticus*

After Crassus had seen that he [Cn. Pompeius Magnus (**111**)] had netted credit from the fact that people assumed that he approved of my consulship, he got to his feet and spoke about my consulship most elaborately, so as to say that he counted it as received from me that he was a senator, a citizen, a free man, and alive. Whenever he saw his wife, his house, his native country, each time he saw a gift of mine. What else? He worked up this whole theme that I am in the habit of painting various ways in my speeches, whose Aristarchus [Aristarchus of Samothrace, Greek grammarian and producer of critical editions] you are, about fire, about the sword (you know that color box), really most impressively.

On Behalf of P. Sestius (F 11)

*Again with Q. Hortensius Hortalus (**92** F 43–45), as well as with C. Licinius Macer Calvus (**165** F 29) and Cicero (Cic. Sest.), Crassus spoke on behalf of P. Sestius (**135**), charged under the* Lex Plautia de vi, *in 56 BC (TLRR 271).*

F 11 Scholia Bobiensia to Cicero, *Pro Sestio*

= **92** F 45.

On Behalf of M. Caelius Rufus (F 12–13)

*When M. Caelius Rufus (**162**) was prosecuted under the*
*Lex Plautia de vi by L. Sempronius Atratinus (**171** F 1–7),*
*also in 56 BC, the defendant spoke on his own behalf (**162***

F 12 Cic. Cael. 18

quo loco possum dicere id quod vir clarissimus, M. Crassus, cum de adventu regis Ptolemaei quereretur, paulo
ante dixit: "utinam ne in nemore Pelio—" [Enn. *Trag.* F
89.1 *TrRF / FRL*] . . .

F 13 Cic. Cael. 23

itaque illam partem causae facile patior graviter et ornate
a M. Crasso peroratam de seditionibus Neapolitanis, de
Alexandrinorum pulsatione Puteolana, de bonis Pallae.
vellem dictum esset ab eodem etiam de Dione.

On Behalf of M. Caelius Rufus (F 12–13)

F 23–28) and was successfully supported by Crassus and Cicero (Cic. Cael.*) (TLRR 275).*

F 12 Cicero, *Pro Caelio*

At this point I can say what that very illustrious man, Crassus, said a little earlier, when he complained about the arrival of king Ptolemy [Ptolemy XII, who came to Rome in 58 BC]: "Would that in the forest of Pelion not—" [Enn. *Trag.* F 89.1 *TrRF / FRL*] . . .

F 13 Cicero, *Pro Caelio*

Accordingly, I am quite content that this part of the case has been fully argued by Crassus with weight and eloquence, that is, concerning the disturbances at Neapolis [modern Naples], the assault on the Alexandrians at Puteoli [modern Pozzuoli],[1] the property of Palla.[2] I would wish that he had also spoken about Dio.

---

[1] An Alexandrian embassy was sent to Italy to make the case against the restoration of King Ptolemy XII. The leader of the embassy, Dio of Alexandria, an Academic philosopher, was murdered in Rome.   [2] Cf. Quint. *Inst.* 4.2.27.—Palla was perhaps the mother or stepmother of L. Gellius Poplicola, the husband of Sempronia Atratina, the adoptive sister of Caelius' prosecutor L. Sempronius Atratinus (**171**).

On Behalf of L. Cornelius Balbus (F 14–15)

F 14 Cic. *Balb.* 17

= **111** F 25.

F 15 Cic. *Balb.* 50

quid? hic qui adest, a quo haec quae ego nunc percurro subtilissime sunt omnia perpolita, M. Crassus, non Aveniensem[1] foederatum civitate donavit, homo cum gravitate et prudentia praestans, tum vel nimium parcus in largienda civitate?

[1] Aveniensem *Reid*: auenniensem *vel* auennensem *vel* anniensem *vel* anomensem *codd.*

103 T. POMPONIUS ATTICUS

T. Pomponius Atticus (110–32 BC; RE Pomponius 102) was a rich and well-educated man, a close friend of Cicero. He spent many years living in Athens and was well versed in Greek, but he did not have any major political roles (on his life see the biography by Cornelius Nepos; FRHist

On Behalf of L. Cornelius Balbus (F 14–15)

*Cicero (Cic. Balb.) and Crassus, as well as Cn. Pompeius Magnus (**111** F 25), successfully defended Cornelius Balbus Gaditanus, prosecuted in relation to his citizenship status, in 56 BC (Cic. Balb.) (TLRR 276).*

F 14 Cicero, *Pro Balbo*

= **111** F 25.

F 15 Cicero, *Pro Balbo*

Further, did not this man who is here, by whom all that I am now touching upon very lightly has been elaborated in great detail, Crassus, bestow citizenship upon a person from Avenio,[1] with federate status, a man [Crassus] distinguished by dignity and sagacity and in particular oversparing in giving out citizenship?

[1] Avenio (modern Avignon) in Gallia Narbonensis had become an *oppidum Latinum*, probably through the activities of C. Iulius Caesar (**121**) (Plin. *HN* 3.36).

103 T. POMPONIUS ATTICUS

1:344–45). Atticus had intellectual interests and is the dedicatee of works by Cicero, Varro, and Cornelius Nepos. Atticus wrote letters (though only those from Cicero to him survive), a Greek memoir on Cicero's consulship, a liber annalis, *and family histories (FRHist 33).*

Funeral Oration for His Mother Caecilia (F 1)

F 1 Nep. *Att.* 17.1

de pietate autem Attici quid plura commemorem? cum
hoc ipsum vere gloriantem audierim in funere matris
suae, quam extulit annorum XC, cum esset VII et LX, se
numquam cum matre in gratiam redisse, numquam cum
sorore fuisse in simultate, quam prope aequalem habebat.

104 M. PUPIUS PISO FRUGI
CALPURNIANUS

M. Pupius Piso Frugi Calpurnianus (cos. 61 BC; RE Pu-
pius 10) had a successful public career (he came from the
family of the Calpurnii Pisones Frugi and was adopted by
a M. Pupius). Although he lived in Cicero's time, he was
so much older that the young Cicero became attached to
him as a model of a traditional way of life and learning (T
6; [Sall.] Inv. in Cic. 2). Cicero praised Piso in one of his
speeches against C. Verres (Cic. Verr. 2.1.37). Yet Cicero
did not approve of Piso's behavior in relation to P. Clodius
Pulcher (137); he therefore criticized the consul's conduct
in letters to Atticus (Cic. Att. 1.13.2, 1.14.6, 1.16.12). Piso
was an adherent of the Peripatetics and is made to explain
the views of this philosophical school in Cicero's De fini-

Funeral Oration for His Mother Caecilia (F 1)

Comments that Atticus is said to have made at his mother's funeral may come from a funeral oration delivered on that occasion.

F 1 Cornelius Nepos, *Atticus*

And as concerns Atticus' devotion to his family, what more should I say? Since I heard him correctly praise himself at the funeral of his mother, whom he buried at the age of ninety, when he was sixty-seven, for the fact that he had never had occasion to seek a reconciliation with his mother and had never quarreled with his sister, who was about his own age.

104 M. PUPIUS PISO FRUGI CALPURNIANUS

bus 5 *(Cic.* Att. *13.19.4;* De or. *1.104;* Nat. D. *1.16;* Fin. *5.1–2).*

In Cicero it is noted that, as an orator, Piso possessed some natural ability and had gone through rigorous training, that he was sharp and witty, but sometimes forced and ill-tempered, that he could not bear the labors of the Forum for long, but enjoyed success and fame as a young man and, after an interruption, again after his speech at a trial of Vestal Virgins in 73 BC (T 1; Cic. Cat. 3.9; see Bätz 2012, 243–44, with further references).

*As consul in 61 BC, Piso proposed a bill concerning P. Clodius Pulcher (**137**) and his involvement in the Bona Dea scandal. Unusually, the consul also spoke against the*

T 1 Cic. *Brut.* 236

[CICERO:] M. Piso quidquid habuit, habuit ex disciplina maximeque ex omnibus, qui ante fuerunt, Graecis doctrinis eruditus fuit. habuit a natura genus quoddam acuminis, quod etiam arte limaverat, quod erat in reprehendendis verbis versutum et sollers, sed saepe stomachosum, non numquam frigidum, interdum etiam facetum. is laborem {quasi cursum}[1] forensem diutius non tulit, quod et corpore erat infirmo et hominum ineptias ac stultitias, quae devorandae nobis sunt, non ferebat iracundiusque respuebat sive morose, ut putabatur, sive ingenuo liberoque fastidio. is cum satis floruisset adulescens, minor haberi est coeptus postea. deinde ex virginum iudicio magnam laudem est adeptus et ex eo tempore quasi revocatus in cursum tenuit locum tam diu quam ferre potuit laborem; postea quantum detraxit ex studio tantum amisit ex gloria.

[1] *del. Jahn*

T 2 Cic. *Brut.* 240
= **105** T 1.

T 3 Cic. *Brut.* 308
= **78** T 3.

bill; he was opposed by M. Porcius Cato and others (126 F 17).

T 1 Cicero, *Brutus*

[CICERO:] Whatever qualities M. Piso possessed, he had them as the result of formal learning, and of all who were before him he was most thoroughly versed in Greek doctrines. He possessed by nature a kind of acumen that he had sharpened also by training, that was adroit and skilled in criticizing words, but often ill-tempered, not infrequently frigid, sometimes also witty. The hard labor of the Forum {as if a race course} he did not endure for very long, because he both had a weak body and could not put up with the human ineptitude and stupidity that we [pleaders] have to swallow, and he rejected it rather angrily, whether from a temper naturally morose, as people believed, or from high-minded scorn and disgust. After he had succeeded quite well as a young man, he began to be less well regarded afterward. Then, as a result of the trial of the [Vestal] Virgins, he won great fame, and from that time, as if called back into the race, he held his position as long as he could bear the labor; afterward, as much as he relaxed in effort, so much he lost in renown.

T 2 Cicero, *Brutus*

= **105** T 1.

T 3 Cicero, *Brutus*

= **78** T 3.

T 4 Cic. *Brut.* 310

[CICERO:] commentabar declamitans—sic enim nunc lo-
quuntur—saepe cum M. Pisone et cum Q. Pompeio aut
cum aliquo cottidie, idque faciebam multum etiam Latine,
sed Graece saepius . . .

T 5 Cic. *Planc.* 12

. . . homini nobilissimo, innocentissimo, eloquentissimo,
M. Pisoni . . .

T 6 Asc. in Cic. *Pis.* 62 (p. 14 KS = 15.13–18 C.)

quis hic M. Piso fuerit credo vos ignorare. fuit autem, ut
puto iam nos dixisse, P⟨upius⟩ Piso[1] eisdem temporibus
quibus Cicero, sed tanto aetate maior ut adulescentulum
Ciceronem pater ad eum deduceret, quod in eo et anti-
quae[2] vitae similitudo et multae erant litterae: orator quoque melior quam frequentior habitus est.

[1] P⟨upius⟩ Piso *Manutius*: P. Piso *codd.*   [2] eo et anti-
quae *codd. rec., Manutius*: eo etiam quae *codd.*

On the Vestal Virgins (F 7A)

F 7A Cic. *Brut.* 236
= T 1.

T 4 Cicero, *Brutus*

[CICERO:] I frequently prepared and delivered declamations—for this is what they now say—often with M. Piso and with Q. Pompeius [Q. Pompeius Bithynicus (**105**)] or with anyone, daily, and I generally did this a lot even in Latin, but more often in Greek . . .

T 5 Cicero, *Pro Plancio*

. . . a most noble, most incorruptible, and most eloquent man, M. Piso . . .

T 6 Asconius on Cicero, *Against Piso*

Who this M. Piso was, I believe you do not know. In fact, as I think we have already said, a P‹upius› Piso was around in the same period as Cicero, but so much older that his father brought the young Cicero to him, since there was the semblance of an ancient way of life in him and much knowledge of literature: also, he was regarded as a good rather than a frequent orator.

On the Vestal Virgins (F 7A)

F 7A Cicero, *Brutus*

= T 1.

105 Q. POMPEIUS BITHYNICUS

*Q. Pompeius Bithynicus (b. ca. 108 BC; RE Pompeius 25)
obtained his cognomen because he was instrumental in
organizing Bithynia as a Roman province after the country was bequeathed to the Romans by King Nicomedes IV
Philopator in 74 BC. In the civil war he sided with Cn.
Pompeius Magnus (111). In 48 BC, when Bithynicus went*

T 1 Cic. *Brut.* 240

[CICERO:] Q. Pompeius A. f., qui Bithynicus dictus
est, biennio quam nos fortasse maior, summo studio
di‹s›cendi[1] multaque doctrina, incredibili labore atque
industria; quod scire possum: fuit enim mecum et cum M.
Pisone cum amicitia tum studiis exercitationibusque coniunctus. huius actio non satis commendabat orationem; in
hac enim satis erat copiae, in illa autem leporis parum.

[1] di‹s›cendi *Lambinus:* dicendi *codd.*

T 2 Cic. *Brut.* 310

= **104** T 4.

106 P. SATURIUS

*P. Saturius (RE Saturius 1) was a judge in the first case of
A. Cluentius Habitus (against Statius Albius Oppianicus,
charged with poison attempts) in 74 BC (TLRR 149; T 2;
Cic. Clu. 182). In 77/76 BC he defended C. Fannius Chae-*

105 Q. POMPEIUS BITHYNICUS

to Egypt after the battle of Pharsalus, he was killed (Oros. 6.15.28).

Cicero notes that Bithynicus was an ambitious, hard-working, and well-trained orator but that his delivery did not do justice to his style (T 1). Bithynicus was acquainted with Cicero (T 1–2); a letter from him to Cicero and a letter from Cicero to him survive (Cic. Fam. 6.16, 6.17).

T 1 Cicero, *Brutus*

[CICERO:] Q. Pompeius, Aulus' son, who was called Bithynicus, perhaps two years older than me, had great eagerness to study, much training, and incredible application and industry. And I should know: for he was associated with me and with M. Piso [M. Pupius Piso Frugi Calpurnianus (**104**)] both in friendship and also through studies and exercises. His delivery did not do justice to his style; for in the latter there was sufficient fullness, but in the former there was little charm.

T 2 Cicero, *Brutus*

= **104** T 4.

106 P. SATURIUS

rea against Q. Roscius, the comic actor; Roscius was represented by Cicero (Cic. Q Rosc.), who commented on the opponent's statements in his speech (TLRR 166).

T 1 Cic. *Q Rosc.* 22

subridet Saturius, veterator, ut sibi videtur . . .

T 2 Cic. *Clu.* 107

atque in his omnibus natu minimus, ingenio et diligentia et religione par eis quos antea commemoravi, P. Saturius, in eadem sententia fuit.

On Behalf of C. Fannius Chaerea Against Q. Roscius, the Comic Actor (F 3)

F 3 Cic. *Q Rosc.* 18, 19, 27–28, 51, 52, 56

quid? tu, Saturi, qui contra hunc venis, existimas aliter? nonne, quotienscumque in causa in nomen huius incidisti, totiens hunc et virum bonum esse dixisti et honoris causa appellasti? . . . [19] qua in re mihi ridicule es visus esse inconstans qui eundem et laederes et laudares, et virum optimum et hominem improbissimum esse diceres. eundem tu et honoris causa appellabas et virum primarium esse dicebas et socium fraudasse arguebas? . . . [27] . . . exorditur magna cum exspectatione veteris histrionis exponere societatem. "Panurgus," inquit, "fuit Fanni; is f{u}it[1] ei cum Roscio communis." hic primum questus est non leviter Saturius communem factum esse gratis cum Ros-

---

[1] f{u}it *Passow*: fuit *codd.*

T 1 Cicero, *Pro Quinctio Roscio Comoedo*

Saturius smiles, the cunning old fellow, as he thinks himself to be . . .

T 2 Cicero, *Pro Cluentio*

And among them all, P. Saturius, the youngest in years, an equal in ability, earnestness, and devotion to duty of those I mentioned earlier [other judges], was of the same opinion [i.e., a verdict of guilty].

On Behalf of C. Fannius Chaerea Against
Q. Roscius, the Comic Actor (F 3)

F 3 Cicero, *Pro Quinctio Roscio Comoedo*

Well? Do you, Saturius, who appear against this man here [Q. Roscius], think differently? As often as you happened to mention his name in the case, each time did you not both declare that he was an honorable man and mentioned him by name out of respect? . . . [19] In this matter you seemed to me to be ridiculous and inconsistent, as you both attacked and praised the same man, as you called him both a most excellent man and a thorough rascal. As regards the same person, did you mention him by name out of respect and call him a most distinguished man and accuse him of having cheated his business partner? . . . [27] . . . Amid great expectation he [Saturius] begins to set forth the partnership concerning the old actor. "Panurgus," he says, "was the slave of Fannius; he becomes the common property of him and Roscius." At this point Saturius first complained rather strongly that he [the slave] was made common property for Roscius for nothing, as he had been

cio, qui pretio proprius fuisset Fanni. largitus est scilicet
homo liberalis et dissolutus et bonitate adfluens Fannius
Roscio. sic puto. [28] quoniam ille hic constitit paulisper,
mihi quoque necesse est paulum commorari. Panurgum
tu, Saturi, proprium Fanni dicis fuisse. . . . [51] . . . iam
intellegis, C. Piso, sibi soli, societati nihil Roscium petisse.
hoc quoniam sentit Saturius esse apertum, resistere et
repugnare contra veritatem non audet, aliud fraudis et
insidiarum in eodem vestigio deverticulum reperit. [52]
"petisse," inquit,[2] "suam partem Roscium a Flavio confiteor, vacuam et integram reliquisse Fanni concedo; sed,
quod sibi exegit, id commune societatis factum esse
contendo." . . . [56] . . . perstat in sententia Saturius, quod-
cumque sibi petat socius, id societatis fieri.

[2] inquit *Angelius*: inquam *codd.*

107 L. QUINCTIUS

T 1 Cic. *Brut.* 223

[Cicero:] Cn. Carbonem M. Marium et ex eodem genere

bought by Fannius and was his property. Of course, Fannius, that generous man, careless about money, overflowing with kindness, made a present of him to Roscius. I suppose so! [28] Since that man [Saturius] dwelt on this point for a little bit of time, I also must linger a little. You say, Saturius, that Panurgus was the private property of Fannius. . . . [51] . . . You can now understand, C. Piso [C. Calpurnius Piso (**108**), the judge], that Roscius claimed for himself alone, nothing for the partnership [in compensation from Q. Flavius for the killing of Panurgus]. Since Saturius feels that this is clear, he does not venture to resist and fight against the truth; he discovers another byway for fraud and treachery in the same vein. [52] "I admit," he says, "that Roscius claimed his share from Flavius; I grant that he left Fannius' share free and untouched. But I maintain that what he obtained for himself became the common property of the partnership." . . . [56] . . . Saturius persistently maintains the view that whatever a partner claims for himself becomes the property of the partnership.

107 L. QUINCTIUS

L. Quinctius (tr. pl. 74, praet. 68 BC; RE Quinctius 12) appears in Cicero not as a great orator or lawyer, but as an active speaker before the People, able to move a crowd, with an arrogant manner (T 1–3; cf. Quint. Inst. 5.13.39).

T 1 Cicero, *Brutus*

[CICERO:] Cn. Carbo [Cn. Papirius Carbo, cos. 85, 84, 82 BC], M. Marius [M. Marius Gratidianus], and several oth-

compluris minime dignos elegantis conventus auribus aptissimos cognovi turbulentis contionibus.[1] quo in genere, ut in his perturbem aetatum ordinem, nuper L. Quinctius fuit; aptior etiam Palicanus auribus imperitorum.

[1] contionibus *edd.*: cognitionibus *codd.*

T 2 Cic. *Clu.* 109–11

iam insolentiam noratis hominis, noratis animos eius ac spiritus tribunicios. quod erat odium, di immortales! quae superbia, quanta ignoratio sui, quam gravis atque intolerabilis adrogantia! . . . [110] nam Quinctius quidem quam causam umquam antea dixerat, cum annos ad quinquaginta natus esset? quis eum umquam non modo in patroni, sed in lautioris[1] advocati loco viderat? qui quod rostra iam diu vacua locumque illum post adventum L. Sullae a tribunicia voce desertum oppresserat multitudinemque desuefactam iam a contionibus ad veteris consuetudinis similitudinem revocarat, idcirco cuidam hominum generi paulisper iucundior fuit. atque idem quanto in odio postea fuit illis ipsis[2] per quos in altiorem locum ascenderat! neque iniuria. [111] facite enim ut non solum mores et adrogantiam eius sed etiam voltum atque amictum atque etiam illam usque ad talos demissam purpuram recordemini.

[1] lautioris *vel* laudatoris aut *codd.*   [2] fuit illis ipsis *Baiter*: suis ipsis *vel* suis illis ipsis *codd.*

ers of the same type I regard as not at all as worthy of the ears of a cultivated audience, but as very well suited to turbulent meetings of the People. Of this type, to disturb the chronological order with respect to these, was recently L. Quinctius; Palicanus [M. Lollius Palicanus (**117**)], too, was better suited to the ears of the ignorant.

T 2 Cicero, *Pro Cluentio*

Once you had gotten to know the fellow's insolence, you had gotten to know his pride and his airs as a Tribune. By the gods, what odious behavior there was! What haughtiness, what lack of knowledge of himself, what troublesome and unendurable arrogance! . . . [110] For as to Quinctius, what case had he ever undertaken before, although he had lived to an age of almost fifty years? Who had ever seen him not just in the role of a pleader, but in that of a more respected legal adviser? Because he had seized upon the Rostra, long unoccupied, and upon that place abandoned by a Tribune's voice since the arrival of L. Sulla [L. Cornelius Sulla], and had recalled the populace, now unused to public meetings, to a semblance of its former practice, for that reason he was rather popular with a certain class of people for a short while. And the same person, how much hatred he later experienced from those very men through whom he had climbed to a higher place! Nor was this an injustice. [111] For make an effort to recall not only his manners and arrogance, but also his expression and clothing, and even that purple robe running down to his heels.

T 3 Cic. *Clu.* 79

. . . L. Quinctius, homo cum summa potestate praeditus tum ad inflammandos animos multitudinis accommodatus . . .

On Behalf of Statius Albius Oppianicus (F 4–5)

*In 74 BC, as Tribune of the People, Quinctius spoke (unsuccessfully) in support of Statius Albius Oppianicus, in the first case, against the prosecutor A. Cluentius Habitus and his supporter P. Cannutius (**114** F 5–8), when C. Iu-*

F 4 Ps.-Asc. in Cic. *Verr.* 1.2 (p. 206.17–19 Stangl)

"contionibus": Quintium dicit tr. pl., qui veneficii reum Oppianicum Cluentio accusatore defendens victus erat illo damnato . . .

F 5 Cic. *Clu.* 74

atque etiam casu tum, quod illud repente erat factum, Staienus ipse non aderat; causam nescio quam apud iudicem defendebat. facile hoc Habitus patiebatur, facile Cannutius, at non Oppianicus neque patronus eius L. Quinctius; qui, cum esset illo tempore tribunus plebis, convicium C. Iunio iudici quaestionis maximum fecit ut ne sine illo

T 3 Cicero, *Pro Cluentio*

... L. Quinctius, a man endowed with the greatest authority of office and also skilled in kindling the passions of a crowd ...

On Behalf of Statius Albius Oppianicus (F 4–5)

nius was president of the court (TLRR 149). One of the judges was C. Aelius Paetus Staienus (**107A**), who was involved in another court case at the time (F 5; TLRR 150).

F 4 Pseudo-Asconius on Cicero, *Verrine Orations*

"public meetings": He [Cicero] means Quintius [i.e., Quinctius], a Tribune of the People, who, defending Oppianicus accused of poisoning, when Cluentius [A. Cluentius Habitus] was the prosecutor, was defeated, with his client found guilty ...

F 5 Cicero, *Pro Cluentio*

And indeed by chance then, because that had been enacted suddenly [i.e., the announcement that pleadings are finished], Staienus himself was not present; he was defending some suit before a judge. Habitus [A. Cluentius Habitus] took this lightly, Cannutius [P. Cannutius (**114**)] too took it lightly, but not Oppianicus nor his counsel, L. Quinctius: he, since he was a Tribune of the People at the time [74 BC], protested in the most abusive language to the president of the court, C. Iunius, that one should not withdraw to consider the verdict without that man; and

in consilium iretur; cumque id ei per viatores consulto neglegentius agi videretur, ipse e publico iudicio ad privatum Staieni iudicium profectus est et illud pro potestate dimitti iussit; Staienum ipse ad subsellia adduxit.

On the Courts to the People (F 6)

F 6 Cic. *Clu.* 77, 111, 127

condemnato Oppianico statim L. Quinctius, homo maxime popularis, qui omnis rumorum et contionum ventos conligere consuesset, oblatam sibi facultatem putavit ut ex invidia senatoria posset crescere, quod eius ordinis iudicia minus iam probari populo arbitrabatur. habetur una atque altera contio vehemens et gravis; accepisse pecuniam iudices ut innocentem reum condemnarent tribunus plebis clamitabat; agi fortunas omnium dicebat; nulla esse iudicia; qui pecuniosum inimicum haberet, incolumem esse neminem posse. . . . [111] . . . is, quasi non esset ullo modo ferendum se ex iudicio discessisse victum, rem ab subselliis ad rostra detulit. . . . [127] . . . quid est hoc? duos esse corruptos solos pecunia ⟨iu⟩dicant;[1] ceteri videlicet gratiis condemnarunt. non est igitur circumventus, non oppres-

---

[1] ⟨iu⟩dicant *Madvig*: dicant *codd.*: quid *Angelius*

since this seemed to him to be happening through the intentional negligence of the criers, he himself went from the criminal court to the civil court of Staienus, and by virtue of his official prerogative ordered that one to adjourn: Staienus he led back to his seat himself.

On the Courts to the People (F 6)

Later in 74 BC, Quinctius criticized the courts before the People (CCMR, App. A: 236).

F 6 Cicero, *Pro Cluentio*

Immediately upon the conviction of Oppianicus, L. Quinctius, very much active in the political interests of the People, who was accustomed to catch every breath of private gossip or public harangue, felt that a chance for advancement had presented itself to him as a result of the unpopularity of the Senate, since he believed that the courts of that order had a rather poor reputation with the People at the time. A series of violent and impressive speeches to the People were delivered: he protested loudly as Tribune of the People [74 BC] that the judges had accepted money to condemn an innocent man; he said that the fortunes of all were being dealt with; there were no courts; nobody could be safe who had a rich enemy. . . . [111] . . . He then, as if it were not to be tolerated in any way that he should leave the court defeated, carried the case from the benches to the Rostra. . . . [127] . . . What does this mean? They [censors investigating the case] judge that two [judges] only had been bribed with money; the others, I guess, found him [Oppianicus] guilty for no

279

sus pecunia, non, ut in illa Quinctiana contione habebatur,[2] omnes qui Oppianicum condemnarunt in culpa sunt
ac suspicione ponendi. duos solos video auctoritate censo-
rum adfinis ei turpitudini iudicari.

[2] in illa Quinctiana contione habebatur *Graevius*: illa Quinctiana contiones habebantur (haberebantur) *vel* illae Quinctianae
contiones habebantur *codd.*

Against C. Iunius (F 7)

F 7 Cic. *Clu.* 89, 90–91, 92, 93,108

condemnatus est C. Iunius qui ei quaestioni praefuerat;
adde etiam illud, si placet: tum est condemnatus cum esset
iudex quaestionis. non modo causae sed ne legi quidem
quicquam per tribunum plebis laxamenti datum est. quo
tempore illum a quaestione ad nullum aliud rei publicae
munus abduci licebat, eo tempore ad quaestionem ipse
abreptus est. at ad quam quaestionem? . . . [90] . . . dicat
qui volt hodie de illo populo concitato, cui tum populo
mos gestus est, qua de re Iunius causam dixerit; quem-
cumque rogaveris, hoc respondebit, quod pecuniam acceperit, quod innocentem circumvenerit. est haec opinio. at,
si ita esset, hac lege accusatum oportuit qua accusatur

bribe. Therefore, he was not the victim of intrigue, not overwhelmed by bribery; nor are all those who found Oppianicus guilty, as was claimed at that public meeting of Quinctius, to be regarded as guilty and suspicious. I observe that only two were judged by the official pronouncement of the censors to be accomplices in that scandal.

Against C. Iunius (F 7)

Also in 74 BC Quinctius prosecuted (CCMR, App. A: 237) C. Iunius, the president of the court in the case of Statius Albius Oppianicus (TLRR 153; Gruen 1974, 33–34).

F 7 Cicero, *Pro Cluentio*

C. Iunius was convicted, who had presided at that trial. Add this also, if you please: he was convicted at the time when he was president of the court. No indulgence was given by the Tribune of the People [L. Quinctius], not only to the case, but even to the law. At a time when it was unlawful for him to be withdrawn from court to any other public duty, at that time he was himself haled away to court. But to what court? . . . [90] . . . Let any willing member of that excited mob, whose demands were then accommodated, say today on what charge Iunius stood trial. Whomsoever you ask, he will give this reply, namely that he [Iunius] accepted a bribe, that he convicted an innocent man unjustly. This is the general opinion. But, if it were so, he ought to have been prosecuted under that law under which Habitus [A. Cluentius Habitus] is being prosecuted. But he himself presided over the court ad-

Habitus. at ipse ea lege quaerebat. paucos dies exspectas-
set Quinctius. at neque privatus accusare nec sedata iam
invidia volebat. videtis igitur non in causa sed in tempore
ac potestate spem omnem accusatoris fuisse. [91] multam
petivit. qua lege? quod in legem non iurasset, quae res
nemini umquam fraudi fuit, et quod C. Verres, praetor
urbanus, homo sanctus et diligens, subsortitionem eius in
eo codice non haberet qui tum interlitus proferebatur. his
de causis C. Iunius condemnatus est, iudices, levissimis et
infirmissimis, quas omnino in iudicium adferri non oportuit. . . . [92] hoc vos Cluentio iudicium putatis obesse
oportere? quam ob causam? si ex lege subsortitus non erat
Iunius aut si in aliquam legem aliquando non iuraverat,
idcirco illius damnatione aliquid de Cluentio iudicabatur?
"non" inquit; "sed ille idcirco illis legibus condemnatus
est, quod contra aliam legem commiserat." qui hoc
confitentur, possunt idem illud iudicium fuisse defendere? "ergo" inquit "idcirco infestus tum populus Romanus fuit C. Iunio, quod illud iudicium corruptum per eum
putabatur." . . . [93] . . . accusabat tribunus plebis idem in
contionibus, idem ad subsellia; ad iudicium non modo de
contione sed etiam cum ipsa contione veniebat. gradus illi
Aurelii tum novi quasi pro theatro illi iudicio aedificati

ministering that law. Quinctius should have waited a few days. But he did not wish to prosecute as a private person [after the end of his term of office] or when the popular prejudice had already subsided. So you see that the entire hope of the prosecutor relied not on the merits of his case, but on the timing and his power. [91] He demanded a fine. Under what law? Because he had not taken the official oath on the law, a matter that has never been held criminal in anyone, and because C. Verres, the city praetor [in 74 BC], an upright and scrupulous man, did not have a note of his having filled up a vacancy among the judges in that record that was then produced, full of erasures [cf. Cic. *Verr.* 2.1.157–58]. For these reasons, very trivial and very insubstantial, C. Iunius was convicted, judges, reasons that ought not to have been admitted before the court at all. . . . [92] Do you think that this trial ought to do harm to Cluentius? For what reason? If Iunius had not appointed a substitute according to the law or if at some point he had not taken an official oath on some law, then, for that reason, by his conviction, was any judgment made about Cluentius? "No," he [Quinctius] says; "but he [Iunius] was convicted under those laws for the reason that he had committed an offense against another law." Can those who admit this maintain equally that this was a trial? "Well," he says, "the Roman People were then hostile to C. Iunius for the reason that this court [at Oppianicus' trial] was believed to have been corrupted through him." . . . [93] . . . A Tribune of the People prosecuted him [Iunius], at public meetings as well as at the benches in court; he came into court not only straight from a public meeting, but even along with the meeting itself. Those Aurelian steps, new then, seemed to have been built as an audito-

videbantur; quos ubi accusator concitatis hominibus com-
plerat, non modo dicendi ab reo sed ne surgendi quidem
potestas erat. [94] . . . [108] . . . haec tum agente Quinctio
neque in contione neque in iudicio demonstrata sunt; neque enim ipse dici patiebatur nec per multitudinem conci-
tatam consistere cuiquam in dicendo licebat. itaque ipse
postquam Iunium pervertit, totam causam reliquit; paucis
enim diebus illis et ipse privatus est factus et hominum
studia defervisse intellegebat.

Against C. Fidiculanius Falcula (F 8)

*Quinctius accused C. Fidiculanius Falcula (a judge in the
trial of Statius Albius Oppianicus) of a corrupt verdict
(TLRR 154); the defendant was acquitted and was later a*

F 8 Cic. *Clu.* 103, 104, 108, 112–13

videamus ecquod aliud iudicium, quod pro Cluentio sit
proferre possimus. dixitne tandem causam C. Fidiculanius
Falcula qui Oppianicum condemnarat, cum praesertim, id
quod fuit in illo iudicio invidiosissimum, paucos dies ex
subsortitione sedisset? dixit et bis quidem dixit. in summam enim L. Quinctius invidiam contionibus eum cotidianis seditiosis et turbulentis adduxerat. uno iudicio
multa est ab eo petita, sicut ab Iunio, quod non suae decu-
riae munere neque ex lege sedisset. paulo sedatiore tempore est accusatus quam Iunius, sed eadem fere lege et

rium for that trial; when the prosecutor had filled them with excited people, there was not only no possibility of speaking for the defendant but not even of rising to speak. [94] . . . [108] . . . Through the activities of Quinctius, at the time, this [the judges' views on Oppianicus] was not pointed out either at a meeting of the People or in court. For he himself allowed no mention of it, nor was it possible for anyone, owing to the excitement of the mob, to stand their ground when speaking. Thus, after he had ruined Iunius, he let the whole case drop. For, a few days afterward, he both became a private man himself and realized that the heat of popular feeling had abated.

Against C. Fidiculanius Falcula (F 8)

witness in the case of A. Caecina (Cic. Caec. 28–30; TLRR 189).

F 8 Cicero, *Pro Cluentio*

Let us see if we can bring forward any other trial that is in support of Cluentius [A. Cluentius Habitus]. Did not C. Fidiculanius Falcula, who had voted for Oppianicus' condemnation, eventually plead his case, especially since he had only sat for a few days as a substitute, a fact that excited much prejudice against him at that trial? He pleaded, and in fact he pleaded twice: for L. Quinctius, with lawless and unruly daily meetings of the People, had created a strong prejudice against him. At one trial a fine was sought from him, as from Iunius, because he had taken his seat when it was not the turn of his panel and not according to the law. He [C. Fidiculanius Falcula] was accused at a

crimine. quia nulla in iudicio seditio neque vis nec turba
versata est, prima actione facillime est absolutus. . . . [104]
Fidiculanius quid fecisse dicebatur? accepisse a Cluentio
HS C̄C̄C̄C̄. cuius erat ordinis? senatorii. qua lege in eo
genere a senatore ratio repeti solet, de pecuniis repetundis, ea lege accusatus honestissime est absolutus. . . . [108]
. . . quod si, per quos dies Iunium accusavit Fidiculanium
accusare voluisset, respondendi Fidiculanio potestas facta
non esset. ac primo quidem omnibus illis iudicibus, qui
Oppianicum condemnarant minabatur. [109] . . . [112] . . .
sed ut illuc revertar, quo tempore Fidiculanius est absolutus, tu qui iudicia facta commemoras quid tum esse existimas iudicatum? certe gratiis iudicasse. [113] at condemnarat, at causam totam non audierat, at in contionibus a L.
Quinctio, tribuno plebis, vehementer erat et saepe vexatus. illa igitur omnia Quinctiana iniqua, falsa, turbulenta,
popularia, seditiosa ⟨iudices⟩[1] iudicaverunt.

[1] *add. Clark*

On Behalf of P. Fabius (F 9)

In 72 or 71 BC Quinctius defended P. Fabius against M.
Tullius, who was supported by Cicero (Cic. Tull. I and II:
Crawford 1984, 47–50). The case, dealt with in two hear-
*ings (*actiones*), concerned the recovery of damages for the*

slightly quieter time than Iunius [cf. F 7], but under much
the same law and on much the same charge. Because at
his trial there was no unrest, violence, or disorder, he was
very easily acquitted at the first hearing. . . . [104] What
was Fidiculanius alleged to have done? To have accepted
400,000 sesterces from Cluentius. To what order did he
belong? The senatorial. He was accused under the law by
which a senator is usually brought to trial in such a case,
that regarding the recovery of extorted money, and was
very honorably acquitted under that law. . . . [108] . . . But
had he [Quinctius] chosen to accuse Fidiculanius during
the days in which he accused Iunius, there would not have
been the chance for Fidiculanius to make a reply. And
indeed he began by threatening all those judges who had
voted for Oppianicus' conviction. [109] . . . [112] . . . But
to return to that point in time at which Fidiculanius was
acquitted, what do you [T. Attius Pisaurensis (**145**), the
prosecutor in 66 BC] imagine to have been proved by
the verdict then, you who are so fond of quoting verdicts
made? Assuredly, that a verdict was reached without any
money. [113] Yet he had voted for conviction; yet he had
not listened to the whole case; yet at public meetings he
had been assailed by L. Quinctius, a Tribune of the People, furiously and often. Thus, all those activities of Quinctius were decided by the ‹judges› to be unjust, false, riot-
ous, designed to appeal to the People, and seditious.

On Behalf of P. Fabius (F 9)

*murder of Tullius' slaves by Fabius' men, after Fabius' at-
tempts to lay claim to land owned by Tullius had not pro-
ceeded successfully (TLRR 173).*

F 9 Cic. *Tull.* 3, 6, 35, 38, 39, 47, 49

nunc quoniam Quinctius ad causam pertinere putavit res
ita multas, falsas praesertim et inique confictas, proferre
de vita et moribus et existimatione M. Tulli . . . [6] unum
hoc abs te, L. Quincti, pervelim impetrare . . . ut ita tibi
multum temporis ad dicendum sumas ut his aliquid ad
iudicandum relinquas. namque antea non defensionis
tuae modus sed nox tibi finem dicendi fecit . . . [35] quid
ad haec Quinctius? sane nihil certum neque unum in quo
non modo possit verum putet se posse consistere. primum
enim illud iniecit,[1] nihil posse dolo malo familiae fieri. hoc
loco non solum fecit ut defenderet Fabium, sed ut omnino
huiusce modi iudicia dissolveret. . . . [38] dicis oportere
quaeri, homines M. Tulli iniuria occisi sint[2] necne. de quo
hoc primum quaero, venerit ea res in hoc iudicium necne.
si non venit, quid attinet aut nos dicere aut hos quaerere?
si autem venit, quid attinuit te tam multis verbis a praetore
postulare ut adderet in iudicium "iniuria," et, quia non
impetrasses, tribunos pl. appellare et hic in iudicio queri
praetoris iniquitatem, quod de iniuria non addidisset?[3]
[39] haec cum praetorem postulabas, cum tribunos appellabas, nempe ita[4] dicebas, potestatem tibi fieri oportere ut,

[1] iniecit *Peyron*: ini . c . t *cod.*
[2] sint *Madvig*: essent *cod.*
[3] addidisset *Huschke*: addiderit (*vel* addidebat) *cod.*
[4] nempe ita *Peyron*: . . . m . . . .a *cod.*

F 9 Cicero, *Pro Tullio*

Now since Quinctius believed that it was relevant to the case to bring forward so many matters, false ones, in particular, and unjustly put together, concerning the life, character, and reputation of M. Tullius . . . [6] This one thing I would really like to obtain from you, L. Quinctius, . . . that you take only so much time for yourself to speak that you leave some to these men here [the judges] for making a judgment. For previously [at the first hearing] not the measure of your defense, but the night brought an end to your speaking . . . [35] What [will] Quinctius [say] to this [i.e., that the deed was done with malice]? Obviously nothing certain, nor the one thing on which he not only could, but believes that he could, base his case. For he first threw out that reproach that nothing could happen to a household by bad trickery. At this point he not only brought it to pass that he defended Fabius, but that he dissolved trials of this sort altogether. . . . [38] You say that it is necessary to ask whether or not men of M. Tullius have been killed by injustice. About this I first ask this, whether or not that matter has come to this court. If it has not come, what difference does it make that either we talk about it or these men here [the judges] inquire? But if it has come, what difference did it make that you demanded from the praetor with so many words that he added the charge of injustice to the trial, and, because you had not achieved this, that you called on the Tribunes of the People and complained here in court about the unfairness of the praetor, since he did not add the charge of injustice? [39] When you asked this from the praetor, when you called on the Tribunes, obviously you spoke in such a way

si posses, recuperatoribus[5] persuaderes non esse iniuria
M. Tullio damnum datum. quod ergo ideo in iudicium
addi voluisti, ut de eo tibi apud recuperatores dicere liceret, eo non addito nihilo minus tamen ita dicis, quasi id
ipsum a quo depulsus[6] es impetraris? at quibus verbis in
decernendo Metellus usus est ceteri‹que›[7] quos appellasti? nonne haec omnium fuit oratio, quod vi hominibus
armatis coactisve familia fecisse diceretur, id tametsi nullo
iure fieri potuerit, tamen se nihil addituros? . . . [47] atque
ille legem mihi de XII tabulis recitavit, quae permittit ut
furem noctu liceat occidere et luce,[8] si se telo defendat, et
legem antiquam de legibus sacratis, quae iubeat impune
occidi eum qui tribunum pl. pulsaverit. . . . [48] . . . ergo
istis legibus quas recitasti certe non potuit istius familia
servos M. Tulli occidere. [49] "non," inquit, "ad eam rem
recitavi, sed ut hoc intellegeres, non visum esse maioribus
nostris tam indignum istuc nescio quid quam tu putas,
hominem occidi."

---

[5] recuperatoribus *Beier*: reciperatores *cod.*   [6] depulsus
Peyron: . e . . . s . s *cod.*   [7] *add. Madvig*   [8] luce *Peyron*:
luci *cod.*

that the opportunity ought to be given to you so that, if you could, you might persuade the recovery judges that damage was done to M. Tullius not by injustice. Therefore, as regards the matter that you wanted to be added to the trial, so that it would be possible for you to speak about that in front of the recovery judges, after it has not been added, are you, nevertheless, still talking about it in such a way as if you achieved that very thing from which you have been thrust away? But what words did Metellus [the presiding praetor, probably L. Caecilius Metellus, cos. 68 BC] use in making a decision ⟨and⟩ the others that you have called upon? Was not this the language of them all, that, even though what a household was said to have done by men armed and recruited, this could in no way be done rightly, still they would not add anything? . . . [47] And that man [Quinctius] read out to me the law from the Twelve Tables that grants that it is permitted to kill a thief by night and by day if he defends himself with a weapon, and an old law from the sacred laws that decrees that he is killed with impunity who has assaulted a Tribune of the People. . . . [48] . . . Therefore, according to those laws that you have read out that man's household could not kill the slaves of M. Tullius. [49] "Not," he says, "for that reason have I read these out, but so that you understand this, that such a matter did not seem as scandalous to our ancestors as you think, that a man should be killed."

107A C. AELIUS PAETUS STAIENUS

C. Aelius Paetus Staienus (quaest. 77 BC; RE Aelius 98; Staienus) was originally called C. Staienus; he had himself adopted into the gens Aelia *and then took the name C. Aelius Staienus Paetus (T 1; Cic.* Clu. *72), though the full name does not appear in the sources (Shackleton Bailey 1991, 65).*

T 1 Cic. *Brut.* 241, 244

[CICERO:] ". . . et C. Staienus, qui se ipse adoptaverat et de Staieno Aelium fecerat, fervido quodam et petulanti et furioso genere dicendi; quod quia multis gratum erat et probabatur, ascendisset ad honores, nisi in facinore manifesto deprehensus poenas legibus et iudicio dedisset. [242] . . ." [244] tum ATTICUS: "tu quidem de faece," inquit, "hauris idque iam dudum, sed tacebam; hoc vero non putabam, te usque ad Staienos et Autronios esse venturum."

108 C. CALPURNIUS PISO

*C. Calpurnius Piso (cos. 67 BC; RE Calpurnius 63) administered the province of Gallia Narbonensis for two years after his consulship. Upon his return, he was accused in the extortion court by C. Iulius Caesar (**121**), in relation to unlawful punishment of a Transpadane Gaul; defended by Cicero (Cic. Pro C. Calpurnio Pisone: Crawford 1984, 77–78), Piso was acquitted (TLRR 225; Cic. Flacc. 98;*

107A C. AELIUS PAETUS STAIENUS

*Staienus was active as a pleader (Cic. Clu. 74) and is mentioned as an example of someone influencing trials by corrupt practices, particularly in the court case between A. Cluentius Habitus and Statius Albius Oppianicus (Cic. Clu. 69–76; cf. **107**, **114**). In 76 BC Staienus took on the case concerning the property of Safinius Atella (TLRR 142; Cic. Clu. 68, 99).*

T 1 Cicero, *Brutus*

[CICERO:] ". . . and C. Staienus, who had himself adopted and from a Staienus made himself into an Aelius, with a certain intense, insolent, and wild style of speaking; since that was welcomed and approved by many, he would have obtained higher honors if he had not been caught in an evident misdeed and paid the penalty exacted by the laws and the courts. [242] . . ." [244] Here ATTICUS said: "You are drawing from the dregs, and that for some time, but I have kept quiet. In fact, I did not think that you would get down to men like Staienus and Autronius [P. Autronius]."

108 C. CALPURNIUS PISO

Sall. Cat. 49.2). Earlier, Piso had been accused of misconduct in the campaign for the consulship, but the trial was abandoned owing to bribery (TLRR 190). In 63 BC Piso supported the punishment of the Catilinarian conspirators (Cic. Att. 12.21.1; Phil. 2.12; Plut. Cic. 19.1). Piso served as a judge in the trial of the actor Q. Roscius Gallus, when Cicero spoke for the defense (Cic. Q Rosc.; TLRR 166).

T 1 Cic. *Brut.* 239

[CICERO:] C. deinde Piso statarius et sermonis plenus orator, minime ille quidem tardus in excogitando, verum tamen vultu et simulatione multo etiam acutior quam erat videbatur.

On Behalf of Sex. Aebutius (F 2)

In 69 BC Piso defended Sex. Aebutius against A. Caecina, who was represented by Cicero (Cic. Caec.), in a dispute over land claimed by Aebutius (TLRR 189): when the two men had arranged to meet on the land in question, so that

F 2 Cic. *Caec.* 34–35, 41, 64, 65, 66

nondum de Caecinae causa disputo, nondum de iure possessionis nostrae loquor; tantum de tua defensione, C. Piso, quaero. [35] quoniam ita dicis et ita constituis, si Caecina, cum in fundo esset, inde deiectus esset, tum per hoc interdictum eum restitui oportuisse; nunc vero deiectum nullo modo esse inde ubi non fuerit; hoc interdicto nihil nos adsecutos esse: quaero . . . [41] "queramur," inquit, "licet; tamen hoc interdicto Aebutius non tenetur." quid ita? "quod vis Caecinae facta non est." . . . "nemo," inquit, "occisus est neque saucius ‹factus›."[1] . . . [64] venio

[1] *add.* Zielinski: sauci‹at›us *Ernesti*

In Cicero, Piso is described as a stationary and conversational orator, good at finding material and appearing to be of greater acumen than he was (T 1).

T 1 Cicero, *Brutus*

[CICERO:] Then there was C. Piso, an orator of the stationary type and practicing the conversational style; he was by no means slow in invention, yet by his countenance and assumed appearance he even seemed to be of much greater acumen than he was.

On Behalf of Sex. Aebutius (F 2)

Caecina would submit to a formal "ejection," he was denied access by Aebutius' armed men; thereupon, Caecina obtained a praetorial interdict against Aebutius. Cicero comments on Piso's defense in his speech.

F 2 Cicero, *Pro Caecina*

I am not yet arguing about Caecina's case, I am not yet speaking of the right to our possession; I am only asking about your defense, C. Piso. [35] Seeing that you speak thus and conclude thus, that, if Caecina had been ejected from the farm when he was there, then he would have had the right to restitution by means of this interdict; but that, as it is, he was in no way ejected from a place in which he was not; that by this interdict we have gained nothing: I ask . . . [41] "We may regret it," he [Piso] says; "nevertheless, Aebutius is not covered by this interdict." How so? "Because force was not used upon Caecina." . . . "No one," he says, "was killed or <became> wounded." . . . [64] I

nunc ad illud tuum: "non deieci; non enim sivi accedere."
puto te ipsum, Piso, perspicere quanto ista sit angustior
iniquiorque defensio quam si illa uterere: "non fuerunt
armati, cum fustibus et cum saxis fuerunt." . . . [65] atque
illud in tota defensione tua mihi maxime mirum videbatur,
te dicere iuris consultorum auctoritati obtemperari non
oportere. . . . [66] in ista vero causa cum tu sis is qui te
verbo litteraque defendas, cum tuae sint hae partes: "unde
<d>eiectus² es? an inde quo prohibitus es accedere? reiec-
tus es, non deiectus," cum tua sit haec oratio: "fateor me
homines coegisse, fateor armasse, fateor tibi mortem esse
minitatum,³ fateor hoc interdicto⁴ praetoris vindicari,⁵ si
voluntas et aequitas valeat; sed ego invenio in interdicto
verbum unum ubi delitiscam: non deieci te ex eo loco
quem in locum prohibui ne venires"—in ista defensione
accusas eos qui consuluntur, quod aequitatis censeant rationem, non verbi haberi oportere?

2 <d>eiectus *Camerarius*: eiectus *codd.*   3 minitatum
Angelius: immutatum *vel* minitatam *codd.*   4 interdicto *ed.*
Ascens.: interdictum *codd.*   5 vindicari *ed.* V: vindicavi *vel*
violavi *codd.*

109 L. MANLIUS TORQUATUS PATER

*L. Manlius Torquatus pater (cos. 65 BC; RE Manlius 79)
became consul in 65 BC, after the consuls originally elected
for that year had been convicted of ambitus (TLRR 201;
cf. 146). After his consulship Torquatus administered the
province of Macedonia and was awarded the title of im-
perator by the Senate in 63 BC (Cic. Pis. 44).*

come now to that argument of yours: "I did not drive him out; for I did not let him draw near." I believe you realize yourself, Piso, how much more quibbling and inequitable such a defense is than if you used that one: "they were not armed; they had sticks and stones." . . . [65] And that point seemed to me the most astounding in the whole of your defense, that you said that we ought not to defer to the authority of legal experts. . . . [66] But in this case of yours, when you are the one who uses a defense based upon the words and the letter [of the law], when this is your position: "Whence were you driven out? From a place which you were prevented from reaching? You were driven away, not driven out," while this is your speech: "I admit that I collected men together; I admit that I armed them; I admit that I threatened you with death; I admit that I am liable under this praetorian interdict if its intention and fair interpretation prevail; but I find a single word in the interdict where I can find shelter: I have not driven you out of that place that I have prevented you from entering"—in that defense are you accusing those who are being consulted because they believe that account should be taken of equity, not of a word?

109 L. MANLIUS TORQUATUS PATER

*Torquatus was a friend of T. Pomponius Atticus (**103**) (Nep. Att. 1.4). Like his son L. Manlius Torquatus (**146**), he favored the Epicurean philosophical school (Cic. Fin. 1.39) and wrote playful poetry (Plin. Ep. 5.3.5).*

In Cicero, Torquatus is described as an orator with polished style and sound judgment (T 1).

T 1 Cic. *Brut.* 239

[CICERO:] etiam L. Torquatus elegans in dicendo, in existimando admodum prudens, toto genere perurbanus.

On Behalf of L. Sergius Catilina (F 2)

F 2 Cic. *Sull.* 81

quin etiam parens tuus, Torquate, consul reo de pecuniis repetundis Catilinae fuit advocatus, improbo homini, at supplici, fortasse audaci, at aliquando amico. cui cum adfuit post delatam ad eum primam illam coniurationem, indicavit se audisse aliquid, non credidisse.

110 C. LICINIUS MACER

C. Licinius Macer (tr. pl. 73 BC; RE Licinius 112), the father of C. Licinius Macer Calvus (165), fought as Tribune of the People for the restoration to the People of the powers that L. Cornelius Sulla had taken away from them. Later, when he came back from a provincial governorship, Macer was charged with extortion before the praetor Cicero in 66 BC and either took his own life in advance of the condemnation or died suddenly (TLRR 195; Plut. Cic. 9.2;

T 1 Cicero, *Brutus*

[CICERO:] Also L. Torquatus, elegant in speaking, very sound in critical judgment, in all respects a man of perfect urbanity.

On Behalf of L. Sergius Catilina (F 2)

*As consul in 65 BC, Torquatus spoke in support of L. Sergius Catilina (**112**), prosecuted by P. Clodius Pulcher (**137**) on a charge of extortion (TLRR 212).*

F 2 Cicero, *Pro Sulla*

Furthermore, your father, Torquatus [L. Manlius Torquatus (**146**)], when he was consul [65 BC] defended Catiline—an immoderate man, but a suppliant; reckless perhaps, but once a friend—concerning a charge of extorting money. Inasmuch as he [Torquatus] appeared for him [Catiline] after that first conspiracy had been reported to him, he indicated that he had heard something, but did not believe it.

110 C. LICINIUS MACER

Cic. Att. 1.4.2; Val. Max. 9.12.7; on his life see FRHist 1:320–31.

*Macer was a friend of L. Cornelius Sisenna (**89**) and also wrote an historical work (T 2; FRHist 27). In Cicero, Macer is described as an able pleader, while his fame was marred by his character. His language was unremarkable, and his delivery was not particularly impressive; his speeches were characterized by careful collection and arrangement of the material (T 1).*

T 1 Cic. *Brut.* 238

[CICERO:] C. Macer auctoritate semper eguit, sed fuit patronus propemodum diligentissimus. huius si vita, si mores, si vultus denique non omnem commendationem ingeni everteret, maius nomen in patronis fuisset. non erat abundans, non inops tamen; non valde nitens, non plane horrida oratio; vox gestus et omnis actio sine lepore; at in inveniendis componendisque rebus mira accuratio, ut non facile in ullo diligentiorem maioremque cognoverim, sed eam ut citius veteratoriam quam oratoriam diceres. hic etsi etiam in publicis causis probabatur, tamen in privatis inlustriorem obtinebat locum.

T 2 Cic. *Leg.* 1.7

[ATTICUS:] nam quid <M>acrum[1] numerem? cuius loquacitas habet aliquid argutiarum, nec id tamen ex illa erudita Graecorum copia, sed ex librariolis Latinis; in orationibus autem multas ineptias, et adeo[2] summam impudentiam.

[1] <M>acrum *Sigonius:* acrum *codd.*   [2] et adeo *Zumpt:* datio *vel* elatio *vel* ad *codd.*: in mendacio *Sigonius: lac. ind. Reifferscheid*

On the Restitution of Tribunician Powers to the People (F 3)

The historian Sallust has Macer, as Tribune of the People in 73 BC, deliver a speech in front of the People; it is directed against the nobility and supports the restitution of

T 1 Cicero, *Brutus*

[CICERO:] C. Macer was always deficient in authority, but as a pleader he was almost the most diligent. If his way of life, if his character, if even his mien had not taken away any recommendation of his talent, he would have had a greater name among the pleaders. His language was not copious, yet not meager; not too brilliant, not completely crude; his voice, his gesture, and his whole delivery were without charm; but in collection and arrangement of material there was an amazing care, so that I have scarcely seen it more diligent and greater in anyone, but of such a kind that you would rather call it characteristic of adroit routine than oratory. Though he won recognition also in criminal cases, he nonetheless held a more conspicuous place in civil suits.

T 2 Cicero, *On the Laws*

[ATTICUS:] For why should I mention ‹M›acer [in a list of historiographers]? His loquacity has some adroitness of expression, and that not from that wealth of knowledge of the Greeks, though, but from the Roman copyists; yet in his speeches there are many absurdities and even the greatest impudence. [continued by **89 T 2**]

*On the Restitution of Tribunician Powers to
the People (F 3)*

tribunician powers (CCMR, App. A: 239; Walt 1997, 9–28).

F 3 Sall. *Hist.* 3.48 M. = 3.15 R.

Macer outlines the terrible circumstances resulting from the "slavery" imposed by L. Cornelius Sulla and his followers on the People and the other magistrates and points out that in the past the People had managed to establish Tribunes of the People for the defense of their rights. In his view all other magistrates, persuaded by personal interest,

Against C. Rabirius (F 4)

*Perhaps in his year as Tribune of the People, Macer prosecuted C. Rabirius for having been involved in killing L. Appuleius Saturninus (**64A**), who, along with his followers, had had to withdraw to the Capitol, then had surrendered and been brought to the Senate house; the defendant was acquitted (TLRR 171; Walt 1997, 29–30). In 63 BC*

F 4 Cic. *Rab. perd.* 7

nisi forte de locis religiosis ac de lucis quos ab hoc violatos esse dixisti pluribus verbis tibi respondendum putas; quo in crimine nihil est umquam abs te dictum, nisi a C. Macro obiectum esse crimen id C. Rabirio. in quo ego demiror meminisse te quid obiecerit C. Rabirio Macer inimicus, oblitum esse quid aequi[1] et iurati iudices iudicarint.

---

[1] aequi *Angelius*: aeque *codd.*

F 3 Sallust, *Histories*

hope, or bribery, have now turned their power and authority against the People. Since the situation will get
worse for the People, Macer appeals to them to shake off
their slothfulness, take back their power, refuse to serve
the powerful, and aim for the restoration of tribunician
powers.

Against C. Rabirius (F 4)

C. Rabirius was prosecuted by T. Labienus (**133** F 1–2) for
the same reason, now charged with treason; he was again
acquitted, on that occasion defended by Q. Hortensius
Hortalus (**92** F 34–35) and Cicero (Cic. Rab. perd.; TLRR
220, 221).

F 4 Cicero, *Pro Rabirio Perduellionis Reo*

Or perhaps you [T. Labienus, the present prosecutor] believe that I should reply at some length to you concerning
the holy places and groves that you have said had been
violated by this man here [Rabirius]; as regards this charge
nothing has ever been said by you, except that this charge
was brought against C. Rabirius by C. Macer. With respect
to this, I am amazed that you remembered what Macer,
his enemy, charged C. Rabirius with but forgot what im-
partial judges decided under oath.

On Behalf of the Tusci (F 5)

F 5 Prisc., *GL* II, p. 532.22–25

. . . "verro" enim secundum Servium [ad Verg. *Aen.* 1.59] "versi" facit, secundum Charisium [*GL* I, p. 246.9 = p. 320.13 B.] autem "verri," quod et usus comprobat. Licinius Macer pro Tuscis: "quis[1] oportuit amissa restituere, hisce etiam reliquias averrerunt."

---

[1] quis *Hertz*: quos *codd.*: quibus *Meyer*

111 CN. POMPEIUS MAGNUS

*Cn. Pompeius Magnus (106–48 BC; RE Pompeius 31) was consul three times (cos. 70, 55, 52 BC) and celebrated three triumphs (79, 71, 61 BC). He freed the Mediterranean Sea from pirates in 67 BC and concluded the Mithridatic War in 66 BC. In 60 BC he formed an alliance with C. Iulius Caesar (**121**) and M. Licinius Crassus Dives (**102**). During the civil war Pompey was an opponent of Caesar; he was killed after the battle of Pharsalus, in 48 BC (on his life see, e.g., Seager 2002; Gelzer 2005; on his career and oratory see van der Blom 2016, 113–45; on his speeches, pp. 296–304).*

Pompey is said to have studied rhetoric with M'. Otacilius Pitholaus (T 9). In Cicero, Pompey is praised as a great speaker whose fame as an orator was surpassed only

On Behalf of the Tusci (F 5)

Macer spoke on behalf of the Tusci (Etruscans) (F 5 = F 26 Walt = 26 HRR); this intervention may be linked to colonies of veterans established by L. Cornelius Sulla in Etruria (Walt 1997, 28–29).

F 5 Priscian

. . . for *verro* ["I sweep"], according to Servius, creates *versi*, but, according to Charisius, *verri* [different forms of perfect], which usage also confirms. Licinius Macer [in the speech] on behalf of the Tuscans: "to whom one ought to restore what has been lost, from them they have swept away even what was left."

111 CN. POMPEIUS MAGNUS

by his military achievements: he was eloquent and had a splendid style of delivery; however, he is also presented as shy and reluctant, taking lessons in oratory (T 1–2; Cic. Balb. 2; cf. T 3–6, 8–9; Plut. Pomp. 1.4). Quintilian claims that Cicero wrote speeches for Pompey, as he did for others (T 11; cf. F 27).

*As a young man, Pompey was prosecuted in a civil case and defended by Q. Hortensius Hortalus (**92** F 15), L. Marcius Philippus (**70** F 12–13), and Cn. Papirius Carbo (TLRR 120).*

Copies of letters by Pompey survive (Cic. Att. 8.11A, C; cf. T 10). A number of speeches in the Senate and at public meetings are known (F 16–18: CCMR, App. A: 276; cf. Cic. Att. 1.14.6, 1.19.7), such as support for Caesar's

agrarian bill (F 20b). Also mentioned are statements at further public meetings (Cic. Att. 2.21.3, 7.21.1; Red. sen. 29; Red. pop. 16–17; Sest. 107; Pis. 34; Plut. Pomp. 51.6–7), at trials (Cic. Q Fr. 2.3.2), appearances in the Senate (Cic. Har. resp. 45; Dom. 69; Sest. 74, 129; Pis. 35, 80; Rab. post. 13; Fam. 8.4.4, 8.9.5; Caes. BCiv. 1.32.8, 1.33.2), and addresses to soldiers (Caes. BCiv. 3.82.1; Plut. Pomp. 41.7, 43.3; App. B Civ. 2.50.205–52.212, 2.72.299–302). Brief utterances on various occasions, such as his discharge from military service (Plut. Pomp. 22.4–9), or the presentation of the proposal to extend Caesar's command (Vell. Pat. 2.64.2), are attested (see also Quint. Inst.

T 1 Cic. *Brut.* 239

[CICERO:] meus autem aequalis Cn. Pompeius vir ad omnia summa natus maiorem dicendi gloriam habuisset, nisi eum maioris gloriae cupiditas ad bellicas laudes abstraxisset. erat oratione satis amplus, rem prudenter videbat; actio vero eius habebat et in voce magnum splendorem et in motu summam dignitatem.

T 2 Cic. *Leg. Man.* 42

iam quantum consilio, quantum dicendi gravitate et copia valeat, in quo ipso inest quaedam dignitas imperatoria, vos, Quirites, hoc ipso ex loco saepe cognostis.

6.3.111; Vell. Pat. 2.33.2, 2.33.4; Caes. BCiv. 3.45.6, 3.94.5). When Pompey was offered the command in the fight against the pirates in 67 BC, Cassius Dio puts a long deceptive speech into his mouth, so that accepting it would appear to be thrust upon him (Cass. Dio 36.25–36; CCMR, App. A: 246). Pompey may not have delivered public speeches as frequently as other Republican politicians because of his focus on military exploits. According to Plutarch, Pompey had prepared a speech in Greek for addressing Ptolemy XIII in 48 BC, but was murdered before he was able to deliver it (Plut. Pomp. 79.2–4).

T 1 Cicero, *Brutus*

[CICERO:] And my contemporary Pompey, a man born to all the most outstanding achievements, would have enjoyed greater glory for eloquence had not ambition for still greater glory drawn him off to military fame. In his language he was sufficiently elevated, he saw matters sagaciously; his delivery, indeed, possessed much splendor in his voice and great dignity in his movement.

T 2 Cicero, *Pro Lege Manilia*

How great his [Pompey's] powers are in counsel, how great in the weight and command of eloquence, which itself contains a certain dignity belonging to a commander, you have often observed, Romans, from this very place [the Rostra in the Forum].

T 3 Vell. Pat. 2.29.2–3

fuit hic . . . [3] . . . eloquentia medius . . .

T 4 Quint. *Inst.* 11.1.36

imperatorum ac triumphalium separata est aliqua ex parte ratio eloquentiae, sicut Pompeius abunde disertus rerum suarum narrator, et hic qui bello civili se interfecit Cato eloquens senator fuit.

T 5 Sen. *Ep.* 1.11.4

nihil erat mollius ore Pompei; numquam non coram pluribus rubuit, utique in contionibus.

T 6 Tac. *Dial.* 37.2–3

= **47** T 5.

T 7 Plut. *Crass.* 7.4

= **102** T 7.

T 8 Suet. *Gram. et rhet.* 25.3

. . . Cn. Pompeium quidam historici tradiderunt sub ipsum civile bellum, quo facilius C. Curioni promptissimo iuveni causam Caesaris defendenti contradiceret, repetisse declamandi consuetudinem; M. Antonium, item Augustum ne Mutinensi quidem bello omisisse . . .

T 3 Velleius Paterculus, *Compendium of Roman History*

He [Pompey] was . . . [3] . . . of moderate talent as regards eloquence . . .

T 4 Quintilian, *The Orator's Education*

The type of eloquence of generals and triumphant conquerors is to some extent set apart; thus, Pompey was a very articulate narrator of his own deeds, and the Cato who committed suicide in the civil war [M. Porcius Cato (**126**)] was an eloquent senator.

T 5 Seneca, *Epistles*

Nothing was more sensitive than Pompey's face; he always blushed in the presence of a gathering, especially at meetings of the People.

T 6 Tacitus, *Dialogue on Oratory*

= **47** T 5.

T 7 Plutarch, *Life of Crassus*

= **102** T 7.

T 8 Suetonius, *Lives of Illustrious Men. Grammarians and Rhetoricians*

. . . some historians have recorded that Pompey, on the very eve of the civil war, had taken up again the habit of declaiming so that he could speak more easily against C. Curio [C. Scribonius Curio (**170**)], a young man and very fluent speaker defending the cause of Caesar [as tr. pl. 50 BC]; that Antony [**159**], and Augustus as well, did not give it up even during the war at Mutina [in 43 BC] . . .

T 9 Suet. *Gram. et rhet.* 27.3

deinde rhetoricam professus Cn. Pompeium Magnum docuit patrisque eius res gestas nec minus ipsius compluribus libris exposuit . . .

T 10 Cic. *Att.* 7.17.2

scire iam te oportet L. Caesar quae responsa referat a Pompeio, quas ab eodem ad Caesarem ferat litteras; scriptae enim et datae ita sunt ut proponerentur in publico. in quo accusavi mecum ipse Pompeium qui, cum scriptor luculentus esset, tantas res atque eas quae in omnium manus venturae essent Sestio nostro scribendas dederit; itaque nihil umquam legi scriptum Σηστιωδέστερον.

T 11 Quint. *Inst.* 3.8.50

nam sunt multae a Graecis Latinisque compositae orationes quibus alii uterentur, ad quorum condicionem vitamque aptanda quae dicebantur fuerunt. an eodem modo cogitavit aut eandem personam induit Cicero cum scriberet Cn. Pompeio et cum T. Ampio ceterisve, ac non unius cuiusque eorum fortunam, dignitatem, res gestas intuitus omnium quibus vocem dabat etiam imaginem expressit, ut melius quidem sed tamen ipsi dicere viderentur?

T 9 Suetonius, *Lives of Illustrious Men. Grammarians and Rhetoricians*

Then, lecturing on rhetoric, he [M'. Otacilius Pitholaus (restored name)] taught Pompey and outlined the deeds of that man's father and also of [Pompey] himself in several books . . .

T 10 Cicero, *Letters to Atticus*

You ought to know by now what reply L. Caesar [L. Iulius Caesar, proquaestor in Africa in 47/46 BC] is taking back from Pompey, what letter he is carrying from the latter to Caesar [C. Iulius Caesar (**121**)]; for it was written and dispatched in such a way that it would be displayed in public. For that, in my own mind, I blamed Pompey, who, although he is a splendid writer, granted to our Sestius [P. Sestius (**135**)] to write up such great matters and of such a kind that will come into the hands of everyone. And so I have never read anything written "in a more Sestian style."

T 11 Quintilian, *The Orator's Education*

For there are many speeches composed by Greeks and Romans for others to deliver, to whose circumstances and way of life what was said had to be adapted. Did Cicero think in the same way or assume the same character when he wrote for Pompey and for T. Ampius [T. Ampius Balbus; cf. F 27] or others, and did he not consider the fortune, position, and achievements of each single one of them, and thus produce also an image of all those to whom he was lending his voice, so that they seemed to speak better, but still as themselves?

On Tribunician Powers to the People (F 12–14)

F 12 Cic. *Verr.* 1.44–45

neque enim ullam aliam ob causam populus Romanus tribuniciam potestatem tanto studio requisivit; quam cum poscebat, verbo illam poscere videbatur, re vera iudicia poscebat. neque hoc Q. Catulum, hominem sapientissimum atque amplissimum, fugit, qui Cn. Pompeio, viro fortissimo et clarissimo, de tribunicia potestate referente cum esset sententiam rogatus, hoc initio est summa cum auctoritate usus; . . . [45] ipse denique Cn. Pompeius cum primum contionem ad urbem consul designatus habuit, ubi, id quod maxime exspectari videbatur, ostendit se tribuniciam potestatem restituturum, factus est in eo strepitus et grata contionis admurmuratio. idem in eadem contione cum dixisset populatas vexatasque esse provincias, iudicia autem turpia ac flagitiosa fieri, ei rei se providere ac consulere velle, tum vero non strepitu, sed maximo clamore suam populus Romanus significavit voluntatem.

On Tribunician Powers to the People (F 12–14)

*When consul designate for his first consulship (71 BC), Pompey delivered a speech (*CCMR, App. A: 241*) to a public meeting on the restitution of tribunician powers (*App. B Civ. 1.121.560*).*

F 12 Cicero, *Verrine Orations*

For no other reason [viz., distrust of courts] have the Roman People requested tribunician power with such eagerness. When they demanded this, they appeared to demand that nominally; in fact, they demanded law courts. And this fact did not escape Q. Catulus [Q. Lutatius Catulus (**96**), F 4], that very wise and very eminent individual: when Pompey, that very valiant and very distinguished man, was putting forward a proposal on tribunician power,[1] he [Catulus], when he was asked for his opinion, had recourse to this opening with the greatest authority; . . . [45] Finally, when Pompey himself, as consul designate [end of 71 BC], for the first time addressed a public meeting near the city [of Rome], where, in accordance with what appeared to be very widely expected, he indicated that he would restore tribunician power, upon that, a murmuring noise of grateful approval arose from the meeting. When, in the same speech to the People, he had said that the provinces had been wasted and laid desolate, that the law courts had become scandalous and wicked, that he intended to take measures and to deal with this matter, then it was with no mere murmur, but with a mighty roar that the Roman People showed their favorable attitude.

[1] Pompey's *contio* was apparently preceded by a discussion in the Senate about the same issue, initiated by him.

F 13 Ps.-Asc. in Cic. *Verr.* 1.45 (p. 220.18–20 Stangl)

Pompeius autem pro consule de Hispania Sertorio victo nuper venerat et statim habuerat contionem de restituenda tribunicia potestate, Palicano tr. pl.

F 14 Sall. *Hist.* 4.44–47 M. = 4.34–37 R.

. . . magnam exorsus orationem . . . [45] si nihil ante adventum suum inter plebem et patres convenisset, coram se daturum operam . . . [46] qui quidem mos ut tabes in urbem coniectus . . . [47] multitudini ostendens, quam colere plurumum, ut mox cupitis ministram haberet, decreverat . . .

On Theophanes of Mytilene (F 15–15A)

F 15 Cic. *Arch.* 24

quid? noster hic Magnus qui cum virtute fortunam adaequavit, nonne Theophanem Mytilenaeum, scriptorem re-

F 13 Pseudo-Asconius on Cicero, *Verrine Orations*

But Pompey had recently come as proconsul from Hispania after the defeat of Sertorius and immediately delivered a speech before the People about the restitution of tribunician powers, when Palicanus [M. Lollius Palicanus (**117**)] was Tribune of the People [71 BC].

F 14 Sallust, *Histories*

. . . having commenced a long speech . . . [45] that if no understanding had been achieved between the commons and the senators before his arrival, he would in person devote effort . . . [46] which habit, in truth, foisted upon the city, like a plague . . . [47] showing to the throng, which he had resolved to cultivate very assiduously, so as to have it soon as an agent for furthering his wishes . . .[1]

[1] These fragments from Sallust's *Histories* (transmitted by different sources) might come from a version of the speech as given by Sallust in his historical work.

On Theophanes of Mytilene (F 15–15A)

When Pompey presented Theophanes of Mytilene, a writer and close associate of his, with Roman citizenship at a public meeting of the soldiers in 62 BC, he accompanied this action with a speech.

F 15 Cicero, *Pro Archia*

Again, did not this Great man here [Pompey], who has put his good fortune on a level with his high qualities, present Theophanes of Mytilene, the historian of his campaigns,

rum suarum, in contione militum civitate donavit; et nostri illi fortes viri, sed rustici ac milites, dulcedine quadam
gloriae commoti quasi participes eiusdem laudis magno
illud clamore approbaverunt?

F 15A Val. Max. 8.14.3

ne Pompeius quidem Magnus ab hoc adfectu gloriae aversus, qui Theophanen Mitylenaeum scriptorem rerum suarum in contione militum civitate donavit, beneficium per
se amplum accurata etiam et testata oratione prosecutus.
quo effectum est ut ne quis dubitaret quin referret potius
gratiam quam incoharet.

To the People (F 16–18)

F 16 Cic. *Att.* 1.14.1–2

prima contio Pompei qualis fuisset scripsi ad te antea: non
iucunda miseris, inanis improbis, beatis non grata, bonis
non gravis; itaque frigebat. tum Pisonis consulis impulsu
levissimus tribunus pl. Fufius in contionem producit Pompeium. res agebatur in circo Flaminio, et erat in eo ipso
loco illo die nundinarum πανήγυρις. quaesivit ex eo pla-

with citizenship before a public meeting of the soldiers? And did not those brave men of ours, though peasants and soldiers, moved by a certain sweetness of renown, loudly applaud that [action], as if they too had a share in the same glory?

F 15A Valerius Maximus, *Memorable Doings and Sayings*

Not even Pompeius Magnus was averse to this eagerness for glory: he bestowed citizenship on Theophanes of Mytilene, the chronicler of his exploits, in a public meeting of the soldiers, and he followed up the gift, ample in itself, with a carefully prepared and well publicized speech. Thereby it was achieved that no one doubted that he [Pompey] was repaying a favor rather than initiating one.

To the People (F 16–18)

F 16 Cicero, *Letters to Atticus*

What Pompey's first public speech [an earlier *contio*] was like, I wrote to you earlier [in a lost letter]: of no comfort to the poor, of no interest to the rascals, not pleasing to the rich, not sufficiently serious to the loyal men; thus he was frozen. Then, on the encouragement of consul Piso [M. Pupius Piso Frugi Calpurnianus (**104**), cos. 61 BC], a very irresponsible Tribune of the People, Fufius [Q. Fufius Calenus], called Pompey out into a meeting of the People. This was taking place in the Circus Flaminius [in the Campus Martius, outside the city boundary], and there was in that very spot, on that market day, a holiday crowd. He [Fufius] asked him [Pompey] whether he

ceretne ei iudices a praetore legi, quo consilio idem praetor uteretur. id autem erat de Clodiana religione ab senatu
constitutum. [2] tum Pompeius μάλ' ἀριστοκρατικῶς
locutus est senatusque auctoritatem sibi omnibus in rebus
maximi videri semperque visam esse respondit, et id multis verbis.

F 17 Oros. *Hist.* 6.6.4

hoc bellum Orientis cum viginti et duobus regibus sese
gessisse ipse Pompeius pro contione narravit.

F 18 Plut. *Pomp.* 54.1

καίτοι Πομπήιος εἶπέ ποτε δημηγορῶν ὅτι πᾶσαν ἀρ-
χὴν λάβοι πρότερον ἢ προσεδόκησε, καὶ κατάθοιτο
θᾶττον ἢ προσεδοκήθη . . .

In the Senate (F 19)

F 19 Cic. *Att.* 1.14.2

postea Messalla consul in senatu de Pompeio quaesivit
quid de religione et de promulgata rogatione sentiret. lo-

thought it right for judges to be selected by a praetor if the same praetor presided over this panel. This procedure had been determined by the Senate in the sacrilege case [i.e., the Bona Dea scandal] of Clodius [P. Clodius Pulcher (**137**)]. [2] Pompey then replied very much *en bon aristo-crate* and said that in all matters he held and had always held the Senate's authority in the highest respect, and he did so at considerable length. [continued by F 19]

F 17 Orosius, *Histories*

That he had waged this war against twenty-two kings of the east was recounted by Pompey himself before a meeting of the People.[1]

[1] To which of the speeches at meetings of the People attested for Pompey this note should be assigned is uncertain.

F 18 Plutarch, *Life of Pompey*

Still, Pompey once said, when addressing the People, that he had received every office earlier than he had expected and had laid it down more quickly than he had been expected . . .[1]

[1] To which of the speeches at meetings of the People attested for Pompey this note should be assigned is uncertain.

In the Senate (F 19)

F 19 Cicero, *Letters to Atticus*

[continued from F 16] Subsequently Messalla, the consul [M. Valerius Messalla Niger (**124**), cos. 61 BC], asked Pompey in the Senate what he thought about the sacrilege

cutus ita est in senatu ut omnia illius ordinis consulta
γενικῶς laudaret, mihique, ut adsedit, dixit se putare satis
ab se {et}iam[1] de istis rebus esse responsum.

1 {et}iam *Shackleton Bailey*: etiam *codd.*

On His Achievements to the People (F 20)

F 20   Plin. *HN* 7.98–99

triumphi vero, quem duxit a. d. III kal. Oct. M. Pisone M.
Messala cos., praefatio haec fuit: "cum oram maritimam
praedonibus liberasset et imperium maris populo Romano
restituisset, ex Asia Ponto Armenia Paphlagonia Cappadocia Cilicia Syria Scythis Iudaeis Albanis Hiberia insula
Creta Basternis et super haec de rege[1] Mithridate atque
Tigrane triumphavit." [99] summa summarum in illa gloria fuit (ut ipse in contione dixit, cum de rebus suis disse-
ret) Asiam ultimam provinciarum accepisse eandemque
mediam patriae reddidisse.

1 regibus *edd. vet.*

Cf. Plin. *HN* 37.12–16.

On Lex Iulia agraria (F 20b)

*When C. Iulius Caesar (**121**), as consul in 59 BC, put
forward an agrarian bill (Lex Iulia agraria: LPPR,
pp. 387–88; cf. Vell. Pat. 2.44.4; App. B Civ. 2.10.35–36;
Plut. Pomp. 47.6–8), he had Pompey and M. Licinius*

and the promulgated bill. He spoke thus in the Senate that he commended all decrees of that body in general terms, and he remarked to me, as he sat down, that he believed he had now replied sufficiently with respect to those matters.

On His Achievements to the People (F 20)

F 20 Pliny the Elder, *Natural History*

Indeed the preamble of the triumph that he [Pompey] celebrated on the third day before the Kalends of October [September 28] in the consulship [61 BC] of M. Piso [M. Pupius Piso Frugi Calpurnianus (**104**)] and M. Messalla [M. Valerius Messalla Niger (**124**)] was as follows: "After he had freed the sea coast from pirates and restored the command over the sea to the Roman People, he celebrated a triumph over Asia, Pontus, Armenia, Paphlagonia, Cappadocia, Cilicia, Syria, the Scythians, the Jews, the Albanians, Iberia, the island of Crete, the Basternae and, in addition, over King Mithridates and Tigranes." [99] The crowning pinnacle in that glorious record was (as he himself declared in a public meeting when he spoke about his achievements) to have found Asia the remotest of the provinces and to have turned the same place into a central one for his country.

On Lex Iulia agraria (F 20b)

*Crassus Dives (**102**) speak in support before the meeting of the People (CCMR, App. A: 285), although both were private citizens at the time (Cass. Dio 38.4.4).*

F 20b Cass. Dio 38.5.1–5

ὅ τε οὖν Πομπήιος μάλα ἀσμένως "οὐκ ἐγώ" ἔφη "μό-
νος, ὦ Κυιρῖται, τὰ γεγραμμένα δοκιμάζω, ἀλλὰ καὶ
ἡ ἄλλη βουλὴ πᾶσα, δι' ὧν οὐχ ὅτι τοῖς μετ' ἐμοῦ
ἀλλὰ καὶ τοῖς μετὰ τοῦ Μετέλλου συστρατευσαμένοις
ποτὲ γῆν δοθῆναι ἐψηφίσατο. [2] τότε μὲν οὖν (οὐ γὰρ
ηὐπόρει τὸ δημόσιον) εἰκότως ἡ δόσις αὐτῆς ἀνε-
βλήθη· ἐν δὲ δὴ τῷ παρόντι (παμπλούσιον γὰρ ὑπ'
ἐμοῦ γέγονε) προσήκει καὶ ἐκείνοις τὴν ὑπόσχεσιν
καὶ τοῖς ἄλλοις τὴν ἐπικαρπίαν τῶν κοινῶν πόνων
ἀποδοθῆναι." [3] ταῦτ' εἰπὼν ἐπεξῆλθέ τε καθ' ἕκαστον τῶν γεγραμμένων, καὶ πάντα αὐτὰ ἐπήνεσεν,
ὥστε τὸν ὅμιλον ἰσχυρῶς ἡσθῆναι. ὁ οὖν Καῖσαρ
ἰδὼν τοῦτο ἐκεῖνόν τε ἐπήρετο εἰ βοηθήσοι οἱ προθύ-
μως ἐπὶ τοὺς τἀναντία σφίσι πράττοντας, καὶ τῷ
πλήθει παρήνεσε προσδεηθῆναι πρὸς τοῦτο αὐτοῦ. [4]
γενομένου δὲ τούτου ἐπαρθεὶς ὁ Πομπήιος, ὅτι τῆς
παρ' ἑαυτοῦ ἐπικουρίας, καίπερ μηδεμίαν ἡγεμονίαν
ἔχοντος, καὶ ὁ ὕπατος καὶ ὁ ὅμιλος ἔχρηζεν, ἄλλα τε
πολλὰ ἀνατιμῶν τε καὶ ἀποσεμνύνων ἑαυτὸν διελέ-
ξατο, καὶ τέλος εἶπεν ὅτι, ἄν τις τολμήσῃ ξίφος
ἀνελέσθαι, καὶ ἐγὼ τὴν ἀσπίδα ἀναλήψομαι. [5] ταῦθ'
οὕτως ὑπὸ τοῦ Πομπηίου λεχθέντα καὶ Κράσσος ἐπήνεσεν.

F 20b Cassius Dio, *Roman History*

Pompey then very gladly said: "It is not I alone, Romans, who approve this measure, but also all the rest of the Senate, inasmuch as it has voted for land to be given not only to my soldiers but also to those who once fought with Metellus [Q. Caecilius Metellus Pius, cos. 80 BC, who fought with Pompey in the Sertorian War]. [2] On the former occasion (for the treasury had no great means) its granting was naturally postponed; but at present (for it has become exceedingly rich through me) it is right that the promise made to those [soldiers] be fulfilled and that the rest also reap the fruit of the common toils." [3] After having said this, he went over the details of the measure, and he praised them all, so that the crowd was mightily pleased. Seeing this, Caesar [C. Iulius Caesar (**121**)] therefore asked him if he would willingly assist him against those who were working in opposition, and he also urged the populace to join in asking him for aid for this purpose. [4] When this had happened, Pompey felt elated over the fact that both the consul [Caesar, 59 BC] and the multitude desired his help, although he was holding no position of command, and so, with an added opinion of his own worth and assuming much dignity, he spoke at some length, and he said at the end: "If anyone dares to raise a sword, I also will snatch up my shield." [5] Crassus [M. Licinius Crassus Dives (**102**)] too approved of what was thus said by Pompey.

On Behalf of T. Annius Milo (F 21–22A)

F 21 Asc. in Cic. *Mil.* (p. 43 KS = 48.23–27 C.)

. . . Pompeius tamen cum defenderet Milonem apud populum, de vi accusante Clodio, obiecit ei, ut[1] legimus apud
Tironem libertum Ciceronis in libro IIII de vita eius, oppressum {Clodio}[2] L. Caecilium praetorem.

    [1] ei ut *Clark*: et ut *codd.*: ut *Baiter*   [2] *del. Clark*: Clodio
codd.: a Clodio *Lodoicus*

F 22 Cic. *Q Fr.* 2.3.1–2

a. d. IIII Non. Febr. Milo adfuit. ei Pompeius advocatus
venit. dixit M. Marcellus a me rogatus. honeste discessimus. prodicta[1] dies est in VII Id. Febr. . . . [2] a. d. VII[2]
Id. Febr. Milo adfuit. dixit Pompeius sive voluit. nam ut
surrexit, operae Clodianae clamorem sustulerunt, idque ei
perpetua oratione contigit, non modo ut acclamatione sed
ut convicio et maledictis impediretur. qui ut peroravit
(nam in eo sane fortis fuit, non est deterritus, dixit omnia

    [1] prodicta *Drakenborch*: producta *codd.*   [2] VII *vel* IIII
codd.: VIII *Manutius*

On Behalf of T. Annius Milo (F 21–22A)

In 56 BC Pompey spoke on behalf of T. Annius Milo (138),
who was prosecuted by P. Clodius Pulcher (137 F 6–7),
amid disruptions steered by Clodius (TLRR 266; Cic. Mil.
40; Cass. Dio 39.18–19).

F 21 Asconius on Cicero, *Pro Milone*

. . . yet Pompey, while he defended Milo [T. Annius Milo
(**138**)] before the People, upon Clodius' [P. Clodius Pulcher (**137**), F 6–7] prosecution for violence, charged him
[Clodius] with having harassed L. Caecilius, the praetor
[L. Caecilius Rufus, praet. 57 BC] {for Clodius}, as we
read in Tiro, Cicero's freedman, in Book Four on the latter's life [*FRHist* 46 F 1].

F 22 Cicero, *Letters to Quintus*

On the fourth day before the Nones of February [Febru-
ary 2, 56 BC] Milo [T. Annius Milo (**138**)] appeared. Pompey came as a supporting counselor for him. M. Marcellus
[M. Claudius Marcellus (**155**)] spoke, asked by me. We
came off honorably. The case was adjourned to the seventh day before the Ides of February [February 7]. . . . [2]
On the seventh day before the Ides of February Milo appeared. Pompey spoke or rather tried to speak. For, as
soon as he got to his feet, Clodius' [P. Clodius Pulcher
(**137**)] gang raised a clamor, and it happened throughout
the entire speech that he was interrupted, not merely by
shouting, but by booing and abuse. When he came to the
end (for in that matter he was indeed courageous; he was
not put off; he said everything and sometimes even amid

atque interdum etiam silentio, cum auctoritate pervicerat[3])—sed ut peroravit, surrexit Clodius. ei tantus clamor
a nostris (placuerat enim referre gratiam) ut neque mente
nec lingua neque ore consisteret.

[3] pervicerat *Watt*: pergerat *codd*.: perfregerat *Gulielmius*

F 22A Cic. *Fam.* 1.5b.1 [ad P. Cornelium Lentulum Spin-
therem]

postea quam Pompeius et apud populum a. d. VII[1] Id.
Febr., cum pro Milone diceret, clamore convicioque
iact‹at›us[2] est in senatuque a Catone aspere et acerbe
‹i›nimi‹cor›um[3] magno silentio est accusatus, visus est
mihi vehementer esse perturbatus.

[1] a. d. VII *Sjögren*: at octavo *vel* ab octavo *vel* ad VIIII *vel* a.d.
VIII *codd*.   [2] iact‹at›us *codd. det*.: iactus *codd*.   [3] ‹i›n-
imi‹cor›um *Weinhold*: nimium *codd*.: omnium *Manutius*

In the Senate (F 23)

F 23 Cic. *Q Fr.* 2.3.3

a. d. VI[1] Id. Febr. senatus ad Apollinis fuit, ut Pompeius
adesset. acta res est graviter a Pompeio. eo die nihil perfectum est.

[1] VI *vel* III *codd*.: VII *Manutius*

silence, when he had won the upper hand by his personal authority)—but when he came to the end, Clodius rose: he received such a clamor from our side (for it had been decided to repay the compliment) that he lost command of thoughts, tongue, and countenance.

F 22A Cicero, *Letters to Friends* [to P. Cornelius Lentulus Spinther]

After Pompey had been harassed with noise and abuse among the People on the seventh day before the Ides of February [February 7, 56 BC], when he was speaking for Milo [T. Annius Milo (**138**)], and had been attacked by Cato [C. Porcius Cato (**136**), F 3A] bitterly and vehemently in the Senate amid portentous silence of his enemies, he appeared to me much shaken.

In the Senate (F 23)

F 23 Cicero, *Letters to Quintus*

On the sixth day before the Ides of February [February 8, 56 BC] the Senate met in the Temple of Apollo, so that Pompey could be present.[1] The matter was handled impressively by Pompey. On that day nothing was concluded.

[1] Since Pompey was still holding *imperium*, he was not permitted to cross the ancient city boundary (*pomerium*) and could not have attended a meeting in a venue within this area (cf. F 29).

About Himself in the Senate (F 24)

F 24 Cic. *Q Fr.* 2.3.3

a. d. V[1] Id. Febr. senatus ad Apollinis. . . . eo die Cato
vehementer est in Pompeium invectus et eum oratione
perpetua tamquam reum accusavit . . . respondit ei vehementer Pompeius Crassumque descripsit dixitque aperte
se munitiorem ad custodiendam vitam suam fore quam
Africanus fuisset, quem C. Carbo[2] interemisset.

---

[1] V *Tunstall*: VI *vel* III *codd.*   [2] carbo *unus cod. corr.*:
cato *codd.*

On Behalf of L. Cornelius Balbus (F 25)

*In 56 BC, along with M. Licinius Crassus Dives (**102**
F 14–15) and Cicero (Cic. Balb.), Pompey successfully
defended L. Cornelius Balbus Gaditanus, prosecuted in*

F 25 Cic. *Balb.* 2–5, 17, 19, 59

quae fuerit hesterno die Cn. Pompei gravitas in dicendo,
iudices, quae facultas, quae copia, non opinione tacita ves-
trorum animorum, sed perspicua admiratione declarari
videbatur. nihil enim umquam audivi quod mihi de iure
subtilius dici videretur, nihil {de}[1] memoria maiore de
exemplis, nihil peritius de foederibus, nihil inlustriore
auctoritate de bellis, nihil de re publica gravius, nihil de
ipso modestius, nihil de causa et crimine ornatius: [3] ut

---

[1] *del. Garatoni*

About Himself in the Senate (F 24)

F 24 Cicero, *Letters to Quintus*

On the fifth day before the Ides of February [February 9, 56 BC] Senate in Temple of Apollo. . . . That day Cato [C. Porcius Cato (**136**), F 3] inveighed against Pompey with great force and prosecuted him in a set speech like a defendant . . . Pompey replied energetically to him, alluded to Crassus [M. Licinius Crassus Dives (**102**)], and said plainly that he would be better guarded as regards protecting his life than Africanus [P. Cornelius Scipio Aemilianus Africanus minor (**21**)] had been, whom C. Carbo [C. Papirius Carbo (**35**)] had murdered.

On Behalf of L. Cornelius Balbus (F 25)

relation to his having been granted Roman citizenship. As the final speaker, Cicero picks up on what he claims Pompey said (TLRR 276).

F 25 Cicero, *Pro Balbo*

What weightiness was there yesterday in Pompey's speech, judges, what eloquence, what copiousness was clearly manifested, not by the tacit approval of your minds, but by evident admiration. For I have never heard anything said that seemed to me more subtle concerning the law, nothing with a fuller recollection of precedents, nothing more learned in regard to treaties, nothing more brilliant and authoritative concerning warfare, nothing more weighty concerning public affairs, nothing more modest as to the speaker himself, nothing more elaborate about the case

mihi iam verum videatur illud esse quod non nulli litteris
ac studiis doctrinae dediti quasi quiddam incredibile dicere putabantur, ei qui omnis animo virtutes penitus com-
prehendisset omnia quae faceret recte procedere.[2] quae
enim in L. Crasso potuit, homine nato ad dicendi singularem quandam facultatem, si hanc causam ageret, maior
esse ubertas, varietas, copia quam fuit in eo qui tantum
potuit impertire huic studio temporis quantum ipse a pue-
ritia usque ad hanc aetatem a continuis bellis et victoriis
conquievit? [4] quo mihi difficilior est hic extremus perorandi locus. etenim ei succedo orationi quae non prae-
tervecta sit aures vestras, sed in animis omnium penitus
insederit, ut plus voluptatis ex recordatione illius orationis
quam non modo ex mea, sed ex cuiusquam oratione capere possitis. sed mos est gerundus non modo Cornelio,
cuius ego voluntati in eius periculis nullo modo deesse
possum, sed etiam Cn. Pompeio, qui sui facti, sui iudici,
sui benefici voluit me esse, ut apud eosdem vos, iudices,
nuper in alia causa fuerim, et praedicatorem et actorem.
[5] ac mihi quidem hoc dignum re publica videtur, hoc
deberi huius excellentis viri praestantissimae gloriae, hoc
proprium esse vestri offici, hoc satis esse causae ut, quod
fecisse Cn. Pompeium constet, id omnes ei licuisse conce-
dant. nam verius nihil est quam quod hesterno die dixit
ipse, ita L. Cornelium de fortunis omnibus dimicare ut
nullius in delicti crimen vocaretur. . . . [17] . . . de lege, de

<hr />

[2] recte (praeclare?) procedere *Peterson*: tractare *codd.*: procedere *Müller*: recte se dare *Madvig*: recte cadere *Reid*: recte
habere *Paul*

and the charge: [3] so that it now appears to be true to me, the saying that some of those devoted to literature and the study of philosophy [Stoics] were believed to put forward as something almost incredible [*paradoxon*], that for a man who has a grasp of all the virtues deep in his soul, everything that he does turns out well. For could even L. Crassus [L. Licinius Crassus (**66**)], a man born for a certain outstanding quality as an orator, if he were pleading this case, have shown greater richness, variety, and copiousness than was shown by him who has only been able to devote to this study just so much time as he could rest from the continuous wars and victories from his boyhood to the present time? [4] Therefore, this last position of making the final speech is more difficult for me. For I come after such a speech that has not passed over your ears, but has sunk deeply into the minds of all, so that from the recollection of that speech you can derive more pleasure not only than from my own, but than from anyone's speech. But I must accommodate the wishes not only of Cornelius, whose will in his troubled situation I can in no way fail to comply with, but also those of Pompey, who wanted me, as I recently did in another case [reference unclear], also before you, judges, to eulogize and defend his action, his judgment, and his rendering of service. [5] And in my view at least this is worthy of the Republic, this is owed to the outstanding renown of this eminent man, this is a true part of your duty, and this is a sufficient plea, that what is known to have been done by Pompey should be admitted by all to have been lawfully done. For nothing is truer than what he himself said yesterday, that L. Cornelius was fighting for his very existence in such a situation that he was not charged with any offense. . . . [17] . . . As for the law,

foedere, de exemplis, de perpetua consuetudine civitatis nostrae renovabo ea quae dicta sunt; nihil enim mihi novi, nihil integri neque M. Crassus, qui totam causam et pro facultate et pro fide sua diligentissime vobis explicavit, neque Cn. Pompeius, cuius oratio omnibus ornamentis abundavit, ad dicendum reliquit.... [19] ... donatum esse L. Cornelium praesens Pompeius dicit, indicant publicae tabulae.... [59] ... non igitur a suis, quos nullos habet, sed a suorum, qui et multi et potentes sunt, urgetur inimicis; quos quidem hesterno die Cn. Pompeius copiosa oratione et gravi secum, si vellent, contendere iubebat, ab hoc impari certamine atque iniusta contentione avocabat.

On Behalf of L. Scribonius Libo Against
Helvius Mancia (F 26)

F 26 Val. Max. 6.2.8
= **71** F 1.

the treaty, the precedents, the unchanging custom of our community, I will reiterate what has been said. For nothing new, nothing fresh has been left for me to say, either by Crassus [M. Licinius Crassus Dives (**102**), F 14], who has set forth to you the whole case in great detail in line with his ability and his sincerity, or by Pompey, whose speech showed all ornaments of eloquence in abundance. . . . [19] . . . That L. Cornelius was endowed with it [Roman citizenship], Pompey, being present here, states, public records attest. . . . [59] . . . Therefore he [Balbus] is not attacked by his own enemies, of whom he has none, but by the enemies of his friends, who are both many and powerful; whom, in fact, Pompey yesterday, in his eloquent and weighty speech, asked to fight with himself, if they wished, and whom he endeavored to draw away from this unequal contest and unjust struggle.

On Behalf of L. Scribonius Libo Against Helvius Mancia (F 26)

*Pompey supported L. Scribonius Libo (cos. 34 BC), accused by Helvius Mancia (**71** F 1) before the censors (probably at the census of 55–54 BC).*

F 26 Valerius Maximus, *Memorable Doings and Sayings* = **71** F 1.

On Behalf of T. Ampius Balbus (F 27)

F 27 Cic. *Leg.* 2.6

ATTICUS: recte igitur Magnus ille noster, me audiente, posuit in iudicio, quom pro Ampio[1] tecum simul diceret, rempublicam nostram iustissimas huic municipio gratias agere posse, quod ex eo duo sui conservatores exstitissent . . .

1 Ampio *quidam ap. Turnebum 1557*: ambio (-u) *codd.*: Balbo *Paul. Man. ex cod.*

On T. Annius Milo to the People (F 28)

F 28 Asc. in Cic. *Mil.* 67 (p. 45 KS = 51.8–24 C.)

prius etiam quam Pompeius ter consul crearetur, tres tribuni, Q. Pompeius Rufus, C. Sallustius Crispus, T. Munatius Plancus, cum cotidianis contionibus suis magnam invidiam Miloni propter occisum Clodium excitarent, produxerant ad populum Cn. Pompeium et ab eo quaesierant num ad eum delatum esset illius quoque ⟨rei⟩[1] indicium, suae vitae insidiari Milonem. responderat Pompeius: Licinium quendam de plebe sacrificulum,[2] qui solitus esset

1 *add. Mommsen*   2 sacrificulum *Manutius*: sacrificorum *codd.*

On Behalf of T. Ampius Balbus (F 27)

Pompey spoke on behalf of T. Ampius Balbus along with Cicero (Cic. Pro T. Ampio Balbo: *Crawford 1984, 175–77; TLRR 281).*

F 27 Cicero, *On the Laws*

ATTICUS: Indeed, then, our famous friend Magnus [Pompey] rightly stated in court, in my hearing, when he spoke on behalf of Ampius in company with you [Cicero], that our Republic could pay the most justified thanks to this municipality [Arpinum], because two of her saviors [Marius and Cicero] had come from it . . .

On T. Annius Milo to the People (F 28)

F 28 Asconius on Cicero, *Pro Milone*

Even before Pompey was elected consul three times [consul for the third time in 52 BC], when three Tribunes [of 52 BC], Q. Pompeius Rufus, C. Sallustius Crispus [**152**], and T. Munatius Plancus [**150** F 5], with their daily speeches to the People, aroused great resentment against Milo [T. Annius Milo (**138**)] because of the killing of Clodius [P. Clodius Pulcher (**137**)], they had produced Pompey before the People and asked him whether evidence about that ‹matter› too had been reported to him, namely that Milo was plotting against his life. Pompey had answered: that a certain Licinius, a sacrificial priest from the commons, who was accustomed to cleanse households,

familias purgare, ad se detulisse servos quosdam Milonis itemque libertos comparatos esse ad caedem suam, nomina quoque servorum edidisse; ⟨se⟩[3] ad Milonem misisse utrum[4] in potestate sua haberet; a Milone responsum esse, ex iis servis quos nominasset partim neminem se umquam habuisse, partim manumisisse; dein, cum Licinium apud se haberet . . . Lucium quendam de plebe ad corrumpendum indicem venisse; qua re cognita in vincla eum publica esse coniectum.

[3] *add. Baiter*   [4] utrum *Clark*: ut eum *codd.*: ut eos *Beraldus*

On the Political Situation in the Senate (F 29)

F 29 Caes. *BCiv.* 1.6.1–2

proximis diebus habetur extra urbem senatus. Pompeius eadem illa quae per Scipionem ostenderat agit; senatus virtutem constantiamque collaudat; copias suas exponit; legiones habere sese paratas X; [2] praeterea cognitum compertumque sibi alieno esse animo in Caesarem milites neque eis posse persuaderi uti eum defendant aut sequantur saltem.

had reported to him that some slaves of Milo and likewise freedmen had been set up for his murder, he had also revealed the names of the slaves; <he> [Pompey] had sent to Milo [to ask] whether he had them in his power; by Milo the answer had been given that out of those slaves that he had named some he had never owned, some he had manumitted; then, while he had Licinius with him . . . [apparently gap in the text] One Lucius from the commons had come to bribe the informer; when this matter had been discovered, he had been taken into custody on behalf of the state.

On the Political Situation in the Senate (F 29)

F 29 Caesar, *Civil War*

On the following days [in early January 49 BC] the Senate was held outside the city.[1] Pompey made the same points that he had indicated through Scipio [Q. Caecilius Metellus Pius Scipio Nasica (**154**), F 3]: he praised the Senate's courage and firmness; he set forth an account of his troops: he had ten legions ready; [2] furthermore, [he said] that he had established on good evidence that the soldiers were estranged from Caesar [C. Iulius Caesar (**121**)] and could not be persuaded to defend or even follow him.

[1] To enable Pompey, who was still holding *imperium*, to attend (see F 23 n.).

On Behalf of Manilius Crispus (F 29A)

F 29A Val. Max. 6.2.4

Cn. Piso, cum Manilium Crispum reum ageret eumque evidenter nocentem gratia Pompeii eripi videret, iuvenili impetu ac studio accusationis provectus multa et gravia crimina praepotenti defensori obiecit. interrogatus deinde ab eo cur non se quoque accusaret, "da" inquit "praedes rei publicae te, si postulatus fueris, civile bellum non excitaturum, et iam de tuo prius quam de Manili capite in consilium iudices mittam." ita eodem iudicio duos sustinuit reos, accusatione Manilium libertate Pompeium, et eorum alterum lege peregit alterum professione, qua solum poterat.

Unplaced Fragment (F 30)

F 30 Victorin. *GL* VI, p. 8.14–15

Gn. Pompeius Magnus et scribebat et dicebat kadamitatem pro calamitate.[1]

[1] pro c/kalamitate *vel* pro kalamitatem *codd.*: pro kalamitatem *edd. vet.*

On Behalf of Manilius Crispus (F 29A)

Pompey seems to have intervened on behalf of Manilius Crispus, prosecuted by Cn. Calpurnius Piso, promagistrate in Spain in 65–64 BC (TLRR 188).

F 29A Valerius Maximus, *Memorable Doings and Sayings*

When Cn. Piso [Cn. Calpurnius Piso] was prosecuting Manilius Crispus and saw that he, though evidently guilty, was being snatched away by Pompey's influence, he [Piso], carried away by youthful impetuosity and accusatory zeal, put forward many grave charges against the overpowerful defender. Then asked by him [Pompey] why he did not prosecute him [Pompey] as well, he said: "Give sureties to the Republic that, if you have been challenged, you will not start a civil war, and I will now send judges to consider a capital indictment against you ahead of that against Manilius." So, in the same trial, he coped with two defendants, Manilius by prosecution, Pompey by unfettered speech; and the former of these he dealt with by law, the latter by declaration, the only way in which he could do so.

Unplaced Fragment (F 30)

F 30 Marius Victorinus

Cn. Pompeius Magnus generally wrote and said *kadamitas* instead of *calamitas* ["calamity"].

112 L. SERGIUS CATILINA

L. Sergius Catilina (praet. 68 BC; RE Sergius 23) twice stood for election to the consulship unsuccessfully; he raised the so-called Catilinarian Conspiracy in 63 BC (Sall. Cat.; Cic. Cat.) and fell fighting in Etruria in early 62 BC (on his life see, e.g., Levick 2015).

T 1 Sall. *Cat.* 5.4

animus audax, subdolus, varius, quoius rei lubet simulator ac dissimulator, alieni adpetens sui profusus, ardens in cupiditatibus; satis eloquentiae, sapientiae parum.

Against M. Tullius Cicero (F 2–4)

F 2 Asc. in Cic. *Tog. cand.* (pp. 84 KS = 93.24–94.3 C.)

huic orationi Ciceronis et Catilina et Antonius contumeliose responderunt,[1] quod solum poterant invecti in novitatem eius. feruntur quoque orationes nomine illorum editae, non ab ipsis scriptae sed ab Ciceronis obtrectatoribus: quas nescio an satius sit ignorare.

[1] responderunt *Manutius*: responderant *codd.*

112 L. SERGIUS CATILINA

Sallust describes Catiline as reasonably eloquent (T 1).
Catiline was prosecuted on various occasions (TLRR 212,
217, 222, 223, 379).

T 1 Sallust, *The War with Catiline*

His mind was reckless, cunning, adaptable, capable of any
form of pretense or concealment; covetous of others' possessions, prodigal of his own; intense in his passions; with
adequate eloquence, too little soundness of judgment.

Against M. Tullius Cicero (F 2–4)

In 64 BC, before and after the elections to the consulship
of 63 BC, for which they were both candidates, Catiline
delivered orations against Cicero.

F 2 Asconius on Cicero, *In Toga Candida*

To this speech of Cicero [*In toga candida*] both Catiline
and Antonius [C. Antonius Hybrida (**113**), F 1A] replied
in a manner full of abuse, which was the only thing they
were able to do, attacking his status as a newcomer. There
are in circulation also speeches published in their name,
not written by the men themselves, but by detractors of
Cicero: perhaps it would be better to ignore these.

341

FRL IV: ORATORY, PART 2

F 3 Schol. Bob. ad Cic. *Sull.* 22 (p. 80.13–16 Stangl)

novitatem Ciceronis multi quidem per illa tempora contu-
meliis agitare voluerunt, ut Catilina et Clodius et ipse,
quamvis collega fuerit, C. Antonius: ⟨cuius⟩[1] virtutibus
obtrectare non poterant, eius humilitatem natalium male-
dica insectatione carpebant.

[1] ⟨cuius⟩ *ed. Turicensis 1833:* ⟨nam quia⟩ *ed. Romana 1828*

F 4 App. *B Civ.* 2.2.5

πάγχυ δ᾽ ἐλπίσας αἱρεθήσεσθαι διὰ τὴν ὑποψίαν
τήνδε ἀπεκρούσθη, καὶ Κικέρων μὲν ἦρχεν ἀντ᾽ αὐτοῦ, ἀνὴρ ἥδιστος εἰπεῖν τε καὶ ῥητορεῦσαι, Κατιλίνας δ᾽ αὐτὸν ἐς ὕβριν τῶν ἑλομένων ἐπέσκωπτεν, ἐς
μὲν ἀγνωσίαν γένους καινὸν ὀνομάζων (καλοῦσι δ᾽
οὕτω τοὺς ἀφ᾽ ἑαυτῶν, ἀλλ᾽ οὐ τῶν προγόνων γνωρί-
μους), ἐς δὲ ξενίαν τῆς πόλεως ἰγκουΐλινον, ᾧ ῥήματι
καλοῦσι τοὺς ἐνοικοῦντας ἐν ἀλλοτρίαις οἰκίαις.

To His Followers in His House (F 5–5A)

F 5 Cic. *Mur.* 50–51

meministis enim, cum illius nefarii gladiatoris voces per-
crebruissent quas habuisse in contione domestica diceba-

F 3 Scholia Bobiensia to Cicero, *Pro Sulla*

At that time many indeed wished to attack Cicero's status as a newcomer with insults, such as Catiline and Clodius [P. Clodius Pulcher (**137**)] and even C. Antonius [C. Antonius Hybrida (**113**), F 1B], although he was his colleague [as consul in 63 BC]: as they were unable to disparage ⟨his⟩ abilities, they slandered the humility of his birth with foul-mouthed calumny.

F 4 Appian, *Civil Wars*

Though he [Catiline] confidently expected to be elected, he was driven off because of this suspicion [that he was aiming at absolute power], and Cicero, the most pleasing man in making speeches and public orations, won instead of him. And Catiline insultingly mocked those who voted for him [Cicero], calling him a "new man" on account of his obscure birth (so they call those who achieve distinction by their own merits, and not by those of their ancestors), and because he was not born in the city, "lodger," by which term they designate those living in houses belonging to others.

To His Followers in His House (F 5–5A)

Catiline's encouraging speech to his followers, given in his house before the consular elections in 63 BC, was known in Rome (F 5); a version of this speech is put into Catiline's mouth in Sallust's historiographical work (F 5A).

F 5 Cicero, *Pro Murena*

For you remember how the words of that evil cut-throat [Catiline] that he was said to have delivered in a meeting

tur, cum miserorum fidelem defensorem negasset inveniri
posse nisi eum qui ipse miser esset; integrorum et fortu-
natorum promissis saucios et miseros credere non oportere; qua re qui consumpta replere, erepta reciperare
vellent, spectarent quid ipse deberet, quid possideret,
quid auderet; minime timidum et valde calamitosum esse
oportere eum qui esset futurus dux et signifer calamitoso-
rum. [51] tum igitur, his rebus auditis, meministis fieri
senatus consultum referente me ne postero die comitia
haberentur, ut de his rebus in senatu agere possemus.

F 5A Sall. *Cat.* 20–21

*Catiline regards it as advantageous to encourage all his
followers together with a speech: he begins by praising
their courage and loyalty, which have given him the confidence to think of a great and glorious enterprise, which
they have heard about individually before. He goes on to
claim that all influence, power, office, and wealth in the
Republic are in the hands of a few, while the majority of
people have a subservient position and live in poor circumstances. Catiline appeals to the men not to put up with that*

in his house became widely known: when he had denied that a trustworthy protector of the poor could be found other than him, who was poor himself; [he said] that broken and poor men should not trust the promises of the prosperous and successful; therefore, those who wished to replace what they had spent and to recover what had been taken from them should consider what he himself owed, what he possessed, what he dared; the man who was to be the leader and the standard-bearer of ruined men ought to be himself the least timid and the most completely ruined. [51] Then, you recall that, therefore, on receipt of this news, a decree of the Senate was made on my initiative that voting assemblies would not be held on the following day, so that we could debate these matters in the Senate. [continued by F 6]

F 5A Sallust, *The War with Catiline*

any longer; he insinuates that they are likely to win since they are strong and determined; they will win freedom as well as riches, honor, and glory. Catiline announces that he is ready to serve them in this enterprise. When asked to do so, Catiline promises the cancellation of debts, proscriptions of the wealthy, public offices, priesthoods, and plunder, and he outlines the favorable situation for taking action. Catiline finishes by urging the men to make his candidacy their concern.

About Himself and the Republic in the
Senate (F 6)

F 6 Cic. *Mur.* 51

itaque postridie frequenti senatu Catilinam excitavi atque
eum de his rebus iussi, si quid vellet, quae ad me adlatae
essent dicere. atque ille, ut semper fuit apertissimus, non
se purgavit sed indicavit atque induit. tum enim dixit duo
corpora esse rei publicae, unum debile infirmo capite,
alterum firmum sine capite; huic, si ita de se meritum esset, caput se vivo non defuturum. congemuit senatus fre-
quens neque tamen satis severe pro rei indignitate decre-
vit; nam partim ideo fortes in decernendo non erant, quia
nihil timebant, partim, quia omnia.[1] erupit e senatu trium-
phans gaudio quem omnino vivum illinc exire non opor-
tuerat, praesertim cum idem ille in eodem ordine paucis
diebus ante Catoni, fortissimo viro, iudicium minitanti ac
denuntianti respondisset, si quod esset in suas fortunas
incendium excitatum, id se non aqua sed ruina restinctu-
rum.

[1] omnia *Clark*: timebant *codd.*: timebant nimium *Müller*

Cf. Plut. *Cic.* 14.6.

About Himself and the Republic in the
Senate (F 6)

When challenged about his behavior in advance of the
elections in 63 BC, Catiline defiantly defended his actions
in the Senate.

F 6 Cicero, *Pro Murena*

[continued from F 5] On the following day, then, in a well-
attended Senate, I called upon Catiline to rise and asked
him, if he wished, to speak about those matters that had
been reported to me. And he, absolutely frank as he always
was, did not justify himself, but rather incriminated and
entangled himself. For he then said that there were two
bodies of the Republic [i.e., Senate and People], one frail
with a weak head, the other strong but without a head; and
the latter, if it behaved accordingly toward him, would not
lack a head while he was alive. The well-attended Senate
groaned, but still did not pass a decree sufficiently severe
in relation to the vileness of the matter; for some senators
were not firm in passing decrees for the reason that they
did not fear anything, others because [they feared] everything. He [Catiline] dashed from the Senate triumphant
with delight although he should not have left from there
alive at all, especially because in this same Senate, a few
days previously, he had replied to Cato [M. Porcius Cato
(**126**)], a very courageous man, who was threatening and
announcing to bring him to court, that, if any fire was set
to his property, he would put it out not with water, but
by destroying everything [cf. F 9; Val. Max. 9.11.3; Flor.
2.12.7].

To His Followers in Laeca's House (F 7–8)

F 7 Cic. *Cat.* 1.9

fuisti igitur apud Laecam illa nocte, Catilina, distribuisti partis Italiae, statuisti quo quemque proficisci placeret, delegisti quos Romae relinqueres, quos tecum educeres, discripsisti urbis partis ad incendia, confirmasti te ipsum iam esse exiturum, dixisti paulum tibi esse etiam nunc morae, quod ego viverem.

Cf. Cic. *Sull.* 52.

F 8 Sall. *Cat.* 27.3–4

postremo, ubi multa agitanti nihil procedit, rursus intempesta nocte coniurationis principes convocat per M. Porcium Laecam, [4] ibique multa de ignavia eorum questus docet se Manlium praemisisse ad eam multitudinem quam ad capiunda arma paraverat, item alios in alia loca opportuna qui initium belli facerent, seque ad exercitum proficisci cupere, si prius Ciceronem oppressisset: eum suis consiliis multum officere.

To His Followers in Laeca's House (F 7–8)

In preparing the conspiracy, Catiline delivered a speech to his followers in the house of his supporter M. Porcius Laeca in November 63 BC.

F 7 Cicero, *Against Catiline*

You were, then, at the house of Laeca [M. Porcius Laeca] on that night [November 6–7, 63 BC], Catiline, you allocated the regions of Italy, you decided where you wanted each man to go, you chose those whom you were leaving at Rome and those whom you were taking with you, you assigned the parts of the city to be burned, you confirmed that you were on the point of departure yourself, you said that even now there was a little delay for you because I was alive.

F 8 Sallust, *The War with Catiline*

Finally, when his many efforts came to naught, with the help of M. Porcius Laeca he summoned the leaders of the conspiracy again in the dead of night, [4] and there, after having made many complaints about their lethargy, he informed them that he had sent Manlius [C. Manlius, follower of Catiline] on ahead [to Etruria] to the large throng that he had prepared for taking up arms, that likewise he had sent to other suitable places other men who were to start the fighting, and that he himself was eager to set out for the army if only he had first crushed Cicero; that man was a major obstacle to his plans.

About Himself Against Cicero in the Senate (F 9)

F 9 Sall. *Cat.* 31.5–9

postremo dissimulandi causa aut sui expurgandi, sicut iurgio lacessitus foret, in senatum venit. [6] tum M. Tullius
consul, sive praesentiam eius timens sive ira conmotus,
orationem habuit luculentam atque utilem rei publicae,
quam postea scriptam edidit. [7] sed ubi ille adsedit, Catilina, ut erat paratus ad dissimulanda omnia, demisso voltu,
voce supplici postulare a patribus coepit ne quid de se
temere crederent: ea familia ortum, ita se ab adulescentia
vitam instituisse ut omnia bona in spe haberet; ne existu-
marent sibi, patricio homini, quoius ipsius atque maiorum
pluruma beneficia in plebem Romanam essent, perdita re
publica opus esse, quom eam servaret M. Tullius, inquili-
nus civis urbis Romae. [8] ad hoc maledicta alia quom
adderet, obstrepere omnes, hostem atque parricidam vo-
care. [9] tum ille furibundus "quoniam quidem circumventus" inquit "ab inimicis praeceps agor, incendium
meum ruina restinguam."

About Himself Against Cicero in the Senate (F 9)

A little later in November 63 BC, Catiline gave a speech in the Senate in response to Cicero's First Catilinarian Oration. *The contents of Catiline's speech can be inferred from the summary given by Sallust.*

F 9 Sallust, *The War with Catiline*

Finally, in order to conceal his designs or to clear himself, as though he had been provoked by abuse, he came into the Senate. [6] Then M. Tullius [Cicero], the consul [63 BC], whether fearing his presence or roused by indignation, delivered a speech brilliant and of great service to the Republic, which he later circulated in written form [Cic. *Cat.* 1]. [7] But as soon as he [Cicero] took his seat, Catiline, prepared as he was to conceal everything, with downcast face and suppliant voice, began to beg the senators not to believe rashly anything concerning him: he was sprung from such a family, had so ordered his life from youth up that he had all the best prospects; they should not suppose that he, a patrician, from whom and from whose forefathers there were a great many good services to the commons of Rome, had any need for the overthrow of the Republic, while its savior was M. Tullius, a resident alien in the city of Rome. [8] When he tried to add other insults on top of this, everyone raised an uproar, called him traitor and assassin. [9] Then in a rage he said: "Since I have been cornered and am being driven to desperation by my enemies, I shall put out the fire besetting me with demolition [cf. F 6]."

113 C. ANTONIUS HYBRIDA

*C. Antonius Hybrida (cos. 63 BC; RE Antonius 19), a son
of the orator M. Antonius (65) and an uncle of the trium-
vir M. Antonius (159), was consul with Cicero in 63 BC,
although he originally ran an election campaign with L.
Sergius Catilina (112). Therefore, Cicero attacked both
Antonius and Catiline in his speech* In toga candida *in 64
BC (Crawford 1994, 159–99); during the election campaign, Antonius voiced criticism of Cicero (F 1A–C), along
with L. Sergius Catilina (112 F 2–3). After the elections,
by offering Antonius Macedonia as his consular province,
Cicero managed to obtain his support in fighting the Catilinarian Conspiracy; Antonius, however, did not assume
an active role and let his legate M. Petreius command the
army in the decisive battles in Etruria.*

Against M. Tullius Cicero (F 1A–C)

F 1A Asc. in Cic. *Tog. cand.* (pp. 84 KS = 93.24–94.3 C.)
= **112** F 2.

F 1B Schol. Bob. ad Cic. *Sull.* 22 (p. 80.13–16 Stangl)
= **112** F 3.

F 1C Quint. *Inst.* 9.3.93–95

nam de illo dubitari possit, an schema sit in distributis
subiecta ratio, quod apud eundem primo loco positum est:
[94] προσαπόδοσιν dicit, quae, ut maxime, servetur sane

113 C. ANTONIUS HYBRIDA

*In 76 BC Antonius had been taken to court for extortion by some Greeks and was supported by C. Iulius Caesar (**121** F 24–25) when he called on the Tribunes for assistance to have his conviction overturned (TLRR 141). In 70 BC Antonius had been expelled from the Senate by the censors (**121** F 24); later, he was reinstated. In 59 BC Antonius was prosecuted by M. Caelius Rufus (**162** F 13– 18), presumably for treason and extortion (though the sources are unclear), and was unsuccessfully defended by Cicero (Cic. Pro C. Antonio collega: Crawford 1984, 124– 31) (TLRR 241). Thereupon, Antonius went into exile, but he was called back by C. Iulius Caesar (**121**) and became censor in 42 BC.*

Against M. Tullius Cicero (F 1A–C)

F 1A Asconius on Cicero, *In Toga Candida*

= **112** F 2.

F 1B Scholia Bobiensia to Cicero, *Pro Sulla*

= **112** F 3.

F 1C Quintilian, *The Orator's Education*

Moreover, one could even have doubts about that, namely whether "reason assigned to each point separately," which in his work [Rutilius Lupus 1.1, *RLM*, pp. 3–4] is put in first place, is a figure:[1] [94] he calls it "prosapodosis"; it

---

[1] See Lausberg 1998, §§861–66.

in pluribus propositis, cum[1] aut singulis statim ratio subiciatur, ut est apud Gaium Antonium: "sed neque accusatorem eum metuo, quod sum innocens, neque competitorem vereor, quod sum Antonius, neque consulem spero, quod est Cicero": [95] aut . . .

---

[1] cum *Winterbottom*: quia *cod.*: quibus *Radermacher*

114 P. CANNUTIUS

T 1 Cic. *Brut.* 205
= **76** T 10.

T 2 Cic. *Clu.* 29, 50, 73 (cf. F 5, 6, 8)

. . . a P. Cannutio, homine eloquentissimo . . . [50] . . . P. Cannutius, homo in primis ingeniosus et in dicendo exercitatus . . . [73] . . . Cannutio, perito homini . . .

could be kept up certainly in a number of propositions, when either the reason is given immediately for each one, as in Gaius Antonius' [remark]: "But neither do I dread him as an accuser, because I am innocent, nor do I fear him as a rival candidate, because I am Antonius, nor do I expect to see him consul, because he is Cicero";[2] [95] or . . .

---

[2] Because of its contents, this remark must be connected with the election campaign in 64 BC. Malcovati doubts its authenticity and considers that it might come from one of the spurious speeches written by detractors of Cicero (cf. F 1A).

114 P. CANNUTIUS

P. Cannutius (RE *Cannutius* 2) *is described in Cicero as his contemporary and the best orator of those not of senatorial rank (T 1–2).*

T 1 Cicero, *Brutus*

= **76** T 10.

T 2 Cicero, *Pro Cluentio* (cf. F 5, 6, 8)

. . . P. Cannutius, a most eloquent man . . . [50] . . . P. Cannutius, a man particularly gifted and proficient in speaking . . . [73] . . . Cannutius, an experienced man . . .

T 3 Tac. *Dial.* 21.1

[APER:] nec unum de populo, Canuti‹um ›[1] aut Atti‹um,[2] dico, ne quid loquar›[3] de Furnio et Toranio[4] quosque alios in eodem valetudinario haec ossa et haec macies[5] probant . . .

1 Canuti‹um› *Gronovius*: canuti *vel* ganuti *codd.*
2 Atti‹um› *Michaelis*: atti *codd.*: Arrium *Gronovius*
3 ‹dico, ne quid loquar› *suppl. John*: alii alia
4 toranio *vel* coranio *codd.*
5 quosque alios . . . haec macies *Gronovius*: quique alios: hanc maciem *codd.*

In the Name of P. Sulpicius Rufus (F 4)

F 4 Cic. *Brut.* 205

= **76** T 10.

Against Statius Albius Oppianicus and His Accomplices (F 5–8)

*Cannutius assisted A. Cluentius Habitus in the first trial before C. Iunius in 74 BC, when Cluentius prosecuted his stepfather, the elder Statius Albius Oppianicus, defended by L. Quinctius (**107** F 4–5), for having attempted to poi-*

T 3 Tacitus, *Dialogue on Oratory*

[APER:] And I am not ⟨naming⟩ someone from the rank and file, a Canuti⟨us⟩[1] or an Atti⟨us, not to mention⟩ Furnius and Toranius, and any others who, in the same infirmary, are recommended by such bones and such skin [i.e., by speeches consisting just of "bare bones"] . . .

[1] The text is corrupt: a reference to P. Cannutius has been assumed. Some of the other men mentioned might be Q. Arrius (Cic. *Brut.* 242) and C. Furnius (**151**). Or all of them could be orators otherwise unknown.

In the Name of P. Sulpicius Rufus (F 4)

*According to Cicero, Cannutius was believed to have written speeches circulating in the name of P. Sulpicius Rufus (***76***) after Sulpicius' death.*

F 4 Cicero, *Brutus*

= **76** T 10.

Against Statius Albius Oppianicus and His Accomplices (F 5–8)

son him (TLRR 149). *The case included charges by Cannutius against Scamander, a freedman of C. Fabricius (F 6; TLRR 147), and against C. Fabricius, an accomplice of Oppianicus (F 7; cf.* **115** + **116** *F 2; TLRR 148).*

F 5 Cic. *Clu.* 29

. . . audiebant ab accusatoribus, audiebant verba multorum testium, audiebant cum una quaque de re a P. Cannutio, homine eloquentissimo, graviter et diu diceretur.

F 6 Cic. *Clu.* 50

res agi coepta est; citatus est Scamander reus. accusabat
P. Cannutius, homo in primis ingeniosus et in dicendo
exercitatus; accusabat autem ille quidem Scamandrum
verbis tribus, "venenum esse deprehensum." omnia tela
totius accusationis in Oppianicum coniciebantur, aperie-
batur causa insidiarum, Fabriciorum familiaritas comme-
morabatur, hominis vita et audacia proferebatur, denique
omnis accusatio varie graviterque tractata ad extremum
manifesta veneni deprehensione conclusa est.

F 7 Cic. *Clu.* 58

citatur reus, agitur causa;[1] paucis verbis accusat ut de re
iudicata Cannutius . . .

[1] agitur causa *om. unus cod., post* paucis *hab. alius cod., del.*
Baiter

F 8 Cic. *Clu.* 73

in ea obscuritate ac dubitatione omnium Cannutio, perito
homini, qui quodam odore suspicionis Staienum corruptum esse sensisset neque dum rem perfectam arbitraretur,
placuit repente pronuntiari "dixerunt."

F 5 Cicero, *Pro Cluentio*

. . . they [judges of the first trial] were listening [to the story told] by the accusers; they were listening to the words of many witnesses; they were listening when P. Cannutius, a most eloquent man, spoke about each individual point gravely and at length.

F 6 Cicero, *Pro Cluentio*

The trial began; the defendant Scamander was summoned. The prosecutor was P. Cannutius, a man particularly gifted and proficient in speaking; and he charged Scamander in three words: "Poison was detected." All the weapons of the entire accusation were thrown against Oppianicus, the motive for the plot was revealed, the friendship with the Fabricii was recalled, the audacious life of the man was set forth; finally, the entire indictment, presented in a diversified and serious manner, was eventually concluded by the overt discovery of the poison.

F 7 Cicero, *Pro Cluentio*

The defendant [C. Fabricius] is summoned, the case is being dealt with; Cannutius brings forward the charge in a few words, as for a case that has already been judged . . .

F 8 Cicero, *Pro Cluentio*

In this obscurity and uncertainty of all, Cannutius, an experienced man, who had noticed by some wind of suspicion that Staienus [C. Aelius Paetus Staienus (**107A**), one of the judges] had taken a bribe, but did not think that the matter had yet been completed, decided to have it suddenly announced: "The pleadings are finished."

Unplaced Fragment (F 9)

F 9 Prisc., *GL* II, p. 381.12–14

Cannutius: "turpe est propter venustatem vestimentorum admirari, ut propter turpissime vitam actam non contempnere,"[1] "admirari" θαυμάζεσθαι.

[1] condemnare *vel* condemnari *vel* contempnare *vel* non contempnere *codd.*: contemni *ed. Ald. Ven. 1527, Putschius*: non contemni *Meyer: fort.* non tempnere *Hertz*

115 + 116 C. ET L. CAEPASII FRATRES

T 1 Cic. *Brut.* 242

[CICERO:] eodem tempore C. L. Caepasii fratres fuerunt, qui multa opera, ignoti homines et repentini, quaestores celeriter facti sunt, oppidano quodam et incondito genere dicendi.

On Behalf of C. Fabricius (F 2)

The brothers Caepasii, the elder in particular, defended C. Fabricius, an accomplice of the elder Statius Albius Oppianicus, when he was charged with attempted poision-

Unplaced Fragment (F 9)

F 9 Priscian

Cannutius: "It is disgraceful to be admired because of the elegance of one's clothes, as it is [disgraceful] not to regard people with contempt [?] because of a life very disgracefully lived," "to be admired," to be admired [in Greek: deponent verb here with passive sense].

115 + 116 C. ET L. CAEPASII FRATRES

The brothers C. and L. Caepasius seem to have been quaestors in around 70 BC (RE Caepasius). In Cicero they are described as upstarts, whose eloquence was rather provincial and unpolished (T 1).

T 1 Cicero, *Brutus*

[CICERO:] In the same period there were the brothers C. and L. Caepasius, who, through much effort, though unknown men and having emerged suddenly, were soon elected quaestors; their style of speaking was of a certain provincial nature and unpolished.

On Behalf of C. Fabricius (F 2)

ings (TLRR 148) in 74 BC by A. Cluentius Habitus, assisted by P. Cannutius (**114** F 7).

F 2 Cic. *Clu.* 57–59

itaque tum ille inopia et necessitate coactus in causa eius
modi ad Caepasios fratres confugit, homines industrios
atque eo animo ut quaecumque dicendi potestas esset
data in honore atque in beneficio ponerent. nam hoc
prope iniquissime comparatum est quod in morbis corporis, ut quisque est difficillimus, ita medicus nobilissimus
atque optimus quaeritur, in periculis capitis, ut quaeque
causa difficillima est, ita deterrimus obscurissimusque
patronus adhibetur. nisi forte hoc causa⟨e⟩[1] est quod me-
dici nihil praeter artificium, oratores etiam auctoritatem
praestare debent. [58] citatur reus, agitur causa;[2] paucis
verbis accusat ut de re iudicata Cannutius; incipit longo et
alte petito prooemio respondere maior Caepasius. primo
attente auditur eius oratio. erigebat animum iam demis-
sum et oppressum Oppianicus; gaudebat ipse Fabricius;
non intellegebat animos iudicum non illius eloquentia sed
defensionis impudentia commoveri. postea quam de re
coepit dicere, ad ea quae erant in causa addebat etiam ipse
nova quaedam volnera ut, quamquam sedulo faciebat, tamen interdum non defendere sed praevaricari[3] videretur.
itaque cum callidissime se dicere putaret et cum illa verba
gravissima ex intimo artificio deprompsisset: "respicite,
iudices, hominum fortunas, respicite dubios variosque

---

[1] hoc causa⟨e⟩ *Lambinus*: hoc causa *codd. plerique*: haec
causa *Naugerius*   [2] agitur causa *om. unus cod., post* paucis
hab. alius cod., del. Baiter   [3] accusationi *add. codd. plerique, del. Lambinus*

Cf. Quint. *Inst.* 6.3.39–40; Iul. Vict., *RLM*, p. 428.218–21.

F 2 Cicero, *Pro Cluentio*

And so then that man [C. Fabricius], driven by want and necessity in such a case, took refuge with the brothers Caepasii, hardworking men and of such a mind that they regarded whatever opportunity for speaking was given to them as a compliment and as a favor. For this comparison has been made most unfairly, as it were, namely that, with respect to diseases of the body, for the most difficult, the most distinguished and best doctor is called, whereas with respect to life-threatening trials, for the most difficult cases, the most incompetent and most obscure advocate is engaged. Unless this is perhaps the reason that doctors should provide nothing but their skill, orators also their good name. [58] The defendant [C. Fabricius] is summoned, the case is being dealt with; Cannutius [P. Cannutius (**114**), F 7] brings forward the charge in a few words, as for a case that has already been judged; the elder Caepasius begins to answer with a long and far-fetched exordium. At first his speech has an attentive hearing. Oppianicus began to raise his already drooping and dejected spirits; Fabricius himself began to feel happy; he did not realize that the minds of the judges were moved not by his eloquence, but by the effrontery of the plea. After he had started to talk about the matter, he [Caepasius] even added some fresh wounds to those that were inherent in the case, so that, though he was doing his best, he still seemed at times not to be defending, but to be acting in collusion with the prosecutor. Thus, when he thought he was pleading very cleverly and when he had produced from the secrets of his stock-in-trade these very weighty words: "Look back, judges, upon the lot of mortal man;

casus, respicite C. Fabrici senectutem"—cum hoc "respicite" ornandae orationis causa saepe dixisset, respexit ipse.
at C. Fabricius a subselliis demisso capite discesserat. [59]
hic iudices ridere, stomachari atque acerbe ferre patronus
causam sibi eripi et se cetera de illo loco "respicite, iudices" non posse dicere; nec quicquam propius est factum
quam ut illum persequeretur et collo obtorto ad subsellia
reduceret ut reliqua posset perorare. ita tum Fabricius
primum suo iudicio, quod est gravissimum, deinde legis vi
et sententiis iudicum est condemnatus.

117 M. LOLLIUS PALICANUS

T 1 Sall. *Hist.* 4.43 M. = 4.33 R.

M. Lollius Palicanus, humili loco Picens, loquax magis
quam facundus

T 2 Cic. *Brut.* 223
= **107** T 1.

look back upon its changeable and uncertain states; look back upon the old age of C. Fabricius!"—when he had repeated the phrase "look back" frequently to ornament his speech, he looked back himself. But C. Fabricius had left his seat with hanging head. [59] Thereupon the judges burst out laughing; the pleader lost his temper and was annoyed that the case was slipping through his fingers and that he could not say the rest from this stock passage beginning "look back, judges"; and he was almost at the point that he pursued him and dragged him back to his seat by the scruff of his neck, so that he could deliver the rest of his peroration. Thus Fabricius was then found guilty, firstly by his own verdict, which is the most serious, then by the force of law and the votes of the judges.

117 M. LOLLIUS PALICANUS

M. Lollius Palicanus (tr. pl. 71, praet. 69 BC; RE Lollius 21) was not highly regarded as an orator: in Cicero his eloquence is described as better suited to the ears of the uneducated (T 2; cf. T 1).

T 1 Sallust, *Histories*

M. Lollius Palicanus, of low birth, from Picenum [region in Italy between the Apennines and the Adriatic Sea], loquacious rather than eloquent

T 2 Cicero, *Brutus*

= **107** T 1.

As Tribune Against C. Verres to the People (F 3–4)

As Tribune of the People in 71 BC, Palicanus delivered a
speech at a public meeting (CCMR, App. A: 240) criticiz-
ing C. Verres' cruelness toward Roman citizens (e.g., Cic.

F 3 Cic. *Verr.* 2.1.122

oblitosne igitur hos putatis esse quem ad modum sit iste
solitus virgis plebem Romanam concidere? quam rem
etiam tribunus plebis in contione egit, cum eum quem iste
virgis ceciderat in conspectu populi Romani produxit.

F 4 Cic. *Verr.* 2.2.100

nuntiabatur illi primis illis temporibus, id quod pater quoque ad eum pluribus verbis scripserat, agitatam rem esse
in senatu; etiam in contione tribunum plebis de causa
Stheni, M. Palicanum, esse questum . . .

118 SER. SULPICIUS RUFUS

Ser. Sulpicius Rufus (cos. 51 BC; RE Sulpicius 95) was
regarded as an accomplished orator and an outstanding
jurist, who had devoted effort to training in both arts
(T 1–5; Quint. Inst. 12.3.9, 12.10.11). Cicero implies that
Sulpicius left legal writings (T 2); according to Pomponius,
there were almost 180 books (T 5).

As Tribune Against C. Verres to the People (F 3–4)

Verr. *2.5.140) and his treatment of Sthenius of Thermae
(Cic.* Verr. *2.2.83–99).*

F 3 Cicero, *Verrine Orations*

Do you [the judges] think then that these men here have
forgotten how that man [C. Verres] was accustomed to
beat ordinary Roman folk with rods? That matter was even
addressed in a public meeting by a Tribune of the People,[1]
when he produced before the eyes of the Roman People
someone whom that man had beaten with rods.

[1] Pseudo-Asconius *(ad loc.* [p. 250.21 St.]) identifies the Tribune as M. Lollius Palicanus.

F 4 Cicero, *Verrine Orations*

At the very outset news was brought to that man [C.
Verres], as his father too had written to him in great detail,
that the matter had been discussed in the Senate; further,
that a Tribune of the People, M. Palicanus, had complained about the case of Sthenius at a public meeting . . .

118 SER. SULPICIUS RUFUS

*Three speeches by Sulpicius were known to Quintilian;
he also mentions rather elaborate collections of notes for
cases pleaded by Sulpicius (T 3–4). Two letters from Sulpicius to Cicero are extant (Cic.* Fam. *4.5, 4.12).*

*In 43 BC Sulpicius was sent as a member of an embassy
to negotiate with Marc Antony (M. Antonius [**159**]); en*

T 1 Cic. *Brut.* 151–53

et ego [CICERO] ". . . de Servio autem et tu probe dicis et
ego dicam quod sentio. non enim facile quem dixerim plus
studi quam illum et ad dicendum et ad omnis bonarum
rerum disciplinas adhibuisse. nam et in isdem exercitationibus ineunte aetate fuimus et postea una Rhodum ille
etiam profectus est, quo melior esset et doctior; et inde ut
rediit, videtur mihi in secunda arte primus esse maluisse
quam in prima secundus. atque haud scio an par principibus esse potuisset; sed fortasse maluit, id quod est adeptus, longe omnium non eiusdem modo aetatis sed eorum
etiam qui fuissent in iure civili esse princeps." [152] hic
BRUTUS: "ain tu?" inquit. "etiamne Q. Scaevolae Servium
nostrum anteponis?" "sic enim," inquam [CICERO],
"Brute, existimo, iuris civilis magnum usum et apud Scae-
volam et apud multos fuisse, artem in hoc uno; quod numquam effecisset ipsius iuris scientia, nisi eam praeterea
didicisset artem quae doceret rem universam tribuere in
partis, latentem explicare definiendo, obscuram explanare
interpretando, ambigua{m}[1] primum videre, deinde dis-
tinguere, postremo habere regulam qua vera et falsa iudi-

---

[1] ambigua{m} *Lambinus*: ambiguam *codd.*

*route he died of an illness. Thereupon, Cicero argued (Cic.
Phil. 9) that Sulpicius should be honored with a statue
because he died while on public service (cf. T 5).*

T 1 Cicero, *Brutus*

And I [CICERO] said: ". . . but about Servius you [Brutus]
speak well, and I will tell you what I think. For I could not
easily name anyone who has devoted more attention to the
art of speaking and to all other subjects of liberal study
than him. For in our youth we occupied ourselves with the
same [rhetorical] exercises, and afterward he also went
with me to Rhodes to become better and more perfectly
trained. And once he returned from there, he seems to me
to have preferred to be first in the second art [law] rather
than second in the first [oratory]. And he could probably
have been the equal of those of the first rank; but perhaps
he preferred what he did attain, to be first by far not only
of all those in his own time but also of those who had gone
before, in mastery of the civil law." [152] Here BRUTUS
said: "Do you say so? Do you place our Servius even above
Q. Scaevola [Q. Mucius Scaevola (**67**)]?" "This is what I
think, Brutus," I [CICERO] said, "that there was great
practical knowledge of civil law both in Scaevola and in
many others, the theoretical art of it in this man alone: he
would have never attained that through knowledge merely
of the law if he had not acquired in addition that art that
teaches one to divide a general matter into its parts, to set
forth and define a latent matter, to interpret and make
clear an obscure [matter], first to recognize, then to dis-
tinguish the ambiguous, finally, to apply a rule for adjudg-
ing what is true and false and for determining what con-

carentur et quae quibus propositis essent quaeque non
essent consequentia. [153] hic enim adtulit hanc artem
omnium artium maximam quasi lucem ad ea quae confuse
ab aliis aut respondebantur aut agebantur." "dialecticam
mihi videris dicere," inquit [BRUTUS].

T 2 Cic. *Brut.* 153–55

[CICERO:] . . . sed adiunxit etiam et litterarum scientiam
et loquendi elegantiam, quae ex scriptis eius, quorum
similia nulla sunt, facillime perspici potest. [154] cumque
discendi causa duobus peritissimis operam dedisset, L.
Lucilio Balbo C. Aquilio Gallo, Galli hominis acuti et exer-
citati promptam et paratam in agendo et in respondendo
celeritatem subtilitate diligentiaque superavit; Balbi docti
et eruditi hominis in utraque re consideratam tarditatem
vicit expediendis conficiendisque rebus. sic et habet quod
uterque eorum habuit, et explevit quod utrique defuit.
[155] itaque ut Crassus mihi videtur sapientius fecisse
quam Scaevola . . . sic Servius sapientissime,[1] cum duae
civiles artes ac forenses plurimum et laudis haberent et
gratiae, perfecit ut altera praestaret omnibus, ex altera
tantum assumeret quantum esset et ad tuendum ius civile
et ad obtinendam consularem dignitatem satis.

---

[1] sapientissime *edd.*: apsentissume *codd.*

clusions follow from what premises and what do not. [153] For this art, the greatest of all arts, he brought to bear, like a light, on what had been given as legal opinions or said in trials in a disorderly manner by others." "The art of logic I suppose you mean," he [BRUTUS] said.

T 2 Cicero, *Brutus*

[CICERO:] . . . but he also added both a knowledge of letters and a finished style of speaking, which can be seen very easily from his writings, for which there is nothing comparable. [154] And when, for the sake of learning, he had devoted his attention to two of the ablest jurists, L. Lucilius Balbus and C. Aquillius Gallus [both pupils of Q. Mucius Scaevola (**67**)], he surpassed the acute and ready quickness of Gallus, a precise and experienced man, in court and in consultation, by penetration and accuracy; to the well-considered slowness of Balbus, a learned and erudite man, in both cases, he was superior in preparing and finishing matters. Thus, he both has what each of them possessed, and supplied what each of them lacked. [155] Therefore, just as Crassus [L. Licinius Crassus (**66**)] seems to me to have acted more wisely than Scaevola [Q. Mucius Scaevola (**67**)] . . . so Servius acted most wisely: seeing that two civic and forensic arts led to the greatest fame and favor, he achieved that he was supreme beyond everybody in the one and from the other borrowed as much as was required both to uphold civil law and to maintain consular dignity.

T 3 Quint. *Inst.* 10.1.116

et Servius Sulpicius insignem non inmerito famam tribus orationibus meruit.

T 4 Quint. *Inst.* 10.7.30

sed feruntur aliorum quoque et inventi forte, ut eos dicturus quisque composuerat, et in libros digesti, ut causarum quae sunt actae a Servio Sulpicio, cuius tres orationes extant: sed hi de quibus loquor commentarii ita sunt exacti ut ab ipso mihi in memoriam posteritatis videantur esse compositi.

T 5 Pompon. *Dig.* 1.2.2.43

Servius autem Sulpicius cum in causis orandis primum locum aut pro certo post M. Tullium optineret, traditur ad consulendum Quintum Mucium de re amici sui pervenisse cumque eum sibi respondisse de iure Servius parum intellexisset, iterum Quintum interrogasse et a Quinto Mucio responsum esse nec tamen percepisse, et ita obiurgatum esse a Quinto Mucio: namque eum dixisse turpe esse patricio et nobili et causas oranti ius in quo versaretur ignorare. ea velut contumelia Servius tactus operam dedit iuri civili et plurimum eos, de quibus locuti sumus, audiit, institutus a Balbo Lucilio, instructus autem maxime a Gallo Aquilio, qui fuit Cercinae: itaque libri complures

T 3 Quintilian, *The Orator's Education*

And Servius Sulpicius not undeservedly won great fame with three speeches.

T 4 Quintilian, *The Orator's Education*

But those [the notes] of others are also in circulation, both some discovered by chance, just as each person had composed them when about to speak, and some collected into books, like those of the cases that were pleaded by Servius Sulpicius, of whom three speeches are extant: but these notes about which I speak are so accomplished that they seem to me to have been composed by the man himself as a record for posterity.

T 5 Pomponius, *Digest*

And when Servius Sulpicius held the first place in pleading cases, or certainly the place after M. Tullius [Cicero], he is said to have come to Quintus Mucius [Q. Mucius Scaevola (**67**)] to consult him about a matter of a friend of his and, when Servius had hardly understood what he replied to him about the law, to have asked Quintus again and received an answer from Quintus Mucius and still not to have understood it, and to have been criticized by Quintus Mucius in the following manner: for he [Quintus Mucius] reportedly said that it was disgraceful for a patrician nobleman pleading cases not to know the law with which he was concerned. Stung by this as if by an insult, Servius spent effort on civil law and listened particularly to those about whom we have spoken, taught by Balbus Lucilius [L. Lucilius Balbus] and trained particularly by Gallus Aquilius [C. Aquillius Gallus], who was based on Cercina

373

eius extant Cercinae confecti. hic cum in legatione peris-
set, statuam ei populus Romanus pro rostris posuit, et
hodieque exstat pro rostris Augusti. huius volumina com-
plura exstant: reliquit enim prope centum et octoginta libros.

Against L. Licinius Murena (F 6)

*In 63 BC, when he had unsuccessfully stood as a candidate
for the consulship, Sulpicius, along with M. Porcius Cato
(**126** F 11–12), prosecuted L. Licinius Murena, the consul
elect, for* ambitus; *Murena was successfully defended by*

F 6 Cic. *Mur.* 7, 11, 15, 18, 21, 35, 73

sed me, iudices, non minus hominis sapientissimi atque
ornatissimi, Ser. Sulpici, conquestio quam Catonis accusatio commovebat qui gravissime et acerbissime ‹se› ferre[1]
dixit me familiaritatis necessitudinisque oblitum causam
L. Murenae contra se defendere. . . . [11] intellego, iudices, tris totius accusationis partis fuisse, et earum unam
in reprehensione vitae, alteram in contentione dignitatis,
tertiam in criminibus ambitus esse versatam. atque harum
trium partium prima illa quae gravissima debebat esse ita
fuit infirma et levis ut illos lex magis quaedam accusatoria
quam vera male dicendi facultas de vita L. Murenae dicere aliquid coegerit. . . . [15] . . . contempsisti L. Murenae

---

[1] ‹se› ferre *Lambinus:* ferme *codd.*

[island off Tunisia]: therefore, quite a number of his books having been finished on Cercina are extant. When he [Servius] had died on an embassy, the Roman People erected a statue to him in front of the Rostra, and today it still exists in front of Augustus' Rostra. By him [Servius] quite a number of volumes are extant: for he left almost one hundred and eighty books.

Against L. Licinius Murena (F 6)

*Q. Hortensius Hortalus (**92** F 36–37), M. Licinius Crassus Dives (**102** F 8–9), and Cicero, who commented in his speech on what the prosecutors allegedly said (Cic. Mur.) (TLRR 224).*

F 6 Cicero, *Pro Murena*

But the complaint, judges, of this very learned and very eminent man, Ser. Sulpicius, affected me no less than the accusation of Cato [M. Porcius Cato (**126**), F 11–12], who said that <he> felt very aggrieved and very bitterly hurt that I, having forgotten the ties of friendship, was defending the case of L. Murena against him. . . . [11] I see, judges, that there were three parts of the prosecution as a whole, and that one of these focused on an attack upon his private life, another on disputing his fitness for office, and the third on charges of bribery. And of these three parts, that first one, which should have been the most serious, was so feeble and trivial that a sort of convention of accusers rather than any true opportunity for abuse compelled them to say something about L. Murena's private life. . . . [15] . . . You poured scorn on L. Murena's family, you ex-

genus, extulisti tuum. . . . [18] . . . "quaesturam una petiit
et sum ego factus prior." . . . [21] summa in utroque est
honestas, summa dignitas; quam ego, si mihi per Servium
liceat, pari atque eadem in² laude ponam. sed non licet;
agitat rem militarem, insectatur totam hanc legationem,
adsiduitatis et operarum harum cotidianarum putat esse
consulatum. "apud exercitum mihi fueris" inquit; "tot annos forum³ non attigeris; afueris tam diu et,⁴ cum longo
intervallo veneris, cum his qui in foro habitarint⁵ de dignitate contendas?" . . . [35] "at enim in praeturae petitione
prior renuntiatus est Servius." pergitisne vos tamquam ex
syngrapha agere cum populo ut, quem locum semel honoris cuipiam dederit, eundem ⟨in⟩⁶ reliquis honoribus debeat? . . . [73] . . . haec omnia sectatorum, spectaculorum,
prandiorum item crimina a multitudine in tuam nimiam
diligentiam, Servi, coniecta sunt, in quibus tamen Murena
ab senatus auctoritate defenditur. quid enim? senatus
num obviam prodire crimen putat? "non, sed mercede."
convince. num sectari⁷ multos? "non, sed conductos."
doce. num locum ad spectandum dare aut ad⁸ prandium
invitare? "minime, sed volgo, passim." quid est "volgo"?
"universos."

² eadem in *Lambinus*: in eadem *codd.*

³ tot annos forum *Halm*: tot annis *Quint. Inst.* 5.13.27

⁴ et *Quint.*: ut *codd.*

⁵ habitarint *vel* habitarunt *codd.*: habitarunt *Quint.*

⁶ *add. Ernesti*

⁷ sectari *ed. Guar.*: sectare *codd.*

⁸ aut ad *vel* aut *codd.*

Cf. Quint. *Inst.* 5.13.27.

alted your own. . . . [18] . . . "He was a candidate for the quaestorship at the same time, and I was elected first [alleged statement of Sulpicius; quaest. prob. 74 BC]." . . . [21] The highest distinction, the greatest prestige can be found in both of them [Sulpicius and Murena]; for my part, if Servius permitted me to do so, I should assign the same and equal praise. But he does not permit it; he ridicules the profession of arms, he attacks the whole of this legateship, he thinks that the consulship is a matter of persistent attention to these daily tasks. "You [Murena] have been away with the army," he [Sulpicius] says; "for so many years you have not approached the Forum; you have been away for such a long time and, now that you have come after such a long gap, are you competing for office with these men who have made their homes in the Forum?" . . . [35] "But in the election for the praetorship [of 65 BC] Servius was declared elected first." [alleged objection] Are you going to suggest to the People that they are obliged, as if under contract, to give a man ⟨in⟩ all subsequent magistracies the same position for a magistracy that they have given him once? . . . [73] . . . These charges relating to retinues, shows, dinners, have all alike been put down by the population to your excessive officiousness, Servius; yet, as regards those, Murena is defended by the authority of the Senate. What then? Surely the Senate does not regard it as a crime to go out to meet a candidate? "No; only for payment." Prove that it was. To have many escorting? "No; only if they were hired." Show that they were. To provide a seat at a show or give an invitation to dinner? "Not at all; unless it was given indiscriminately, throughout the city." What does "indiscriminately" mean? "To everybody."

377

On Behalf of Aufidia (F 7–10)

F 7 Quint. *Inst.* 10.1.22–23

= **92** F 28.

F 8 Quint. *Inst.* 4.2.106

sermo vero aversus a iudice et brevius indicat interim et coarguit magis: qua de re idem quod in prohoemio dixeram sentio, sicut de prosopopoeia quoque, qua tamen non Servius modo Sulpicius utitur pro Aufidia: "somnone te languidum an gravi lethargo putem pressum?", sed M. quoque Tullius [Cic. *Verr.* 2.5.118] circa navarchos (nam ea quoque rei expositio est): "ut adeas, tantum dabis" et reliqua.

F 9 Fest., p. 140.12–17 L.

ut patri‹s› sui heres e [– – –] | tet,[1] tam heres est quam[2] [– – –] | in potestate alie‹na› [– – –] | et suus heres, ut p [– – –] ‹Ser.› | Sulpicius in ea oratio‹ne, quam habuit contra Messalam›[3] | pro Aufidia.

---

[1] ‹mancipatus et adoptatus› ut patri‹s› sui heres e‹sse desinit, ita eius qui adop›tet *Huschke*   [2] quam ‹ex eo natus. sed et arrogatus› *Huschke*   [3] *suppl. Müller*

On Behalf of Aufidia (F 7–10)

*Sulpicius spoke on behalf of Aufidia against M. Valerius Messalla Corvinus (**176** F 12–13) in what seems to have been a case of inheritance (Quint. Inst. 6.1.20 [corrupt text]).*

F 7 Quintilian, *The Orator's Education*

= **92** F 28.

F 8 Quintilian, *The Orator's Education*

In fact, a remark turned away from the judge [i.e., apostrophe] sometimes makes a point more briefly or proves it more cogently: about this matter I am of the same opinion that I expressed with respect to the prooemium [Quint. Inst. 4.1.63–64], as also with respect to prosopopoeia, which was used, however, not only by Servius Sulpicius on behalf of Aufidia: "Am I to think that you were drowsy with sleep or weighed down by some heavy lethargy?", but also by M. Tullius [Cicero] in the passage about the ships' captains (for this too is a narrative of the matter): "to be admitted, you must give so much" and so on [Cic. Verr. 2.5.118].

F 9 Festus

So that he e[merg]es as the heir of his father, is heir in the same way as . . . in an⟨other⟩'s power . . . and his heir, as . . . ⟨Ser.⟩ Sulpicius in that spee⟨ch that he delivered against Messalla [M. Valerius Messalla Corvinus (**176**), F 12–13]⟩ on behalf of Aufidia.[1]

---

[1] The text is corrupt, and the remark attributed to Sulpicius cannot be recovered. The passage confirms that Sulpicius spoke on behalf of Aufidia.

F 10 Fest., p. 194.18–21 L.

ORBA apud poel|tas significatur privata aliqua|[1] persona cara: apud | ｜oratores, quae patrem|[2] [– – – e – – –], ut Ser. | ｜Sulpicius ait, quae filios|[3] [– – –] ulos[4] orba est

[1] *suppl. ex Epit.*   [2] *suppl. ex Epit.*   [3] *suppl. ex Epit.*
[4] <amisit parv>ulos *Huschke*: <quasi oc>ulos *Ursinus*

118A M. PONTIDIUS

M. Pontidius from Arpinum (RE Pontidius 3) is otherwise unknown, but included in Cicero's Brutus *as a man frequently pleading in private suits (T 1). If anachronism can*

T 1 Cic. *Brut.* 246

[CICERO:] etiam M. Pontidius municeps noster multas privatas causas actitavit, celeriter sane verba volvens nec hebes in causis vel dicam plus etiam quam non hebes, sed effervescens in dicendo stomacho saepe iracundiaque vehementius; ut non cum adversario solum sed etiam, quod mirabile esset, cum iudice ipso, cuius delenitor esse debet orator, iurgio saepe contenderet.

119 Q. CAECILIUS METELLUS CELER

*Q. Caecilius Metellus Celer (cos. 60 BC; RE Caecilius 86), a brother of Q. Caecilius Metellus Nepos (**120**), was married to Clodia, by whom he is said to have been killed in*

F 10 Festus

orba ["bereaved"; feminine], in the poets, means "deprived of some beloved person"; in the orators, a woman who [has lost] her father ... as Ser. Sulpicius says, a woman who [has lost young] sons is bereaved.[1]

----

[1] The (lacunose) fragment has been attributed to this speech on the basis of the assumed context.

118A M. PONTIDIUS

be assumed, the Pontidius (RE Pontidius 1) mentioned in Cicero's De oratore because of a witty answer (Cic. De or. 2.275) might be the same person.

T 1 Cicero, *Brutus*

[CICERO:] M. Pontidius also, my fellow townsman, was active in many private suits, certainly reeling off words quickly and in court cases not dull-witted, or I should rather say even more than "not dull-witted", since in speaking he would frequently become greatly worked up with vexation and resentment; thus, he would frequently wrangle not only with the opponent, but also, what is remarkable, with the judge himself, whom the orator ought to conciliate.

119 Q. CAECILIUS METELLUS CELER

59 BC because of his opposition to her brother P. Clodius Pulcher (137) (Cic. Cael. 59; Schol. Bob. ad Cic. Sest. 131 [p. 139.8–10 St.]).

*In Cicero the brothers Metelli (**119** + **120**) are described as not without natural ability or training and cultivating a style of speaking appealing to the People (T 1).*

T 1 Cic. *Brut.* 247

[CICERO:] duo etiam Metelli, Celer et Nepos, ⟨non⟩ nihil[1] in causis versati nec sine ingenio nec indocti, hoc erant populare dicendi genus adsecuti.

1 ⟨non⟩ nihil *edd.*: nihil *codd.*

Against M. Aemilius Lepidus (F 2)

F 2 Ps.-Asc. in Cic. *Div. Caec.* 2 (p. 187.9–14 Stangl); in Cic. *Verr.* 2.2.8 (p. 259.1–3 Stangl)

Siculi veteres patronos habent: in quibus . . . Metellos, quorum familia proxime Siculis patrocinium praebuit, cum fuit Lepidus in ea provincia praetor, instantibus ad accusandum eum Metellis duobus, Celere et Nepote.

"etsi illum annum": M. Lepidi praetoris, qui accusari coeperat a duobus Metellis, Celere et Nepote: qui cum legibus interrogassent, victi eius apud populum gratia destiterunt.

---

1 In the procedure *legibus / lege interrogari*, the prosecutor interrogates the defendant to establish a preliminary assessment of the case and to enable the presiding magistrate to decide whether to go further (Ps.-Asc. in Cic. *Verr.* 1.5 [p. 207.10–14 St.]; Greenidge 1901, 463–65).

A letter from Metellus Celer to Cicero is extant (Cic. Fam. *5.1), as are letters from Cicero to him (cf.* **120** *F 2–3).*

T 1 Cicero, *Brutus*

[CICERO:] The two Metelli as well, Celer and Nepos [**120**], ‹not› inexperienced in private suits, nor without talent, nor uneducated, cultivated that style of speaking intended to win favor with the People.

Against M. Aemilius Lepidus (F 2)

*After M. Aemilius Lepidus (***95***) had served as provincial governor in Sicily in 80 BC, Metellus Celer, along with Nepos (***120*** F 2A), was ready to prosecute him on a charge of extortion, but did not carry it through (*TLRR *131).*

F 2 Pseudo-Asconius on Cicero, *Against Caecilius*; on Cicero, *Verrine Orations*

The Sicilians have long-standing patrons: among them . . . the Metelli, whose family provided very close patronage for the Sicilians, when Lepidus was praetor in that province, as two Metelli, Celer and Nepos [**120**], threatened to prosecute him.

"even if that year": Of the praetor M. Lepidus, whose prosecution by two Metelli, Celer and Nepos, had just started: when they had interrogated him before the presiding magistrate according to procedure,[1] they left off, defeated by his popularity among the People.

383

Against Cn. Sergius Silus (F 3)

F 3 Val. Max. 6.1.8

Metellus quoque Celer stuprosae mentis acer poenitor
exstitit Cn. Sergio Silo promissorum matri familiae num-
morum gratia diem ad populum dicendo eumque hoc uno
crimine damnando: non enim factum tunc, sed animus in
quaestionem deductus est, plusque voluisse peccare no-
cuit quam non peccasse profuit.

120 Q. CAECILIUS METELLUS NEPOS

*Q. Caecilius Metellus Nepos (cos. 57 BC; RE Caecilius 96),
a brother of Q. Caecilius Metellus Celer (**119**), as Tribune
of the People in 62 BC opposed Cicero; by the time Metellus Nepos became consul for 57 BC, he was reconciled
with Cicero and supported his recall from exile. As proconsul, Metellus Nepos administered Hispania citerior; a*

T 1 Cic. *Brut.* 247

= **119** T 1.

Against Cn. Sergius Silus (F 3)

Cn. Sergius Silus, possibly an official mentioned by Cicero (Cic. Verr. 2.3.102), was prosecuted by a Metellus Celer (TLRR 371), who may have been this Metellus or his adoptive father, Metellus Celer (tr. pl. 90 BC).

F 3 Valerius Maximus, *Memorable Doings and Sayings*

Metellus Celer too appeared as a stern chastiser of lascivious intent by summoning Cn. Sergius Silus to trial before the People on account of money promised to the matron of a household and convicting him on this sole charge: for not an act, but a state of mind was then brought to the judicial investigation, and having wished to do wrong hurt more than not having done wrong helped.

120 Q. CAECILIUS METELLUS NEPOS

letter written from there to Cicero in 56 BC is extant (Cic. Fam. 5.3), as are letters to him from Cicero (F 5).

*In Cicero, the brothers Metelli (**119** + **120**) are described as not without natural ability or training and cultivating a style of speaking appealing to the People (T 1).*

T 1 Cicero, *Brutus*

= **119** T 1.

Against M. Aemilius Lepidus (F 2A)

F 2A Ps.-Asc. in Cic. *Div. Caec.* 2 (p. 187.9–14 Stangl);
in Cic. *Verr.* 2.2.8 (p. 259.1–3 Stangl)

= **119** F 2.

On Cicero to the People (F 2)

*At the end of Cicero's consulship in 63 BC, Metellus Nepos,
as Tribune of the People for 62 BC, prevented Cicero from
delivering the customary final speech (Cic. Pis. 6–7; Asc.
in Cic. Pis. 6 [p. 6 C.]; Plut. Cic. 23.1–3; Cass. Dio 37.38;*

F 2 Cic. *Fam.* 5.2.6–8 [ad Q. Metellum Celerem]

quod scribis non oportuisse Metellum, fratrem tuum, ob
dictum a me oppugnari, primum hoc velim existimes, animum mihi istum tuum vehementer probari et fraternam
plenam humanitatis ac pietatis voluntatem; deinde, si qua
ego in re fratri tuo rei publicae causa restiterim, ut mihi
ignoscas (tam enim sum amicus rei publicae, quam qui
maxime); si vero meam salutem contra illius impetum in
me crudelissimum defenderim, satis habeas nihil me
etiam tecum de tui fratris iniuria conqueri. quem ego cum
comperissem omnem sui tribunatus conatum in meam
perniciem parare atque meditari, egi cum Claudia, uxore
tua, et cum vestra sorore Mucia, cuius erga me studium

Against M. Aemilius Lepidus (F 2A)

*After M. Aemilius Lepidus (**95**) had served as provincial governor in Sicily in 80 BC, Metellus Nepos, along with Celer (**119** F 2), was ready to prosecute him on a charge of extortion, but did not carry it through (TLRR 131).*

F 2A Pseudo-Asconius on Cicero, *Against Caecilius*; on Cicero, *Verrine Orations*

= **119** F 2.

On Cicero to the People (F 2)

CCMR, *App. A: 268; cf. also Cic. Mur. 81). This was followed by an altercation in the Senate between Metellus Nepos and Cicero over several days in January 62 BC (cf. F 3).*

F 2 Cicero, *Letters to Friends* [to Q. Caecilius Metellus Celer]

As regards the fact that you write that Metellus, your brother, should not have been attacked by me because of an utterance, in the first place I would wish you to believe that your sentiment here and your fraternal spirit full of good feeling and affection are strongly approved by me; secondly, if in any matter I have opposed your brother because of the Republic, I would wish you to forgive me (for I am as great a supporter of the Republic as one possibly can be). But if I have defended my well-being against a very savage onslaught on his part, you should be content that I do not protest also to you about your brother's ill usage. When I had learned that he was preparing and

pro Cn. Pompei necessitudine multis in rebus perspexeram, ut eum ab illa iniuria deterrerent. [7] atqui ille, quod te audisse credo, prid. Kal. Ian., qua iniuria nemo umquam in ullo[1] magistratu improbissimus civis adfectus est ea me consulem adfecit, cum rem publicam conservassem, atque abeuntem magistratu contionis habendae potestate privavit. cuius iniuria mihi tamen honori summo fuit; nam cum ille mihi nihil nisi ut iurarem permitteret, magna voce iuravi verissimum pulcherrimumque ius iurandum, quod populus idem magna voce me vere iurasse iuravit. [8] hac accepta tam insigni iniuria tamen illo ipso die misi ad Metellum communis amicos qui agerent cum eo ut de illa mente desisteret. quibus ille respondit sibi non esse integrum; etenim paulo ante in contione dixerat ei qui in alios animum advertisset indicta causa {a}dic{i}endi[2] ipsi potestatem fieri non oportere.

---

[1] ullo *Shackleton Bailey* (*noluit Orelli*): animo *vel* aliquo *codd.*: minimo *Bandinelli*: infimo *Orelli*   [2] {a}dic{i}endi *Manutius*: adiciendi *codd.*

Against Cicero in the Senate (F 3)

In January 62 BC there was an altercation in the Senate between Metellus Nepos, Tribune of the People for that year, and Cicero over several days (cf. Plut. Cic. 26.6, 26.9;

planning the entire endeavor of his Tribunate [62 BC] for my destruction, I addressed myself to Claudia, your wife, and to your [half-]sister Mucia, whose friendly disposition toward me on account of my friendship with Pompey [Cn. Pompeius Magnus (**111**), husband of Mucia] I had noticed in many matters, so that they should deter him from that injurious design. [7] And yet, as I believe you have heard, on the day before the Kalends of January [last day of December 63 BC] he laid an insult that has never been laid upon anyone in any magistracy, even the most disloyal citizen, upon me, a consul, although I had saved the Republic: he deprived me of the opportunity to address a public meeting when retiring from office. His affront, however, was a source of the greatest honor to me: for, when he permitted me nothing except my taking the oath, I swore in loud tones the truest and finest oath, and the People likewise in loud tones swore that I had sworn the truth. [8] Even after receiving so signal an insult, still, on that very same day, I sent mutual friends to Metellus, who were to negotiate with him so that he might drop this attitude. He replied to them that his hands were no longer free; and, in fact, he had declared at a public meeting a little earlier that one who had punished others without a hearing ought not to be given the opportunity to speak himself.

Against Cicero in the Senate (F 3)

Apophth. Cic. 5–6). *Fragments of Cicero's second response* Oratio contra contionem Q. Metelli *have been preserved* (*Crawford 1994, 219–31*).

F 3 Cic. *Fam.* 5.2.8 [ad Q. Metellum Celerem]

itaque ego Metello, fratri tuo, praesenti restiti. nam in
senatu Kal. Ian. sic cum eo de re publica disputavi ut
sentiret sibi cum viro forti et constanti esse pugnandum.
a. d. III Non. Ian. cum agere coepisset, tertio quoque
verbo orationis suae me appellabat, mihi minabatur, neque illi quicquam deliberatius fuit quam me, quacumque
ratione posset, non iudicio neque disceptatione sed vi atque impressione evertere.

On Cicero's Recall in the Senate (F 4–5)

*As consul in 57 BC, Metellus Nepos spoke (CCMR, App.
A: 308) in favor of Cicero's recall from exile (Cic. Sest. 87;
Red. sen. 5, 9, 26; Red. pop. 10, 15; Dom. 7, 70). Further*

F 4 Cic. *Sest.* 72

veniunt Kalendae Ianuariae. vos haec melius scire pot-
estis, equidem audita dico: quae tum frequentia senatus,
quae exspectatio populi, qui concursus legatorum ex Italia
cuncta, quae virtus, actio, gravitas P. Lentuli consulis fuerit, quae etiam conlegae eius moderatio de me. qui cum
inimicitias sibi mecum ex rei publicae dissensione suscep-
tas esse dixisset, eas se patribus conscriptis dixit et temporibus rei publicae permissurum.

F 3 Cicero, *Letters to Friends* [to Q. Caecilius Metellus Celer]

Accordingly, I stood up to Metellus, your brother, face to face. For in the Senate on the Kalends of January [January 1, 62 BC] I argued with him about the state of the Republic in such a way that he felt that he had to fight with a man of courage and resolution. In a speech on the third day before the Nones of January [January 3], when he had started to argue, he named me at every third word of his speech, he threatened me; for nothing was more certainly decided for him than to bring me down, in whatever way he could, not through due process of law, but by aggressive violence.

On Cicero's Recall in the Senate (F 4–5)

contiones *in 57 BC are mentioned (Cic.* Att. *4.3.4; CCMR, App. A: 311).*

F 4 Cicero, *Pro Sestio*

The Kalends of January [January 1, 57 BC] arrive. You can know this better. I say what I have heard: what the turnout of the Senate then was; how great was the expectation of the People; what a gathering of delegates from all of Italy; what courage, delivery, and weighty words from P. Lentulus, the consul [P. Cornelius Lentulus Spinther, cos. 57 BC]; what moderation also from his colleague [Q. Caecilius Metellus Nepos] toward me; when he [Metellus Nepos] had said that his enmity against me had arisen from differences in political opinion, he said that he would give it up for the sake of the senators and the condition of the Republic.

F 5 Cic. *Fam.* 5.4.2 [ad Q. Metellum Nepotem]

nunc mihi Quintus frater meus mitissimam tuam orationem, quam in senatu habuisses, perscripsit . . .

121 C. IULIUS CAESAR

*C. Iulius Caesar (100–44 BC; cos. 59, 48, 46, 45, 44 BC;
RE Iulius 131) formed an alliance with M. Licinius
Crassus Dives (**102**) and Cn. Pompeius Magnus (**111**) in
60 BC; later he became consul several times and dictator
(perpetuus). He was assassinated on the Ides of March 44
BC in the Curia Pompeia (on his life see, e.g., Weinstock
1971; Meier 1995; Gelzer 2008; Stevenson 2015; on his
career and oratory, see Lowrie 2008; van der Blom 2016,
146–80; on his speeches, pp. 305–12; 2017; on his style, see
von Albrecht 1989, 54–58 [esp. on F 29]; see also L. Grillo
and C. B. Krebs [eds.],* The Cambridge Companion to the
Writings of Julius Caesar *[Cambridge, 2017]).*

*Caesar studied oratory with M. Antonius Gnipho (Suet.
Gram. et rhet. 7.2) and later with Apollonius Molo of
Rhodes (T 11; F 17). In addition, Caesar wrote playful
poetry (Plin. Ep. 5.3.5; Tac. Dial. 21.6); a tragedy (TrRF
1:140); letters (Cic. Att. 9.6A, 9.7C, 9.13A.1, 9.16.2, 10.8B);
two volumes of* Anticatones *following the suicide of M.
Porcius Cato (**126**); a work* De analogia, *dedicated to Cicero, about the correct use of Latin (T 1; GRF, pp. 145–57);
and* commentarii *on his military and political achievements (T 2; Caes. BGall.; BCiv.). These* commentarii *in-
clude speeches put into the mouths of characters (esp.*

F 5 Cicero, *Letters to Friends* [to Q. Caecilius Metellus Nepos]

Now Quintus, my brother, has written out for me your most gentle speech that you had delivered in the Senate [on January 1, 57 BC] . . .

121 C. IULIUS CAESAR

Caes. BGall. 7.77; BCiv. 2.31–32) and indications of some of Caesar's own speeches (on Caesar's literary output, see Suet. Iul. 55–56).

In Cicero, Caesar is praised for his pure and elegant Latinity and well-chosen vocabulary (T 1–2; cf. T 4, 13). He was regarded as a great and gifted orator, renowned for his style, delivery, and force, and as almost as accomplished in this area as in the field of war (T 2–8, 10–13; Quint. Inst. 12.10.11).

In addition to numerous routine announcements during his consulships, Caesar is attested as having made various utterances as a politician and general (for speeches in the Senate, see, e.g., Vell. Pat. 2.50.2; in public meetings, see, e.g., Plut. Caes. 55.1; Vell. Pat. 2.50.2; Cass. Dio 41.16.1; to soldiers, see, e.g., Cass. Dio 42.53.1–54.3; Plut. Caes. 43.1–2, 51.2; Suet. Iul. 67.2, 70; Tac. Ann. 1.42.3; App. B Civ. 2.92.388–94.396; Caes. BCiv. 3.90; BHisp. 42; Polyaenus, Strat. 8.23.15–17, 22, 29; Frontin. Str. 1.9.4). Caesar is also attested as having spoken in support of Cn. Pompeius Magnus (111) being given extraordinary powers (Plut. Pomp. 25.8; Cass. Dio 36.43.2). He clashed with Q. Lutatius Catulus (96) on several occasions (Vell. Pat. 2.43.3–4; Plut. Caes. 6.6–7; Cic. Att. 2.24.3; Suet. Iul. 15),

*defended himself against allegations of involvement in the Catilinarian Conspiracy (Suet. Iul. 17; Plut. Caes. 8.5), boasted of his Gallic command (Suet. Iul. 22.2), spoke to the People against his consular colleague M. Calpurnius Bibulus (**122**) (Cic. Att. 2.21.5; CCMR, App. A: 288), and delivered a speech at Aquileia (Cic. Vat. 38; for a collection of sources for speeches by Caesar beyond ORF, see Dobesch 1975).*

Cicero claims that Caesar appeared alongside him in

T 1 Cic. *Brut.* 252–53

"sed tamen, Brute," inquit ATTICUS, "de Caesare et ipse ita iudico et de hoc huius generis acerrimo existimatore saepissime audio, illum omnium fere oratorum Latine loqui elegantissime; nec id solum domestica consuetudine ... sed quamquam id quoque credo fuisse, tamen, ut esset perfecta illa bene loquendi laus multis litteris et eis quidem reconditis et exquisitis summoque studio et diligentia est consecutus: [253] qui{n}[1] etiam in maximis occupationibus ad te ipsum," inquit in me intuens, "de ratione Latine loquendi accuratissime scripserit primoque in libro dixerit verborum dilectum originem esse eloquentiae ..."

[1] qui{n} *Schneider*: quin *codd.*

T 2 Cic. *Brut.* 261–62

[ATTICUS:] "Caesar autem rationem adhibens consuetudinem vitiosam et corruptam pura et incorrupta consuetudine emendat. itaque cum ad hanc elegantiam verborum Latinorum—quae, etiam si orator non sis et sis ingenuus

many trials (Cic. Lig. 30; cf. also Deiot. 7). In 63 BC,
*however, Caesar prosecuted C. Calpurnius Piso (**108**)*
for extortion in relation to unlawful punishment of a
Transpadane Gaul (Sall. Cat. 49.2), and the accused was
defended by Cicero (Cic. Pro C. Calpurnio Pisone: Craw-
ford 1984, 77–78) (TLRR 225). In 61/60 BC Caesar sup-
ported a request of the tax collectors against M. Porcius
*Cato (**126** F 18).*

T 1 Cicero, *Brutus*

"But still, Brutus," said ATTICUS, "of Caesar I myself have
the following opinion, and I also hear very frequently from
this most astute judge of this matter [Cicero], that of almost all orators he speaks Latin most elegantly, and this
not only by family habit . . . but, though I believe that this
was present too, still, he has achieved that this merit of
speaking correctly was perfected by much reading of literature and that of a recondite and esoteric kind as well
as by the greatest enthusiasm and diligence: [253] even in
the midst of the most important commitments he wrote,
dedicated to you," he said, looking at me [Cicero], "a most
careful treatise on the principles of speaking a pure Latin,
and he said in the first book that the choice of words is the
foundation of eloquence . . ."

T 2 Cicero, *Brutus*

[ATTICUS:] "Caesar, however [in contrast to orators using
incorrect or unusual words], by invoking rational theory,
corrects distorted and corrupt usage with pure and uncor-
rupted usage. Thus, when he joins to this elegant selection
of Latin words—which, even if you are not an orator and

395

civis Romanus, tamen necessaria est—adiungit illa orato-
ria ornamenta dicendi, tum videtur tamquam tabulas bene
pictas conlocare in bono lumine. hanc cum habeat praeci-
puam laudem, in communibus non video cui debeat cedere. splendidam quandam minimeque veteratoriam rationem dicendi tenet, voce, motu, forma etiam magnifica‹m›
et generosa‹m›[1] quodam modo." [262] tum BRUTUS:
"orationes quidem eius mihi vehementer probantur. compluris autem legi atque etiam commentarios, quos ‹i›dem[2]
scripsit rerum suarum." "valde quidem," inquam [CIC-
ERO], "probandos; nudi enim sunt, recti et venusti, omni
ornatu orationis tamquam veste detracta. sed dum voluit
alios habere parata, unde sumerent qui vellent scribere
historiam, ineptis gratum fortasse fecit, qui illa volent[3]
calamistris inurere: sanos quidem homines a scribendo
deterruit; nihil est enim in historia pura et inlustri brevitate dulcius. . . ."

[1] magnifica‹m› et generosa‹m› *Lambinus*: magnifica et generosa *codd.*   [2] quos ‹i›dem *Stangl*: quosdam *codd.*: quos
Bake   [3] illa volent *Suet.*: volunt illa *codd.*

T 3 Sall. *Cat.* 54.1

igitur iis genus, aetas, eloquentia prope aequalia fuere,
magnitudo animi par, item gloria, sed alia alii.

are a freeborn Roman citizen, is still necessary—the characteristic embellishments of oratorical style, then he almost seems to place well-painted pictures in a good light. Since he has this peculiar merit, I do not see to whom he should give place in regard to the standard qualities. He has a method of speaking that is brilliant and with no suggestion of routine, and which in respect of voice, movement, and appearance is even somehow noble and highbred." [262] At this point BRUTUS [said]: "His orations certainly are highly regarded by me. And I have read a number of them and also the *Commentaries*, which he wrote about his own deeds." "Indeed worthy of high regard," I [CICERO] said; "for they are like nude figures, straight and beautiful, stripped of all ornament of style as if of a garment. But while he wished others to have material ready, from which those who wished to write history could take, he perhaps gratified the inept, who may wish to apply their curling irons to that [material]: men of sound judgment certainly he has deterred from writing; for in history there is nothing more pleasing than clear and brilliant brevity. . . ."

T 3 Sallust, *The War with Catiline*

Now, their ancestry, age, and eloquence were almost equal; on a par was their magnanimity, likewise their renown, but of a different sort for each of them [Caesar and M. Porcius Cato (**126**)].

T 4 Quint. *Inst.* 10.1.114

C. vero Caesar si foro tantum vacasset, non alius ex nostris
contra Ciceronem nominaretur: tanta in eo vis est, id acumen, ea concitatio, ut illum eodem animo dixisse quo bel-
lavit appareat; exornat tamen haec omnia mira sermonis,
cuius proprie studiosus fuit, elegantia.

T 5 Quint. *Inst.* 10.2.25–26

quid ergo? non est satis omnia sic dicere quo modo M.
Tullius dixit? mihi quidem satis esset si omnia consequi
possem. quid tamen noceret vim Caesaris, asperitatem
Caeli, diligentiam Pollionis, iudicium Calvi quibusdam in
locis adsumere? [26] nam praeter id quod prudentis est
quod in quoque optimum est, si possit, suum facere, tum
in tanta rei difficultate unum intuentis vix aliqua pars se-
quitur . . .

T 6 Tac. *Dial.* 21.5

= F 46.

T 7 Tac. *Dial.* 25.3–4

[MESSALLA:] . . . sic apud nos Cicero quidem ceteros
eorundem temporum disertos antecessit, Calvus autem et
Asinius et Caesar et Caelius et Brutus iure et prioribus et

T 4 Quintilian, *The Orator's Education*

But if C. Caesar had only been free to spend time in the Forum, no other of our countrymen could have been named as a rival to Cicero: so much force, such a shrewdness, such a drive is in him that it is obvious that he spoke with the same spirit as he waged war; yet he dressed all this up with a wonderful elegance of language, which he studied in particular.

T 5 Quintilian, *The Orator's Education*

"What then? Is it not sufficient to speak always in the way in which Cicero spoke?" For me at any rate this would be sufficient if I could always achieve it. Still, what harm would there be in taking up Caesar's force, Caelius' asperity [M. Caelius Rufus (**162**)], Pollio's precision [C. Asinius Pollio (**174**)], Calvus' good judgment [C. Licinius Macer Calvus (**165**)] in some places? [26] For apart from the fact that it is appropriate for a wise man to make his own what is best in any model, if he can, then, with regard to such a difficult matter, hardly any part will go well for those who look to a single model . . .

T 6 Tacitus, *Dialogue on Oratory*

= F 46.

T 7 Tacitus, *Dialogue on Oratory*

[MESSALLA:] . . . so among our countrymen Cicero certainly surpassed the other orators of the same period; Calvus [C. Licinius Macer Calvus (**165**)], however, and Asinius [C. Asinius Pollio (**174**)] and Caesar and Caelius [M.

sequentibus anteponuntur. [4] nec refert quod inter se
specie differunt,[1] cum genere consentiant. adstrictior[2]
Calvus, nervosior[3] Asinius, splendidior Caesar, amarior
Caelius, gravior Brutus, vehementior et plenior et valen-
tior Cicero: omnes tamen eandem san{ct}itatem[4] eloquentiae ⟨prae se⟩ ferunt,[5] ut si omnium pariter libros in ma-
num sumpseris, scias, quamvis in diversis ingeniis, esse
quandam iudicii ac voluntatis similitudinem et cogna-
tionem.

[1] differunt *Halm*: differant *codd.*   [2] adstrictior *Acida-*
lius: at strictior *codd.*   [3] nervosior *Meiser*: nūosior *vel* nu-
merosior *codd.*   [4] san{ct}itatem *Rhenanus*: sanctitatem *codd.*
[5] ⟨prae se⟩ ferunt *Andresen*: serunt *vel* ferunt *codd.*

T 8 Tac. *Ann.* 13.3.2

nam dictator Caesar summis oratoribus aemulus . . .

T 9 Plin. *Ep.* 1.20.4

hic ille mecum auctoritatibus agit ac mihi ex Graecis orationes Lysiae ostentat, ex nostris Gracchorum Catonisque,
quorum sane plurimae sunt circumcisae et breves: ego
Lysiae Demosthenen Aeschinen Hyperiden multosque
praeterea, Gracchis et Catoni Pollionem Caesarem Cae-
lium, in primis M. Tullium oppono, cuius oratio optima
fertur esse quae maxima.

Caelius Rufus (**162**)] and Brutus [M. Iunius Brutus (**158**)] are rightly classed above both their predecessors and their successors. [4] And it does not matter that they differ among themselves in the species while they agree in genus. Calvus is more concise, Asinius more vigorous, Caesar brighter, Caelius more pungent, Brutus more dignified, Cicero more impassioned, fuller, and more forceful: yet they all exhibit the same healthiness of style, so that, if you took up the volumes of all of them at the same time, you would find that, in spite of their diverse talents, there is a certain family likeness in opinion and inclination.

T 8 Tacitus, *Annals*

For the dictator Caesar was a rival of the greatest orators . . .

T 9 Pliny the Younger, *Letters*

Here he [an admirer of brevity in oratory] produces his authorities to me and shows me from the Greeks the orations of Lysias and from our countrymen those of the brothers Gracchi [Ti. Sempronius Gracchus (**34**) and C. Sempronius Gracchus (**48**)] and Cato [M. Porcius Cato (**8**)], of whom most are indeed short and concise: I, for my part, counter Lysias with Demosthenes, Aeschines, Hyperides, and many others besides, and the Gracchi and Cato with Pollio [C. Asinius Pollio (**174**)], Caesar, Caelius [M. Caelius Rufus (**162**)], and above all M. Tullius [Cicero], whose best speech is generally thought to be the one that is longest.

T 10 Suet. *Iul.* 55.1–3

eloquentia militarique re aut aequavit praestantissimorum
gloriam aut excessit. post accusationem Dolabellae haud
dubie principibus patronis adnumeratus est. certe Cicero
ad Brutum oratores enumerans negat se videre, cui debeat
Caesar cedere, aitque eum elegantem, splendidam quoque atque etiam magnificam et generosam quodam modo
rationem dicendi tenere; et ad Cornelium Nepotem de
eodem ita scripsit: [2] "quid? oratorem quem huic ante-
pones eorum, qui nihil aliud egerunt? quis sententiis aut
acutior aut crebrior? quis verbis aut ornatior aut elegan-
tior?" genus eloquentiae dum taxat adulescens adhuc Stra-
bonis Caesaris secutus videtur, cuius etiam ex oratione,
quae inscribitur "pro Sardis," ad verbum nonnulla trans-
tulit in divinationem suam. pronuntiasse autem dicitur
voce acuta, ardenti motu gestuque, non sine venustate.
[3] orationes aliquas reliquit, inter quas temere quaedam
feruntur.

T 10 Suetonius, *Life of Caesar*

In eloquence and in the art of war he [Caesar] either equaled or surpassed the fame of the most eminent men. After the prosecution of Dolabella [F 15–23] he was without question numbered among the leading advocates. At all events, when Cicero reviews the orators in the work dedicated to Brutus [M. Iunius Brutus (**158**)], he states that he does not see to whom Caesar ought to yield [T 2], and he says that he has an elegant, also bright, and even grand and in some sense noble way of speaking. And to Cornelius Nepos he [Cicero] writes about him again as follows [letter fragment]: [2] "Come now, what orator would you rank above him of those who have done nothing else? Who has cleverer or more frequent pointed statements? Who is more elaborate or more elegant in diction?" At least while still a young man, he [Caesar] appears to have imitated the manner of speaking of Caesar Strabo, from whose speech that is entitled "On behalf of the Sardinians" [C. Iulius Caesar Strabo (**73**), F 7–10] he even transferred some passages word for word to a speech of his own in which he presented himself as an advocate.[1] He is said to have declaimed in a high-pitched voice with impassioned movement and gestures, not without grace. [3] He left several speeches, including some that are referred to as his on insufficient evidence [cf. F 48].

[1] A *divinatio* is a speech in which someone presents himself in competition with other advocates to win the right to conduct a prosecution. Since this procedure is different from the prosecution of Dolabella (F 15–23), this must therefore be a reference to another speech by Caesar, also dating to his youth.

T 11 Plut. *Caes.* 3.1–4

ἐκ δὲ τούτου τῆς Σύλλα δυνάμεως ἤδη μαραινομένης
καὶ τῶν οἴκοι καλούντων αὐτὸν, ἔπλευσεν εἰς Ῥόδον
ἐπὶ σχολὴν πρὸς Ἀπολλώνιον τὸν τοῦ Μόλωνος, οὗ
καὶ Κικέρων ἠκρόατο,[1] σοφιστεύοντος ἐπιφανῶς καὶ
τὸν τρόπον ἐπιεικοῦς εἶναι δοκοῦντος. [2] λέγεται δὲ
καὶ φῦναι πρὸς λόγους πολιτικοὺς ὁ Καῖσαρ ἄριστα
καὶ διαπονῆσαι φιλοτιμότατα τὴν φύσιν, ὡς τὰ δευ-
τερεῖα μὲν ἀδηρίτως ἔχειν, τὸ δὲ πρωτεῖον, [3] ὅπως
τῇ δυνάμει καὶ τοῖς ὅπλοις πρῶτος εἴη μᾶλλον {ἀλλ'}[2]
ἀσχοληθείς, ἀφεῖναι, πρὸς ὅπερ ἡ φύσις ὑφηγεῖτο
τῆς ἐν τῷ λέγειν δεινότητος, ὑπὸ στρατειῶν καὶ πολιτείας, ᾗ κατεκτήσατο τὴν ἡγεμονίαν, οὐκ ἐξικόμενος.
[4] αὐτὸς δ' οὖν ὕστερον ἐν τῇ πρὸς Κικέρωνα περὶ
Κάτωνος ἀντιγραφῇ παραιτεῖται, μὴ στρατιωτικοῦ
λόγον ἀνδρὸς ἀντεξετάζειν πρὸς δεινότητα ῥήτορος
εὐφυοῦς καὶ σχολὴν ἐπὶ τοῦτο πολλὴν ἄγοντος.

[1] ἠκρόατο *Cobet*: ἠκροᾶτο *codd.*   [2] *del. Stephanus*

T 12 Fronto, *Ad Verum imp.* 2.10 (p. 123.4–5 van den
Hout)

. . . Caesari quidem facultatem dicendi video imperato-
riam fuisse . . .

T 13 Gell. *NA* 19.8.3

Gaius enim Caesar, ille perpetuus dictator, Cn. Pompei
socer . . . vir ingenii praecellentis, sermonis praeter alios
suae aetatis castissimi . . .

T 11 Plutarch, *Life of Caesar*

Afterward, as Sulla's [L. Cornelius Sulla] power was now losing strength, and those at home were inviting him back, he [Caesar] sailed to Rhodes to study with Apollonius, the son of Molo, a well-known teacher and regarded as being of worthy character, whose pupil Cicero also was. [2] It is said, too, that Caesar had the greatest natural talent for political oratory and cultivated his talent most ambitiously, so that he had an undisputed second rank; the first rank, however, [3] he let go, because he rather devoted his efforts to being first in political power and in battle, and did not achieve that effectiveness in oratory to which his natural talent directed him, because of his campaigns and political activities, through which he acquired supremacy. [4] And so later, in his reply to Cicero about Cato [Caesar's *Anticato*], he himself demanded that the diction of a soldier should not be compared with the eloquence of an orator, gifted by nature and having plenty of leisure for this.

T 12 Fronto, *Correspondence*

[FRONTO to L. Verus:] . . . I see that Caesar had an ability in speaking characteristic of a general . . .

T 13 Gellius, *Attic Nights*

For Gaius Caesar, the famous dictator for life and Pompey's father-in-law [Cn. Pompeius Magnus (**111**), as Caesar's daughter was his fourth wife] . . . a man of wonderful talent, of an extremely pure diction surpassing the others of his time . . .

T 14 Apul. *Apol.* 95

= **92** T 11.

Against Cn. Cornelius Dolabella (F 15–23)

*As a young man (age slightly incorrect in F 15), Caesar prosecuted Cn. Cornelius Dolabella (**94** F 1) on a charge of extortion and won great fame for this intervention (in several parts, if the text is constituted correctly: F 23) even though the defendant, supported by C. Aurelius Cotta (**80***

F 15 Tac. *Dial.* 34.7

[MESSALLA:] nono decimo aetatis anno L. Crassus C. Carbonem, uno et vicesimo Caesar Dolabellam, altero et vicesimo Asinius Pollio C. Catonem, non multum aetate antecedens Calvus Vatinium iis orationibus insecuti sunt, quas hodieque cum admiratione legimus.

F 16 Quint. *Inst.* 12.6.1

neque ego annos definiam, cum Demosthenen puerum admodum actiones pupillares habuisse manifestum sit, Calvus Caesar Pollio multum ante quaestoriam omnes aetatem gravissima iudicia susceperint, praetextatos egisse quosdam sit traditum, Caesar Augustus duodecim natus annos aviam pro rostris laudaverit.

T 14 Apuleius, *Apologia*
= **92** T 11.

Against Cn. Cornelius Dolabella (F 15–23)

*F 13–14) and Q. Hortensius Hortalus (***92** *F 20A), was
acquitted (F 17, 20, 21; TLRR 140; Asc. in Cic.* Corn.
[p. 74.11–12 C.]; Vir. ill. 78.2; Empor., RLM, *p. 568.30–
31; Ps.-Asc. in Cic.* Div. Caec. *24 [p. 194.1–8 St.], in Cic.*
Verr. *2.1.41 [p. 234.30–32 St.]).*

F 15 Tacitus, *Dialogue on Oratory*

[MESSALLA:] In the nineteenth year of his life L. Crassus
[L. Licinius Crassus (**66**), F 13–14] prosecuted C. Carbo
[C. Papirius Carbo (**35**)], in his twenty-first year Caesar
Dolabella, in his twenty-second year Asinius Pollio [C.
Asinius Pollio (**174**), F 15–18] C. Cato [C. Porcius Cato
(**136**)], and, being not much further on in age, Calvus [C.
Licinius Macer Calvus (**165**), F 14–28] Vatinius [P. Vati-
nius] with those speeches that we read with admiration
even today.

F 16 Quintilian, *The Orator's Education*

And I shall not specify a particular age [at which to start
pleading], when it is well known that Demosthenes
pleaded against his guardians when still a boy, Calvus [C.
Licinius Macer Calvus (**165**), F 14–28], Caesar, and Pollio
[C. Asinius Pollio (**174**), F 15–18] all undertook very important cases long before the age of the quaestorship, it is
attested that some pleaded while wearing boys' clothing,
and Caesar Augustus gave the funeral eulogy of his grand-
mother from the front of the Rostra at the age of twelve.

F 17 Suet. *Iul.* 4.1

ceterum composita seditione civili Cornelium Dolabellam consularem et triumphalem repetundarum postulavit; absolutoque Rhodum secedere statuit, et ad declinandam invidiam et ut per otium ac requiem Apollonio Moloni clarissimo tunc dicendi magistro operam daret.

F 18 Suet. *Iul.* 55.1

= T 10.

F 19 Val. Max. 8.9.3

divus quoque Iulius, quam caelestis numinis tam etiam humani ingenii perfectissimum columen, vim facundiae proprie expressit dicendo in accusatione Cn. Dolabellae, quem reum egit, extorqueri sibi causam optimam C.[1] Cottae patrocinio, si quidem maxima tunc † eloquentiae † questa[2] est.

[1] C. *Pighi*: L. *codd.*   [2] eloquentiae questa *codd.*: eloquentia questa *unus cod. corr.*: ei maxima eloquentiae laus quaesita *vel* vis eloquentiae questa *vel* maxima tunc eloquentiae (ei) laus quaesita *vel* maxima tunc eloquentia questa *codd. det.*: eloquentiae ei laus questa *edd. vet.*: tum maxima eloquentiae laus quaesita *Perizonius*: <eloquentia de vi> eloquentiae questa *Kempf*

F 20 Asc. in Cic. *Scaur.* II.45 (p. 23 KS = 26.13–18 C.)

ne forte erretis et eundum hunc Cn. Dolabellam putetis esse in quem C. Caesaris orationes legitis, scire vos opor-

F 17 Suetonius, *Life of Caesar*

Then, after the civil disturbance had been quieted, he [Caesar] brought a charge of extortion against Cornelius Dolabella, an ex-consul [cos. 81 BC] and former triumphator [ca. 77 BC]. And upon his acquittal, he [Caesar] decided to withdraw to Rhodes, both to escape from ill will and so that, in leisure and quiet, he could devote attention to studying with Apollonius Molo, the most eminent teacher of oratory at the time.

F 18 Suetonius, *Life of Caesar*

= T 10.

F 19 Valerius Maximus, *Memorable Doings and Sayings*

The divine Iulius too, the most perfect pinnacle of celestial divinity as well as also of human genius, aptly expressed the force of eloquence when he said in the prosecution of Cn. Dolabella, whom he was taking to court, that this most valid case was being wrenched away from him by C. Cotta's advocacy [C. Aurelius Cotta (**80**), F 13–14], if indeed on that occasion eloquence at its greatest complained of the power of eloquence.[1]

[1] The text of the final clause is uncertain; the translation is based on Kempf's conjecture.

F 20 Asconius on Cicero, *Pro Scauro*

Lest you may make a mistake and believe that this Cn. Dolabella is the same as the one against whom you read the orations of C. Caesar, you ought to know that at ⟨that⟩

tet duos eodem ‹eo› tempore[1] fuisse et praenomine et nomine et cognomine Dolabellas. horum igitur alterum {Dolabellam}[2] Caesar accusavit nec damnavit; alterum M. Scaurus et accusavit et damnavit.

[1] eodem ‹eo› tempore *Clark*: eodem tempore *codd.*: eodem tempore eodem *Baiter*   [2] *del. Manutius*

F 21   Plut. *Caes.* 4.1–2

ἐπανελθὼν δ' ἀπὸ τῆς Ἑλλάδος[1] εἰς Ῥώμην, Δολοβέλλαν ἔκρινε κακώσεως ἐπαρχίας, καὶ πολλαὶ τῶν πόλεων μαρτυρίας αὐτῷ παρέσχον. [2] ὁ μὲν οὖν Δολοβέλλας ἀπέφυγε τὴν δίκην, ὁ δὲ Καῖσαρ . . .

[1] ἀπὸ τῆς Ἑλλάδος *huc transp. Schaefer, post* πολλαὶ *hab. codd.* (πολλαὶ τῶν ἀπὸ τῆς Ἑλλάδος *Reiske*)

F 22   Vell. Pat. 2.43.3

reliqua eius acta in urbe, nobilissima Cn. Dolabellae accusatio et maior civitatis in ea favor quam reis praestari solet . . .

F 23   Gell. *NA* 4.16.8–9

C. etiam Caesar, gravis auctor linguae Latinae, in Anticatone: "unius" inquit "arrogantiae, superbiae dominatuque." item in Dolabellam actionis I. lib. I.: "isti,[1] quorum in aedibus fanisque posita et honori erant et ornatu." [9] in libris quoque analogicis [F 26 *GRF*] omnia istiusmodi sine ‹i›[2] littera dicenda censet.

[1] I. lib. I.: isti *Hertz*: in libusti *vel* in libuisti *codd.*   [2] *add. codd. rec.*

very time there were two Dolabellae with the same first name, name, and nickname. One of these {Dolabella} Caesar prosecuted and did not get convicted, the other [praet. 81 BC] M. Scaurus [M. Aemilius Scaurus (**139**), F 1–3] both prosecuted and got convicted.

F 21 Plutarch, *Life of Caesar*

Having come back from Greece to Rome, he [Caesar] brought Dolabella to trial for maladministration of the province, and many of the cities supplied him with testimony. [2] Dolabella, it is true, was acquitted, but Caesar ... [continued by F 25]

F 22 Velleius Paterculus, *Compendium of Roman History*

His [Caesar's] remaining acts in the city of Rome: the very famous prosecution of Cn. Dolabella and the greater favor of the population in that [prosecution] than is usually shown to the accused ...

F 23 Gellius, *Attic Nights*

C. Caesar, too, a weighty authority on the Latin language, says in the *Anticato*: "for the arrogance, haughtiness, and tyranny of one man." Likewise in the first book of the first action against Dolabella: "those in whose temples and shrines they had been placed for honor and adornment." [9] In his books on analogy [F 26 *GRF*] as well he recommends that everything of that sort should be said without the letter ‹*i*›.[1]

---

[1] That is, the dative of words like *dominatus* and *ornatus* should be *dominatu* and *ornatu*, rather than the standard *dominatui* and *ornatui*.

Against C. Antonius Hybrida on Behalf of
the Greeks (F 24–25)

F 24 Asc. in Cic. *Tog. cand.* (p. 75 KS = 84.12–25 C.)

clientem autem negavit[1] habere posse C. Antonium: nam
is multos in Achaia spoliaverat nactus de exercitu Sullano
equitum turmas. deinde Graeci qui[2] spoliati erant[3] edux-
erunt Antonium in ius ad M. Lucullum praetorem qui ius
inter peregrinos dicebat. egit pro Graecis ⟨C. Caesar⟩[4]
etiam tum adulescentulus, de quo paulo ante mentionem
fecimus; et cum Lucullus id quod Graeci postulabant de-
crevisset, appellavit tribunos Antonius iuravitque se ideo
⟨e⟩iurare[5] quod aequo iure[6] uti non posset. hunc Antonium Gellius et Lentulus censores sexennio quo haec dicerentur senatu moverunt causasque[7] subscripserunt,
quod socios diripuerit, quod iudicium recusarit, quod
propter aeris alieni magnitudinem praedia manciparit[8]
bonaque sua in potestate non habeat.

[1] negavit *Baiter*: negabat *vel* negabit *codd.*: negat *Manutius*

[2] qui *codd.*: quos *Poggius*   [3] spoliati erant *Madvig*: spo-
liaverant *vel* spoliaverunt *codd.*: spoliaverat *Poggius*

[4] *add. Manutius*   [5] ⟨e⟩iurare *Baiter*: iurare *codd.*

[6] aequo iure *Lodoicus*: equa in re *codd.*   [7] catulisque *vel*
causasque *codd.*: titulosque *Clark*   [8] recusarit . . . manciparit *Manutius*: recusavit . . . mancipavit *codd.*

*Against C. Antonius Hybrida on Behalf of
the Greeks (F 24–25)*

In 76 BC Caesar supported some Greeks when they took
C. Antonius Hybrida (**113**) to court for appropriating assets and resources (TLRR 141).

F 24 Asconius on Cicero, *In Toga Candida*

But he [Cicero] denied that C. Antonius [C. Antonius
Hybrida (**113**)] could have a client: for he had robbed
many in Greece, after having obtained squadrons of cav-
alry from Sulla's [L. Cornelius Sulla] army. Then the
Greeks, who had been robbed, took Antonius to court
before the praetor M. Lucullus [M. Licinius Lucullus
(**91**)], who administered justice in cases involving foreign-
ers. ⟨C. Caesar⟩, then still a very young man, whom we
have mentioned a little earlier, pleaded the case on behalf
of the Greeks; and when Lucullus had decreed what the
Greeks demanded, Antonius appealed to the Tribunes and
swore that he rejected upon oath the court for the reason
that he could not have a fair application of the law. This
Antonius was removed from the Senate by the censors
Gellius [L. Gellius Poplicola (**101**)] and Lentulus [Cn.
Cornelius Lentulus Clodianus (**99**)] six years after this was
said [censors in 70 BC], and they entered on the roll as
explanations that he robbed the allies, that he rejected the
judgment of the court, that he, because of the size of his
debt, sold his estates and did not have any possessions in
his power.

F 25 Plut. *Caes.* 4.2–4

ὁ μὲν οὖν Δολοβέλλας ἀπέφυγε τὴν δίκην, ὁ δὲ Καῖσαρ, ἀμειβόμενος τὴν Ἑλλάδα τῆς προθυμίας, συνηγόρευσεν αὐτῇ Πόπλιον Ἀντώνιον διωκούσῃ δωροδοκίας ἐπὶ Λευκούλλου Μάρκου τοῦ Μακεδονίας στρατηγοῦ. [3] καὶ τοσοῦτον ἴσχυσεν, ὥστε τὸν Ἀντώνιον ἐπικαλέσασθαι τοὺς δημάρχους, σκηψάμενον οὐκ ἔχειν τὸ ἴσον ἐν τῇ Ἑλλάδι πρὸς Ἕλληνας. [4] ἐν δὲ Ῥώμῃ πολλὴ μὲν ἐπὶ τῷ λόγῳ περὶ τὰς συνηγορίας αὐτοῦ χάρις ἐξέλαμπε, πολλὴ δὲ τῆς περὶ τὰς δεξιώσεις καὶ ὁμιλίας φιλοφροσύνης εὔνοια παρὰ τῶν δημοτῶν ἀπήντα, θεραπευτικοῦ παρ' ἡλικίαν ὄντος.

On the Return of Lepidus' Followers (F 26–27)

In the 70s BC, during or after his military tribunate, Caesar supported the Lex Plautia de reditu Lepidanorum *(LPPR, p. 366, dated to 73 BC [70 BC in MRR II, pp. 128,*

F 26 Suet. *Iul.* 5

tribunatu militum, qui primus Romam reverso per suffragia populi honor optigit, actores restituendae tribuniciae potestatis, cuius vim Sulla deminuerat, enixissime iuvit. L.

F 25 Plutarch, *Life of Caesar*

[continued from F 21] Dolabella, it is true, was acquitted, but Caesar, repaying Greece for her zealous efforts, served as her advocate when she prosecuted Publius Antonius for corruption before Marcus Lucullus, the governor of Macedonia.[1] [3] And he was so effective that Antonius appealed to the Tribunes, alleging that he could not have a fair trial in Greece against Greeks. [4] And at Rome great popularity for him [Caesar] shone forth because of his eloquence as an advocate, and much goodwill from the common people for the friendliness of his manners in dealing with them, since he was ingratiating beyond his years.

[1] Plutarch calls C. Antonius Hybrida (**113**) Publius Antonius.—M. Licinius Lucullus (**91**) was praetor in 76 BC and governor of Macedonia after his consulship (73 BC). Plutarch seems to confuse these two roles and erroneously to locate the trial in Greece.

On the Return of Lepidus' Followers (F 26–27)

130]) and arranged for the return of the followers of M. Aemilius Lepidus (**95**), including Caesar's brother-in-law L. Cornelius Cinna (Cass. Dio 44.74.4).

F 26 Suetonius, *Life of Caesar*

During his term as military tribune, the first office that was conferred on him by vote of the People after his return to Rome, he [Caesar] very ardently supported the organizers of the plan to reestablish tribunician power, the influence of which Sulla [L. Cornelius Sulla] had reduced. Further-

etiam Cinnae uxoris fratri, et qui cum eo civili discordia Lepidum secuti post necem consulis ad Sertorium confugerant, reditum in civitatem rogatione Plotia confecit habuitque et ipse super ea re contionem.

F 27 Gell. *NA* 13.3.5

repperi tamen in oratione C. Caesaris, qua Plautiam rogationem suasit, "necessitatem" dictam pro "necessitudine," id est iure adfinitatis. verba haec sunt: "equidem mihi videor pro nostra necessitate non labore, non opera, non industria defuisse."

Cf. Non., p. 354.7–11 M. = 561 L.

Funeral Oration for His Aunt Iulia (F 28–29)

F 28 Plut. *Caes.* 5.1–3

τοῦ δὲ δήμου πρώτην μὲν ἀπόδειξιν τῆς πρὸς αὐτὸν εὐνοίας ἔλαβεν, ὅτε πρὸς Γάιον Ποπίλιον ἐρίσας ὑπὲρ χιλιαρχίας πρότερος ἀνηγορεύθη· [2] δευτέραν δὲ καὶ καταφανεστέραν, ὅτε τῆς Μαρίου γυναικὸς Ἰουλίας ἀποθανούσης, ἀδελφιδοῦς ὢν αὐτῆς, ἐγκώμιόν τε

more, he achieved the return of L. Cinna [L. Cornelius Cinna], his wife's [Cornelia, Caesar's first wife] brother, and of those who, together with that man, had followed Lepidus [M. Aemilius Lepidus (**95**), cos. 78 BC] in the civil conflict and, after the consul's death, had fled to Sertorius [Q. Sertorius, based in Spain], into the community through a bill proposed by Plotius, and he even delivered personally a speech at a public meeting about that matter.

F 27 Gellius, *Attic Nights*

Yet in a speech of C. Caesar, however, by which he supported a bill of Plautius, I found *necessitas* used for *necessitudo*, that is for the bond of relationship. The words are as follows: "To me indeed it seems that, in view of our kinship, I have failed not in labor, not in pains, not in industry."

When quaestor in 69 BC, Caesar delivered the funeral orations for his aunt Iulia (F 28–29; Kierdorf 1980, 114–16) and his wife Cornelia (F 30–31; CCMR, App. A: 244).

Funeral Oration for His Aunt Iulia (F 28–29)

F 28 Plutarch, *Life of Caesar*

The first proof of the People's goodwill toward him he [Caesar] received when he competed against Gaius Popilius [*RE* Popillius 5] for a military tribuneship and was elected ahead of him; [2] a second and more conspicuous proof when, being the nephew of Iulia, the deceased wife of Marius [C. Marius, seven-time consul], he delivered a splendid encomium on her in the Forum, and in her fu-

417

λαμπρὸν ἐν ἀγορᾷ διῆλθε, καὶ περὶ τὴν ἐκφορὰν
ἐτόλμησεν εἰκόνας Μαρίων προθέσθαι, τότε πρῶτον
ὀφθείσας μετὰ τὴν ἐπὶ Σύλλα πολιτείαν, πολεμίων
τῶν ἀνδρῶν κριθέντων. [3] ἐπὶ τούτῳ γὰρ ἐνίων κατα-
βοησάντων τοῦ Καίσαρος, ὁ δῆμος ἀντήχησε, λαμ-
πρῷ δεξάμενος κρότῳ καὶ θαυμάσας ὥσπερ ἐξ Ἅιδου
διὰ χρόνων πολλῶν ἀνάγοντα τὰς Μαρίου τιμὰς εἰς
τὴν πόλιν.

F 29 Suet. *Iul.* 6.1

quaestor Iuliam amitam uxoremque Corneliam defunctas
laudavit e more pro rostris. {s}et[1] in amitae quidem lauda-
tione de eius ac patris sui utraque origine sic refert: "amitae meae Iuliae maternum genus ab regibus ortum, pater-
num cum diis inmortalibus coniunctum est. nam ab Anco
Marcio sunt Marcii Reges, quo nomine fuit mater; a
Venere Iulii, cuius gentis familia est nostra. est ergo in
genere et sanctitas regum, qui plurimum inter homines
pollent, et caerimonia deorum, quorum ipsi in potestate
sunt reges."

[1] {s}et *Casaubon*: sed *codd.*

Funeral Oration for His Wife Cornelia (F 30–31)

F 30 Suet. *Iul.* 6.1

= F 29.

neral procession ventured to display portraits of Marians,
then seen for the first time since the administration of
Sulla [L. Cornelius Sulla], because the men had been regarded as public enemies. [3] For, when some cried out
against Caesar because of this, the People answered them
with loud shouts, received him with great applause, and
admired him for bringing back after so long a time, as it
were from Hades, the honors of Marius into the city.

F 29 Suetonius, *Life of Caesar*

When quaestor [69 BC], he [Caesar] delivered eulogies,
as was customary, from the front of the Rostra for his aunt
Iulia and his wife Cornelia, who had both died. And in the
eulogy of his aunt he spoke in the following terms of the
paternal and maternal ancestry of her and his father: "The
family of my aunt Iulia is descended on her mother's side
from the kings, on her father's side is linked to the immortal gods. For the Marcii Reges, which was her mother's name, stem from Ancus Marcius, and the Iulii, the
family of which ours is a branch, from Venus.[1] Our stock
therefore has both the sanctity of kings, who have the
supreme power among mortal men, and the sacredness of
gods, in whose power even kings are."

[1] For Caesar referring his origin back to Venus, cf. also Schol.
Gronov. ad Cic. *Marc.* 1 (p. 296.15–16 St.); Serv. ad Verg. *Aen.*
1.267 = *Orig. gent. Rom.* 15.5.

Funeral Oration for His Wife Cornelia (F 30–31)

F 30 Suetonius, *Life of Caesar*

= F 29.

F 31 Plut. *Caes.* 5.4–5

τὸ μὲν οὖν ἐπὶ γυναιξὶ πρεσβυτέραις λόγους ἐπιταφί-
ους διεξιέναι πάτριον ἦν Ῥωμαίοις, ⟨ἐπὶ⟩¹ νέαις δ' οὐκ
ὂν ἐν ἔθει, πρῶτος εἶπε Καῖσαρ ἐπὶ τῆς ἑαυτοῦ γυναικὸς ἀποθανούσης. [5] καὶ τοῦτ' ἤνεγκεν αὐτῷ χάριν
τινα καὶ συνεδημαγώγησε τῷ πάθει τοὺς πολλοὺς ὡς
ἥμερον ἄνδρα καὶ περίμεστον ἤθους ἀγαπᾶν.

¹ add. Hess

On the Catilinarian Conspirators (F 32–36A)

*In the debate in the Senate about the fate of the captured
Catilinarian conspirators at the end of 63 BC, Caesar, then
a praetor elect, proposed life imprisonment, rather than
the death penalty as previous speakers had done (Cic. Att.*

F 32 Cic. *Cat.* 4.7–10

video duas adhuc esse sententias, unam D. Silani qui censet eos qui haec delere conati sunt morte esse multandos,
alteram C. Caesaris qui mortis poenam removet, ceterorum suppliciorum omnis acerbitates amplectitur. uterque
et pro sua dignitate et pro rerum magnitudine in summa
severitate versatur. . . . alter intellegit mortem a dis im-
mortalibus non esse supplici causa constitutam, sed aut
necessitatem naturae aut laborum ac miseriarum quie-
tem. itaque eam sapientes numquam inviti, fortes saepe
etiam libenter oppetiverunt. vincula vero et ea sempiterna

F 31 Plutarch, *Life of Caesar*

Now, in the case of elderly women, it was a tradition for
the Romans to deliver funeral orations over them; but it
was not a custom in the case ⟨of⟩ young women, and
Caesar was the first to speak in that way upon the death of
his own wife. [5] And this brought him considerable favor
and helped with winning the sympathies of the multitude,
so that they were fond of him, as a man who was gentle
and full of feeling.

On the Catilinarian Conspirators (F 32–36A)

*12.21.1; Suet. Iul. 14; App. B Civ. 2.6.21); Sallust presents
a version of Caesar's speech in his historiographical work
(F 36A; cf.* **126** *F 16A).*

F 32 Cicero, *Against Catiline*

I see that so far there are two proposals: one of D. Silanus
[D. Iunius Silanus, cos. 62 BC], who proposes that those
who have attempted to destroy this [the political system]
should be punished by death, the other of C. Caesar, who
removes the death penalty and advocates all types of
harshness relating to other punishments. Each of the two,
in relation to both their position and the gravity of the
matter, is concerned with the utmost severity. . . . The
other [Caesar] recognizes that death has been ordained by
the immortal gods not for the sake of punishment, but
either as a necessity of nature or as a relief from all kinds
of toil and woe. That is why philosophers have never faced
it unwillingly, brave men often even gladly. Confinement,

certe ad singularem poenam nefarii sceleris inventa sunt.
municipiis dispertiri iubet. . . . [8] . . . adiungit gravem
poenam municipiis, si quis eorum vincula ruperit; horri-
bilis custodias circumdat et dignas scelere hominum per-
ditorum; sancit ne quis eorum poenam quos condemnat
aut per senatum aut per populum levare possit; eripit
etiam spem quae sola hominem in miseriis consolari solet.
bona praeterea publicari iubet; vitam solam relinquit ne-
fariis hominibus: quam si eripuisset, multas uno dolore
animi atque corporis ⟨miserias⟩[1] et omnis scelerum poenas ademisset. . . . [10] . . . at vero C. Caesar intellegit
legem Semproniam esse de civibus Romanis constitutam;
qui autem rei publicae sit hostis eum civem esse nullo
modo posse; denique ipsum latorem Semproniae legis
iussu populi poenas rei publicae dependisse. idem ipsum
Lentulum, largitorem et prodigum, non putat, cum de
pernicie populi Romani, exitio huius urbis tam acerbe,
tam crudeliter cogitarit, etiam appellari posse popularem.
itaque homo mitissimus atque lenissimus non dubitat P.
Lentulum aeternis tenebris vinculisque mandare et sancit
in posterum ne quis huius supplicio levando se iactare et

[1] *add. Clark*: aerumnas *add. Halm*

however, and for life at that, has certainly been invented
as an exemplary punishment for a heinous crime. He proposes that they be dispersed among the towns of Italy. . . .
[8] . . . He also proposes a heavy penalty for the towns if
any of the men should escape the confinement; he sur-
rounds them with grim guards, matching the crime of the
corrupt men; he prescribes that nobody can mitigate the
penalty of the men whom he condemns, neither through
the Senate nor through the People; he removes even hope,
which usually is the only thing to console men in misfor-
tune. He further orders their property to be confiscated;
he leaves only their lives to these wicked men: if he had
taken that from them, he would in one painful act have
relieved them of much mental and bodily ‹suffering› and
of all the penalties for their crimes. . . . [10] . . . But C.
Caesar recognizes that the *Lex Sempronia* [*Lex Sempronia
de capite civis Romani*: *LPPR*, pp. 309–10; ensured the
right of appeal to the citizen assembly for Roman citizens
facing the death penalty] was put in place for Roman citizens; but that he who is an enemy of the Republic cannot
be a citizen in any way; finally, that the author of the *Lex
Sempronia* himself [C. Sempronius Gracchus (**48**)] paid
the supreme penalty to the Republic on the order of the
People. At the same time he [Caesar] does not think that
Lentulus himself [P. Cornelius Lentulus Sura (**100**)],
prodigal and spendthrift, can even be called a friend of the
People because he planned the massacre of the Roman
People and the destruction of this city so viciously and so
cruelly. Thus the kindest and gentlest of men does not
hesitate to consign P. Lentulus to permanent darkness and
chains and prescribes for the future that nobody could find
glory by lightening his punishment and subsequently win

in pernicie populi Romani posthac popularis esse possit.
adiungit etiam publicationem bonorum, ut omnis animi
cruciatus et corporis etiam egestas ac mendicitas conse-
quatur.

F 33 Plut. *Caes.* 7.7–9

. . . οἷς εἰ μὲν κρύφα παρεῖχέ τι θάρσους καὶ δυνάμεως ὁ Καῖσαρ, ἄδηλόν ἐστιν, ἐν δὲ τῇ βουλῇ κατὰ
κράτος ἐξελεγχθέντων, καὶ Κικέρωνος τοῦ ὑπάτου
γνώμας ἐρωτῶντος περὶ κολάσεως ἕκαστον, οἱ μὲν
ἄλλοι μέχρι Καίσαρος θανατοῦν ἐκέλευον, [8] ὁ δὲ
Καῖσαρ ἀναστὰς λόγον διῆλθε πεφροντισμένον, ὡς
ἀποκτεῖναι μὲν ἀκρίτους ἄνδρας ἀξιώματι καὶ γένει
λαμπροὺς οὐ δοκεῖ πάτριον οὐδὲ δίκαιον εἶναι μὴ
μετὰ τῆς ἐσχάτης ἀνάγκης· [9] εἰ δὲ φρουροῦντο δε-
θέντες ἐν πόλεσι τῆς Ἰταλίας, ἃς ἂν αὐτὸς ἕληται
Κικέρων, μέχρι ⟨ἂν⟩[1] οὗ καταπολεμηθῇ Κατιλίνας,
ὕστερον ἐν εἰρήνῃ καὶ καθ᾽ ἡσυχίαν περὶ ἑκάστου τῇ
βουλῇ γνῶναι παρέξειν.

[1] *add. Ziegler ex Plut. Cic. 21.1 (ubi* ἄχρι ἂν οὗ)

Cf. Plut. *Cic.* 21.1.

F 34 Cass. Dio 37.36.1–2

ὁ γὰρ Καῖσαρ, πάντων τῶν πρὸ αὐτοῦ ψηφισαμένων
ἀποθανεῖν σφας, γνώμην ἔδωκε δῆσαί τε αὐτοὺς καὶ
ἐς πόλεις ἄλλους ἄλλῃ καταθέσθαι, [2] τῶν οὐσιῶν
ἐστερημένους, ἐπὶ τῷ μήτε περὶ ἀδείας ἔτι αὐτῶν χρη-
ματισθῆναί τί ποτε, κἂν διαδρᾷ τις, ἐν πολεμίων
μοίρᾳ τὴν πόλιν ἐξ ἧς ἂν φύγῃ εἶναι· . . .

popularity through the destruction of the Roman People. He also adds the confiscation of their property, so that every mental and physical torment may be followed even by poverty and beggary.

F 33 Plutarch, *Life of Caesar*

. . . whether Caesar secretly gave these men [some of the captured Catilinarian conspirators] any encouragement and help, is uncertain; but after they had been overwhelmingly convicted in the Senate, and Cicero the consul [63 BC] asked each senator to give his opinion on the punishment, the others, down to Caesar, urged that they be put to death, [8] but Caesar rose and delivered a long and studied speech: that to put to death without trial men distinguished by their rank and lineage did not seem traditional or just, unless under the most extreme necessity; [9] but that, if they should be bound and kept in custody, in towns of Italy, which Cicero himself might select, until Catiline [L. Sergius Catilina (**112**)] had been exhausted by war, the Senate could afterward, in peace and at leisure, vote upon the case of each of them.

F 34 Cassius Dio, *Roman History*

For while all before Caesar had voted that they [the captured Catilinarian conspirators] should be put to death, he expressed the opinion that they should be kept in bonds and each placed in different towns, [2] after having their property confiscated, on the condition that there should never be any further deliberation concerning their pardon, and that if any one of them should escape, the town from which he fled should be considered as being an enemy. . . .

F 35 App. *B Civ.* 2.6.20

Γάιός τε Καῖσαρ οὐ καθαρεύων μὲν ὑπονοίας μὴ συν-
εγνωκέναι τοῖς ἀνδράσι, Κικέρωνος δ' οὐ θαρροῦντος
καὶ τόνδε, ὑπεραρέσκοντα τῷ δήμῳ, ἐς τὸν ἀγῶνα
προβαλέσθαι, προσετίθει διαθέσθαι τοὺς ἄνδρας Κικέρωνα τῆς Ἰταλίας ἐν πόλεσιν αἷς ἂν αὐτὸς δοκι-
μάσῃ, μέχρι Κατιλίνα καταπολεμηθέντος ἐς δικαστή-
ριον ὑπαχθῶσι, καὶ μηδὲν ἀνήκεστον ἐς ἄνδρας
ἐπιφανεῖς ᾗ πρὸ λόγου καὶ δίκης ἐξειργασμένος.

F 36 Iul. Vict., *RLM*, p. 379.14–20

et ut breviter explicem, quaecumque controversia versatur in aestimatione[1] vel pretii vel quantitatis vel numeri vel
alicuius huiusmodi rei, ea cadit in statum negotialem;
sicut etiam de aestimatione litis aut de modo poenae
constituendo iis, quorum de culpa iam pronuntiatum est,
quales sunt duae orationes Catonis et Caesaris de poena
coniuratorum; quaeritur enim illic, quanti lis coniuratorum debeat aestimari.

[1] litis *post* aestimatione *add. Mai, Orelli, Halm*

F 36A Sall. *Cat.* 50.5–52.1

*Caesar stresses that the decision about the fate of the cap-
tured conspirators should be made objectively, with minds
free from passion. To illustrate that, he recalls examples of
ancestors who, in decreeing punishments, took into consideration what conduct would be consistent with their
dignity rather than what action could be justified. Simi-*

F 35 Appian, *Civil Wars*

Gaius Caesar was not free from the suspicion of complic-
ity with these men [the Catilinarians], but Cicero did not
venture to bring into the controversy even him, since he
[Caesar] was so popular with the People; he [Caesar] proposed that Cicero should distribute the men among towns
of Italy, which he himself should approve, until, after Catiline [L. Sergius Catilina (**112**)] had been exhausted by
war, they should be brought to trial, and nothing irremedi-
able should be inflicted upon distinguished men in place
of argument and trial.

F 36 Iulius Victor

And, so that I explain it briefly, whatever controversy sur-
rounds the assessment of value or size or quantity or another matter of this kind, this falls under the *status ne-
gotialis* [i.e., "pragmatic issue"]; thus, too, as regards the
assessment of the damage or the fixing of the kind of penalty for those whose guilt has already been declared: such
as the two speeches of Cato [M. Porcius Cato (**126**),
F 13–16A] and Caesar about the penalty of the conspirators; for there it is asked at how much the damage of the
conspirators should be assessed.

F 36A Sallust, *The War with Catiline*

*larly, for the current Senate the villainy of the conspirators
should not have more weight than their own dignity. Caesar therefore advises applying such penalties as have been
established by law and following the principles introduced
by the wise ancestors, although he agrees that no punishment is too great for the crimes committed. He points out*

*that death is a relief from woes, not a torment, and that
such a decision might be misinterpreted. Thus Caesar concludes by moving that the conspirators' assets be confis-*

On Behalf of Masintha (F 37)

F 37 Suet. *Iul.* 71

studium et fides erga clientis ne iuveni quidem defuerunt.
Masintham nobilem iuvenem, cum adversus Hiempsalem
regem tam enixe defendisset, ut Iubae regis filio in altercatione barbam invaserit, stipendiarium quoque pronuntiatum et abstrahentibus statim eripuit occultavitque apud
se diu et mox ex praetura proficiscens in Hispaniam inter
officia prosequentium fascesque lictorum lectica sua
avexit.

In Response to the Praetors C. Memmius and
L. Domitius Ahenobarbus (F 38–41)

*At the end of Caesar's first consulship (59 BC), the prae-
tors for 58 BC, C. Memmius (**125** F 7–10) and L. Domitius
Ahenobarbus (**131** F 2–3), questioned some initiatives of*

*cated, that the men be kept in bonds throughout the towns
of Italy, and that nobody refer their case to the Senate or
bring it before the People subsequently.*

On Behalf of Masintha (F 37)

*Caesar defended the young Masintha, a noble Numidian,
against King Hiempsal of Numidia.*

F 37 Suetonius, *Life of Caesar*

Even when a young man, he [Caesar] showed no lack of
devotion and fidelity to his dependents. When he had defended Masintha, a noble young man, against king Hiempsal so energetically that in the dispute he caught the beard
of Juba, the king's son, he [Caesar] at once rescued him
[Masintha]—having also been declared a tributary [to the
king]—from those who would carry him off, and kept him
hidden for a long time in his house, and, later, when he set
off for Hispania after his praetorship [62 BC], he carried
him off in his own litter, amid the courtesies of those seeing him off and the *fasces* of the lictors.

In Response to the Praetors C. Memmius and L. Domitius Ahenobarbus (F 38–41)

*the past year, including the agrarian law; Caesar replied
to the Tribunes in three speeches in the Senate (F 39–40).*

F 38 Suet. *Iul.* 23.1

functus consulatu Gaio Memmio Lucioque Domitio prae-
toribus de superioris anni actis referentibus cognitionem
senatui detulit; nec illo suscipiente triduoque per inritas
altercationes absumpto in provinciam abiit.

F 39 Schol. Bob. ad Cic. *Sest.* 40 (p. 130.9–12 Stangl)

de actis loquitur quae habuit in consulatu C. Caesar inaus-
picato, ut videbatur, qua de re adversus eum egerant in
senatu C. Memmius et L. Domitius praetores. et ipsius
Caesaris orationes contra hos extant ‹tres quibus›[1] et sua
acta defendit et illos insectatur.

[1] ‹tres quibus› *vel* ‹tres quis› *Stangl (cf. F 40)*: ‹quibus› *edd.*
Romana, Turicensis, Teubneriana

F 40 Schol. Bob. ad Cic. *Vat.* 15 (p. 146.19–21 Stangl)

commiserat autem senatui causam suam C. Caesar, id est
ut de lege agraria patres iudicarent. ibi enim habitae sunt
tres illae orationes contra Domitium et Memmium.

F 41 Suet. *Iul.* 73.1

simultates contra nullas tam graves excepit umquam, ut
non occasione oblata libens deponeret. Gai Memmi, cuius

F 38 Suetonius, *Life of Caesar*

At the close of his consulship [59 BC], when the praetors [58 BC] Gaius Memmius [C. Memmius (**125**), F 7–10] and Lucius Domitius [L. Domitius Ahenobarbus (**131**), F 2–3] raised the acts of the past year, he [Caesar] brought the inquiry to the Senate; and when it failed to take it up, and three days had been wasted in fruitless wrangling, he went off to his province.

F 39 Scholia Bobiensia to Cicero, *Pro Sestio*

He [Cicero] speaks about the acts that C. Caesar initiated during his consulship [59 BC], without luck, as it seems, as the praetors [58 BC] C. Memmius [C. Memmius (**125**), F 7–10] and L. Domitius [L. Domitius Ahenobarbus (**131**), F 2–3] raised this matter against him in the Senate. And there are extant from Caesar himself ‹three› speeches against these men, ‹in which› he both defends his acts and inveighs against them.

F 40 Scholia Bobiensia to Cicero, *Against Vatinius*

But C. Caesar had handed his case over to the Senate, that is, so that the senators should decide about the agrarian law. For it was there that those three speeches against Domitius [L. Domitius Ahenobarbus (**131**), F 2–3] and Memmius [C. Memmius (**125**), F 7–10] were delivered.

F 41 Suetonius, *Life of Caesar*

On the other hand, he never formed such bitter enmities that he was not glad to lay them aside when opportunity offered. As for Gaius Memmius [C. Memmius (**125**),

asperrimis orationibus non minore acerbitate rescripserat, etiam suffragator mox in petitione consulatus fuit.

On the Political Situation in the Senate (F 41A)

In his commentarii *Caesar reports the argument of a speech of his, delivered in the Senate in spring 49 BC, about his political activities and the actions of opponents*

F 41A Caes. *BCiv.* 1.32

ipse ad urbem proficiscitur. [2] coacto senatu iniurias inimicorum commemorat. docet se nullum extraordinarium honorem appetisse sed expectato legitimo tempore consulatus eo fuisse contentum quod omnibus civibus pateret; [3] latum ab X tribunis plebis—contradicentibus inimicis, Catone{m} vero acerrime repugnante{m} et pristina consuetudine dicendi mora dies extrahente{m}[1]—ut sui ratio absentis haberetur ipso consule Pompeio; qui si improbasset cur ferri passus esset? si probasset cur se uti populi

---

[1] Catone{m} . . . repugnante{m} . . . extrahente{m} *Aldus:* Catonem . . . repugnantem . . . extrahentem *codd.*

F 7–10], to whose very harsh speeches he had replied (in writing)[1] with no less bitterness, soon afterward he [Caesar] was even a supporter in his campaign for the consulship [in 54 BC].

[1] If *rescripserat* is to be taken in a literal sense, this passage refers to another reply in addition to the speeches specified in F 39–40.

On the Political Situation in the Senate (F 41A)

(Cass. Dio 41.15.2–4), followed by a speech of similar content to the People (Cass. Dio 41.16.1; Vell. Pat. 2.50.2; App. B Civ. 2.41.163).

F 41A Caesar, *Civil War*

He himself [Caesar] sets out for the city [of Rome]. [2] When the Senate has been summoned, he recounts the injuries done by his enemies. He explains that he had not been standing for an extraordinary office, but, having waited until the legal time for a consulship, he had been content with what was open to all citizens; [3] that a law had been proposed by the ten Tribunes of the People—while his enemies were arguing against it and Cato [M. Porcius Cato (**126**), F 27] indeed resisted with the utmost vehemence and with his old tactic of speaking to drag the time out with delay—saying that account should be taken of his candidacy in absentia, when Pompey [Cn. Pompeius Magnus (**111**), cos. 70, 55, 52 BC] himself was consul [52 BC; cf. Cass. Dio 40.51.2]. If he [Pompey] had disapproved, why had he allowed it to be proposed? If he had approved, why had he prevented him from enjoying a fa-

beneficio prohibuisset? [4] patientiam proponit suam cum
de exercitibus dimittendis ultro postulavisset, in quo iac-
turam dignitatis atque honoris ipse facturus esset. [5]
acerbitatem inimicorum docet, qui quod ab altero postu-
larent in se recusarent atque omnia permisceri mallent
quam imperium exercitusque dimittere. [6] iniuriam in
eripiendis legionibus praedicat, crudelitatem et insolentiam in circumscribendis tribunis plebis. conditiones a se
latas, expetita colloquia et denegata commemorat. [7] pro
quibus rebus hortatur ac postulat ut rem publicam susci-
piant atque una secum administrent; sin timore defugiant
illis se oneri non futurum et per se rem publicam admi-
nistraturum; [8] legatos ad Pompeium de compositione
mitti oportere; neque se reformidare quod in senatu Pompeius paulo ante dixisset: ad quos legati mitterentur his
auctoritatem attribui timoremque eorum qui mitterent
significari; [9] tenuis atque infirmi haec animi videri; se
vero ut opibus anteire studuerit sic iustitia et aequitate
velle superare.

To Soldiers at Placentia (F 41B)

vor of the Roman People? [4] He [Caesar] cites his own patience, since of his own accord he had proposed that the armies be dismissed, a matter in which he would experience the loss of dignity and prestige. [5] He shows the harshness of his enemies, who were refusing for themselves what they asked from the other side and preferred creating total confusion to giving up power and armies. [6] He singles out the injury done in depriving him of his legions, and the brutality and highhandedness in obstructing the Tribunes of the People. He recounts the terms proposed by him, the negotiations requested and refused. [7] For all these reasons he exhorts and asks that they take charge of the state and administer it with him; but if they are shirking their duty out of fear, he will not be a burden to them and will administer the Republic on his own. [8] Envoys, he says, ought to be sent to Pompey about a settlement; he does not fear what Pompey had mentioned in the Senate a little earlier: that authority was granted to those to whom envoys were sent, and the fear of those who sent them was demonstrated. [9] This looked like a sign of a petty and feeble character, but he, just as he had made an effort to get ahead in resources, so he wished to outdo others in justice and equity.

To Soldiers at Placentia (F 41B)

Versions of an oration given to unruly soldiers at Placentia (modern Piacenza) in 49 BC are provided by Cassius Dio and (more briefly) by Appian (App. B Civ. 2.47.191–95; CCMR, App. C: 94).

F 41B Cass. Dio 41.26–35

*After some soldiers have mutinied at Placentia, Caesar
addresses the whole army: Caesar starts by assuring the
soldiers that he is keen to support them and have their
affection, but would not wish to share in their errors. He
reminds them that they have provisions in abundance and
that those who have rebelled are not looking for advantage
with reference to what is permanently beneficial; he states
that it is absurd, after conquering the enemy, to be over-
come by pleasures. Caesar concedes that most of the soldiers do their duty scrupulously and satisfactorily, abiding
by ancestral customs, but he points out that a few are
bringing disgrace and dishonor upon everyone. This has
now reached such a stage that he can no longer ignore the
misconduct of a minority, as they are trying to make the
rest mutinous as well and their actions may have a bad*

To Soldiers in Africa (F 42)

F 42 Suet. *Iul.* 66

fama vero hostilium copiarum perterritos non negando
minuendove, sed insuper amplificando ementiendoque
confirmabat. itaque cum expectatio adventus Iubae terri-
bilis esset, convocatis ad contionem militibus: "scitote,"

F 41B Cassius Dio, *Roman History*

*effect on the entire group. For everyone who learned of
these incidents would refer the errors of the few to all.
Moreover, such conduct is not worthy of Romans, particularly since their aim is to assist the outraged country and
defend it against oppressors; accordingly, they should not
show themselves as greedy of gain as the wrongdoers. Caesar also points out that, by natural law, ruling and being
ruled have been placed upon men: one discovers and com-
mands what is required, and the other should obey without questioning. In conclusion, Caesar announces that he
will never yield to these agitators under compulsion and
even tells these men to quit the military service. After the
speech Caesar executes the most audacious and dismisses
the rest.*

To Soldiers in Africa (F 42)

*Suetonius reports a short speech given by Caesar to his
soldiers when fighting in Africa (CCMR, App. C: 115). It
is said to illustrate his approach to arousing the army's
courage (see Polyaenus, Strat. 8.23.19).*

F 42 Suetonius, *Life of Caesar*

In fact, when they [the soldiers] were in a panic on account
of reports about the numbers of the enemy's troops, he
[Caesar] used to reassure them, not by denying or dis-
counting, but even by exaggerating and fabricating. Accordingly, when the anticipation of Juba's [king of Nu-
midia] coming created fear, he called the soldiers together

437

inquit, "paucissimis his diebus regem adfuturum cum decem legionibus, equitum triginta, levis armaturae centum milibus, elephantis trecentis. proinde desinant quidam quaerere ultra aut opinari mihique, qui compertum habeo, credant; aut quidem vetustissima nave impositos quocumque vento in quascumque terras iubebo avehi."

About Himself and the Political Situation (F 42A)

Cassius Dio reports that, after decrees to honor Caesar and to give him extensive political power had been passed in 46 BC, he entered Rome and delivered a reassuring

F 42A Cass. Dio 43.15.1–18.6

After Caesar has entered Rome and noticed that people were apprehensive of his power and therefore voted him extravagant honors through flattery, he delivers a speech in the Senate: Caesar starts by reassuring the senators that, in contrast to predecessors, he will not do anything harsh just because he is victorious and in power. He stresses that he has always been open and honest and that his nature has always been and will be the same. Caesar claims that he has only aimed to secure power so that he might punish all enemies, and he would not want to be convicted of doing those things he rebuked in others with a different opinion. He announces that he would like to be not their master, but their champion, not their tyrant, but their leader; he confirms that he does not intend to kill

to a meeting and said: "You should know that within the next few days the king will be here with ten legions, thirty thousand horsemen, a hundred thousand light-armed troops, and three hundred elephants. Therefore, some of you may cease to ask further questions or to make surmises and may rather believe me, since I have certain information. Otherwise, I will give orders to have people put on a very old ship and carried off to whatever lands any wind may blow them."

About Himself and the Political Situation (F 42A)

speech in the Senate, followed by a similar one before the People, confirming that he would not abuse this power.

F 42A Cassius Dio, *Roman History*

anyone. Caesar therefore tells the senators that they should confidently unite their interests, forgetting all past events and beginning to love each other without suspicion; there should be a relationship between them like that between a father and his children. The soldiers will be guardians of their shared empire. Caesar assures them that any taxes raised have not resulted in private gain for him, but have been spent on the wars and the citizens; he promises that taxes will not be increased further. With this speech in the Senate and a similar one afterward to the People, Caesar relieves the population of their fears to some extent; but he has to confirm the promises by deeds before he is able to win them over completely.

Against the Tribunes C. Epidius Marullus and
L. Caesetius Flavus in the Senate (F 42b)

*In 44 BC Caesar attacked the Tribunes of the People C.
Epidius Marullus and L. Caesetius Flavus as they were
taking action against men who presented Caesar as king*

F 42b App. *B Civ.* 2.108.449–109.454

ἀλλὰ τοῦδε μὲν ἐσφάλησαν, εἰκόνα δ᾽ αὐτοῦ τις τῶν
ὑπερεθιζόντων τὸ λογοποίημα τῆς βασιλείας ἐστεφά-
νωσε δάφναις, ἀναπεπλεγμένης ταινίας λευκῆς· καὶ
αὐτὸν οἱ δήμαρχοι Μάρυλλός τε καὶ Καισήτιος ἀνευ-
ρόντες ἐς τὴν φυλακὴν ἐσέβαλον, ὑποκρινάμενοί τι
καὶ τῷ Καίσαρι χαρίζεσθαι, προαπειλήσαντι τοῖς
περὶ βασιλείας λέγουσιν. [450] ὁ δὲ τοῦτο μὲν ἤνεγκεν
εὐσταθῶς, ἑτέρων δ᾽ αὐτὸν ἀμφὶ τὰς πύλας ἰόντα πο-
θὲν βασιλέα προσειπόντων καὶ τοῦ δήμου στεναξάν-
τος, εὐμηχάνως εἶπε τοῖς ἀσπασαμένοις· "οὐκ εἰμὶ
Βασιλεύς, ἀλλὰ Καῖσαρ," ὡς δὴ περὶ τὸ ὄνομα
ἐσφαλμένοις. [451] οἱ δ᾽ ἀμφὶ τὸν Μάρυλλον καὶ
τῶνδε τῶν ἀνδρῶν τὸν ἀρξάμενον ἐξεῦρον καὶ τοῖς
ὑπηρέταις ἐκέλευον ἄγειν ἐς δίκην ἐπὶ τὸ ἀρχεῖον
αὐτῶν. [452] καὶ ὁ Καῖσαρ οὐκέτι ἐνεγκὼν κατηγόρη-
σεν ἐπὶ τῆς βουλῆς τῶν περὶ τὸν Μάρυλλον ὡς ἐπι-
βουλευόντων οἱ μετὰ τέχνης ἐς τυραννίδος διαβολήν,
καὶ ἐπήνεγκεν ἀξίους μὲν αὐτοὺς εἶναι θανάτου, μόνης
δ᾽ αὐτοὺς ἀφαιρεῖσθαι καὶ παραλύειν τῆς τε ἀρχῆς

Against the Tribunes C. Epidius Marullus and
L. Caesetius Flavus in the Senate (F 42b)

(*Cass. Dio 44.10; Suet.* Iul. *79.1; Plut.* Caes. *61.8–10; Nic.*
Dam. Caes. *20.69 [FGrHist 90 F 130]; Vell. Pat. 2.68.4*).

F 42b Appian, *Civil Wars*

Yet in this [in the hope that Caesar would restore the
Republic] they [the People] were disappointed, but some
person among those who wished to spread the report of
his desire to be king wreathed his statue with a crown of
laurel, bound with a white fillet. And the Tribunes, Marullus and Caesetius [C. Epidius Marullus and L. Caesetius
Flavus, tr. pl. 44 BC, later in the year deprived of their
tribunician power], sought out this person and put him in
prison, pretending thereby to gratify Caesar too, since he
had threatened any who should talk about kingship. [450]
He bore this with a calm mind, and when others who met
him at the city gates as he was returning from somewhere
greeted him as king and the People groaned, he said cleverly to those who had saluted him: "I am not King, but
Caesar," as though they made a mistake with his name.
[451] The attendants of Marullus again found out the person who began the shouting among these men and ordered the officers to bring him to trial before their tribu-
nal. [452] And Caesar no longer put up with it and accused
the faction of Marullus before the Senate of artfully con-
spiring to cast upon him the charge of kingship; and he
added that they [the Tribunes] were deserving of death,
but that it would be sufficient to deprive them of their

441

καὶ τοῦ βουλευτηρίου. [453] ὃ δὴ καὶ μάλιστα αὐτὸν
διέβαλεν ὡς ἐπιθυμοῦντα τῆς ἐπικλήσεως καὶ τὰς ἐς
τοῦτο πείρας καθιέντα καὶ τυραννικὸν ὅλως γεγονότα·
ἥ τε γὰρ πρόφασις τῆς κολάσεως περὶ τῆς βασιλικῆς
ἐπωνυμίας ἦν, ἥ τε τῶν δημάρχων ἀρχὴ ἱερὰ καὶ
ἄσυλος ἦν ἐκ νόμου καὶ ὅρκου παλαιοῦ· τήν τε ὀργὴν
ὀξεῖαν ἐποίει τὸ μηδ᾽ ἀναμεῖναι τῆς ἀρχῆς τὸ ὑπόλοι-
πον. [454] ὧν καὶ αὐτὸς αἰσθανόμενος καὶ μετανοῶν
. . .

To Soldiers about Their Advantages (F 43)

F 43 Diom., *GL* I, p. 400.20–21

frustro ait Gaius Caesar apud milites de commodis eorum:
"non frustrabo vos, milites."

On Behalf of the Bithynians (F 44–45)

*It is unclear in what context Caesar spoke on behalf of the
Bithynians; the matter presumably concerned some financial injustice done to them, with M. (Iunius?) Iuncus (RE*

office and expel them from the Senate. [453] This unam-
biguously made him suspect of desiring the title and being
aware of the attempts to that end, and [suggested] that the
tyranny was already complete; for the pretext of their punishment was the matter concerning the title of king, and
the office of Tribune was sacred and inviolable according
to law and the ancient oath. By not even waiting for the
expiration of their office he made the public indignation
sharper. [454] When he had also perceived this himself
and repented . . .

To Soldiers about Their Advantages (F 43)

*The context of this speech to soldiers about their advan-
tages is unknown (CCMR, App. C: 99). It might be identical with one of the known speeches to soldiers given on
particular occasions.*

F 43 Diomedes

Gaius Caesar uses *frustro* ["I disappoint"; deponent form
more common] [in the speech] before soldiers about their
advantages: "I will not disappoint you, soldiers."

On Behalf of the Bithynians (F 44–45)

*Iuncus 4; proconsul in Asia / Bithynia in 75/74 BC) either
the judge or the accused in this case, raised in the late
70s BC.*

F 44 Gell. *NA* 5.13.2–6

conveniebat autem facile constabatque ex moribus populi
Romani primum iuxta parentes locum tenere pupillos
debere fidei tutelaeque nostrae creditos; secundum eos
proximum locum clientes habere, qui sese itidem in fidem
patrociniumque nostrum dediderunt; tum in tertio loco
esse hospites; postea esse cognatos adfinesque. [3] . . . [6]
firmum atque clarum isti rei testimonium perhibet auctoritas C. Caesaris pontificis maximi, qui in oratione, quam
pro Bithynis dixit, hoc principio usus est: "vel pro hospitio
regis Nicomedis vel pro horum necessitate, quorum res
agitur, refugere hoc munus, M. Iunce, non potui. nam
neque hominum morte memoria deleri debet, quin a
proximis retineatur, neque clientes sine summa infamia
deseri possunt, quibus etiam a propinquis nostris opem
ferre instituimus."

F 45 Iul. Rufin., *RLM*, p. 40.23–25

Caesar pro Bithynis: "quid ergo? syngraphae non sunt, sed
res aliena est."

On Behalf of Decius the Samnite (F 46)

F 44 Gellius, *Attic Nights*

But it was readily agreed and accepted that, in accordance with the usage of the Roman People, the first place next after parents should be held by wards entrusted to our trustworthiness and protection; the second place very close to them should be held by clients, who also had committed themselves to our trustworthiness and guardianship; then, in the third place were guests; finally, there were relations by blood and by marriage. [3] . . . [6] A strong and clear testimony of this matter is furnished by the authority of C. Caesar, *pontifex maximus* [from 63 BC]; in the speech that he delivered on behalf of the Bithynians he used the following opening: "In consideration either of my guest friendship with king Nicomedes [Nicomedes IV Philopator, king of Bithynia, d. 74 BC] or my relationship to those whose case is on trial, M. Iuncus, I could not refuse this duty. For neither ought the remembrance of men to be so obliterated by their death as not to be retained by those nearest to them, nor can we forsake, without the highest disgrace, clients, to whom we are bound to render aid even against our kinsfolk."

F 45 Iulius Rufinianus

Caesar [in the speech] on behalf of the Bithynians: "What then? There are no written agreements to pay, but this is the property of another."

On Behalf of Decius the Samnite (F 46)

Details of Caesar's defense of Decius the Samnite are uncertain (TLRR 376).

F 46 Tac. *Dial.* 21.5–6

[APER:] concedamus sane C. Caesari, ut propter magnitudinem cogitationum et occupationes rerum minus in eloquentia effecerit, quam divinum eius ingenium postulabat, tam hercule quam Brutum philosophiae suae relinquamus; nam in orationibus minorem esse fama sua etiam admiratores eius fatentur. [6] nisi forte quisquam aut Caesaris pro Decio[1] Samnite aut Bruti pro Deiotaro rege ceterosque eiusdem lentitudinis ac te{m}poris[2] libros legit, nisi qui et carmina eorundem miratur.

¹ Deci‹di›o *John*   ² te{m}poris *Lipsius*: temporis *codd.*

On Behalf of Nysa, Daughter of Nicomedes, in the Senate (F 47)

F 47 Suet. *Iul.* 49.3

Cicero vero non contentus in quibusdam epistulis scripsisse a satellitibus eum in cubiculum regium eductum in aureo lecto veste purpurea decubuisse floremque aetatis a Venere orti in Bithynia contaminatum, quondam etiam in senatu defendenti ei Nysae causam, filiae Nicomedis,

F 46 Tacitus, *Dialogue on Oratory*

[APER:] We must certainly make allowances to C. Caesar, that, owing to the extent of his considerations and the preoccupation with important matters, he accomplished less in eloquence than his divine genius called for, just as, by Hercules, we must leave Brutus [M. Iunius Brutus (**158**)] to his philosophy; for even his admirers admit that in his speeches he was beneath his own reputation. [6] Unless anybody by chance reads either Caesar's oration on behalf of Decius the Samnite[1] or Brutus' on behalf of king Deiotarus [**158** F 24–26], and other volumes of the same slowness and tepidity, or unless it be someone who is an admirer also of the same men's poetry.

[1] The name is often restored as *Deci‹di›us* to create a link to a person mentioned by Cicero (Cic. *Clu.* 161: *Cn. Decidio Samniti, ei qui proscriptus est . . .*).

On Behalf of Nysa, Daughter of Nicomedes, in the Senate (F 47)

In the Senate Caesar supported Nysa, the daughter of Nicomedes III and sister of Nicomedes IV Philopator, kings of Bithynia.

F 47 Suetonius, *Life of Caesar*

Cicero, indeed, was not content with having written in some letters that he [Caesar] was led by attendants to the royal apartments, that he lay on a golden couch in a purple gown, and that the virginity of this son of Venus was lost in Bithynia; when he [Caesar] was once defending the case of Nysa, daughter of Nicomedes, in the Senate and was

beneficiaque regis in se commemoranti: "remove," inquit, "istaec, oro te, quando notum est et quid ille tibi et quid illi tute dederis."

Potentially Spurious Speeches (F 48)

F 48 Suet. *Iul.* 55.3–4

orationes aliquas reliquit, inter quas temere quaedam feruntur. pro Quinto Metello non immerito Augustus existimat magis ab actuaris exceptam male subsequentibus verba dicentis, quam ab ipso editam; nam in quibusdam exemplaribus invenio ne inscriptam quidem pro Metello, sed quam scripsit Metello, cum ex persona Caesaris sermo sit Metellum seque adversus communium obtrectatorum criminationes purgantis. [4] apud milites quoque in Hispania idem Augustus vix ipsius putat, quae tamen duplex fertur: una quasi priore habita proelio, altera posteriore, quo Asinius Pollio ne tempus quidem contionandi habuisse eum dicit subita hostium incursione.

enumerating his obligations to the king, he [Cicero] even said to him: "Stop this, please, since it is well known both what he gave to you and what you gave to him."

Potentially Spurious Speeches (F 48)

Suetonius notes that among the speeches attributed to Caesar some are not genuine and provides examples of speeches that Augustus regarded as spurious, at least in the form in which they circulated.

F 48 Suetonius, *Life of Caesar*

He [Caesar] left several speeches, including some that are referred to as his on insufficient evidence [cf. T 10]. Augustus believes, not without reason, that [the speech] on behalf of Quintus Metellus [Q. Caecilius Metellus Nepos, cos. 57 BC] was rather taken down by shorthand writers, who were scarcely following the words he was speaking, than published by the man [Caesar] himself; for in some copies I find even that it is not entitled "For Metellus," but "Which he wrote for Metellus," although the discourse purports to be from Caesar's lips, defending Metellus and himself against the charges of their shared detractors. [4] Augustus also believes that [the address] to the soldiers in Hispania is hardly his; this speech, however, circulates in two versions, one purporting to have been spoken at the first battle, the other at the second, about which Asinius Pollio [C. Asinius Pollio (**174**), *FRHist* 56 F 6] says that, because of the sudden onslaught of the enemy, he did not even have time to deliver a speech.[1]

---

[1] It is unclear which two battles Suetonius might refer to.

122 M. CALPURNIUS BIBULUS

*M. Calpurnius Bibulus (cos. 59 BC; RE Calpurnius 28) was a contemporary of C. Iulius Caesar (**121**) and held several offices together with him (notwithstanding some tensions). Bibulus joined Cn. Pompeius Magnus (**111**) in*

T 1 Cic. *Brut.* 267

[CICERO:] sunt etiam ex eis, qui eodem bello occiderunt, M. Bibulus, qui et scriptitavit accurate, cum praesertim non esset orator, et egit multa constanter . . .

Speeches and Edicts Against C. Iulius Caesar and Cn. Pompeius Magnus (F 2–6)

*During his consulship in 59 BC, Bibulus clashed with his colleague C. Iulius Caesar (**121**); he spoke out against him and Cn. Pompeius Magnus (**111**) in speeches and edicts,*

F 2 Cic. *Att.* 2.19.2, 5

Bibulus in caelo est, nec qua re scio, sed ita laudatur quasi ⟨qui⟩[1] "unus homo nobis cunctando restituit rem." [Enn. *Ann.* 363 Sk. = 12 *Ann.* F 1 *FRL*] . . . [5] . . . edicta Bibuli audio ad te missa. iis ardet dolore et ira noster Pompeius.

---

[1] *add. Watt (post* homo *Wesenberg)*

122 M. CALPURNIUS BIBULUS

the civil war and died before the battle of Dyrrhachium in
48 BC.

In Cicero, Bibulus' accuracy in writing is noted, but he
is not judged to be a true orator (T 1).

T 1 Cicero, *Brutus*

[CICERO:] Among those who fell in the same war [civil war
in the 40s BC] were also M. Bibulus, who both wrote in
an accurate manner, especially since he was not an orator,
and pleaded many cases with determination . . .

Speeches and Edicts Against C. Iulius Caesar and
Cn. Pompeius Magnus (F 2–6)

using the latter particularly after he had stopped leaving
his house in response to violence and political controver-
sies (F 6).

F 2 Cicero, *Letters to Atticus*

Bibulus is in heaven, and I do not know why, but he is
praised in such a way as if he was the man ‹who› "alone
by delaying restored the state to us." [Enn. *Ann.* 363 Sk.
= 12 *Ann.* F 1 *FRL*] . . . [5] . . . I hear Bibulus' edicts have
been sent to you. Because of them our Pompey [Cn. Pompeius Magnus (**111**)] is burning with anguish and rage.

F 3 Cic. *Att.* 2.20.4

Bibulus hominum admiratione et benevolentia in caelo est. edicta eius et contiones describunt et legunt. novo quodam genere in summam gloriam venit. populare nunc nihil tam est quam odium popularium.

F 4 Suet. *Iul.* 9.2

= **86** F 12.

F 5 Suet. *Iul.* 49.2

= **158** F 17.

F 6 Plut. *Pomp.* 48.5

πραττομένων δὲ τούτων, Βύβλος μὲν εἰς τὴν οἰκίαν κατακλεισάμενος ὀκτὼ μηνῶν οὐ προῆλθεν ὑπατεύων, ἀλλ᾿ ἐξέπεμπε διαγράμματα βλασφημίας ἀμφοῖν ἔχοντα καὶ κατηγορίας . . .

On Behalf of the People of Tenedos (F 7)

F 3 Cicero, *Letters to Atticus*

Bibulus is in heaven with public admiration and favor. They take down his edicts and public speeches and read them. By some new method he has come to the greatest glory. Nothing is so popular nowadays as hatred of "popular" politicians.

F 4 Suetonius, *Life of Caesar*

= **86** F 12.

F 5 Suetonius, *Life of Caesar*

= **158** F 17.

F 6 Plutarch, *Life of Pompey*

While this [political unrest and decisions made by others] was going on, Bibulus shut himself up in his house and, for his last eight months as consul [59 BC], did not appear in public, but issued edicts full of accusations and slanders against both men [Cn. Pompeius Magnus (**111**) and C. Iulius Caesar (**121**)] . . .

On Behalf of the People of Tenedos (F 7)

In 54 BC Bibulus was among the men who spoke on behalf of the liberty of the people of Tenedos (island in the Aegean Sea), who seem to have asked the Senate for the status of a free community and to have been refused.

FRL IV: ORATORY, PART 2

F 7 Cic. *Q Fr.* 2.10(9).2

Tenediorum igitur libertas securi Tenedia praecisa est,
cum eos praeter me et Bibulum et Calidium et Favonium
nemo defenderet.

Speeches in the Senate (F 7A)

F 7A Plut. *Pomp.* 54.6–7

καὶ Βύβλος ἐχθρὸς ὢν Πομπηΐῳ πρῶτος ἀπεφήνατο
γνώμην ἐν συγκλήτῳ, μόνον ἑλέσθαι Πομπήϊον ὕπα-
τον·¹ ἢ γὰρ ἀπαλλαγήσεσθαι τῆς παρούσης τὴν πόλιν ἀκοσμίας ἢ δουλεύσειν τῷ κρατίστῳ. [7] φανέντος
δὲ παραδόξου τοῦ λόγου διὰ τὸν εἰπόντα . . .

¹ Πομπήϊον μόνον ἑλέσθαι ὕπατον transp. Ziegler

Cf. Plut. *Cat. min.* 47.3; Cass. Dio 40.50.4; Asc. in Cic. *Mil.*, *arg.*
(p. 36.2–5 C.).

F 7 Cicero, *Letters to Quintus*

The liberty of the people of Tenedos, then, was chopped by an ax from Tenedos,[1] when nobody came to their defense except myself, Bibulus, Calidius [M. Calidius (**140**), F 8], and Favonius [M. Favonius (**166**), F 6].

[1] This proverbial expression has been referred to the eponym of the island, Ten(ne)es, but also been explained in many other ways (*Suda* s.v. Τενέδιος πέλεκυς).

Speeches in the Senate (F 7A)

Further interventions of Bibulus in the Senate are attested for the 50s BC (Cic. Dom. 69; Fam. 1.1.3, 1.2.1–3).

F 7A Plutarch, *Life of Pompey*

And Bibulus, an enemy of Pompey's [Cn. Pompeius Magnus (**111**)], was the first to propose in the Senate that Pompey be chosen sole consul; for thus, he said, the city would either be set free from the current disorder or would become the slave of its strongest man. [7] The motion seemed strange because of its proposer . . .

123 L. LUCCEIUS

*L. Lucceius (praet. 67 BC; RE Lucceius 6) unsuccessfully
stood for the consulship in 60 BC; afterward, he withdrew
from public life and devoted his time to writing history;
he wrote a historical work starting with the Social War
(FRHist 30). A letter from Lucceius to Cicero is extant
(Cic.* Fam. *5.14), as are three by Cicero to him (Cic.* Fam.

T 1 Cic. *Cael.* 54

habeo enim, iudices, quem vos socium vestrae religionis
iurisque iurandi facile esse patiamini, L. Lucceium, sanc-
tissimum hominem et gravissimum testem, qui . . . an ille
vir illa humanitate praeditus, illis studiis, illis artibus atque
doctrina . . . ? . . . homo eruditus . . . ?

T 2 Cic. *Fam.* 5.12.7 [ad Lucceium]

atque hoc praestantius mihi fuerit et ad laetitiam animi et
ad memoriae dignitatem si in tua scripta pervenero quam
si in ceterorum quod non ingenium mihi solum suppedi-
tatum fuerit tuum . . . sed etiam auctoritas clarissimi et
spectatissimi viri et in rei publicae maximis gravissimisque
causis cogniti atque in primis probati, ut mihi non solum
praeconium . . . sed etiam grave testimonium impertitum
clari hominis magnique videatur.

123 L. LUCCEIUS

5.12, 5.13, 5.15), including one in which Cicero tries to persuade Lucceius to write a historical work about his consulship (Cic. Fam. 5.12).

In Cicero, Lucceius' learning, qualities as a writer, and reputation are highlighted (T 1–2).

T 1 Cicero, *Pro Caelio*

For I can produce, judges, a man whom you would readily allow to be associated with you in the sanctity of your oath, L. Lucceius, a most upright man and a most respected witness, who . . . Could such a man, endowed with such a civilized character, such learning, such culture and knowledge . . . ? . . . an educated man . . . ?

T 2 Cicero, *Letters to Friends* [to Lucceius]

And therefore it would be preferable both for the pleasure of my mind and for the dignity of my memory if I should obtain a place in your writings rather than in those of others because not only your talent would be supplied to me in abundance . . . but also your authority as a most illustrious and much admired man, tried and notably approved in the greatest and most serious public affairs, so that I would seem to have received not only the duties of a herald . . . but also the weighty testimony of an illustrious and great man.

Against L. Sergius Catilina (F 3–4)

Lucceius prosecuted L. Sergius Catilina (**112**) for murder after the latter's unsuccessful candidacy for the consulship in 64 BC. Asconius (F 4) seems to imply that there was

F 3 Asc. in Cic. *Tog. cand.* (p. 81 KS = 91.9–13 C.)

huius autem criminis periculum quod obicit Cicero paucos post menses Catilina subiit. post effecta enim comitia consularia et Catilinae repulsam fecit eum reum inter sicarios L. Lucceius paratus eruditusque, qui postea consulatum quoque petiit.

F 4 Asc. in Cic. *Tog. cand.* (pp. 82 KS = 91.27–92.3 C.)

dicitur Catilina adulterium commisisse cum ea quae ei postea socrus fuit, et ex eo natam stupro duxisse uxorem, cum filia eius esset. hoc Lucceius quoque Catilinae obicit in orationibus quas in eum scripsit. nomina harum mulierum nondum inveni.

Against L. Sergius Catilina (F 3–4)

more than one speech against Catiline; not all of them,
however, need to be connected with this trial (TLRR 217).

F 3 Asconius on Cicero, *In Toga Candida*

But Catiline endured the peril of this charge, which Cicero brings up against him, a few months later. For after
the election assembly for the consulship had taken place
and after Catiline's defeat [in 64 BC], L. Lucceius, a
trained and educated man, who later stood as a candidate
for the consulship too [in 60 BC], prosecuted him in the
court for murder cases.

F 4 Asconius on Cicero, *In Toga Candida*

Catiline is said to have committed adultery with that
woman who later was his mother-in-law and to have married the woman who was born from this illicit relationship
although she was his daughter. Lucceius too reproached
Catiline with this in the speeches that he wrote against
him. I have not yet found out the names of these women.[1]

[1] The identity of these women is indeed uncertain. The wife
of Catiline alluded to might be Aurelia Orestilla (Sall. *Cat.* 15.1–
2, 35.3).

124 M. VALERIUS MESSALLA NIGER

M. Valerius Messalla Niger (cos. 61, censor 55 BC; RE
Valerius 266) seems to have entrusted Cicero with the case
of Sex. Roscius from Ameria in 80 BC (T 1) and was him-
self involved in many trials (T 2).

T 1 Cic. *Rosc. Am.* 149

quae domi gerenda sunt, ea per Caeciliam transiguntur,
fori iudicique rationem ⟨M.⟩[1] Messala,[2] ut videtis, iudices,
suscepit; qui, si iam satis aetatis ac roboris haberet, ipse
pro Sex. Roscio diceret. quoniam ad dicendum impedi-
mento est aetas et pudor qui ornat aetatem causam mihi
tradidit quem sua causa cupere ac debere intellegebat,
ipse adsiduitate, consilio, auctoritate, diligentia perfecit,
ut Sex. Rosci vita erepta de manibus sectorum sententiis
iudicum permitteretur.

[1] M. *Garatoni*: om. *codd.*   [2] Messala *codd.*: Messalla
Lambinus

T 2 Cic. *Brut.* 246

[Cicero:] M. Messalla minor natu quam nos, nullo modo
inops, sed non nimis ornatus genere verborum; prudens,
acutus, minime incautus patronus, in causis cognoscendis
componendisque diligens, magni laboris, multae operae
multarumque causarum.

124 M. VALERIUS MESSALLA NIGER

In Cicero, Messalla is described as an orator of not particularly ornate diction, and as a shrewd, cautious, and industrious pleader, diligent in mastering and arranging the material (T 2).

T 1 Cicero, *Pro Sexto Roscio Amerino*

As for his [Sex. Roscius'] domestic affairs, they are settled by Caecilia [friend of Roscius' father]; the conduct of his affairs in the Forum and in court, as you see, judges, has been undertaken by ‹M.› Messalla.[1] If that man already had sufficient age and strength, he would plead himself for Sex. Roscius. Since his age and his modesty, which is an ornament to his age, prevent him from speaking, he has entrusted the case to me, whom he knew desired and was under an obligation to undertake it in his interest. Personally, by his constant presence, advice, influence, and unwearied attention, he succeeded in snatching away the life of Sex. Roscius from the hands of the brokers and handing it over to the verdict of the judges.

[1] Generally seen as a reference to M. Valerius Messalla Niger, though it might refer to M. Valerius Messalla Rufus (cos. 53 BC).

T 2 Cicero, *Brutus*

[CICERO:] M. Messalla, younger in age than us, not deficient in any way, but not very elaborate in diction; a sagacious, shrewd, and certainly not incautious pleader, diligent in mastering and arranging cases, with great industry, great devotion, and engaged in many cases.

461

T 3 Schol. Gron. ad Cic. *Rosc. Am.* 5 (p. 303.6–7 Stangl)

"maximo ingenio": Messalam maxime significat, cuius {maxime}[1] extant orationes.

[1] *del. Schuetz*

On Behalf of M. Aemilius Scaurus (F 4)

F 4 Asc. in Cic. *Scaur.*, *arg.* (p. 18 KS = 20.13–18 C.)
= **92** F 48.

125 C. MEMMIUS

C. Memmius (praet. 58 BC; RE Memmius 8) unsuccessfully stood for the consulship in 54 BC; accused of ambitus and found guilty, he eventually withdrew into exile to Athens (TLRR 320; Cic. Fam. 13.1.1; App. B Civ. 2.24.90).

Besides having a public career, Memmius was a poet (FPL[4], pp. 191–92) and a supporter of poets: Catullus and Cinna accompanied him during his governorship of Bithynia in 57 BC, and Lucretius dedicated his poem De rerum natura (on Epicurean natural philosophy) to him.

T 3 Scholia Gronoviana to Cicero, *Pro Sexto Roscio Amerino*

"with the greatest talent": He [Cicero] means Messalla[1] in particular, of whom orations {in particular} are extant.

[1] The scholion describes a Messalla known as an orator but does not identify him further and may misinterpret Cicero's reference.

On Behalf of M. Aemilius Scaurus (F 4)

*In 54 BC Messalla was one of six advocates defending M. Aemilius Scaurus (**139**), who also spoke on his own behalf (**139** F 5), when P. Valerius Triarius (**148** F 1–2) prosecuted him for extortion (cf. **148**).*

F 4 Asconius on Cicero, *Pro Scauro*
= **92** F 48.

125 C. MEMMIUS

Letters to Memmius from Cicero are extant (Cic. Fam. 13.1–3).

In Cicero, Memmius is described as learned in Greek literature, as an adroit orator with a pleasing diction, but averse to the labor required, so that his skill did not come fully to the fore (T 1).

*Memmius charged Q. Caecilius Metellus Pius Cornelianus Scipio Nasica, Cn. Pompeius Magnus' (**111**) father-in-law, with ambitus, but withdrew the accusation before a trial was held (App. B Civ. 2.24.93–94).*

T 1 Cic. *Brut.* 247

[CICERO:] C. Memmius L. f. perfectus litteris, sed Graecis, fastidiosus sane Latinarum, argutus orator verbisque dulcis sed fugiens non modo dicendi verum etiam cogitandi laborem, tantum sibi de facultate detraxit quantum imminuit industriae.

Against M. Licinius Lucullus (F 2)

F 2 Plut. *Luc.* 37.1–2

ὁ δὲ Λεύκολλος ἀναβὰς εἰς Ῥώμην, πρῶτον μὲν κατέλαβε τὸν ἀδελφὸν Μάρκον ὑπὸ Γαΐου Μεμμίου κατηγορούμενον ἐφ᾽ οἷς ἔπραξε ταμιεύων Σύλλα προστάξαντος. [2] ἐκείνου δ᾽ ἀποφυγόντος . . .

Against L. Licinius Lucullus (F 3–6)

F 3 Plut. *Luc.* 37.2–3

ἐκείνου δ᾽ ἀποφυγόντος, ἐπὶ τοῦτον αὐτὸν ὁ Μέμμιος μεταβαλόμενος παρώξυνε τὸν δῆμον, καὶ ὡς πολλὰ

125 C. MEMMIUS

T 1 Cicero, *Brutus*

[CICERO:] C. Memmius, Lucius' son, highly educated in literature, albeit Greek [literature], disdainful indeed toward Latin [literature], an adroit orator with a pleasing diction, though averse to the labor not only of speaking, but even of thinking: he took away from his skill to the same degree that he reduced his effort.

As Tribune of the People in 66 BC, Memmius attacked (F 2, 3–6) the brothers L. and M. Licinius Lucullus (90 + 91) because of alleged political misbehavior (TLRR 204, 206; on the possible political context, see Gruen 1971, 56–58).

Against M. Licinius Lucullus (F 2)

F 2 Plutarch, *Life of Lucullus*

When Lucullus [L. Licinius Lucullus (**90**)] had returned to Rome [from fighting in the east], he found, in the first place, that his brother Marcus [M. Licinius Lucullus (**91**)] was being prosecuted by Gaius Memmius for what he did as quaestor under Sulla's [L. Cornelius Sulla] rule. [2] When he [Marcus] was acquitted . . . [continued by F 3]

Against L. Licinius Lucullus (F 3–6)

F 3 Plutarch, *Life of Lucullus*

When he [M. Licinius Lucullus (**91**)] was acquitted [continued from F 2], Memmius turned his attack upon that man himself [L. Licinius Lucullus (**90**)] and strove to spur on the People, and by describing him as someone who had

νενοσφισμένῳ καὶ μηκύναντι τὸν πόλεμον ἔπειθεν
αὐτῷ μὴ δοῦναι θρίαμβον. [3] ἐλθόντος δ' εἰς ἀγῶνα
τοῦ Λευκόλλου μέγαν, οἱ πρῶτοι καὶ δυνατώτατοι
καταμείξαντες ἑαυτοὺς ταῖς φυλαῖς, πολλῇ δεήσει καὶ
σπουδῇ μόλις ἔπεισαν[1] τὸν δῆμον ἐπιτρέψαι θριαμ-
βεῦσαι ‹. . .›[2] οὐχ ὥσπερ ἔνιοι μήκει τε πομπῆς καὶ
πλήθει τῶν κομιζομένων ἐκπληκτικὸν καὶ ὀχλώδη
θρίαμβον, ἀλλὰ τοῖς μὲν ὅπλοις τῶν πολεμίων οὖσι
παμπόλλοις καὶ τοῖς βασιλικοῖς μηχανήμασι τὸν
Φλαμίνειον ἱππόδρομον διεκόσμησε· καὶ θέα τις ἦν
αὐτὴ καθ' ἑαυτὴν οὐκ εὐκαταφρόνητος . . .

1 ἔπεισαν Schaefer, Richards: ἔπεισεν codd.   2 lac. stat.
Ziegler, e.g. κατῆγεν οὖν excidisse ratus

Cf. Plut. Cat. min. 29.5–6.

F 4 + 5 Serv. Dan. ad Verg. Aen. 1.161

C. Memmius de triumpho Luculli Asiatico[1] "inque luxu-
riosissimis Asiae oppidis consedisse" et mox "inque Gallo-
graeciam redierunt."

1 Luculli Asiatico Duebner: luciliaca IIII. cod.

F 6 Serv. Dan. ad Verg. Aen. 4.261

Gaius Memmius de triumpho Luculli: "Syriaci calceoli
gemmarum stellati coloribus": participium sine verbo.

diverted much property to his own uses and protracted the war, he persuaded them not to grant him a triumph. [3] Lucullus entered a great fight about this, and the foremost and most influential men mingled with the tribes, and by much entreaty and exertion at last persuaded the People to allow him to celebrate a triumph [in 63 BC]; <. . .> not, however, like some, a triumph striking and tumultuous from the length of the procession and the multitude of objects displayed. Instead, he decorated the Circus Flaminius with the arms of the enemy, which were very numerous, and with the royal engines of war; and this was a great spectacle in itself, and far from contemptible. . . .

F 4 + 5 Servius Danielis, *Commentary on Virgil*

C. Memmius [says in the speech] on the triumph of Lucullus over Asia "and that they had settled down in the most luxurious towns of Asia" and a little later "and they returned to Gallograecia [Galatia, in modern Turkey]."

F 6 Servius Danielis, *Commentary on Virgil*

Gaius Memmius [says in the speech] on the triumph of Lucullus: "Syrian half-boots, covered starlike with the colors of precious stones": a participle without a verb [*stellatus*, as the verb *stello* is rare].

On C. Iulius Caesar (F 7–10)

*Having come into office as praetor (for 58 BC), Memmius,
along with his colleague L. Domitius Ahenobarbus (**131** F
2–3), questioned some of C. Iulius Caesar's (**121**) activities*

F 7 Suet. *Iul.* 23.1

= **121** F 38.

F 8 Suet. *Iul.* 49.2

sed C. Memmius etiam ad cyathum † et vi[1] Nicomedi
stetisse obicit, cum reliquis exoletis, pleno convivio, accu-
bantibus nonnullis urbicis negotiatoribus, quorum refert
nomina.

[1] et uina *unus cod.*: et uinum *codd. plerique*: *om. codd. rec.*:
eum *Salmasius*

F 9 Suet. *Iul.* 73.1

= **121** F 41.

F 10 Schol. Bob. ad Cic. *Sest.* 40 (p. 130.9–12 Stangl)

= **121** F 39.

*The election campaign for the consulship in 54 BC wit-
nessed a good deal of bribery; all candidates were accused
of* ambitus *(Cic. Q Fr. 3.1.16, 3.3.2; Att. 4.17.2–3): Memmius prosecuted (F 11) the co-competitor Cn. Domitius*

On C. Iulius Caesar (F 7–10)

during his (first) consulship in the past year (59 BC),
which triggered replies by Caesar (121 F 38–41).

F 7 Suetonius, *Life of Caesar*

= **121** F 38.

F 8 Suetonius, *Life of Caesar*

But C. Memmius makes the charge that he [C. Iulius Caesar (**121**)] even acted as cupbearer [?] to Nicomedes [Nicomedes IV Philopator, king of Bithynia] with the other male prostitutes, at a large dinner party, while among the guests were some merchants from the city [of Rome], whose names he gives.

F 9 Suetonius, *Life of Caesar*

= **121** F 41.

F 10 Scholia Bobiensia to Cicero, *Pro Sestio*

= **121** F 39.

Calvinus (praet. 56 BC) for ambitus (TLRR 301) and defended himself (F 12–14) when brought to trial on the same charge by Q. Acutius (TLRR 298).

Against Cn. Domitius Calvinus (F 11)

F 11 Cic. *Q Fr.* 3.2.3

de ambitu postulati sunt omnes qui consulatum petunt: a Memmio Domitius, a Q. Acutio, bono et erudito adulescente, Memmius, a Q. Pompeio Messalla, a Triario Scaurus.

On His Own Behalf (F 12–14)

F 12 Cic. *Q Fr.* 3.2.3
= F 11.

F 13 Suet. *De poetis*, pp. 30.14–31.2 Reifferscheid

C. Memmius in oratione pro se:[1] "P. Africanus," ⟨in⟩qui⟨t⟩,[2] "qui a Terentio personam mutuatus, quae domi luserat[3] ipse, nomine illius in scaenam detulit."

[1] se *unus cod.*: se ait *codd. cet.*   [2] ⟨in⟩qui⟨t⟩ *Ritschelius cum Schopeno*: qui *codd.*   [3] domui luserat *Roth*: domi luxerat *vel* demulus erat *codd.*

Against Cn. Domitius Calvinus (F 11)

F 11 Cicero, *Letters to Quintus*

All the candidates for the consulship have been charged with bribery: Domitius [Cn. Domitius Calvinus] by Memmius, Memmius by Q. Acutius, a good and well-instructed young man, Messalla [M. Valerius Messalla Rufus] by Q. Pompeius [Q. Pompeius Rufus (**153**)], Scaurus [M. Aemilius Scaurus (**139**)] by Triarius [P. Valerius Triarius (**148**)].

On His Own Behalf (F 12–14)

F 12 Cicero, *Letters to Quintus*

= F 11.[1]

[1] This passage confirms that Memmius was prosecuted for *ambitus* but does not reveal whether he delivered a speech on that occasion (cf. F 13).

F 13 Suetonius, *Lives of Illustrious Men. Poets*

C. Memmius says in the speech on his own behalf:[1] "P. Africanus [P. Cornelius Scipio Aemilianus Africanus minor (**21**)], who had borrowed a character from Terence, brought on stage under that man's name what he himself had playfully written at home."

[1] Since only one trial at which Memmius would have defended himself is known (cf. F 12), the fragment has been assigned to that context and taken as evidence for a speech by Memmius in the trial for *ambitus*.

F 14 Prisc., *GL* II, p. 386.4–5

Gaius Memmius: "quam stulte conficta, quam aperte sunt ementita," ἐψευσμένα.

F 14 Priscian

Gaius Memmius: "how stupidly has it been invented, how openly put together as a lie," "put together as a lie" [in Greek; deponent used in passive sense].[1]

[1] Whether the fragment is to be attributed to this speech is uncertain.